Derivatives Law
and
Regulation

International Banking, Finance and Economic Law

VOLUME 20

Series Editor

Joseph J. Norton

Centre for Commercial Law Studies, University of London
Southern Methodist University School of Law, Dallas, Texas
Asian Institute of International Financial Law,
University of Hong Kong

Derivatives Law and Regulation

By

RASIAH GENGATHAREN

KLUWER LAW INTERNATIONAL

THE HAGUE/LONDON/BOSTON

Published by
Kluwer Law International Ltd
Sterling House
66 Wilton Road
London SW1V 1DE
United Kingdom

Kluwer Law International incorporates
the publishing programmes of
Graham & Trotman Ltd,
Kluwer Law & Taxation Publishers
and Martinus Nijhoff Publishers

Sold and distributed in
the USA and Canada by
Kluwer Law International
675 Massachusetts Avenue
Cambridge MA 02139
USA

In all other countries, sold and distributed by
Kluwer Law International
PO Box 322
3300 AH Dordrecht
The Netherlands

ISBN 90-411-9836-9
© Kluwer Law International 2001
First published 2001

Library of Congress Cataloging-in-Publication Data

Gengatharen, Rasiah.
  Derivatives law and regulation / by Rasiah Gengatharen.
    p. cm.—(International banking, finance, and economic law ; v. 20)
  Includes bibliographical references and index.
  ISBN 9041198369 (hardbound : alk. paper)
   1. Derivative securities—Law and legislation—Australia. 2. Derivative securities—Law
and legislation—New Zealand. 3. Derivative securities—Law and legislation—Malaysia.
4. Derivative securities—Law and legislation—Singapore. 5. Derivative securities—Law and
legislation—China—Hong Kong. I. Title. II. Series.

K1114 .G46 2001
346′.092—dc21   00-067180

Printed and bound in Great Britain by Antony Rowe Limited.

Sponsoring Organisations

Centre for Commercial Law Studies
The Centre was established in 1980 as a distinct department within the Faculty of Laws of Queen Mary College, University of London. The primary objectives of the Centre are to promote systematic study and research in national and international commercial law and its social and economic implications, and to develop a body of knowledge, information and skills that can be placed at the service of government, public bodies, overseas institutions, the legal profession, industry and commerce. The International Financial Law Unit is one of the four internationally-renowned post-graduate research and teaching units at the CCLS.

London Institute of International Banking,
Finance and Development Law
The London Institute is a privately incorporated educational institution. Among other functions, the Institute assists the International Financial Law Unit at the Centre for Commercial Law Studies at Queen Mary and Westfield College, University of London, in directing research seminars, professional conferences, executive training sessions, law reform and consulting projects, and the publication of major journals and book series. This legal think-tank is also responsible for conducting research and publishing articles and essays on an array of important legal issues concerning banking, finance and development.

SMU Institute of International Banking and Finance
The Southern Methodist University Law School in Dallas, Texas has one of the oldest and most comprehensive international law programmes in the United States. Its Institute of International Banking and Finance was established in 1982. The institute serves as an interdisciplinary forum for research, publications, conferences and research seminars in the area of international finance, with input from SMU's Law School, Political Science and Economic Departments, and the Edwin L. Cox School of Business. The Institute conducts major international conferences, is actively involved in economic law reform projects in relating to emerging economies, and regularly produces books and other scholarly articles and papers.

Asian Institute of International Financial Law, University of Hong Kong Chinese Law Group and Centre for Comparative and Public Law
The University of Hong Kong Law Faculty is the oldest and most respected law faculty in Hong Kong. Its Asian Institute (AIIFL) was established in 1999 in cooperation with HKU's school of Business and Management and Department of Economics and is committed to postgraduate programmes, research, publications, conferences, short courses and seminars in the international financial law area, with emphasis on the East Asian and Greater China Areas. The AIIFL works closely with the Law Faculty's Chinese Law Group, one of the few such groups outside of Mainland China, and the Centre for Comparative and Public Law, which was founded by the Law Faculty in 1996.

Table of Contents

5. FUTURE DEVELOPMENTS AND CHALLENGES

Acknowledgements

This book originated as a doctoral thesis that I submitted to The University of Western Australia in 1999. Substantial modifications and changes have been made to parts of the thesis for publication in its present form.

I wish to express my gratitude to several individuals for their help and support. In alphabetical order, I thank the following individuals: Mr Allan Au-Yong, Mr Greg Boland, Associate Professor Ian Campbell, Mr David Chow, Mr David Dass, Professor Dianne Everett, Mr Tjio Hans, Mr A. Jayanath, Mr Lai Kim Leong, Associate Professor Lian Kwen Fee, Mr S. Loganathan, Mr William Loong, Associate Professor Sheelagh McCracken, Dr Paul Moyle, Mr Ng Hock Chuan, Professor James O'Donovan, Mr S. Sagadeva, Mr Gopal Sundaram, Dr Nii Wallace-Bruce, Mr William Weeks, Associate Professor Wickrema Weerasooria and Professor Wu Min Aun.

Any shortcomings or errors that this book may contain are my sole responsibility and are not attributed to any of the above-mentioned individuals.

My doctoral studies were financed by a generous scholarship awarded by the Banking Law Association and this book was funded by a research grant from the UWA Law School. I would like to thank both the Banking Law Association and the Law School for funding my research efforts.

I am grateful to Kluwer Law International for publishing my work. The staff at the United Kingdom office has been most helpful. I would like to thank Mr Lukas Claerhout and Ms Jo Fisher for their valuable suggestions and friendly support. I would also like to thank the editorial and production team for compiling the Index and Table of Cases.

Finally, I owe an enormous debt to my wife, Denise, and my children, Rohan and Sonia. I have dedicated this book to them.

Table of Cases

Introduction

Derivatives are extremely versatile financial products, as they help to manage risks, lower funding costs, enhance yields and diversify portfolios. The contributions made by derivatives have been so great, that they have been credited with having 'changed the face of finance.'[1] Less than three decades ago, the global market for derivatives barely existed. Today, the market is so large that it is difficult to imagine that it has grown so quickly in so short a space of time. Based on the Bank of International Settlements survey undertaken in 1995, the total value of outstanding derivatives worldwide was approximately USD 57 trillion in size.[2] The actual size of the global derivatives market was probably very much larger considering that only 26 countries were included in the survey. In some cases, the trading of derivatives has even surpassed the trading of the underlying commodity or instrument. Despite derivatives activity scaling new heights every year, it appears that the market still has potential for expansion. In many of the lesser-developed financial markets, derivatives usage is still limited for various reasons. It is in these markets that the potential for growth is greatest.

In the past, most of the growth in derivatives took place in the developed Western financial markets, but it appears that in the future, growth would come largely from the emerging financial markets of the Asia-Pacific region.[3]

---

[1] See Global Derivatives Study Group, *Derivatives: Practices and Principles* (Group of Thirty Report) (Group of Thirty, Washington DC, July 1993), p. 28.

[2] According to the *Central Bank Survey of Derivatives Market Activity* conducted by the Bank of International Settlements, the notional amount of derivatives contracts outstanding as at 31 March 1995 was USD 57.3 trillion. A similar survey was conducted in April 1998, but it did not include exchange-traded data. The results were nevertheless very impressive. For example, over-the-counter interest rate and currency derivatives reached USD 362 billion per day in April 1998. This represented an 85 per cent increase over the same statistic for April 1995. For details of the 1998 survey, see Editors, 'International Roundup: The Derivatives Industry Grows, but not Evenly by Region or Instrument' (1999) 4 *Derivatives* 198.

[3] For a definition of the Asia-Pacific region, see M. S. Dobbs-Higginson, *Asia Pacific: Its Role in The New World Disorder* (William Heinemann Australia, Port Melbourne, 1993), pp. xxiii–xxiv: ' "Asia Pacific" refers to those countries encompassed in the triangular region, from India down to New Zealand and up to China and Japan.' See also, R. F. Watters and T. G. McGee (eds), *Asia-Pacific: New Geographies of the Pacific Rim* (Hurst & Company, London, 1997), p. 3. Countless commentators have asserted that the next century will be that of the Asia and the Pacific. See, for example, J. Naisbitt, *Megatrends Asia* (Nicholas Brealey Publishing, London,

1

In 1985, Asian-Pacific derivatives exchanges accounted for 0.5 per cent of the total global contract volume, but by 1994 the top six exchanges in the region alone accounted for 12 per cent of global volume.[4] Derivatives trading in the developed Asia-Pacific countries of Australia, New Zealand, Singapore, Hong Kong and Japan accounted for about one-third of the global turnover in derivatives in 1995.[5] Although the region has suffered economically from the recent Asian Financial Crisis, it is unlikely that the growth of derivatives would be retarded.[6] There is a strong likelihood that the increased volatility of exchange and interest rates in the region would create a greater demand for sophisticated risk management mechanisms. As an indication of the importance of derivatives in attracting international capital inflows, a significant number of countries in the region have already established their own derivatives exchanges.[7]

The derivatives industry has, however, come under increasing regulatory scrutiny in recent years. There are many reasons why derivatives have attracted so much attention. One major reason is the speed and manner in which derivatives markets have grown. They have grown tremendously in a relatively short period of time. Their activities have become increasingly borderless. The last few years have witnessed increasing linkages between markets. Another no less important reason is the risks created by derivatives. There are many who see derivatives as complex, opaque, difficult to manage, and more risky than other traditional financial products.[8] A significant number of widely reported derivatives-linked losses worldwide have heightened fears about the dangers posed by derivatives. These concerns have not only raised questions about the wisdom of using derivatives, but

---

1996), pp. vi–xiii: 'As we move toward the year 2000, Asia will become the dominant region of the world; economically, politically, and culturally.' See also, D Forbes, 'Towards the "Pacific Century": Integration and Disintegration in the Pacific Basin' in *The Far East and Australasia 1996* (27th ed., Europa Publications Ltd, London, 1996), p. 25: 'The expansion of the Japanese economy, the emergence of the newly-industrialising countries (NICs) and the rise of another group of "near-NICs" in East and South-east Asia in the post-war era have prompted speculation that the Pacific Ocean has replaced the Atlantic as the core of world economic growth, heralding the emergence of the "Pacific century".'

[4] See E. Banks, *Asia Pacific Derivative Markets* (Macmillan Press Ltd, London, 1996), p. 8.

[5] See D. Lynch, 'Growth in Asia-Pacific Markets' in E. Sheedy and S. McCracken (eds), *Derivatives: The Risks That Remain* (Allen & Unwin, St Leonards, NSW, 1997), p. 16.

[6] For an insight into the causes of the Asian Financial Crisis, see for example, S. A. Grenville, 'Exchange Rates and Causes' (February 1998) *Reserve Bank of Australia Bulletin* 29.

[7] See Lynch, above n. 5, pp. 21–22: Countries in the Asia-Pacific region which have their own derivatives exchanges include Japan, Korea, Hong Kong, Singapore, Malaysia, Philippines, New Zealand and Australia. See also, V. L. Chou, 'Derivatives and Dialectics: The Evolution of the Chinese Futures Market' (1997) 72 *New York University Law Review* 175, 176–177: China had more than 60 registered and unregistered futures markets in late 1994. But, by the end of 1995, the number of exchanges had been reduced to 15.

[8] Group of Thirty Report, above n. 1, p. 2. See also M. Rubinstein, *Rubinstein on Derivatives* (Risk Books, London, 1999), p. 1: 'To many, "derivatives" is a mysterious word, connoting the dark and seemingly impenetrable world of modern finance. In fact, the basics of derivatives are easy to understand, in part because most people in developed countries, know it or not, own at least one.'

have led some people to 'demonise' derivatives.[9] However, regulators have generally been slow to introduce sweeping regulatory changes, as they are uncertain about the proper regulatory response to these concerns.

Two main themes have dominated the global regulatory debate in recent years. The first major theme is the extension of regulation to the over-the-counter (OTC) markets.[10] Whenever a large default or near-large default occurs, regulators renew the cry for increased regulation.[11] Those who are in favour of extending the regulatory net argue that regulation would, among other things, minimise systemic risk and provide greater legal predictability. The second major theme is the dismantling of the existing on-exchange regulatory framework.[12] There is widespread acceptance among regulators that some form of reform of the on-exchange derivatives laws is desirable. The last few years have been a period of great change in financial services regulation globally.[13] While there is a growing awareness among regulators that their existing regulatory systems are inadequate, there is considerable uncertainty as to the proper regulatory model that should be adopted. This book will examine these two important themes in the context of the legal and regulatory frameworks of Australia, New Zealand, Singapore, Malaysia, and Hong Kong (jurisdictions under study). These jurisdictions have been selected because they are part of the Asia-Pacific region, have established derivatives markets, and their legal systems are based on English common law. In addition, little has been written about the legal and regulatory issues facing their markets when compared to the availability of literature on developed European and American markets.

This book is divided into five chapters. The first chapter will explain what derivatives are, how they originated, and some of the risks they pose. It is the writer's view that no study of the legal or regulatory issues should be undertaken without a proper understanding of the products involved. The second chapter will trace the development of derivatives markets in the jurisdictions under study. It will also study practices and procedures developed to manage counterparty exposures in OTC markets. The third chapter will analyse the key legal issues arising from the use of derivatives. It will compare the legal responses to these issues in the jurisdictions under study.

---

[9] See J. E. McKown and A. T. Purcell, 'Enforcement Actions Involving Derivatives: *BT Securities Corp. and Beyond*' (1996) 65 *University of Cincinnati Law Review* 117, 119.

[10] The term 'over-the counter markets' (OTC markets) refers to the markets for customised derivatives. For the genesis of the argument that the OTC markets should be regulated, see I. Cullens, 'The Development of Regulation of OTC Derivatives Business' in E. J. Swan (ed.), *Derivative Instruments Law* (Cavendish Publishing Ltd, London, 1995), p. 1: 'The fear that OTC derivatives markets were growing too large and too fast, was first voiced in 1992 by former New York Federal Reserve Bank chairman Gerald Corrigan.'

[11] See M. Philipp and E. Nield, 'Swapclear: A New Mechanism for Enhancing Management of Counterpary Credit Risk from OTC Derivatives Transaction' (1999) 4 *Derivatives* 173. See also A. I. Ogus, *Regulation: Legal Form and Economic Theory* (Clarendon Press, Oxford, 1994), p. 357: One commentator observed that the urge to regulate is stronger than the sex urge.

[12] The term 'on-exchange regulatory framework' refers to the legal framework for standardised derivatives traded on organised exchanges.

[13] See W. Blair, 'The Reform of Financial Regulation in the U.K.' (1998) 13 JIBL 43.

The fourth chapter examines how on-exchange derivatives markets are regulated in the jurisdictions under study. It will not only compare the differences in regulatory approaches, but also highlight the inadequacies of the existing regulatory arrangements. The fifth chapter analyses the changes to the global financial landscape and how they have given rise to new regulatory challenges. It will discuss the regulatory reform currently underway in some of the jurisdictions under study.

1. An Overview of Derivatives

1.1 NATURE OF DERIVATIVES

'Derivatives' is the generic name for legally binding agreements whose values are derived from the value of an underlying commodity, financial instrument or reference rate. The basic purpose of derivatives is to transfer risk arising from a variable factor, such as the price of a commodity or the exchange rate of a currency, from one party to another who is willing or able to accept the risk. It would appear that the term 'derivatives' only gained widespread usage in the 1980s. A United States court first used the term in 1982, but it did not appear in any reported English decision until 1995.[1] Despite extensive press coverage, 'derivatives' remains perhaps the most widely misused and misunderstood financial term. This is, in part due, to the wide range of financial instruments included under the rubric of 'derivatives' and also, to the complex nature of the instruments. There is an unfortunate perception among many that a derivative is anything, which causes loss to an investor. Derivatives have variously been described as 'esoteric', 'arcane', and a subject capable of being understood only by 'rocket scientists'. While it is true that derivatives are complex instruments, they are not conceptually inscrutable. But, quantifying the market risks of derivatives or understanding how they are priced requires an advanced knowledge of mathematics.

In almost all common law jurisdictions, the term 'derivatives' has no precise legal meaning ascribed to it. For example, neither the United States *Commodity Exchange Act* nor the United Kingdom *Financial Services Act* contains a definition for derivatives. Derivatives, unlike futures contracts or securities, have not been statutorily defined, possibly because the expression encompasses far too wide a range of financial instruments.[2] Generally,

---

[1] See E. J. Swan and C. McKenna, 'The Issue of Understanding Derivatives' in E. J. Swan (ed.) *Issues in Derivative Instruments* (Kluwer Law International, The Hague, 1999), p. 3.
[2] Malaysia is an exception as the Malaysian banking legislation contains a statutory definition of 'derivative instrument'. Section 2 (7) of the *Banking and Financial Institutions Act* 1989 provides that:

    (a)   '"derivative instrument" means an instrument the value of which depends upon the value of underlying indices or assets such as currencies, securities, commodities or other

derivatives are regulated on the basis that they are either futures contracts or securities. For example, in countries like Australia, New Zealand, and Malaysia, different regulatory schemes apply to derivatives that are futures contracts and those that are securities. As far back as June 1997, the Australian Companies and Securities Advisory Committee (CASAC) recommended that the *Corporations Law* contain a general definition of derivatives.[3] The adoption of a statutory definition for derivatives would make it easier to regulate derivatives in a more consistent manner. This recommendation will be incorporated in the new regulatory framework for financial products, which is expected to be implemented as early as 2001.[4]

Different industry and regulatory groups have developed their own working definitions of 'derivatives', which provide useful insight into the range of financial instruments covered. CASAC, for example, has defined a 'derivatives instrument' as:

[A] financial instrument whose value is derived from some other thing, such as:
— a physical commodity (for instance, wool, cattle, oil, or gold)
— a financial asset (for instance, shares or bonds)
— an index (for instance, a share price index)
— an interest rate
— a currency
— another derivative.[5]

The Global Study Derivatives Group has adopted a similar definition that has often been quoted:

[A] derivatives transaction is a bilateral contract or payments exchange agreement whose value derives, as its name implies, from the value of an underlying asset or underlying reference rate or index.[6]

---

derivative instruments and includes a derivative financial instrument and a commodity derivative instrument;
(b) "derivative financial instrument" means futures, forward, swap, or option contract, or other financial instrument with similar characteristics but shall not include—
　(i) all on-balance sheet receivables and payables, including those that derive their values or contractually require cash flows from the price of some other security or index, such as mortgage-backed securities, interest-only and principal-only obligations, and indexed debt instruments; and
　(ii) option features that are embedded within an on-balance sheet receivable or payable, such as the conversion feature and call provisions embedded in convertible bonds; and
(c) "commodity derivative instrument" includes, to the extent such instrument is not a derivative financial instrument, commodity futures, commodity forward, commodity swap, commodity option, or other commodity instruments with similar characteristics, that are reasonably possible to be settled in cash or with securities or other derivative instruments.'

[3] See Companies and Securities Advisory Committee, *Regulation of On-exchange and OTC Derivatives Markets* ('CASAC Report on Derivatives Markets') (Sydney, June 1997), p. 64.
[4] See Treasury, *Financial Products, Service Providers and Markets—An Integrated Framework* ('Implementing CLERP 6 Consultation Paper') (AGPS, Canberra, 1999).
[5] See Companies and Securities Advisory Committee, *Law of Derivatives: An International Comparison* (CASAC Research Paper) (Sydney, January 1995), p. 1.
[6] See Global Derivatives Study Group, *Derivatives: Practices and Principles* (Group of Thirty Report) (Group of Thirty, Washington, DC, July 1993), p. 28.

Although the International Swaps and Derivatives Association's definition is not much different from either of the above definitions, it is narrower in scope since it confines the term to instruments designed to manage risks:

Derivatives are bilateral contracts involving the exchange of cash flows and *designed to shift risk between parties.* When transactions mature, the amounts owed by each party are determined by the prices of underlying commodities, securities or indices.[7] [emphasis added]

However, formulating a suitable legal definition of 'derivatives' is a more difficult task. The definition should not be too narrow as it would not be able to accommodate the endless array of new products regularly introduced into the marketplace, many of which possess characteristics that do not easily fit into any established category of financial instruments. At the same time, the definition should not be too wide, as it would cover financial activities that the legislature may have no intention of regulating. This could explain why little effort has been made so far to adopt a statutory definition of 'derivatives'.

Generally, all derivatives are based on one, or both, of two primary elements:

- the forward element, under which there is an obligation to deliver or make a cash adjustment at some time in the future based on the current or future value of the underlying asset or index;
- the option element, which gives the option holder the right, but not the obligation, to buy or sell the underlying asset or instrument, at a certain price, on or before a specified future date.[8]

A derivatives contract with a forward element gives rise to symmetrical obligations because one contracting party must buy and the other party must sell the underlying asset or instrument at a given price, at an agreed future date. On the other hand, a derivatives contract with an option element gives rise to an asymmetrical obligation, as the option holder is not legally obliged to exercise the option. It is only the option writer who has to deliver or take delivery of the underlying asset or instrument.

Derivatives are simply contracts that give rise to rights and obligations, which take a variety of forms such as cash settlement and delivery or transfer of rights to the underlying interest.[9] Generally, they do not themselves grant or transfer the underlying interest from which they are derived.[10] But for some derivatives, the right to transfer the underlying interest arises on maturity of the contract. Counterparties to over-the-counter derivatives transactions are usually selected on the basis of their credit standing. It has

---

[7] See P. Levin, J. Luke, and P. Sundaravej, 'Recent Developments Affecting US Financial Derivatives' (November 1994) *International Financial Law Review* 10.
[8] See CASAC Report on Derivatives Markets, above n. 3, p. 17.
[9] See M. Cashmere, *Tax and Corporate Finance into the New Millennium* (CCH, Sydney, 1999), p. 136.
[10] Ibid.

been suggested that the market value of derivatives is not only derived from the market price of the underlying asset, but also the strength of the promisor's ability to perform.[11] The consent of both contracting parties is usually required before the transfer of contractual interests or obligations to a third party. Most market documentation in use today would contain a transfer clause to this effect.[12]

1.2   HISTORICAL BACKGROUND

Commodity trading is as ancient as the earliest civilisations that flourished in the Middle East. The existence of markets that specialised in the spot and forward delivery of specific commodities in the pre-Christian empires, suggests that forward contracts were used for hedging even in early times.[13] As early as 2000 BC, rice producers in China negotiated with merchants to deliver specified quantities of rice at a future date for an agreed price.[14] These contracts were entered into prior to the planting of the rice so that the merchants were assured of a fixed quantity of rice at an agreed price and the rice growers of a market for their crops.[15]

The origins of options may be traced back to the ancient Greeks.[16] There are claims that the oldest reference to derivatives is found in the works of Aristotle, written some 2400 years ago.[17] Aristotle tells the story of a poor philosopher named Thales, who used his knowledge of astronomy to predict the demand for olive presses. He forecasted that weather conditions would favour the production of olives. So he gained control of the market for olive presses by taking options on them. When his predictions materialised, there was a great demand for olive presses. Since he had a monopoly on the supply of presses, he could charge whatever prices he wanted and soon became very rich. However, the early history of options trading did not always produce such a happy ending. In fact it was characterised by scandals, defaults and other criminal activities as trading was carried out on an over-the-counter basis.[18] It was not until the opening of the Chicago Board Options Exchange in 1973 that options on stocks and physical commodities gained respectability and grew in popularity.[19]

As for futures contracts and swaps, they did not develop until very much later. It is now widely accepted that the first organised futures exchange

---

[11] See Swan and McKenna, above n. 1, p. 16.
[12] See for example, *ISDA Multi-Currency Master Agreement* 1992, clause 7.
[13] See A. D. Seidel and P. M. Ginsberg, *Commodities Trading* (New Jersey, Prentice Hall, 1983), p. 5.
[14] See V. L. Chou, 'Derivatives and Dialectics: The Evolution of the Chinese Futures Market' (1997) 72 *New York University Law Review* 175.
[15] Ibid.
[16] See D. Ford, *The Investor's Guide to Traded Options* (London, Pitman Publishing, 1994), p. 2.
[17] See G. Crawford and B. Sen, *Derivatives for Decision Makers* (John Wiley & Sons, New York, 1996), pp. 7–10.
[18] See M. D. Fitzgerald, *Financial Options* (Euromoney Publications, 1987, London), p. 1.
[19] Ibid.

was the Osaka rice market, which was formed in 1650.[20] This exchange, which later became known as the 'Dojima rice market' was well organised and regulated. It had rules relating to trading, contract standardisation, settlement, and the use of a clearinghouse.[21] For instance, the contract term was limited to four months, only four grades of rice were traded, no physical delivery was allowed, and all trades had to be cleared through a clearinghouse. However, unlike modern exchanges, the Dojima rice market did not impose any margining requirement on its traders. It would appear that the Dojima rice contract was the precursor of the modern futures contract.

Organised futures markets developed later in the Western World. Some commentators argue that a rudimentary form of commodity futures was used by Liverpool cotton traders in the eighteenth century, while others point to the trading of tea and rubber futures in the London coffee houses around that time.[22] There are also reports that futures contracts were traded in Holland and France before 1832, although they were different in nature and specifications from the futures contracts in use today.[23] Despite these various claims, the evidence overwhelmingly suggests that it was the North Americans who developed the first modern futures contract.

In the early part of the nineteenth century, several organised commodities exchanges emerged in the United States, the first of which was the Chicago Board of Trade (CBOT), established in 1842 with 82 members.[24] Modern futures contracts evolved from forward contracts traded on the CBOT. On 13 March 1851 the first forward contract was recorded on the CBOT.[25] It involved 3000 bushels of corn for delivery in June at a price of one cent below the 13 March price per bushel.[26] Initially, forward contracts were made between country merchants and terminal operators, with both parties intending to take and make delivery.[27] By the latter half of the 1850s, the contracts changed hands several times before being sold to someone who had intentions of taking delivery.[28] The popularity of the forward contract stemmed from its detailed and standardised contract specifications.[29] With the increase in business volume, trading was often halted to allow record keeping to catch up.[30] To solve this problem the CBOT devised a new mechanism, the futures contract, which had all the benefits of the forward contract,

---

[20] See J. D. LaPlante, 'Growth and Organisation of Commodity Markets', in P. J. Kaufman (ed.), *Handbook of Futures Markets* (New York, Wiley, 1984), para. 1.7.
[21] Ibid.
[22] See M. Fox-Andrews and N. Meaden, *Derivatives Markets and Investments Management* (Prentice Hall/Woodhead-Faulkner, London, 1995), p. 6.
[23] See LaPlante, above n. 20, para. 1.9.
[24] See R. J. Teweles and F. J. Jones, *The Futures Game* (McGraw-Hill Book Co, New York, 1987), p. 9.
[25] Ibid.
[26] Ibid.
[27] See LaPlante, above n. 20, para. 1.8.
[28] Ibid.
[29] The contract not only specified the quantity and price, but also the quality of the commodity, the place and date of delivery.
[30] See D. Courtney and E. C. Bettelheim, *An Investor's Guide to the Commodity Futures Markets* (Butterworths, London, 1986), p. 11.

but with important additions.[31] The futures contract was transferable, and certain of its terms were standardised. For instance, delivery months were predetermined, and trading lots were standardised.[32] In 1865, the CBOT officially launched the first futures contract and in the same year it also initiated a margining system to eliminate non-fulfilment of contracts.[33]

During the early history of futures trading, the bases of futures contracts were usually commodity prices or stock prices. However, the collapse of the Bretton Woods Agreement on fixed-rates of exchange for currencies in the early 1970s created a demand for financial derivatives.[34] On 16 May 1972 the International Monetary Market, a division of the Chicago Mercantile Exchange introduced six foreign currency futures contracts.[35] At that time few would have foreseen the introduction of futures contracts based on 'interest rates', but by 20 October 1975, a GNMA futures contract began to be traded on the CBOT.[36] The demand for a hedging mechanism for interest rates was fuelled by the increase in interest rate instability.[37] Stock index futures were introduced on 24 February 1982, with the listing of the Value Line Composite Index futures contract by the Kansas City Board of Trade.[38] The delay in the introduction of stock index futures contracts was largely due to uncertainty as to whether the Commodity Futures Trading Commission or the Securities and Exchange Commission had jurisdiction over the contracts.[39]

Swaps originated from the sterling pound and dollar parallel loans arranged between British and American entities in the 1970s.[40] For example, if there was an English company which wanted to finance the operations of its subsidiary in New York, and an American company which wanted to finance its subsidiary in London, both would enter into parallel or back-to-back loans. In other words, the American company would borrow in dollars and lend them to the English company, and the latter would borrow an equivalent amount in pounds sterling and lend them to the American company. These parallel loans were the forerunners of swaps, in particular currency swaps, and were popular as a means of financing investments abroad in the face of foreign exchange controls.[41] Between 1947 and 1979, exchange

---

[31]   Ibid.

[32]   Ibid.

[33]   See Chicago Board of Trade, *Commodity Trading Manual* (1989), p. 5.

[34]   There were also other factors, such as financial sector liberalisation and advances in technology, which stimulated the development of financial derivatives. See D. Lynch, 'Growth in Asia-Pacific Markets' in E. Sheedy and S. McCracken (eds), *Derivatives: The Risks That Remain* (Allen & Unwin, St Leonards, NSW, 1997), pp. 25–27.

[35]   See Teweles and Jones, above n. 24, p. 515.

[36]   Id, pp. 527–528. See also, A. Schick, 'Financial Derivatives Instruments' (1989) 4 JIBFL 403: GNMA certificates are mortgage-backed certificates issued by private lenders and guaranteed by the Government National Mortgage Assistance.

[37]   Two factors contributed to the increase in interest rate instability during that period. The first was the attempt by governments to manage exchange rate fluctuations through the manipulation of short-term interest rates, and the second, was their adoption of money supply targets. See K. Redhead, *Financial Derivatives* (Prentice Hall, London, 1997), p. 2.

[38]   See Teweles and Jones, above n. 24, p. 538.

[39]   Ibid.

[40]   See S. Das, *Swaps and Financial Derivatives* (2nd edn, Law Book Co, Sydney, 1994), pp. 14–15.

[41]   See S. Decovny, *Swaps* (London, Woodhead-Faulkner, 1992), p. 1.

controls were imposed on residents in the United Kingdom. For example, no foreign currency payments could be made to non-residents of the sterling area without Treasury permission.[42]

However, there were two major disadvantages of using this financing technique. First, the English borrower would have to locate an American firm with identical financing needs. Second, if one firm defaulted in its obligation, it was not relieved of its obligation to the other. These problems were resolved by the development of swaps. The swap agreement clarified the set-off rights of the parties, and the emergence of swap dealers who were prepared to act as counterparties alleviated the problem of finding borrowers with reciprocal needs.[43] In 1976, Continental Illinois Limited and Goldman Sachs arranged the first currency swap between Bos Kalis Westminster (a Dutch company) and ICI Finance (a British company).[44] The International Business Machines-World Bank swap in August 1981 was a landmark in the development of the swap market, as the international reputation of the counterparties helped to promote universal acceptance of swaps.[45]

The initial interest rate swaps were almost all based on the United States dollar and had a common theme.[46] In the early 1980s, there were many United States corporations that required fixed-rate financing but had exhausted their domestic funding sources. However, they had no problems obtaining floating-rate funding at favourable rates from United States banks. Coincidentally, around this time there were many European and Japanese banks that required floating rate finance but discovered that they could only obtain fixed rate financing at very favourable rates in the Eurobond market. This mismatch of financing needs created a window of opportunity for investment banks and other financial intermediaries to market their swaps transactions. Swaps allowed these comparative advantages to be exploited and in the process created mutually beneficial outcomes for the counterparties. However, the swap market did not take off until the swap dealers realised that they did not need to find matching counterparties to create swaps. They could commit to one side of an interest rate swap and then go looking for another side as they could hedge their exposures in the futures market. Later it dawned upon them that there was even no necessity to find matching counterparties because the swaps in their portfolios would to some extent cancel out each other's risks.

To a large extent, the growth of derivatives in the Asia-Pacific markets has mirrored the growth of derivatives globally. The key factor behind the development of derivatives in the Asia-Pacific region was its rapid and sustained

---

[42] See P. Ottino, 'London Futures Markets: Self-regulation, or Bureaucratic Centralism?' in E. J. Swan (ed.), *Derivative Instruments Law* (Cavendish Publishing Limited, London, 1995), p. 138.
[43] See R. Romano, 'A Thumbnail Sketch of Derivative Securities and Their Regulation', (1996) 55 *Maryland Law Review* 50.
[44] See Das, above n. 40, p. 15.
[45] See Decovny, above n. 41, p. 2. See also, Das, above n. 40, p. 15: '...the World Bank swapped a US$290 million bond issue into an equivalent amount of DEM and SFR provided by IBM under an arrangement devised by Salomon Brothers.'
[46] See Crawford and Sen, above n. 17, pp. 27–31.

economic growth.[47] As countries in the region expanded their economies, they attracted considerable inflows of capital from the more economically developed countries of the world such as the United States. This in turn created a need for sophisticated risk management instruments to manage the resulting financial exposures. However, the development of derivatives markets has been far from uniform in the region. At one end of the development spectrum there are mature markets like Australia and Singapore, while at the other end, there are under-developed markets like Indonesia and Thailand. Some of the factors which have retarded the growth of derivatives in the less developed markets, are the absence of a 'risk management culture', inadequate infrastructure, and underdeveloped physical or cash markets.[48]

1.3   TYPES OF DERIVATIVES

The traditional approach to categorising derivatives is to classify them according to product type. Under this approach, there are four broad categories of derivatives: forwards, swaps, futures, and options. Forwards and swaps are privately negotiated customised contracts, transacted in the wholesale markets. Futures and options on futures are standardised contracts traded on organised exchanges. Privately negotiated options also exist on a multitude of assets and indices. There is a fifth category of derivatives that have recently emerged. According to the Group of Thirty Report, 'the term 'derivatives' ... is [also] used by some observers to refer to a wide variety of debt instruments which have payoff characteristics reflecting embedded characteristics, or have options characteristics, or are created by 'stripping' particular components of other instruments such as principal or interest payments.'[49] This category of derivatives is referred to as 'derivatives securities' or 'hybrid instruments' since they exhibit characteristics found in more than one type of instrument. Another approach is to divide derivatives into three different groups: exchange-traded futures and options; debt securities with an unusual rate of return; and over-the-counter derivatives.[50] A third approach is to categorise derivatives according to the nature of the underlying commodity, instrument or reference rate. Under this approach, derivatives may be classified as interest and currency rates derivatives, equity derivatives, commodity derivatives, credit derivatives and weather derivatives.

Credit derivatives are a recent innovation and refer to financial instruments whose values are linked to the creditworthiness or perceived creditworthiness of a particular entity. Das has described them as traditional derivatives, such as swaps and options, reengineered to have a credit

---

[47]   See Lynch, above n. 34, pp. 27–30, for a discussion on the factors that have contributed to the development of derivatives in the Asia-Pacific region.
[48]   Ibid.
[49]   See Group of Thirty Report, above n. 6, p. 29.
[50]   See S. K. Henderson, 'Derivatives Law as a Niche Area is Dead' (1997) 12 JIBL 351, 352.

orientation.[51] Although credit derivatives are capable of handling a wide range of credit situations, there are five basic types of credit derivatives: standard credit default swap; total return swap; basket trade; quasi-securitisation structure using credit default swaps; and quasi-securitisation structure with credit-linked note.[52] Weather derivatives are also another very recent financial innovation. They are instruments whose values are linked to changes in weather conditions. They enable end-users to hedge against reduced demand for their products arising from changes in weather conditions.[53]

Classifying derivatives according to the nature of the underlying asset or instrument is useful since each type of 'underlying' gives rise to its own unique legal and regulatory issues. For example, credit derivatives raise interesting issues relating to the banker's duty of confidentiality to its customers.[54] Another issue is whether credit derivatives are insurance contracts and therefore subject to insurance legislation. Similarly, equity derivatives raise issues relating to insider trading, which are not applicable to other derivatives such as interest or currency rate derivatives. This chapter will adopt the traditional approach to the classification of derivatives, as it is still the most popular method in use.

1.3.1 Forward Contracts

A forward contract is defined as an agreement, which 'obligates one counterparty to buy, and the other counterparty to sell, a specific underlying at a specific price, amount, and date in the future.'[55] For example, a farmer may contract in June to sell wheat in December in anticipation of a fall in the price of wheat during harvesting time. The buyer, a miller, may wish to determine in advance the price to be paid for wheat. Both parties will enter into a contract to fix the price, grade of wheat, delivery details and credit terms, if any. The party that agrees to sell assumes what is referred to as a 'short position', and the party that agrees to buy assumes what is referred to as a 'long position'. By selling forward, the 'short' (in this case, the farmer) shifts the risk of selling wheat at a lower price to the 'long' (in this case, the miller). Trading to reduce risk is called hedging, and is a primary reason for the existence of forward markets.[56]

---

[51] See S. Das, 'Credit Derivatives—Instruments' in S. Das (ed.), *Credit Derivatives* (John Wiley & Sons, Singapore, 1998), ch. 1 for a discussion of credit derivatives.
[52] For a description of how each type works, see 'Basic Types of Credit Derivatives and Their U.S. Taxation' (2000) 1 : 10 *Derivatives Report* 20. See also S. K. Henderson, 'Credit Derivatives—Part I: The Context' (1998) 13 JIBFL 332.
[53] For a more detailed discussion of weather derivatives, see for example, P. U. Ali, 'Weather Derivatives, Hedging Volumetric Risk and Directors' Duties' (2000) 18 C&SLJ 151.
[54] For a discussion of the various legal and regulatory issues arising from the use of credit derivatives, see C. Brown, 'Legal, Documentation and Regulatory Issues of Credit Derivatives' (1997) 12 JIBFL 119; S. K. Henderson, 'Credit Derivatives—Part 3: Selected Legal Issues' (1999) 14 JIBFL 193; P. U. Ali, 'Unbundling Credit Risk: The Nature and Regulation of Credit Derivatives' (2000) 11 JBFLP 73.
[55] See Group of Thirty Report, above n. 6, p. 30.
[56] See Romano, above n. 43, 9.

Markets exist for a wide variety of forward contracts, as 'underlyings' range from physical commodities to currencies and interest rates.[57] Terms such as the contract size, grade, credit terms, delivery month and location are subject to negotiation between the parties. Forward contracts are therefore more flexible than futures contracts. However, the credit risk is generally greater for forward contracts as the contract amounts are usually large, and there is no clearinghouse to guarantee against counterparty default. Forward contracts do not necessarily increase the profitability of the parties. Rather, they improve the predictability of variable outcomes. In the above example, the farmer could be worse off if the price of wheat rose in December, as the farmer has agreed to sell the wheat at a lower price. But by selling forward, the farmer is assured of a particular price for his wheat.

1.3.2   Futures Contracts

A futures contract is similar to a forward contract, in that it is an agreement to buy or sell a specified commodity or instrument, at a specified price, at a date in the future.[58] It could also be an agreement to make a cash adjustment based on the change in the value of an index or reference rate, at an agreed future date. For example, the buyer of a Nikkei share index futures contract agrees to pay or receive from the seller an amount of money based on the value of the share index at a predetermined date in the future. Despite the broad similarity, there are a number of commercial and institutional differences between futures contracts and forward contracts, which are worthy of mention.

The first difference is that the contract terms of futures contracts are standardised. For example, all Brent Crude Oil futures traded on the Singapore Monetary International Exchange will have the same contract size, delivery months, minimum price fluctuation, and settlement option. Full standardisation leads to fungibility, which means that contracts of the same maturity are perfect substitutes for each other. In the vast majority of transactions, delivery is not made and they are 'closed-out' or discharged by the investors entering into offsetting transactions.[59] Most investors who trade in futures contracts have no intention of taking delivery.

The second difference is that futures contracts are traded on exchanges. In most jurisdictions it is illegal to trade in futures on an over-the-counter basis. This is often referred to as the 'on-exchange trading rule'. Exchanges

---

[57]   These three categories of forward contracts are usually referred to as 'forward commodity contracts', 'forward foreign exchange contracts', and 'forward rate agreements' respectively.

[58]   See M. Hains, 'Futures Contracts: Do They Include Forward and Swaps?' in G. Walker and B. Fisse (eds), *Securities Regulation in Australia & New Zealand* (Oxford University Press, Auckland, 1994), p. 846: 'It is common to speak of buying and selling futures. Technically, the parties do not buy or sell contracts. They enter contracts to buy or sell commodities for future delivery for deliverable contracts, or to make cash adjustment in the future for cash-settled contracts.'

[59]   See J. S. Currie, *Australian Futures Regulation* (Longman Professional, Melbourne, 1994), p. 5: '... very few futures contracts [less than 2 per cent] are completed by actual physical delivery of the underlying commodity or instrument.'

are organised markets where buyers and sellers meet. They, however, are not public markets, as they exist primarily to provide their members with the facilities to trade in futures.[60] Trading usually takes place on a trading floor using the 'open outcry' method, which involves the use of hand signals and verbal communication to make bids and offers. This is no longer true as more and more exchanges are introducing electronic screen trading to either complement or replace floor trading. Exchanges like the New Zealand Futures and Options Exchange, the Sydney Futures Exchange and the Kuala Lumpur Options and Financial Futures Exchange have discarded the use of the open outcry method.

The third difference is that a clearinghouse, which is either owned by the exchange or independently operated, guarantees the contractual obligations.[61] This is normally achieved by the clearinghouse interposing itself between the parties to a futures contract. Normally, the relationship between the parties would be clarified in the relevant exchange's or clearinghouse's rules.[62] As long as the buyer and seller meet their obligations, the clearinghouse has no exposure. To protect itself against default, the clearinghouse will usually impose margins on its members.[63] These margins, which are either in the form of cash or securities, will be used to cover the obligations of defaulting members. In addition, clearinghouses may also adopt a number of other financial and operational safeguards such as minimum financial requirements, position limits, and segregation of customers' accounts.[64]

Futures contracts are widely used for several reasons. First, they attract lower transaction costs. They are normally only a fraction of the costs of trading in the underlying commodity or instrument. Second, counterparty risk is minimal as it is unlikely that the clearinghouse would collapse, as it is usually well-backed financially. In addition, if a participant defaults, the rules of a typical clearinghouse will provide for the allocation of the losses to the surviving participants according to a predetermined formula. Third,

---

[60] See 73 Am Jur 2d, *Stock and Commodity Exchanges*, section 1.

[61] See Currie, above n. 59, pp. 15–29. There has been some debate in the past whether the futures contract is formed at the time of acceptance of the bid or offer, or at the time of registration of the contract with the clearinghouse. See also, M. Hains, 'Reflections on the Sydney Futures Exchange Clearinghouse: The Rise of the Mirrored Contract Theory' (1994) 5 JBFLP 257 et seq. for a discussion of the legal relationship between market participants.

[62] For example, see the *Consolidated Rules of the Singapore International Monetary Exchange* (1995), Rule 514.

[63] See Romano, above n. 43, 18–19. All members are required to maintain a margin account with the clearinghouse. An 'initial margin', which depending on the volatility of the underlying asset may range between one and twenty per cent of the contract value, will be placed in the account before the start of trading. The balance in the margin account must not fall below the 'maintenance margin', which is typically set at seventy-five percent of the initial margin. Through a process known as 'marking-to-market' the clearinghouse will daily recompute the balance in the margin account based on the previous day's closing price. If the 'initial margin' falls below the 'maintenance margin', the member would be required to place additional funds into the account to restore the balance to the 'initial margin' level. The amount used to 'top-up' the margin account is referred to as the 'variation margin'.

[64] For a discussion of the financial and operational safeguards adopted by clearinghouses, see R. Dale, 'Derivatives Clearinghouses: The Regulatory Challenge' (1997) 12 JIBL 46.

futures contracts permit anonymity of participants as most brokers act for undisclosed principals. Fourth, there is no requirement for large capital outlays as initial deposits range between five and 15 per cent only. Fifth, futures markets are more liquid, and therefore it is easier for participants to 'close-out' or settle their contracts. However, a major disadvantage of using futures contracts is their inflexibility. Any investor using futures contracts for hedging would be exposed to basis risk. 'Basis risk' refers to the risk that the futures contract and the instrument that is being hedged may not be perfectly matched.

The following example illustrates the attractiveness of using futures contracts. An investor expects Malaysian shares to rise because of an improvement in the country's balance of payment, and decides to buy futures contracts because of the low capital outlay involved. On 27 October 1999 when the index stands at 1050, the investor buys one December KLSE CI Futures Contract for MYR 105,000. A deposit of MYR 750 is placed as an initial margin with the futures broker. By 19 December 1999, the last trading day for the contract, the index has risen to 1,100. The investor closes out the contract and (since one index point represents MYR 100) realises a gross profit of MYR 5,000, which is much higher than the initial outlay of MYR 750. Of course, had the market moved in the opposite direction, the investor would have incurred equally large losses. It should be pointed out that futures contracts are only risky if they are traded on a leveraged basis.[65] It is possible for an investor to trade in futures on a non-leveraged basis by using futures as a proxy for the underlying investment. In such a case, the investor is exposed to the same risks as he or she would be if trading in the underlying investment.

1.3.3   Swaps

Swaps like forward contracts, are customised over-the-counter transactions. A swap has been described as 'an agreement between two parties to pay each other a series of cash flows, based on fixed or floating interest rates in the same or different currencies.'[66] The cash flows are either fixed or calculated at each payment date by multiplying the notional principal by a specified price (such as the USD/barrel of oil) or reference rate (such as six-month LIBOR). At the outset, the parties view as equal the present values of the cash flows at the prevailing interest rate or exchange rates. The notional principal is not exchanged, except for currency swaps, and interim payments are generally netted.[67] Although most currency swaps involve an initial and final exchange of currencies, it is possible to eliminate the exchanges through appropriate spot foreign exchange transactions and payment of a currency difference.[68]

---

[65]   'Leverage' is sometimes referred to as 'gearing'.
[66]   See S. K. Henderson, 'Swap Financing' in J. J. Norton and R. M. Auerback (eds), *International Finance in the 1990s* (Blackwell Finance, London, 1993), p. 345.
[67]   See Group of Thirty Report, above n. 6, p. 31.
[68]   See Decovny, above n. 41, p. 73.

Swap transactions are broadly classified into interest rate, currency, commodity, or equity swaps. The most common swap transaction is the fixed-for-floating interest rate swap, often referred to as the 'plain vanilla swap'. In such a swap, a counterparty with fixed-rate liabilities agrees to exchange interest payments with a counterparty with floating-rate liabilities. Commodity and equity swaps are, however, of more recent origin.[69] A commodity swap is basically a variant of the 'plain vanilla swap', except that the floating rate is pegged to the price of a commodity.[70] Equity swaps are more complex than commodity swaps. In some equity swaps, one counterparty pays a rate pegged to the price of a share index or an individual share, while in other equity swaps both counterparties pay rates pegged to different share indices.[71]

It is possible to use swaps for a variety of purposes including the reduction of borrowing costs; asset and liability management; and yield enhancement. The principle of comparative advantage, a concept central to international trade, plays an important role in swap transactions. Each counterparty borrows in the market where it enjoys a comparative advantage, and through the use of a swap obtains financing at a more favourable rate than it would otherwise be able to do so. Swap cash flows can be decomposed into equivalent cash flows from a bundle of simple forward contracts. This has implications for the hedging of swap risks. Swaps are now hedged with a variety of derivative products, and no longer only by matching two identical but opposing swaps.

1.3.4 Options

An option is the 'right to buy or sell a specific quantity of an underlying asset at a specific price on or before a specific date in the future.'[72] The right to buy an asset is a 'call option', while the right to sell an asset is a 'put option'. Each type of option can be bought or sold, so there are four distinct types of option transactions. In other words an investor can buy a 'call option' or 'put option', or sell a 'call option' or a 'put option'. The buyer of an option is usually called the 'option holder', and the seller of the option, the 'option writer'. An American option is one which can be exercised any time until maturity, while a European option can only be exercised on maturity date.[73] The option holder must pay the option writer a price known as the 'premium' in order to acquire the rights under the option. Options are available on a wide range of assets including commodities, foreign currencies, shares, bonds, and even other derivatives.

It is often said that options create rights and not obligations. This is certainly true from the option holder's perspective. If the price moves favourably,

---

[69]   Romano, above n. 43, 51.
[70]   See L. Chew, *Managing Derivative Risks* (John Wiley & Sons, Chichester, 1996), p. 292.
[71]   Id., p. 295.
[72]   See Fitzgerald, above n. 18, p. 1.
[73]   See A. Hudson, *The Law of Financial Derivatives* (Sweet & Maxwell, London, 1996), pp. 333, 336 respectively.

the holder can exercise the option and enjoy the profits. But, if the price of
the underlying asset moves unfavourably, the holder can abandon the
option and forfeit the premium. On the other hand, the option writer is
legally obliged to either buy or sell the underlying asset, even if it involves
incurring losses. Not surprisingly, clearinghouses impose margin requirements on writers of 'naked call options'.[74] It would therefore be more accurate to say that while options create rights but not obligations for option
holders, the same does not necessarily hold true for option writers.

If the option holder will make a profit from the exercise of the option, the
option is described as being 'in-the-money' or having an 'intrinsic value'.
However, if the option holder will incur a loss from the exercise of the option,
the option is described as being 'out-of-money'. The valuation of options is
very complex because the relationship between the value of the option and
the underlying asset is not constant. There are a number of factors that determine the intrinsic value of an option. These factors include the price of the
underlying asset, the time to expiration of the option, and the exercise price
of the option. An option may still have a market value despite not having an
intrinsic value because of the possibility that the value of the underlying
asset may move in favour of the option holder before the expiry date.

The benefit of using options is illustrated in the following example. An
investor expects BHP share prices to rise, as the investor is confident of BHP
reporting an abnormally large profit. On 15 September 1997, when a BHP
share is being traded at $18.96, the investor buys 1000 BHP December call
options with an exercise price of $20 for $0.41. The price of BHP shares rises
to $21 on 21 December 1997 and the investor exercises the option. Assuming
the shares are sold in the cash market for the same price, the investor will
make approximately $590 from an outlay of only $410. The extent of losses
to the option holder is limited to the premium paid. In the above example, if
the price of the shares falls below $20, the investor is unlikely to exercise the
option. Based on the premium of $0.41 per option, the investor would stand
to lose only $410.

Options are regarded as the most versatile and exciting of all financial
engineering tools.[75] They can be broadly classified into exchange-traded
options like options on futures contracts, and privately negotiated options
like commodity and currency options. Collars, caps, and floors also belong
to the category of privately negotiated options. They are usually used in
connection with swap transactions.[76] A 'cap' basically protects the buyer
against a rise in interest rate. In exchange for a premium, the seller agrees to
pay the buyer the difference between the actual interest rate and the cap
rate. A 'floor' is the reverse of a cap and the seller only pays the buyer if the
actual interest rate falls below the floor rate. Buying a 'collar' is equivalent
to buying a cap and selling a floor.[77]

---

[74] The writer of a 'naked option' does not own the underlying stock, whereas the writer of a
'covered option' does.
[75] See L. Galitz, *Financial Engineering* (Pitman Publishing, London, 1994), p. 185.
[76] See Hudson, above n. 73, pp. 28–29.
[77] See Group of Thirty Report, above n. 6, p. 33.

1.3.5   Derivative Securities

According to the Global Derivatives Study Group there are three main categories of derivatives: structured securities and deposits, stripped securities, and securities with option characteristics.[78] Within each category of derivative securities there are various sub-categories. The range of derivatives securities is so large that it would not be possible to describe all of them here. However, one group of derivatives securities in particular, merits closer scrutiny as they were featured in a number of major derivatives-linked losses in the United States. This group of derivatives, which are popularly referred to as 'structured notes', are essentially a form of structured securities.

'Structured notes' are basically debt securities, issued by governmental entities, banks, and corporations with good credit ratings.[79] They offer higher returns than conventional securities because they have payoff characteristics similar to derivatives. They come in a wide variety and include the following:

- 'inverse floaters' whose coupons increase as interest rates decline and decrease as interest rates rise;
- 'index-linked floaters' whose coupons are tied to long-term interest rates such as the ten-year Constant Maturity Treasury (CMT) in the United States; and
- 'leveraged floaters' whose coupons contain a multiplier, which magnifies changes in interest rates.[80]

In the early 1990s, structured notes were popular in the United States for a number of reasons. They offered much higher returns than other investments in a low interest rate environment. Since money managers could only invest in low-yielding public-listed bonds issued by government agencies and similar credits, structured notes were extremely attractive to money managers as they enjoyed the highest credit ratings.[81] However, many buyers of these structured notes failed to realise that these were highly leveraged instruments. To further aggravate matters, some of the buyers did not fully understand the complex mathematical formulae used to calculate the interest charges. As a result, a number of institutional investors lost massive amounts of money from the use of structured notes.[82]

Apart from structured notes, there is another category of derivative securities known as 'collateralised mortgage obligations' (CMOs), which also deserves some mention.[83] These securities are usually referred to as

---

[78]   Id., p. 29.
[79]   See Romano, above n. 43, 74.
[80]   See Chew, above n. 70, pp. 50–51 for a review of the various types of structured notes.
[81]   Id., p. 57.
[82]   Id., p. 55. Bank of America's Pacific Horizon prime money market fund required a cash bailout of USD 67.9 million; fund manager Piper Jaffray reported a loss of USD 700 million; and Paine Webber had to inject USD 268 million into a short-term bond fund.
[83]   See Crawford and Sen, above n. 17, pp. 39–47, for a more detailed discussion of the subject.

'mortgage derivatives', as their values are derived from the values of underlying mortgages. In the United States, most mortgages are insured against default with government-sponsored federal agencies like the Federal National Mortgage Association. These insured mortgages are marketable financial assets, as the originating banks would normally continue to service them for the new owners. The originating bank may sell them in pools or 'tranches' of the same maturity since the risk varies with the maturity of the tranche. Alternatively, the originating bank may repackage the securities in such a way that one class of security holders may only be entitled to interest payments, while another may only be entitled to principal payments. A major risk faced by investors is that when interest rates fall, the homeowners may refinance their loans and prepay their mortgages. Nonetheless, CMOs play an important economic role as they provide cash-strapped banks with an alternative avenue of funds.

1.4   USERS AND USES OF DERIVATIVES

There are two main groups of derivatives users: end-users and dealers. End-users include commercial firms, financial institutions, governmental bodies, and institutional investors (such as pension and mutual funds). In some markets, retail investors are also important users of certain types of derivatives. For example, in Malaysia and Hong Kong, the market for stock index futures contracts has a large retail element. Dealers are mainly large international banks and securities firms, but also include a few insurance companies and corporations with high credit ratings. Sometimes an institution may participate in derivatives activity both as an end-user and dealer. A bank, for instance, may use derivatives to lower its own funding costs, but at the same time trade in derivatives on behalf of end-users to increase its fee-based income.

An international survey of the corporate use of financial derivatives, covering 386 major corporations over 16 countries, released by Price Waterhouse in October 1995, revealed the following findings:

- 73 per cent of all respondents used derivatives to manage their interest rate exposures; and
- 96 per cent of respondents used currency derivatives.[84]

Although the above findings suggest that derivatives are widely used internationally, there is a wide divergence in usage not only between countries but also within countries.[85]

Despite the large number of derivatives users, there are only a limited number of dealers. There is also significant imbalance in the distribution of

---

[84] See R. Allan, 'Inside the Corporate Treasury' in E. Sheedy and S. McCracken (eds), *Derivatives: The Risks that Remain* (Allen & Unwin, St Leonards, NSW, 1997), p. 79.
[85] Id., p. 80.

business among the dealers. For example, although there were about 150 firms acting as derivatives dealers worldwide as at the end of 1992, dealing activity was concentrated only among a few firms.[86] To give some idea of the extent of market concentration, at the end of 1991 over half the world-wide contract amounts of interest rate and currency swaps were dealt through eight United States bank dealers.[87] By the end of 1994, the number of banks in the United States reporting derivatives activity had risen to 633, but only six of them accounted for 83 per cent of the market.[88] This market concentration can be explained in terms of the need to develop complex risk management systems and the pressure to limit counterparty exposure, which has resulted in the concentration of activity among a few large firms.[89]

Derivatives provide numerous and substantial benefits to end-users. It is possible to identify four main uses, namely, risk management, yield enhancement, funding costs reduction, and portfolio diversification. Risk management is by far the most important function of derivatives. Derivatives offer end-users an efficient method of managing risks arising from either fluctuation in interest and exchange rates, or commodity prices. For example, a company that has borrowed floating-rate funds may enter into an interest rate swap to minimise its exposure to interest rate volatility. Or, a Hong Kong exporter that receives payment in Australian dollars may wish to sell Australian dollars forward to hedge against adverse currency movements. Risk management was, and still is, the main reason why derivatives are used.

The second main function of derivatives is yield enhancement. For this reason, derivatives are especially popular among professional funds managers. The leverage element in derivatives makes them particularly attractive for increasing investment returns. Besides, it is generally more economical to trade in the futures markets than in the cash markets. For example, if a funds manager in Singapore has SGD 1.5 million and wishes to invest in Treasury bonds, the manager would be able to buy SGD 1.5 million worth of bonds in the cash market. However, since the up-front payment for Treasury bond futures is only 1.5 per cent, the manager could use the SGD 1.5 million to obtain an exposure of SGD 100 million worth of bonds in the futures market.[90] Generally, the same amount of outlay will bring higher returns in the futures market than in the cash market.

Derivatives, especially swaps, are also used to lower funding costs. For example, an established Australian company, which conducts business in Japan, may require a yen-denominated loan to finance the purchase of an office in Tokyo. Similarly, a Japanese manufacturer may require an Australian

---

[86] See United States General Accounting Office, *Financial Derivatives: Actions Needed to Protect the Financial System* ('GAO Report') (Washington, DC, May 1994), p. 36.
[87] Ibid.
[88] See G. A. Walker, 'Financial Derivatives—Global Regulatory Developments' (January 1996) *Journal of Business Law* 66, 71.
[89] Ibid.
[90] See Chew, above n. 70, p. 15.

dollar loan to finance the expansion of its factory in Adelaide. Since both companies enjoy better credit ratings in their respective countries, they could raise funds in their domestic markets and enter into a currency swap with each other. In this way they could enjoy cheaper funds than would otherwise be possible.

Most institutional investors such as fund managers also use derivatives to diversify their capital portfolios.[91] For example, a large pension fund, which has locked the bulk of its funds in British stocks, may wish to take advantage of the strongly performing Japanese equity market. It could achieve this through the purchase of Nikkei share index futures, rather than liquidating its share portfolio and buying Japanese shares. Not only will it be cheaper and quicker to diversify through futures, there will be no risk of the sale of a large block of shares depressing prices in the cash market.

Derivatives have proven to be extremely versatile financial instruments and have in recent years been used for purposes other than financial management. For example, there is now a growing appreciation of the role of derivatives in mergers and acquisitions. Equity derivatives may be used to build a pre-bid stake, to lock in an acquisition price of an offeror, or to sweeten the consideration to be provided by an offeror.[92] The most notable use of derivatives to build a stake in takeovers in Australia was the Mobil bid for Ampolex, while the high profile bid by Trafalgar House Plc for Northern Electric Plc in the United Kingdom is an example of how derivatives were used to lock in an acquisition price.[93]

While derivatives are mainly used as a financial management tool, they also have an important economic role, which is easily overlooked. Derivatives contribute to the deepening of the financial infrastructure of a country, and form part of its larger capital-raising mechanism. It is therefore unsurprising that newly developing countries have either established or are in the process of establishing their own derivatives exchanges. Derivatives also play an important role in price discovery. Derivatives markets provide price information, which is used as a guide for determining the value of an instrument or commodity. This is because the same factors which influence the price of futures, also influence the price of the underlying instruments or commodities. The price information disseminated by derivatives exchanges significantly influences the way people all over the world make economic decisions.

1.5   SIZE OF GLOBAL MARKET

Despite the early origins of derivatives, their development was prompted by the fundamental changes in global financial markets in the last thirty years.

---

[91]   See Fox-Andrews and Meaden, above n. 22, p. 18.
[92]   See S. Ansell, 'The Application of Equity Derivatives in Mergers and Acquisitions' (1997) 15 C&SLJ 218, 219.
[93]   Id., 223–224.

The increased volatility in currency exchange rates began soon after the major industrialised countries abandoned the Bretton Woods system of fixed currency rates in favour of the floating exchange rate system.[94] Similarly, financial deregulation on a global scale led to increased volatility in interest rates. Financial derivatives developed in response to the need to manage financial risks in a volatile global environment. Although derivatives have long existed, the big explosion in derivatives occurred only after the appearance of financial derivatives in early 1970.[95]

The negative publicity surrounding derivatives in recent years has had little adverse impact on their growth rates. For example, the International Swaps and Derivatives Association's first-half market survey showed that outstanding interest rate swaps, currency swaps and interest rate options as at 30 June 1999 totalled USD 52.7 trillion compared to USD 36.9 trillion a year earlier.[96] The results of the international survey of derivatives market activities in 43 countries coordinated by the Bank of International Settlement revealed that:

- the notional amount of over-the-counter derivatives contracts outstanding as at end December 1998, after adjusting for double-counting, was USD 80 trillion; and
- the notional amount of exchange-traded derivatives contracts as at end December 1998 was USD 13.5 trillion.[97]

A further analysis of the over-the-counter derivatives contracts revealed that interest rate instruments were the largest component of the OTC market (72 per cent), followed by foreign exchange products (26 per cent) and those based on equities (2 per cent).[98]

It is important to recognise that statistical information on derivatives activities is still lacking in two important aspects. First, it is generally difficult to obtain reliable or comprehensive data about the scale of derivatives activities. Currently, there are no mandatory reporting obligations imposed on end-users. While data on exchange-traded derivatives is regularly published, it is difficult to gather data on privately negotiated over-the-counter transactions. The use of different sources of information and methods of computation leads to varying results. For example, there is often a great disparity between the statistical information provided by the International Swap and Derivatives Association and the Bank of International Settlement.

Second, activity in derivatives is usually measured in terms of the notional or contract amounts. While the notional amount provides a useful

---

[94] See GAO Report, above n. 86, p. 24.
[95] See M. Rubinstein, *Rubinstein on Derivatives* (Risk Books, London, 1999), p. 1.
[96] See International Swaps and Derivatives Association, '1999 Year-End ISDA Market Survey' <www.isda.org>, 10 January 2000.
[97] See Bank of International Settlements, 'The Global OTC Derivatives Market at End-December 1998' (BIS Survey) <www.bis.org>, 2 June 1999.
[98] Ibid.

indication of the level of derivatives activities, it suffers from a number of drawbacks:

- There is double counting of some activities, and this can be substantial, depending on the source. For example, an outstanding swap contract is likely to be reported by both parties, and unless an adjustment is made, the same transaction will be counted twice.
- Notional principal is not suitable as a measure of risk exposure for two main reasons: First, notional principal fails to take into account offsetting exposures, resulting in risks exposures being overstated. Second, transactions of different maturities, and involving different 'underlyings' are aggregated without accounting for their different risks profiles.[99]

Concerns about the risks involved with derivatives activities has in part been aggravated by exaggerated estimates of the level of credit exposure. A more meaningful measure of financial risk is the gross market value of derivatives contracts. The gross market value is the cost of replacing the contracts at the prevailing market prices and is usually a small percentage of the notional amount. For example, the gross market value of over-the-counter contracts at the end of December 1998 was only four per cent of the notional amount.[100] This figure fell to 1.6 per cent after taking into account legally enforceable bilateral netting arrangements.[101]

Several international initiatives have already been taken to address the problems faced in obtaining useful information about derivatives activities.[102] Reliable and comprehensive information on derivatives activities is a pre-requisite for any meaningful discussion of the risks posed by derivatives. The derivatives industry could be adversely affected by policies which are based on inaccurate market information. Some progress has been made towards improving the quality of information obtained, especially on over-the-counter derivatives activity. However, additional work needs to be undertaken to make derivatives activities more transparent to investors, dealers, end-users and regulators.[103] Disclosure of derivatives activities should be made mandatory and there must be in place a universally accepted system of reporting derivatives activities.

1.6   RISKS POSED BY DERIVATIVES

There are two conflicting views on the risks posed by derivatives. On the one hand, there are those who believe that derivatives pose risks no different

---

[99]   See Group of Thirty Report, above n. 6, p. 54.
[100]   See BIS Survey, above n. 97.
[101]   Ibid.
[102]   Id., 7–8. See also, Bank of England 'Statistical Information About Derivatives Markets' (May 1995) *Bank of England Quarterly Bulletin*, pp. 185–188.
[103]   See P. A. Barcroft, 'Derivatives and Market Risk Disclosure—Leaving No Stone Unturned?' (1998) 13 JIBFL 131, on the necessity of derivatives disclosure regulation and for a comparative survey of disclosure developments in international capital markets.

from those found in other financial activities. The following comments made by the Global Derivatives Study Group of Thirty are representative of this view:

Derivatives help to manage risks in new ways—an important economic function. Yet the risks involved in derivatives activities are neither new nor unique. They are the same kinds of risks found in traditional financial products: market, credit, legal and operational risks.[104]

It appears that the Reserve Bank of Australia shares a similar view when it stated that:

Derivatives do not, of themselves, create any additional risks. Rather, properly handled they provide a means for managing risks which already exist and which have tended to increase as markets have become more volatile.[105]

On the other hand, there are those who believe that derivatives are more risky than other financial products and difficult to manage. An advocate of this view is the United States Group Accounting Office. In its Report to Congressional Requesters it made the following observations:

These general types [credit, market, legal, and operations] of risks exist for many financial activities, but the specific risks in derivatives are relatively difficult to manage, in part, because of the complexity of some of these products and the difficulties in measuring these risks.[106]

A careful analysis of the various risks faced by derivatives users and dealers would reveal that they are neither new nor unique. However, derivatives possess two characteristics which make them more risky than conventional financial products. Firstly, they are more complex than conventional financial tools, which means that few fully appreciate the risk transformation profile of derivatives. Secondly, derivatives are highly leveraged instruments, which means that losses and gains are out of proportion to the initial outlays. It is these two characteristics that magnify the various risks posed by derivatives. Not surprisingly, several derivatives end-users have suffered crippling losses.

1.6.1 Market Risk

Market risk refers to the risk that a change in market conditions may result in a fall in the value of a derivative contract. For example, the value of a call option on NAB shares will decline if the price of NAB shares fell in the cash market. The danger posed by market risk is that the relationship between the value of a derivative contract and its 'underlying asset' is a complex one, which is not often properly understood by end-users. How the value changes

---

104   See Group of Thirty Report, above n. 6, p. 2.
105   See Reserve Bank of Australia, 'Derivatives—Bank Activities and Supervisory Responses' (May 1995) *Reserve Bank of Australia Bulletin* 1, p. 6.
106   See GAO Report, above n. 86, p. 9.

depends on a number of factors including the type of derivatives contract involved. For example, the relationship between the value of a forward contract and its 'underlying' is generally linear. In other words, a change in the value of the latter would lead to a proportional change in the former. On the other hand, the value of an option depends on several factors, such as the price of the underlying, exercise price of the option, and time to expiration of the option. This means that the relationship between the price of the underlying and the value of an option-based derivative is not constant.

The relationship between the value of the derivatives contract and the value of the underlying asset or index is also determined by the former's profile. The payoff profile is in turn dependant on the extent of leverage embedded into the derivatives contract. Understanding the concept of leverage is the key to understanding derivatives. Leverage is best explained by using the concept of the simple home loan. Under current conditions an individual may be able to buy a residential property worth $100,000 with a simple down payment of $10,000. Assuming the individual is employed and has a satisfactory credit history, he or she may be able to borrow the remaining $90,000 from a bank. Since the debt is equivalent to nine times the value of the initial cash outlay, the leverage ratio is 9:1. Similarly, in derivatives transactions, the investor would normally require only a fraction of the total value of the derivatives transaction. For example, with $1,500 an investor may be able to buy $100,000 worth of equity futures.

The advantage of leverage is obvious. If the value of the house in our earlier example rose to $110,000 and the individual decided to sell it, he or she will make a profit of $10,000. This represents a 100 per cent return on the value of his or her initial cash outlay of $10,000. However, it is always possible that the individual may also lose his or her entire investment if the value of the house fell to $90,000 and for some reason the bank decided to recall the loan. Derivatives are therefore inherently more risky because they all contain some element of leverage. However, they can be just as safe as any other investments if used wisely. A company using all its available cash resources to buy futures contracts would be courting disaster because during the life of the contracts their values would fluctuate significantly. Unless the company has resources to meet the margin calls, it would have to liquidate the contracts at a loss.

Market risk is magnified if the leverage embedded in the derivatives contract is increased. This was amply demonstrated in the Procter & Gamble (P&G) case. P&G entered into a five-year USD 200 million leveraged swap with Bankers Trust (BT) in November 1994 with the objective of achieving lower funding costs.[107] Under the terms of the transaction, BT would pay P&G a fixed rate, and P&G would pay BT a floating rate of 75 basis points below the United States commercial paper rate for the first six-months. For the remaining term of the transaction, P&G would pay BT a floating rate of 75 basis points below the commercial paper rate plus a spread calculated according to an agreed formula. The formula was written in such a way

---

[107]   See Chew, above n. 70, pp. 37–49, for a quantitative analysis of the swap transactions.

that any increase in the Constant Maturity Treasury yield beyond 70 basis point would be magnified 31 times.[108] When interest rates in the United States rose, P&G lost around USD 157 million on the transaction.[109]

Another large American corporation which reported losses from adverse market movements, was Gibson Greetings, a Cincinnati-based greeting card producer.[110] The derivatives involved included 'wedding-band' options (which provided for significant payments by Gibson if interest rates moved out of a specified band); a knock-out call option (which provided for the expiry of the option if at any time during its life a particular interest benchmark rate dropped below a specific level), and several other complex swaps, spread lock and periodic-floor agreements.[111] Gibson Greetings sued Bankers Trust to recover its losses on a number of grounds including violations of federal commodities legislation. Had both parties not reached an out-of-court settlement, Gibson Greetings would have stood to lose USD 27 million.[112]

Non-business entities like local governments have also suffered derivatives-linked losses resulting from a combination of excessive leverage and adverse interest rate movements. For example, in early December 1994, Orange County, one of the wealthiest counties in the United States, disclosed that its USD 20 billion investment fund had fallen by at least USD 1.5 billion.[113] A few days after reporting the losses it filed for bankruptcy. There was public disbelief that the fund, which had invested in high-quality bonds and had produced handsome returns for several years, could suffer such debilitating losses. However, many informed commentators were not surprised considering the fact that Orange County had relied heavily on leverage to enhance its returns on its bonds.[114] It bought more derivative securities than it could afford by borrowing against its pool of financial assets. When interest rates rose, the funds sustained heavy losses, which were made worse when the investment firms liquidated their collateral.

There are several of other risks, which are sometimes included under the umbrella of 'market risk'. They include rollover, liquidity and funding risks, which if not properly managed could also result in losses to end-users, as was the case with Metallgesellschaft A.G. (MG). In the summer of 1993, MG's United States subsidiary, MG Refining and Marketing (MGRM) committed itself to supply approximately 160 million barrels of gasoline and heating oil to its customers over the next ten years at fixed prices.[115] Most of these

---

[108] The Constant Maturity Treasury was the interest rate benchmark used for calculating P&G's rate.

[109] See A. R. Waldman, 'OTC Derivatives & Systemic Risk: Innovative Finance or the Dance Into the Abyss', (1994) 43 *The American University Law Review* 1023, 1040.

[110] See Chew, above n. 70, pp. 37–49, for a quantitative analysis of the various transactions.

[111] See W. J. McSherry and Others, 'Litigation Involving Derivatives' in R. A. Klein and J. Lederman (eds), *Derivatives Risk and Responsibility* (Irwin, Chicago, 1996), p. 665.

[112] See Chew, above n. 70, p. 37.

[113] See J. E. McKown and A. T. Purcell, 'Enforcement Actions Involving Derivatives: BT Securities Corp and Beyond' (1996) 65 *University of Cincinnati Law Review* 117, 119.

[114] See for example, Crawford and Sen, above n. 17, pp. 136–137.

[115] See F. R. Edwards and M. S. Canter, 'The Collapse of Metallgesellschaft: Unhedgeable Risks, Poor Hedging Strategy, or Just Bad Luck?' (1995) 87 *Journal of Applied Corporate Finance* 86.

contracts were negotiated when energy prices were low and falling. MGRM hedged the risk of rising energy prices with short-term energy futures and over-the-counter swaps. This meant it had to 'roll forward' its contracts continuously to maintain its position. As long as spot prices were higher than futures prices, MGRM made profits. But in late 1993, when spot prices fell, MGRM lost money every time it rolled over its contracts. The sharp fall in energy prices forced MGRM to post almost USD 900 million in margins. As rumours of its liquidity crisis surfaced it was forced to post even higher margins. When MGRM was eventually forced to liquidate its position it incurred massive losses. So large were the losses that only a USD 1.9 billion rescue operation mounted by more than 150 banks kept MG from going into insolvency.

1.6.2   Credit Risk

Credit risk generally refers to the risk of sustaining losses as a result of the counterparty's failure to meet its contractual obligations. But, credit risk is more than counterparty default risk. The underlying of a derivative instrument can itself generate credit risk. There is an important difference between credit risk posed by derivatives and that posed by conventional balance sheet items like loans. In the case of the former the credit exposure is dynamic, while in the case of the latter the credit exposure is static.[116] For exchange-traded derivatives such as futures contracts, credit risk is minimal as the clearinghouse guarantees performance of the transaction. The clearinghouse is usually financially sound. A good example is the International Commodity Clearing House, which clears most of the commodity contracts on the London exchanges. It has access to significant financial resources because it is owned by six of the major London banks.[117] Credit risk is in theory greater for over-the-counter derivatives than exchange-traded derivatives. The nature of risk also varies with the type of derivatives. Credit risk is symmetrical for forward contracts and swaps as each counterparty faces the risk that the other will default. On the other hand, credit risk is asymmetrical for options as only the buyer faces the risk of the seller defaulting.

The potential losses that a non-defaulting counterparty could face should not be equated with the notional value of the transaction. When a counterparty defaults, the losses are confined to the costs of replacing the transaction and to the recovery of any sums paid. Contrary to popular belief, the losses are usually only a fraction of the total notional amount. Replacement cost refers to the cost of replacing a contract with a new one and it can either be negative or positive. Only if the replacement cost is positive will the non-defaulting or remaining party incur any losses. While it is relatively straightforward to calculate the current costs of replacing the remaining cash flows, it is much more difficult to calculate the replacement costs at some point of time in the future.[118] This is because calculating potential

---

[116]   See Chew, above n. 70, p. 127.
[117]   See Courtney and Bettelheim, above n. 30, p. 14.
[118]   See Group of Thirty Report, above n. 6, p. 48.

exposure involves not only projecting movements of the 'underlyings' but also the probability of default.

Credit risk is normally a small percentage of the notional amount, usually between two to four per cent. Since in practice, most over-the counter (OTC) derivatives counterparties enjoy good credit ratings, the risk of default is very small. The swaps industry is proud of its extremely low default rate of less than one-half of one per cent of the money at risk in OTC swap transactions.[119] Nonetheless, the derivatives market is not immune to defaults arising from the insolvency of counterparties. For instance, when the British and Commonwealth Merchant Bank went into administration in early June 1990, it held a derivatives portfolio of approximately 200 transactions with more than 50 counterparties.[120] The administrators ceased payment on all International Swaps and Derivatives Association documented swaps on the basis that the automatic termination provision in the 1987 Master Agreement was effective.[121] Other notorious defaults included the collapse of investment bank Drexel Burnham Lambert, and the failure of the Bank of New England.[122]

The most obvious way for a market participant to minimise credit risk is to enter into transactions with only the most highly credit-rated counterparties such as AAA-rated institutions. However, this approach would only limit the potential field of counterparties. Another approach is collateralisation, which involves an exchange of guaranteed cash flows. The key difference between collateralisation of privately negotiated derivatives and collateralisation of other conventional credit transactions is that in the case of the former, either of the counterparties may be the credit support taker, as the valuations of net exposure change from time to time.[123] Collateralisation as a means of minimising credit risks in international derivatives transactions is not without limitations. For example, counterparties often find it difficult to agree on the value of their net exposures. Valuation can be administratively burdensome, depending on the different proprietary models used and the frequency at which the counterparties mark-to-market.[124] A recent Bank of International Settlements Report (BIS Report) said that the use of collateral does not eliminate credit risk and may entail other risks such as legal, liquidity and operational risks.[125] For example, collateral agreements expose counterparties to liquidity pressures if called upon to deliver additional collateral. The risk that the security interest taken may not be enforceable is increased where the transaction involves counterparties

---

[119]   See Waldman, above n. 109, 1052.
[120]   See Das, above n. 40, p. 1150.
[121]   Ibid.
[122]   Ibid.
[123]   See K. Tyson-Quah, 'Collateralisation v Clearinghouse: Credit Risk Management for OTC Derivatives' in E. Bettelheim, H. Parry and W. Rees (eds), *Swaps and Off-Exchange Derivatives Trading: Law and Regulation* (FT Law & Tax, London, 1996), p. 125.
[124]   Id., p. 127.
[125]   See Bank of International Settlements, *OTC Derivatives: Settlement Procedures and Counterparty Risk Management, Report by the Committee on Payment and Settlement Systems and the Euro-currency Committee of the Central Banks of the Group of Ten Countries* (Basle, 1998).

from more than one jurisdiction. Nonetheless, the BIS Report concluded that collateralisation is an effective method of mitigating credit risks provided the associated risks are properly managed.

Another mechanism for managing OTC counterparty credit risk is the use of multilateral clearing systems. Currently the vast majority of OTC derivatives transactions are settled between counterparties on a bilateral basis.[126] A clearinghouse will replace bilateral settlement arrangements with multilateral netting. According to the BIS Report, the use of a clearinghouse has the potential to mitigate the various counterparty risks associated with OTC transactions. Multilateral netting would reduce members' credit exposures on the contracts cleared, while margining would eliminate the net exposure on a daily basis. A clearinghouse, if it employs effective risk management controls, may be financially stronger than most counterparties. However, one of the limitations with multilateral clearing arrangements is that they only clear a limited range of instruments.[127] The use of clearinghouses has the potential to reduce other risks such as legal risks. National law often supports a clearinghouse's default procedures. Clearinghouses have more efficient procedures for dealing with documentation.

1.6.3 Operational Risk

Operational risk is the risk of losses resulting from inadequate systems, controls or human error.[128] With the widespread use of electronic trading, operational risks would include the risk of computer system failure, computer viruses and unauthorised use of terminals.[129] It is important that senior management is not only involved but also understands the nature of the risks inherent in derivatives activities. Any organisation involved in derivatives activities in a significant way should have independent risk management systems to provide early warning signals to management of any potential disasters. In addition, there should also be in place, a system of checks and balances to prevent fraud and excessive risk from taking place.

The Barings debacle has convincingly demonstrated the dire consequences of ignoring the above requirements. On 27 February 1995 the British merchant bank, Barings Plc, was placed under administration due to massive losses incurred by its subsidiary, Barings Futures Singapore (BFS). These losses stemmed from the unauthorised trading activities of Nick Leeson, the General Manager of BFS, on the Singapore and Osaka futures exchanges. According to the Report of the Board of Banking Supervision, 'the fact that

---

[126] See M. Philipp and E. Nield, 'Swapclear: A New Mechanism for Enhancing Management of Counterpary Credit Risk from OTC Derivatives Transaction' (1999) 4 *Derivatives* 173.

[127] Id., 174: London Clearinghouse Limited's multilateral clearing facility, SwapClear, will initially clear 'vanilla' single-currency interest rate swaps of up to ten-years duration and forward rate agreements of up to one year duration.

[128] See Group of Thirty Report, above n. 6, p. 50.

[129] For a discussion of the operational risks that are specific to electronic trading environments, see M. O'Hara, 'Electronic Trading Risks: What Can Go Wrong in Screen-Traded Derivatives Markets' (2000) 5 *Derivatives Use, Trading & Regulation* 316.

Leeson was permitted throughout to remain in charge of front office and back office was the most serious failing.'[130] Leeson was therefore able to take advantage of the lack of internal controls and supervision to conceal his losses from unauthorised trading.

A lack of understanding of the nature of derivatives is also a facet of operational risk. The Barings Report observed that the senior executives of Barings 'did not adequately understand their own business'.[131] In the Procter & Gamble case, there was strong evidence to suggest that the senior management did not fully appreciate how interest was to be determined for the swaps. Considering that derivatives gained widespread usage only in the last two decades, it is not surprising that many bankers are still not familiar with how derivatives function. In many banks, the trading in derivatives is still confined to a specific department or specialist entity. The problem is further compounded by the diversity of derivative instruments and the highly customised nature of off-exchange transactions.

1.6.4   Legal Risk

Legal risk refers to the risk of losses arising from the non-enforceability of a derivatives contract. This risk only exists because a legal body has decided that for some reason, a particular derivatives transaction has characteristics that do not deserve legal protection.[132] For example, a court of law may not award damages for breach because the derivatives contract in question is contrary to public policy. A derivatives contract may be unenforceable for a number of reasons, ranging from lack of capacity on the part of the counter-party, to contravention of the gaming and wagering laws. The decision in *Hazell v Hammersmith and Fulham London Borough Council*[133] has dramatically emphasised to market participants the legal risk arising from the use of derivative instruments. It has been estimated that the losses suffered by swap dealers as a result of this decision represent over 50 per cent of total losses due to defaults on swaps since the inception of swap activities.[134]

In a sense, legal risk is greater for derivatives transactions than other financial transactions. Being relatively new instruments, there is considerable uncertainty whether they fit into the existing legal framework. Legal risks can be broadly categorised into:

- Jurisdictional risk—for example, the risk that the transaction is illegal because it contravenes the wagering and gaming laws, or that the netting provision in the agreement contravenes the insolvency laws;

---

[130]   See C. Brown, 'Report of the Board of Banking Supervision Inquiry into the Circumstances of the Collapse of Barings' (1995) 10 JIBL 446, 450.
[131]   Ibid.
[132]   See C. A. Samuelson, 'The Fall of Barings: Lessons for Legal Oversight of Derivatives Transactions in the United States' (1996) 29 *Cornell International Law Journal* 767, 781.
[133]   [1992] 2 AC 1.
[134]   See Group of Thirty Report, above n. 6, p. 51.

- Counterparty risk—for example, the risk that the counterparty lacks the capacity, or that the signatory did not have the authority to bind the company;
- Selling risk—for example, the risk that the intermediary has misrepresented the benefits of the transaction or failed to consider the desirability of the product.

Each of the above risks would be discussed in greater detail in the next chapter.

1.6.5   Systemic Risk

Systemic risk is by far the most hotly debated and publicised risk of derivatives activities. It generally refers to the effect the failure of one institution may have on other institutions and the financial system as a whole. Systemic risk has two scenarios: in the first, the collapse of one financial institution may result in a domino effect on other financial institutions; and in the second, the widespread reliance on dynamic (continuous) hedging strategies during a market disturbance could turn an otherwise containable market downturn into an illiquidity-driven crisis.[135] According to Professor Dale the 'potential for contagious disorders is one of the main driving forces behind international regulatory co-ordination not only of derivatives activity but of banking and securities business generally'.[136] The devaluation of the Thai Baht in July 1997, which triggered off the recent financial crisis in Asia, is an example of how turmoil in one market can spread to other markets.

There are many factors which have contributed to the concern with systemic risk. They include the scale and lack of transparency of derivatives activities and the illiquidity of customised over-the-counter transactions. The GAO Report emphasised the interrelationship among dealers, and the concentration of dealing activity among a relatively few financial institutions worldwide.[137] More recently, the focus has been on the systemic risk associated with payments, settlement and clearing systems in different segments of the financial market. Yet surprisingly, major derivatives-induced collapses like that involving Barings Plc did not lead to the much-publicised derivatives Armageddon. However, it must be pointed out that Barings Plc was only a modest-sized merchant bank. While it is conceivable that the collapse of a major derivatives dealer or end-user could lead to a number of cross-defaults and even temporarily destabilise financial markets, it is unlikely though that it would lead to the collapse of the global financial system.

---

[135]   See Waldman, above n. 109, 1054. For a broader meaning of 'systemic risk', see A. M. Whittaker, 'Tackling Systemic Risk on Markets: Barings and Beyond' in F. Oditah (ed.), *The Future for the Global Market* (Clarendon Press, Oxford, 1996), p. 257.
[136]   See Richard Dale, 'Derivatives: The New Regulatory Challenge' (1995) 10 JIBFL 11, 12.
[137]   See GAO Report, above n. 86, p. 13.

1.7   CONCLUSION

From the brief review of the development and nature of derivatives, it is possible to conclude that derivatives have made an enormous contribution to financial management in the last three decades. This conclusion is supported by the fact that derivatives have grown at explosive rates, and at times trading in derivatives has even surpassed trading in their underlying instruments. However, derivatives are more risky than other traditional financial products because they are highly leveraged, more complex and less transparent. Being relatively newer instruments, there is a general lack of understanding of how they operate or how they should be managed.

A closer scrutiny of the losses suffered by end-users would reveal that in many cases, the underlying causes were the improper use of derivatives, greed, and ignorance. Losses from derivatives trading could have been reduced if there was proper disclosure of the risks involved, and if the extent of leverage in the products was controlled. More restraint on the part of dealers is called for when approached by customers to develop highly risky products. End-users should also be encouraged to take responsibility for their own investment decisions.[138] If they only engage in those transactions that they fully understand, they are unlikely to face crippling losses. There is the danger that not enough is being done to ensure that those who use derivatives act in a responsible manner.

The following words of Arthur Levitt, Chairman of the United States Securities and Exchange Commission (when testifying before the Senate in January 1995) very aptly summarise the nature of derivatives:

Derivatives are not inherently bad or good. They are a bit like electricity, dangerous if mishandled, but bearing the potential to do tremendous good.[139]

Until there is a proper understanding of the nature of derivatives and more prudent use of derivatives, the risk remains that they will continue to generate sizable losses for end-users.[140] There is now widespread acceptance that the solution lies in encouraging market participants to adopt better risk management procedures, instead of imposing additional regulatory controls.

---

[138]   Decisions such as *Daniels v AWA Limited* (1995) 13 ACLC 614 suggest that the courts could in future impose liability on the senior management of companies for negligent trading in derivatives.

[139]   See McSherry and Others, above n. 111, p. 663. Orange County, California lost more than USD 2 billion as a result of highly leveraged reverse repurchase agreements and derivatives.

[140]   For a recent example, see 'Scudder Kemper Investments Has Barings-Type Scare' (2000) 1 : 5 *Derivatives Report* 1.

2. Derivatives Markets

2.1 CLASSIFYING MARKETS

Derivatives markets fall into two broad categories: exchange-traded derivatives markets and over-the-counter (OTC) derivatives markets.[1] It might be useful at this stage to explain the basic differences between OTC derivatives markets and exchange-traded derivatives markets. The first difference is that OTC derivatives markets are very much larger than exchange-traded derivatives markets. According to the latest Bank of International Settlement Survey, the notional value of outstanding OTC contracts was almost six times larger than that for exchange-traded contracts.[2] The second difference is that OTC derivatives markets are predominantly institutional markets and individual transactions tend to be fairly large in size.[3] Exchange-traded derivatives markets, on the other hand, have a significant retail component and their average transaction size tend to be much smaller. The third difference is that OTC derivatives markets are usually unregulated and operate on a caveat emptor basis.[4] Exchange-traded markets are almost always subject to some form of statutory regulation. The fourth difference is that OTC derivatives markets do not have a formal trading place, are less transparent, have no margining mechanisms, and generally suffer from reduced liquidity.[5] Exchange-traded derivatives markets,

---

[1] For an alternative way of classifying markets, see P. R. Wood, *Title Finance, Derivatives, Securitisations, Set-off and Netting* (Sweet & Maxwell, London, 1995), p. 215: There are three principal markets for derivatives products: organised securities and commodity exchanges, which include the specialised futures and options exchanges; over-the-counter markets, namely private transactions; and new issues markets for primary offerings of debt securities such as index-linked bonds and warrants.

[2] See Bank of International Settlements, 'The Global OTC Derivatives Market at End-December 1998' ('BIS Survey') < www.bis.org>, 2 June 1999.

[3] See J. W. Markham, 'Protecting the Institutional Investor—Jungle Predator or Shorn Lamb' in D. C. Langervoot (ed.), *Securities Law Review—1996* (Clark Boardman Callaghan, New York, 1996), pp. 638–640.

[4] Currently, the OTC markets in Australia, New Zealand, Singapore and Hong Kong are not subject to statutory regulation.

[5] See M. G. Hains, 'Derivatives Regulation in Australia' in G. Walker and Others (eds), *Securities Regulation in Australia and New Zealand* (LBC, Sydney, 1998), pp. 660–661, for a useful comparison of exchange-traded products and OTC products.

on the other hand, are physical markets, provide for margining of unrealised losses, enjoy greater liquidity, and are more transparent.

However, recent developments have seen a blurring of the distinction between both types of markets. As products originally designed for wholesale markets are adapted for retail end-users, retail participation in OTC derivatives markets will increase.[6] Technological advances have contributed to greater transparency in OTC derivatives markets.[7] In Australia, for example, the Australian Financial Markets Association has launched an information service that provides real-time data on OTC financial market activities.[8] Although OTC markets are not regulated the way exchange-traded markets are, they are increasingly subject to various forms of quasi-regulation. Recent years have witnessed a number of national and international initiatives to reduce risks associated with OTC activities. For instance, central banks in a number of jurisdictions issue supervisory guidelines to financial institutions. On an international level, the Basle Committee on Banking Regulations and Supervisory Practices provides guidelines on the calculation of capital adequacy requirements for credit and market risks. International bodies such as the Bank of International Settlements and the International Organisation of Securities Commissions also regularly provide guidance on improving OTC market practices. Although guidelines by international supervisory bodies do not have the force of law, they are widely adopted and regarded as a form of 'soft law'. Standardised market documentation, such as that developed by the International Swap Dealers Association, also play an important regulatory role. They govern how markets should operate and on what terms market participants should do business with each other.

2.2   EXCHANGE-TRADED DERIVATIVES MARKETS

The derivatives exchanges of Australia, New Zealand, Singapore, Malaysia and Hong Kong (exchanges under study) are a vital component of the global market for exchange-traded derivatives. Although they have generally mirrored the growth experienced by the exchanges worldwide, they have not developed at an even pace. They range from the highly developed exchange to the newly emerging exchange. This section will describe how these exchanges have developed, their market structures and the changes that they are currently undergoing. An understanding of how derivatives exchanges operate is a useful prelude to our discussion of the exchanges under study. Although not all exchanges operate in the same manner, all of them share a number of broad similarities.

---

[6] See Companies and Securities Advisory Committee, *Regulation of On-exchange and OTC Derivatives Markets* (CASAC Report on Derivatives Markets), (Sydney, June 1997), p. 36.
[7] See Treasury, *Financial Markets and Investment Products* (CLERP Paper No. 6) (AGPS, Canberra, December 1997), p. 49.
[8] Ibid.

A derivatives exchange may simply be described as an organised market for the trading of derivatives contracts. Until recently, most exchanges had a trading floor and the buying and selling of derivatives contracts was carried out under the 'open outcry' method. 'Open outcry' is a form of auction in which bids and offers are made by voice and recognised patterns of hand signals.[9] Representatives of exchange members gather around in 'pits' to trade in different contracts. Competitive pressures have forced many exchanges to switch to electronic trading. Most exchanges are membership organisations and normally cater only for members.[10] But, not all members are able to receive and execute client orders. For example, in the Sydney Futures Exchange, only floor members may undertake this activity. Exchanges are usually constituted as companies, which are ultimately owned by their members or by other financial institutions.[11] The members are not only entitled to a share of the assets of the exchange if it is being wound up, but also to vote on important policy decisions affecting the future of the exchange.

The public can only buy and sell derivatives contracts through exchange members. Although members enter into contracts on the trading floor as principals, their relationship with their clients is one of agent and principal and not buyer and seller.[12] Members must meet certain specified criteria for membership. By ensuring that traders with approved credit-standing, integrity and competence may gain membership, trading on the exchange is facilitated. Otherwise, individual assessment of creditworthiness would have to be carried out before every trade is executed. The basic element in derivatives trading is the futures contract.[13] However, most exchanges also trade in option contracts. The exchange establishes the specifications for the contract, provides and regulates the facility for trading. It is the members and not the exchange that undertake trading of the contracts. The forces of supply and demand determine the prices paid for contracts.

In a typical transaction, the client's order is routed to a floor member for execution. After the trade is executed, the contract between the two contracting floor members (assuming they are also clearing members) is then sent to the clearinghouse for registration. Once the contract between the two clearing members is registered, the legal nexus between the original

---

[9] See J. S. Currie, *Australian Futures Regulation* (Longman, Melbourne, 1995), pp. 1–2.

[10] Id., p. 9. In the case of demutualised exchanges, trading rights are tied to trading permits and not membership.

[11] See Wood, above n. 1, p. 216. For a comprehensive discussion of how exchanges are managed, see G. Stimson, 'Who Governs an Exchange?' in E. J. Swan (ed.), *Issues in Derivative Instruments* (Kluwer Law International, The Hague, 1999), p. 53.

[12] See *E .Bailey & Co. Ltd v. Balholm Securities Ltd* [1973] 2 Lloyd's Rep. 404 at 408:

Although brokers deal in the markets as principals by concluding contracts of purchase or sale in their own name on which they are personally liable to each other ... the relationship between a broker and his client is that of agent and principal and not of buyer and seller.

[13] See W. Slatyer and E. Carew, *Trading Asia-Pacific Financial Futures Markets* (Allen & Unwin, St. Leonards, 1993), pp. 53–63, for a useful summary of how a futures exchange works and the roles played by the various participants.

buyer and seller is broken. The clearinghouse interposes itself between the buyer and seller and two new contracts come into existence. In one contract, the clearinghouse acts as buyer to the original seller, and in the other contract, the clearinghouse acts as seller to the original buyer. The clearing house does not guarantee the performance of the open contracts. Rather it assumes the responsibility for performance by acting as the counterparty in both the contracts.

Clearinghouses run perfectly matched books, in that every obligation to a clearing member is matched by an equal and offsetting claim against another member.[14] However, they still face the risk that their clearing members may not be able to fulfil their obligations. In the unlikely event that a clearing member defaults, the clearinghouse is at risk. It will still have to perform on the open contract entered into by the defaulting member. To protect itself from potential losses and to ensure the integrity of the market, the clearinghouse imposes margins on clearing members. Apart from initial margins, members must also pay additional margins when their contracts are 'out-of-money'. Contracts are regularly 'marked-to-market' by the clearinghouse to determine the margin required. Margins must be paid promptly and may be in the form of cash or some other readily realisable asset. Clearing members usually pass on these margins to their individual clients. The clearinghouse may seek further protection by obtaining guarantees from its members and requiring that they meet certain financial criteria for continuing membership.

2.2.1   The Sydney Futures Exchange

The origins of the Australian derivatives industry may be traced to the establishment of the Sydney Greasy Wool Futures Exchange in 1960.[15] There was then a need to provide a hedging facility for merino wool, which at that time was Australia's largest export industry. Trading in Greasy Wool Deliverable Futures began on 11 May of the same year. In the first fifteen years of its existence, the Australian futures exchange traded only in wool futures contracts. The volume of wool futures contracts peaked in 1973, but declined thereafter. With the decline in usage of wool, the exchange saw the need to offer futures contracts based on other commodities. In 1972, the Sydney Greasy Wool Futures Exchange changed its name to the Sydney Futures Exchange (SFE) to reflect this change. On 16 July 1975, SFE launched its Trade Steers Deliverable Futures. This was followed by the launch of a gold futures contract on 19 April 1978. On 17 October 1979, SFE became the first exchange outside the United States to introduce a financial futures contract when it launched its 90-Day Bank Accepted Bill contract.

---

[14]   For a useful discussion of how clearinghouses in the US manage risks, see R. Dale, 'Risk Management in US Derivatives Clearing Houses' in E. J. Swan (ed.) *Issues in Derivative Instruments* (Kluwer Law International, The Hague, 1999), p. 101.
[15]   The contents of this section are largely based on the information found in Sydney Futures Exchange, 'Chronological History of the SFE' <www.sfe.com.au/presentation/channel1/index.asp>, 1 November 1999.

The 1980s was a period of significant growth for SFE, as it was with many other exchanges worldwide. Two events played an important role in the rapid growth of SFE. The first event was the collapse of the Bretton Woods Agreement in 1972, which ushered in a new era of variable exchange rates.[16] Greater volatility in exchange and interest rates led to a huge international demand for financial futures contracts. The second event was the deregulation of the Australian financial system, which led to the floating of the Australian dollar, the removal of exchange controls and restrictions on interest rates, and the entry of foreign banks into the Australian market. Against this favourable backdrop, SFE introduced in rapid succession a whole range of financial futures and options contracts.

By the end of the 1980s, SFE had transformed itself from a single-product exchange catering principally for the local wool industry to a multi-product exchange serving the international financial and commodity markets. It had also succeeded in established trading links with the New York Mercantile Exchange and the New Zealand Futures and Options Exchange. SFE is now the largest financial futures and options exchange in the Asia Pacific region.[17] It is also the only active futures exchange in Australia. The Australian Financial Futures Market, which was established in September 1985 to trade in equity futures contracts, is currently inactive.[18] In 1998, a total of 29.9 million contracts were traded, at a nominal value of AUD 10.5 trillion, on SFE. Trading volume on SFE continued its upward trend for the first quarter of 1999. Its strong growth was fuelled by factors such as surging stock markets, low interest rates and greater awareness of the need to properly manage risks.[19]

The exchange is a not-for-profit company, incorporated by guarantee and owned by its members. Despite earlier setbacks, it is continuing with its plans to demutualise.[20] On 22 July 2000, SFE took a significant step towards demutualisation when the overwhelming majority of members voted in favour of the proposal to demutualsie and exchange their membership rights for shares in the company. Earlier attempts by SFE to demutualise and merge with the Australian Stock Exchange (ASX) failed to materialise. The Australian Competition and Consumer Commission's (ACCC) attacked the proposed SFE-ASX merger on the grounds that it would lead to the lessening of competition and pre-empt competition gains likely to be brought about by the proposed changes to the Corporations Law.[21] Under the

---

[16] For an explanation of the Bretton Woods system, see for example, R. Roberts, *Inside International Finance* (Orion Business, London, 1998), pp. 5–10.
[17] See Sydney Futures Exchange, 'First Volume Quarter Up at the SFE' <www.sfe.com.au/presentation/channels/index.asp>, 2 November 1999.
[18] See M. G. Hains, 'Chapter 8: The Futures Industry' in *Australian Corporations Law* (Butterworths, Sydney, Loose-leaf), para. 8.1.0015.
[19] See Sydney Futures Exchange, 'First Volume Quarter Up at the SFE' <www.sfe.com.au/presentation/channels/index.asp>, 2 November 1999.
[20] See A. Main, 'SFE Carve-Up Looks Likely for February', 10 December 1999, *The Australian Financial Review*, p. 58.
[21] See 'ACCC Has Doubts on Proposed ASX/SFE Merger Proposal', *Butterworths Corporations Law Bulletin* No. 14, 24 June 1999, para. 208.

proposed regulatory scheme, each exchange will be allowed to offer the full range of trading services without any distinction made between futures contracts and shares. It is difficult to understand the ACCC's stand considering that more and more countries are moving towards the unification of their exchanges as a way of competing globally.

There are now three classes of SFE membership: floor members, local members, and associate members. Floor members have direct access to the trading floor; voting and board representation rights; and the right to execute client business. They are mainly banks, merchant banks and stock or commodity brokers. Local members have access to the trading floor but may trade only on their own account. They are also allowed to do 'give-up' business for floor members. Local brokers are sometimes referred to as 'scalpers' as they are short-term speculators seeking to 'scalp' a little profit off each small market movement for themselves.[22] Associate members do not have access to the trading floor. Until recently the vast majority of contracts were executed on the physical floor of the exchange. On 12 November 1999, SFE abandoned its open-outcry system and switched to fully electronic trading.

The Sydney Futures Exchange Clearing House (SFECH), a fully owned subsidiary of the SFE, handles the clearing of contracts. It took over the clearing function from the International Commodities Clearing House Limited in December 1991.[23] When a trade is executed, a contract is formed.[24] The contract is then submitted to SFECH for registration. Upon registration two new contracts are formed and the original contract extinguished. SFECH acts as counterparty to both new contracts and therefore assumes responsibility for their performance. Although SFECH is a wholly owned subsidiary of SFE, it enjoys a certain degree of independence. It has adopted the SPAN (or Standard Portfolio Analysis of Risk) margining system developed by the Chicago Mercantile Exchange.

2.2.2   The New Zealand Futures and Options Exchange

The New Zealand futures exchange is the world's first fully computerised futures exchange.[25] Although the New Zealand futures industry began with the establishment of the Futures and Options Exchange Limited on 25 January 1985, its origins can be traced back to the trading of wool futures

---

[22]   See M. K. Lewis, 'Derivative Markets' in M. K. Lewis and R. H. Lewis (eds), *The Australian Financial System* (Longman Cheshire, Melbourne, 1993), p. 398.

[23]   See Currie, above n. 9, p. 4.

[24]   For a discussion of the complex legal relationships that exist in a futures transaction see: M. G. Hains, 'Reflections on the Sydney Futures Exchange Clearing House: The Rise of the Mirrored Contract Theory' (1994) 5 JBFLP 257, and M. Markovic, 'The Legal Status of Futures Market Participants in Australia' (1989) 7 C&SLJ 82.

[25]   See New Zealand Futures and Options Exchange, 'History' <www.nzfoe.co.nz/ overview.htm>, 15 December 1999. Although the International Futures Exchange (Bermuda)

contracts on the London Wool Terminal Market (LWTM).[26] In 1953, LWTM became the first futures market in the United Kingdom to reopen after the Second World War.[27] The wool futures contract traded on LWTM called for the delivery of 500 pounds of 'B' Grade Merino Wool Tops. It was actively used by New Zealand exporters and United Kingdom importers.

In 1979, the London Wool Terminal Market Association (LWTMA) and International Commodities Clearing House, in consultation with seven New Zealand organisations participating in the market, established a new futures contract designed primarily for use by producers and consumers of New Zealand Crossbred Wool. Encouraged by the success of its New Zealand wool contract, LWTMA established in 1982 a local branch in New Zealand and changed its name to the London and New Zealand Futures Exchange (LNZFA).[28] The local brokers of LNZFA eventually split away from the group and formed their own exchange known as the New Zealand Commodity Market (NZCM).[29]

There was little prospect of introducing financial futures contracts during the Muldoon National government's years of strict controls on interest rates and exchange rates.[30] In 1984 the newly elected Lange Labour government set about overhauling the New Zealand economy. The liberalisation of the economy was largely prompted by the country's massive overseas debt, incurred in previous years to finance major infrastructure projects and the government deficit.[31] Economic reform began with the financial system and a number of measures were introduced. They included the removal of all price regulations in the financial sector; freedom of entry to financial markets; and introduction of prudential supervision and liquidity management policies.[32] The deregulation of the financial markets brought in its wake instability in interest rates, exchange rates, commodities and share prices. New Zealand was soon transformed from a neglected financial centre with little foreign investment to a more open capital market with greater international participation. The inflow of capital created a need for risk hedging mechanisms like futures and options. The stage was therefore set for the establishment of a futures exchange in New Zealand.

Early in 1984, after several years of independent trading, NZCM was re-organised as the 'New Zealand Futures Exchange'.[33] Trading in the first

---

Limited, which commenced operations in October 1984, was the world's first computerised futures exchange, the New Zealand exchange lays claim to being the first successful electronic trading system.

[26] See N. Battley (ed.), *The World's Futures & Options Markets* (Probus Publishing Co., Cambridge, 1993), p. 41.
[27] Id., pp. 40–41.
[28] See E. Banks, *Asia Pacific Derivative Markets* (Macmillan, London, 1996), p. 442.
[29] Ibid.
[30] See Slatyer and Carew, above n. 13, p. 67.
[31] See G. Walker, 'The Policy Basis of Securities Regulation in New Zealand', in G. Walker and B. Fisse (eds) *Securities Regulation in Australia & New Zealand* (Oxford University Press, Auckland, 1994), p. 180.
[32] Id., p. 176.
[33] See Banks, above n. 28, p. 442.

futures contracts commenced on 25 January 1985 and trading in options on futures contracts in February 1988.[34] Following the change of name to the 'New Zealand Futures and Options Exchange' (NZFOE) on 26 February 1990, it gained registration as a stock exchange under s. 9 of the *Sharebrokers Act* 1908. At around the same time, the members unanimously agreed in principle to restructure the exchange to facilitate expansion and growth.[35] The business assets of the exchange were sold to the Sydney Futures Exchange (SFE). Following the sale, NZFOE became a wholly owned subsidiary of SFE in December 1992. On 28 February 1994, 18 floor members of SFE installed terminals in their Australian offices and began live trading on the New Zealand markets.[36]

Although one of the smaller financial markets in the Asia Pacific region, New Zealand plays a role disproportionately larger than its size.[37] In view of its geographical position, it is the first financial market in the region to open for trading daily. It is also the first market to react to overnight regional and world news. During the early years of its existence, NZFOE enjoyed strong demand for its products. The New Zealand debt market attracted substantial foreign participation due to its historically high yields, and this in turn bolstered demand for interest rate futures contracts.[38] There was also interest in equity futures contracts because there were a number of reputable companies listed on the New Zealand Stock Exchange.

Despite its geographical advantage and its early entry into the derivatives arena, New Zealand has a much smaller derivatives market than Australia, Singapore and Hong Kong.[39] There are a number of explanations why New Zealand has lagged behind other regional markets. First, activity in interest rate derivatives has been adversely affected by a sustained period of relative stability in New Zealand rates. Second, the New Zealand exchange was badly affected by the October 1987 crash. Third, the shares of New Zealand companies only constitute a small percentage of foreign investors' portfolios.[40] This means that the demand by funds managers for equity derivatives to hedge their portfolios is limited. Fourth, the domestic market for derivatives is small and the products listed on the exchange do not have a wide international market. These factors have all played a significant role in the exchange's decision to sell its assets to SFE.

---

[34] See New Zealand Futures and Options Exchange 'History' <www.nzfoe.co.nz/overview.htm>, 15 December 1999.
[35] See K. K. H. Park and A. Schoenfeld, *The Pacific Rim Futures & Options Markets* (Heinemann Asia, Singapore, 1994), p. 214.
[36] See New Zealand Futures and Options Exchange 'History' <www.nzfoe.co.nz/overview.htm>, 15 December 1999.
[37] See Park and Schoenfeld, above n. 35, p. 211.
[38] Ibid.
[39] For example, in 1995, a total of 0.67 million futures and options contracts were traded on the NZFOE as compared to 25 million for Australia, 24.2 million for Singapore, and 5.2 million for Hong Kong.
[40] See Park & Schoenfeld, above n. 35, p. 212: ' ... the market comprises a minuscule 0.27 of the Morgan Stanley Capital International EAFE [Europe, Australia and Far East] index at the end of 1990.'

The main contracts traded on NZFOE are:

- 90 day Bank Bill Futures and Options Contracts;
- 3 year and 10 year Government Stock Futures and Options Contracts;
- Share Options Contracts.[41]

NZFOE was the first exchange in the world to launch a cash settled electricity futures contract.[42] Since the change of ownership, trading volumes on NZFOE have improved significantly. A total of 1.298 million futures and option contracts were traded on NZFOE in the year to 31 March 1999.[43] The 90-Day Bill Futures Contract accounted for 94 per cent of total turnover. NZFOE is still heavily dependant on a single product for its viability. The New Zealand futures market remains a predominantly wholesale market and has attracted little retail interest.[44]

Prior to the restructure of the exchange in 1992, all trading members were shareholders of the exchange. With the sale of the assets of the exchange to the Sydney Futures Exchange, none of the members are shareholders any longer. Currently, the main classes of dealers on NZFOE are: public brokers, introducing brokers, principal traders, trading permit holders and clearing members. Public brokers and introducing brokers may deal in contracts on behalf of other persons or for their own account. However, only public brokers are authorised to accept and hold client money and property. Principal traders can trade on their own account, but may deal with contracts on a 'give-up' basis on behalf of other brokers. Like introducing brokers, principal traders cannot accept or hold client money or property. Under existing regulations, trading permits may only be granted to public brokers and principal traders. Where a dealer also holds a trading permit, the dealer may deal directly on the automated trading system of NZFOE. A clearing member is a dealer authorised as a clearing member of SFECH.

Clearing services for NZFOE are undertaken by the Sydney Futures Exchange Clearing House (SFECH), which also manages the clearing function for SFE. SFECH guarantees the performance of clearing members by becoming the opposite party in all registered transactions. To reduce the financial risk assumed by SFECH, a system of margin deposits has been established. Unlike many other exchanges, NZFOE never adopted 'open outcry' trading. Its decision to opt for electronic trading at the outset was primarily due to the relatively small size of the market and the geographical spread of the market participants.[45] In October 1995, the original screen-based system was replaced with a New Zealand version of the SFE Overnight Trading System called 'SYCOM-NZ'. Now both SFE and NZFOE share a common trading platform and clearing technology. Despite the fact

---

[41] See New Zealand Futures and Options Exchange, *New Zealand Futures & Options Exchange—A Brief Description* (March 1996).
[42] See New Zealand Futures and Options Exchange 'History' <www.nzfoe.co.nz/overview.htm> 15 December 1999.
[43] See Securities Commission, Annual Report 30 June 1999 <www.sec.com.govt.nz/public/annrep/03.htm#nz >, 15 February 2000.
[44] Ibid.
[45] See Park & Schoenfeld, above n. 35, p. 212.

that both the exchanges are physically located in different countries, they are in reality a single market.

2.2.3   Singapore Exchange Derivatives Trading Limited

Launched on 7 September 1984, the Singapore International Monetary Exchange (SIMEX) was the first financial derivatives exchange in Asia.[46] It has established itself, within a relatively short period, as one of the leading derivatives exchanges in the world. It won the coveted 'International Exchange of the Year' award from the United Kingdom based *International Financing Review* for an unprecedented four times.[47] On 1 December 1999, following a major restructuring exercise, SIMEX was renamed 'Singapore Exchange Derivatives Trading Limited' (SGX-DT). It is now a subsidiary of the Singapore Exchange Limited (Singapore Exchange), which is also the holding company of the Singapore stock exchange.[48]

The Singapore government has been closely involved with the establishment and development of the exchange. This partnership between the government and the industry has often been cited as an important factor behind the exchange's success.[49] The Singapore government has not only been instrumental in the establishment of SGX-DT, it also played a pivotal role in the development of the financial derivatives industry in Singapore. In 1981, a survey among financial institutions conducted by the Monetary Authority of Singapore (MAS), the country's de facto central bank, revealed a significant potential for the trading of financial derivatives.[50] During that period, the Gold Exchange of Singapore (GES) was in difficulties and was struggling for survival. The lack of regulatory supervision had resulted in trading abuses by local participants.

The Singapore government set about revamping GES with the view to establishing a modern exchange for trading derivatives.[51] In May 1982, MAS invited key members of the Chicago Mercantile Exchange (CME) to Singapore to discuss the prospect of restructuring GES into a more broadly

---

[46]   See Singapore International Monetary Exchange, *SIMEX: A Journey of Excellence 1984–1994* (SGX-DT Brochure), p. 10.

[47]   SGX-DT won the award in 1989, 1992, 1993, and 1998. See Singapore Exchange 'Derivatives Trading—Past and Present', <simex.singaporeexchange.com/about.htm>, 15 February 2000.

[48]   The *Exchanges (Demutualisation and Merger) Act* 1999 resulted in the merger of the Stock Exchange of Singapore Limited, the Singapore International Monetary Exchange Limited and the Securities Clearing and Computer Services (Pte) Limited and the formation of a new holding company, Singapore Exchange Limited. The SGX-DT remains a separate legal entity but as a wholly owned subsidiary of the Singapore Exchange Limited. The members of the Singapore International Monetary Exchange, the predecessor to SGX-DT, were allocated shares in the holding company on the basis of each share and seat held. Following the merger, the clearing-house, which was previously a department of the derivatives exchange, became a wholly owned subsidiary of the Singapore Exchange Limited.

[49]   See M. Harrison, *Asia-Pacific Securities Markets* (2nd ed., Longman, Hong Kong, 1994), p. 467.

[50]   Ibid.

[51]   See SGX-DT Brochure, above n. 46, p. 10.

based exchange.[52] GES changed its name to the Singapore International Monetary Exchange in December 1983 when it adopted a fresh constitution and new rules and regulations.[53] The newly constituted exchange retained its predecessor's clearing arrangements as a basis for its clearinghouse.[54] The highly successful CME served as a model for the fledgling exchange, which adopted its open-outcry trading system and other trading practices.

CME played a pivotal role in the early development of SGX-DT by providing training and transfer of technology. In 1984, SGX-DT co-pioneered with CME the Mutual Offset System (MOS), which paved the way for around the clock trading in derivatives. MOS permits clearing members of SGX-DT and CME to establish or liquidate a position on one exchange through the execution or a trade on the other exchange. In hindsight, it would appear that SGX-DT did more than draw upon CME's expertise. By linking its market for Eurodollar interest rate contracts with that of CME, it capitalised on the latter's much greater liquidity to boost its initial trading volumes.[55] Since its establishment SGX-DT has proved to be a highly innovative and forward-looking exchange. For example, in 1986 it became the first exchange in the world to launch the Nikkei 225 Stock Index Futures Contract.[56] In June 1995, SGX-DT began trading the Brent Crude Oil futures contract in a mutual offset linkage with the International Petroleum Exchange.[57]

In view of SGX-DT's high profile, it may come as a surprise to many that Singapore has more than one derivatives exchange. The Singapore Commodities Exchange (SICOM), which is the country's second exchange, has been overshadowed by SGX-DT. SICOM was established in 1992 as part of the government's efforts to develop Singapore into a premier trading centre for a wide range of derivatives based on natural commodities. Currently, SICOM trades rubber futures contracts and coffee futures contracts. Unlike SGX-DT, SICOM is regulated by the Singapore Trade Development Board and governed by the *Commodity Futures Act* 1992.[58] There are no plans at present to merge SICOM with SGX-DT, although there are no good commercial reasons for maintaining two exchanges.

When SGX-DT began operations in 1984, it offered just four products. However within a decade, it had become a comprehensive market, offering 19 different futures and options products covering interest rates, stock indices, energy, currencies and gold.[59] A total of 25.863 million contracts were traded on the exchange in 1999.[60] This represented a 7.1 per cent

---

[52] See Slatyer and Carew, above n. 13, p. 70.

[53] See H. S. Loh, 'SGX-DT: Developing and Regulating a Futures Market' in K. L. Koh and Others (eds) *Current Developments in International Securities, Commodities and Financial Futures Markets*, (Butterworths, Singapore, 1987), p. 351.

[54] See Harrison, above n. 49, p. 467.

[55] Id., p. 27.

[56] See Singapore Exchange 'Derivatives Trading—Past and Present', <simex.singaporeexchange.com/about.htm>, 15 February 2000.

[57] See *SIMEX Annual Report—Excellent 1994 & Beyond* (SGX-DT Annual Report), pp. 6–7.

[58] See S. K. Tan and R. Liew, 'Behind the Barings Debacle' (May 1995) *Asia Law* 37, 38.

[59] See SGX-DT Annual Report, above n. 46, p. 18.

[60] See Singapore Exchange 'Derivatives Trading—Charts and Statistics', <simex.singaporeexchange.com/extotal1t.htm>, 15 February 2000.

decline in volume over the previous year. Around 87 per cent of its trades derive from international customers—mostly from the US, Japan and Europe.[61] The exchange has a mainly institutional customer base. It does not have a derivatives contract denominated in Singapore dollars as this could be due to the government's aversion to the internationalisation of the country's currency.[62]

There are four broad classes of membership on the exchange: Corporate Clearing, Corporate Non-Clearing, Commercial Associates and Individual Non-Clearing.[63] Corporate Clearing members can clear their own trades and customers' trades. They are also jointly and severally liable for the obligations of the clearinghouse. Corporate non-clearing members, commercial associate members and individual non-clearing members have to clear all their trades through a clearing member. With effect from 1 December 1999, trading access is no longer based on membership rights but on trading permits. There are two types of trading permits: Floor Trading Permit (FTP) and ETS Trading Permit (ETP). ETP holders have only access to SGX-DT contracts listed on the Electronic Trading System, launched in October 1999.

The Singapore derivatives exchange's image was recently dented by the collapse of the Barings Group. Despite the widespread publicity given to the collapse, it would be worthwhile to summarise the events that led to it. It all began in 1989 when Nicholas Leeson joined the settlements department of Barings Securities Limited (BSL) in London.[64] Leeson who was from Watford in the UK, left school at 18 with qualifications in English and History, but without a pass in Maths.[65] Shortly after joining BSL, he applied for registration with the Securities and Futures Authority in England. He made a false statement in his application regarding an unsatisfied judgement against him. When was queried by the Securities and Futures Authority, BSL promptly withdrew Leeson's application.

In April 1992, Leeson was posted to Barings Futures (Singapore) Pte Ltd (BFS) to set up its settlement operations. He took with him his wife, but left behind some GBP 3000 in unpaid county-court judgements.[66] His career took a successful turn in Singapore, probably because he was from the head office rather than any unusual ability on his part. By July 1992, Leeson had passed the necessary examinations to trade on the exchange floor and assumed the position of General Manger. Almost as soon as he began

---

[61] See Roberts, above n. 16, p. 185.
[62] See Harrison, above n. 49, p. 468.
[63] See Singapore Exchange, 'Derivatives Trading—Membership', <simex.singaporeexchange.com/member.htm> for details about membership requirements.
[64] See C. Brown, 'Report of the Board of Banking Supervision Enquiry into the Circumstances of the Collapse of Barings' (1995) 10 JIBL 446 at 447: The holding company of Barings Futures (Singapore) Pte Ltd and Barings Securities (Japan) Ltd was BSL, which in turn was a subsidiary of Barings Brothers & Co. Ltd, an authorised deposit-taking institution in the United Kingdom. The ultimate holding company of the entire group of companies was Barings Plc.
[65] See Roberts, above n. 16, p. 218.
[66] Ibid.

trading he opened error account '88888'. The account was set up to carry the minor losses arising from human errors for end of year write-off. It later transpired that the account was used to conceal from detection the massive losses incurred by BFS. Although the Barings Group denied any knowledge of account '88888', Leeson was adamant that it was opened on the instructions of his London office.[67]

While initially Leeson's trading activities were confined to executing clients' orders, by late 1993 he had got himself involved in proprietary trading. It appears that Barings senior management never really understood the true nature of his trading activities. They were under the impression that he was involved in risk-free arbitrage trading, but in actual fact, he was taking unauthorised positions on the exchanges in Singapore and Japan.[68] Had they fully realised the risks that he was taking, they would have in all likelihood stopped him immediately. On the surface, BFS and Leeson were doing a remarkably superb job. To many back in head office, Leeson was the Barings Group's 'wonder-boy' who single-handedly contributed to half of BFS' profits in 1993, and half of the entire firm's 1994 profits.[69]

Leeson took to falsifying client documentation and pretending that he was trading on behalf of clients, when he was trading for BFS. His main vehicle of deception was the cross-trade.[70] A broker 'cross-trades' when he or she executes a client's order by off setting that order against another client's order without routing the transaction through the trading floor. Leeson had no difficulty securing funds from BSL to finance his unauthorised activities. BSL regularly remitted funds to meet the margin requirements of BFS. Incredulously, by the time of the collapse, the Barings Group had remitted about SGD 1.7 billion to BFS.[71]

On 17 February 1995, a supervisor from BSL Settlements sent to Singapore discovered a major discrepancy between funds remitted to BFS and the margins placed by BFS with SGX-DT. When he realised that his deception had been uncovered, Leeson fled Singapore on 23 February 1995. After a massive international hunt for Leeson, he was arrested in Frankfurt while trying to flee to London. On 26 February 1995, Barings Plc went into administration and on the following day, BFS was placed under interim judicial management. In March 1995, the Internationale Nederlanden Groep NV of the Netherlands (ING) took over the main investment banking operations of the Barings Group. BFS was subsequently wound up on the recommendations of the Singapore company inspectors, Price Waterhouse. Leeson was extradited to Singapore where he stood trial. He pleaded guilty

---

[67] See N. Leeson, *Rogue Trader* (Little, Brown & Co., Boston, 1996), p. 39.

[68] 'Risk-free arbitrage' involves taking advantage of the differences in prices between identical contracts quoted on SGX-DT and on the security exchanges in either Tokyo or Osaka. Since the differences are usually very small, the size of the transactions tends to be very large in order to realise a significant profit.

[69] See L. Chew, *Managing Derivatives Risks* (John Wiley & Sons, Chichester, 1996), p. 228.

[70] Id., p. 229.

[71] See The Report of the Inspectors Appointed by the Minister of Finance, Singapore (Price Waterhouse Report) (October 1995), p. Bx.

to three charges of cheating and was sentenced to a total of six and a half years jail by the Singapore District Court.

Investigation into the collapse revealed that as at end of 1994, Barings had suffered cumulative losses of over GBP 200 million but these losses had not been recognised in the account.[72] Further losses were incurred when the Nikkei index fell after the Kobe earthquake of 17 January 1995. Cumulative losses grew threefold between end December 1995 and February 1996. Adding in the costs of closing out all positions, the total losses incurred on unauthorised trading totalled GBP 927 million.[73] It remains a mystery until this day whether Leeson acted on his own accord or in collaboration with others. Although there is no evidence to suggest that he made any illegal gains from his unauthorised activities, he was certainly well rewarded while under the employment of BFS.[74]

There were a number of factors that made it possible for Leeson to carry out his unauthorised activities for so long. First, he was in control of the dealing desk and the back office. Since there was no segregation of front room and back-room duties, he was able to falsify the records. Second, the Barings management were not fully aware of his activities, nor the activities of BFS. Third, there was some confusion as to whether the Singapore or the United Kingdom regulators were responsible for the supervision of BFS. Each was under the impression that the other was supervising BFS' activities. Fourth, despite SGX-DT identifying a number of trading irregularities, it neither acted on them with urgency nor informed MAS of its concerns. Even the external auditors of BFS are in some way to blame. Had they been more thorough and adopted the correct confirmation procedures they would have uncovered the fraud.[75]

The investigation by the Board of Banking Supervision identified Leeson as the individual primarily responsible for the unauthorised trading, but a parallel investigation conducted in Singapore by the government-appointed company inspectors concluded that certain individuals in the Barings Group were wilfully blind to and reckless of the truth.[76] Leeson's version of the facts in his autobiography appears to support the findings of the Singapore inspectors.[77] Contrary to expectations, the collapse of Barings did not lead to a rash of regulatory changes. The Finance Minister of Singapore, Dr Richard Hu, was quick to declare that the regulatory framework of SGX-DT was fundamentally sound.[78] Although the Bank of England acknowledged the need

---

[72] See 'Implications of the Barings Collapse for Bank Supervisors', *Reserve Bank of Australia Bulletin*, November 1995, p. 2.

[73] Ibid.

[74] See the Price Waterhouse Report, above n. 71, p. Bi, n. 1: Based on his performance in 1993, Leeson obtained a bonus of 115,000 pounds, and for 1994 he was to have received 450,000 pounds.

[75] See B. S. Tabalujan, 'Singapore: Barings Revisited—Auditors and the Detection of Corporate Fraud' (1997) 5 *Journal of Financial Crime* 190, 192.

[76] See C. Hadjiemmanuil, *Banking Regulation and the Bank of England* (LLP Ltd, London, 1996) pp. 49–50.

[77] See Leeson, above n. 67, p. 260.

[78] See 'The Barings Debacle and SIMEX' (1995) *Asia Law* 9, 11.

to improve existing supervisory arrangements, it did not take any immediate action to change the regulatory system.[79]

An examination of the causes of the collapse revealed that there was nothing fundamentally wrong with the Singapore regulatory scheme.[80] There were in place restrictions against illegal market practices such as cross-trading and penalties for falsification of records. The problem did not lie so much with the lack of regulation, but the way supervision was carried out. Not only was there a lack of cooperation between the Singapore and UK authorities, it appeared that the authorities may have been lenient with BFS. SGX-DT officials placed undue reliance on Barings' reputation and the infallibility of their own margining system. Although BFS had violated SGX-DT rules on a number of occasions and was fined, no serious investigation was undertaken to ascertain if there were more serious issues at stake.[81]

Immediately after the Barings incident, SGX-DT took a number of steps to prevent the recurrence of a similar crisis, including the following:

- A review of the exchange rules to enhance the monitoring of risk exposure of member firms;
- Adoption of measures to require the head office of member firms to improve the oversight of their derivatives subsidiaries in Singapore;
- Strengthening its supervision and compliance department to enhance floor supervision and compliance by member firms; and
- Requiring member firms to separate their dealing and settlement functions.[82]

The collapse of Barings only serves to reinforce the argument that no amount of regulation can prevent fraud from taking place. When a person in a position of authority is bent of defrauding his or her organisation, there is little that can be done to prevent it from happening. This is the sad reality not only about regulatory controls, but also internal procedures. Of course in the Barings case, it would appear that even the most basic of internal controls were not in place.

2.2.4 Commodity and Monetary Exchange of Malaysia

The Kuala Lumpur Commodity Exchange (KLCE) was established in July 1980. Its fully owned subsidiary, the Kuala Lumpur Commodity Clearing

---

[79] See Hamish Ramsay, Stephenson Harwood, 'Banking Supervision After Barings', (1995) *International Banking and Financial Law* 38, 39–40, for the proposed changes to banking supervision.

[80] See, for example, C. A. Samuelson, 'The Fall of Barings: Lessons for Legal Oversight of Derivatives Transactions in the United States' (1996) 29 *Cornell International Law Journal* 767, 804: 'Baring's Collapse was notable not for the holes that it exposed in the system of regulatory oversight, but for the inability of Baring's managers to discover the fraud in time to save their jobs.'

[81] See Price Waterhouse Report, above n. 71, p. 112.

[82] See Second Reading Speech on Futures Trading (Amendment) Bill by the Minister of Finance of Singapore on 1 March 1995, *Index to Official Debates and Written Answers to Questions*, Vol. 64, para. 63.

House (KLCCH), was formed to undertake its clearing function. KLCE was the first commodity derivatives exchange in Malaysia and also in the ASEAN region.[83] Malaysia had been trading in primary commodities such as rubber, tin and palm oil on a spot basis for decades. The heavy reliance on commodities had made the economy extremely vulnerable to changes in international commodities prices. By establishing a derivatives exchange, local producers and end-users would have a greater influence over price trends in the physical markets.[84] The crude palm oil futures contract was the first contract traded on KLCE. Turnover was strong in the initial years, but receded in 1984 following the suspension of trading in March 1984. The one-week closure of the exchange was due to the failure of a number of brokers to meet higher margin calls.[85] In September 1983, trading in rubber futures[86] was transferred from the Malaysian Rubber Exchange to KLCE.[87] Following the restructuring of KLCE in 1985, KLCCH was replaced by a new clearinghouse, the Malaysian Futures Clearing Corporation (MFCC). Trading in a second contract for rubber was introduced in March 1986.[88] This was followed by the introduction of tin futures contracts and cocoa futures contracts in October 1987 and October 1988, respectively.[89]

In the early 1980s, there were many commodities futures trading firms that engaged in highly questionable practices.[90] Fraudulent activities such as bucketing and churning were rampant. There was no segregation of clients' funds and brokers' representatives were poorly qualified and trained. Clients' funds in some cases were used to pay staff salaries and for making loans to directors of the broking firms. Investors lost large sums of monies and were generally unhappy with the government's inability to control the unscrupulous brokers. The President of the Consumers' Association of Penang summed up the views of a great majority of Malaysians in the following words:

The deeper question that the authorities must finally probe is whether this activity should be encouraged in the first place and in what ways (if any) it has contributed to the development of the country. This is essentially a *gambling activity*.[91] [emphasis provided]

One of the major causes of the collapse of the commodity derivatives market in 1984 was the unsatisfactory legal framework. At that time the

---

[83] See H. Y. Yeo, 'Kuala Lumpur Commodity Exchange (KLCE): Case-Study of Crude Palm Oil Futures Market' in K. L. Koh and Others (eds), *Current Developments in International Securities, Commodities and Financial Futures Markets* (Butterworths, Singapore, 1987), p. 291. 'ASEAN' is the acronym for the Association of South East Asian Nations, which at that time comprised Indonesia, Thailand, Philippines, Malaysia, and Singapore.
[84] Ibid.
[85] See Banks, above n. 28, p. 417.
[86] Ribbed Smoked Sheet No. 1 (RSS 1) grade.
[87] See *Bank Negara Malaysia Annual Report 1995* (BNM Report), p. 57.
[88] Standard Malaysian Rubber No. 20 (SMR 20) grade.
[89] See BNM Report, above n. 87, p. 57.
[90] See Consumers' Association of Penang, *CAP Report No. 3: Malpractices in the Commodities Futures Trading Firms* (April 1984) for details of some of these malpractices.
[91] Ibid.

commodity derivatives industry was regulated by the *Commodities Trading Act* 1980 (CTA). The CTA was an ineffective piece of legislation as it had a number of major weaknesses including the following:

- the licensing system emphasised probity and financial strength at the expense of professional competence;
- the industry watchdog, the Commodity Trading Commission (CTC), had no jurisdiction over the clearing organisation nor powers to enforce compliance of the exchange's business rules;
- there were no controls over undesirable market practices like price manipulation; and
- the CTC lacked the necessary resources to properly supervise the market.[92]

The closure of KLCE seriously damaged the reputation of the exchange both locally and internationally. In a move to regain investor confidence, the government reorganised KLCE and passed the *Commodity Trading Act* 1985 to replace the unsatisfactory 1980 legislation. The exchange eventually returned to normalcy. The exchange has recorded turnovers averaging half a million contracts in the last couple of years. For example, in 1996, 0.498 million contracts were registered and in 1997, 0.484 million contracts.[93] Despite Malaysia's early start in the trading of derivatives it did not venture into the trading of financial futures until very much later. This may have, in part, been due to KLCE's unsatisfactory experience with crude palm oil futures trading in the early 1980s and the lack of expertise in financial derivatives.

In 1992, KLCE created a wholly owned subsidiary, Kuala Lumpur Futures Market (later renamed 'Malaysia Monetary Exchange') to trade money market and interest rate futures.[94] However, it was not until 28 May 1996 that MME finally commenced trading in the Three-month Kuala Lumpur Interbank Offer Rates Futures Contract. The underlying instrument is a ringgit inter-bank deposit of MYR 1 million with three-month maturity. Like other short-term interest rate futures contracts, it is priced on an index basis. The contract is cash settled, and there are limits imposed on position sizes. Trading from the outset has been relatively thin, possibly because of the difficulty in attracting offshore money market participants requiring hedging instruments with longer maturities.[95] Between May and December 1996, a total of 40,933 contracts were traded.[96] In 1997, the number of contracts increased to 76,384. The financial crisis and the imposition of capital controls had a negative influence on the performance of MME. In 1998 the volume of contracts traded fell to 24,738. Although 1999 was a better year, still only 28,994 contracts were traded.

---

[92] See Yeo, above n. 83, pp. 299–303.
[93] See *COMMEX Malaysia's Data* <commex.com.my/new_home/htm/index1.htm>, 15 February 2000.
[94] See Banks, above n. 28, p. 411.
[95] See 'Klibor Futures—a First for Ringgit', *Business Time*, 28 May 1996, p. 20.
[96] See *COMMEX Malaysia's Data* <commex.com.my/new_home/htm/index1.htm>, 15 February 2000.

KLCE changed its name to the Commodity and Monetary Exchange (COMMEX) of Malaysia on 21 October 1998. On 7 December of the same year, it merged its operations with MME. One of the principal reasons behind the merger was the need to reduce the costs of operation. The poor trading volumes could no longer justify the existence of two separate exchanges. COMMEX is a member-owned exchange and constituted as a company limited by guarantee. It has plans to re-list its Crude Palm Kernel Oil futures contract and to introduce a bond futures contract sometime in the near future. The Malaysian Derivatives Clearing House (MDCH) undertakes the clearing of contracts for both COMMEX and the Kuala Lumpur Options and Financial Futures Exchange (KLOFFE). MDCH was formed in December 1995 initially to clear only financial futures contracts. It merged with the MFCC in November 1997 and assumed the clearing function for COMMEX. Currently, it is jointly owned by COMMEX and KLOFFE. Like SFECH, MDCH acts as counterparty to all contracts upon registration.

There are now two broad classes of members: Corporate Members and Individual Members. Corporate members are further sub-divided into General Members, Financial Members and Commodity Members. Not all corporate members are broker members. Broker members are those licensed under the Futures Industry Act 1993 to carry on futures broking business. There are two categories of individual members: Local Members Trading Permit Holders and Trade Affiliates. With the exception of Trading Permit Holders and Trade Affiliates, who pay non-refundable membership fees, trading rights of members are attached to Seats. Seats on the exchange are either owned or leased. They are sub-divided into commodity seats, financial seats and individual seats. Seats may be purchased or leased in accordance with the Business Rules of the exchange. Exchange members who are also members of the MDCH are called clearing members. Membership of the exchange has increased since the merger.[97]

2.2.5 Kuala Lumpur Options and Financial Futures Exchange

Had KLCE introduced financial futures in the late 1980s, there would not have been a need for the establishment of another futures exchange. During that time, the Malaysian Government was keen to develop Kuala Lumpur into a regional financial centre and saw the need for a derivatives exchange. Singapore had already established its own derivatives exchange and the Government was naturally unhappy with KLCE's delay in introducing financial derivatives.[98] In 1991, four public-listed companies, Renong Berhad, New Straits Times Berhad, Rashid Hussain Berhad, and Zalik Berhad (now renamed HLG Capital Berhad), with the support of the

---

[97] See COMMEX MALAYSIA's Annual Report 1998, p. 6, <commix.com.my/new_home/htm>, 15 December 1999. As at 31 December 1998, there were 31 broker members, 46 non-broker members, 47 locals, 53 Trade Permit Holders and 10 Affilliates.

[98] See Park and Schoenfeld, above n. 35, p 246: The then Minister of Finance, Datuk Paduka Daim Zainuddin, was reported to have accused the KLCE officials of 'dragging their feet' in bringing about the needed changes.

Ministry of Finance, submitted a proposal to establish the Kuala Lumpur Options and Financial Futures Exchange (KLOFFE).[99] Commerce International Merchant Bankers conducted the initial feasibility study with the help of foreign consultants like the Stockholm Options Market.[100] However, the project was beset with difficulties from the start and the Kuala Lumpur Options and Financial Futures Exchange (KLOFFE) was only launched on 15 December 1995.

Since its inception, KLOFFE has remained a single-product exchange. The only product traded on the exchange is the KLSE CI Futures Contract. It is a cash-settled stock index futures contract, based on the Kuala Lumpur Stock Exchange Composite Index.[101] Trading in the first year of operation was relatively thin, largely due to the negative reporting of derivatives induced disasters such as the collapse of Barings. In 1996, 77,281 contracts were traded, which translated into an average daily turnover of 312 contracts. Trading volume picked up in 1997 and peaked at 0.771 million in 1998. The financial crisis and the subsequent imposition of capital controls had an adverse impact on KLOFFE's turnover. In 1999, the total number of contracts traded declined to 0.436 million. KLOFFE has plans to introduce trading in options contracts, such as options on the KLSE Composite Index and on individual stocks, in the near future.[102]

KLOFFE was established as a public limited company, wholly owned by KLOFFE Capital Sendirian Berhad. In December 1998, the Kuala Lumpur Stock Exchange (KLSE) acquired KLOFFE from the shareholders of its holding company.[103] In a press statement, the KLSE explained that the integration of both exchanges would enhance efficiency and optimise use of resources.[104] Given the trading volumes achieved by both exchanges, the integration is a step in the right direction. Indications are that the integration of COMMEX and KLSE may be the next logical move. This would be in line with what is happening in other countries. Unlike many other exchanges, KLOFFE began operations as a fully electronic exchange. It operates an integrated trading and clearing (registration) system called KLOFFE Automated Trading System (KATS).[105]

Currently, there are only two categories of membership in KLOFFE: trading members and local members. Trading members are companies incorporated under the *Companies Act* 1965 engaged in licensed futures broking

---

[99] See Banks, above n. 28, p. 160.

[100] See Park & Schoenfeld, above n. 35, p. 247.

[101] See Kuala Lumpur Options & Financial Futures, *Know Your Futures*, p. 26: The KLSE CI was first published by the Kuala Lumpur Stock Exchange in 1986, and has established itself as the benchmark of market performance for the Malaysian equities market. It is a capitalisation-based index, which means that the impact on the index of a price change in any given stock depends on its capitalisation.

[102] See *Kuala Lumpur Stock Exchange Annual Report 1999*, p. 50.

[103] The main shareholders of KLOFFE Capital Sendirian Berhad were four public listed companies: Renong Berhad, Rashid Hussain Berhad, New Straits Times Press (Malaysia) Berhad and HLG Capital Berhad.

[104] See S. S. Habib, 'KLSE to acquire Kloffe Capital for RM35mil', *Star Online*, 2 July 1998 <thestar.com.my/Thursday/02szdeal.html>, 7 July 1998.

[105] See Kuala Lumpur Options & Futures Exchange, *Stepping Into A New Era*, p. 15.

business. Trading members can trade in contracts both for their own accounts and on behalf of customers. They are required to either become Clearing members of MDCH or to have an arrangement with a Clearing member in order to facilitate the clearing of its trades. Local members are individuals who trade only for their own accounts, and have full and direct access to KLOFFE's trading facilities. They are also required to have an arrangement with a clearing member for the clearing of their trades. There is another category of persons who can also trade on the exchange, albeit under restrictive terms, and are not regarded as exchange members. They are individuals who have been issued with trading permits to trade on their own accounts. These non-transferable permits are for fixed periods of up to 12 months, and allow the holders to trade in only specific contracts.

2.2.6   Hong Kong Futures Exchange

Like the Commodity and Monetary Exchange of Malaysia, the Hong Kong Futures Exchange Ltd has a chequered history. It rose to significance with the launch of its highly successful Hang Seng Index futures contract in May 1986.[106] But the Stock Market Crash of October 1987, which led to its closure, badly damaged its reputation. Following this unhappy episode, the exchange was restructured and regulatory supervision strengthened to restore public confidence. The exchange has since recovered much of its lost ground and once again plays an active role in the region. Following a major restructuring exercise in early 2000, the Hong Kong Futures Exchange is now a subsidiary of the newly formed Hong Kong Exchanges and Clearing Limited.

The history of trading of derivatives in Hong Kong dates back to 1975 when the Hong Kong Legislative Council approved in principle a proposal to establish a commodity derivatives exchange in Hong Kong.[107] The *Commodities Trading Ordinance* (CTO) was subsequently enacted to facilitate the establishment of the exchange and the trading of derivatives contracts. On 17 December 1976, Hong Kong's derivatives exchange was officially launched. Initially, it was called the Hong Kong Commodities Exchange Limited as it only offered cotton, sugar, soybeans, and gold futures contracts. The Governor in Council issued the exchange with a licence, which was subject to review after five years. When the Government's Working Party undertook its review in 1982, it found that the exchange had performed badly due to severe management problems. It recommended the renewal of HKCE's licence on condition that it was re-organised and the legislation amended to improve prudential supervision.

---

[106]   See Slatyer and Carew, above n. 13, p. 77. See also, Securities Review Committee, *The Operation and Regulation of the Hong Kong Securities Industry*, (Hay Davidson Report) (Hong Kong, May 1988), para. 6.13: Trading of the HSI futures contract was so active that within a relatively short period, the HSI futures market became the second largest stock index market in the world.

[107]   The contents of this section are largely based on the information obtained from the Hay Davidson Report, id., Appendix 22.

Following its restructure in 1984, HKCE worked with a number of banks to develop a financial derivatives market. To reflect its change in emphasis from commodity derivatives to financial derivatives, HKCE was renamed 'Hong Kong Futures Exchange Limited' (HKFE) in 1985. The United Kingdom based International Commodities Clearing House was appointed to manage the clearing function. The Futures Guarantee Corporation (FGC), whose shareholders comprised the major banks behind the financial derivatives project, guaranteed all contracts. In May 1986, HKFE launched its Hang Seng Index (HSI) futures contract, which later proved to be remarkably successful.

From its inception, turnover at the stock index futures market grew at a remarkable pace. By September 1987, turnover had increased almost twenty fold, making it the second largest index futures contract market in the world.[108] Following the crash of the New York stock market on 19 October 1987, both the HKSE and the HKFE decided to suspend trading for four days. There were serious doubts at that time whether FGC with a capitalisation of around HKD 15 million and accumulated reserves of around HKD 7.5 million would be able to meet its obligations when trading resumed.[109] The government hastily put together a support package of HKD 2 billion over the weekend for FGC. This facility was to be repaid out of recoveries and the imposition of special levies on both exchanges.[110]

When both exchanges re-opened on Monday, 26 October 1987, the Hang Seng index plunged 1,120 points to close at 2,242.[111] This was equivalent to a 33 per cent decline in value. The drastic drop in value of the HSI futures contracts led to widespread defaults. When it became clear that many of the brokers with 'long' (over-bought) positions would be unable to put up further margins, the government raised an additional HKD 2 billion support facility. However, after discounting margins payments made by futures brokers, and liquidation of some of the net long positions, only HKD 1.795 billion was drawn from the support facility.[112]

On 16 November 1987, the Governor of Hong Kong appointed the Securities Review Committee, chaired by Ian Hay Davidson, to review the constitution, powers, management, and operation of the two exchanges and their regulatory bodies. The Committee uncovered a number of market weaknesses which contributed to the October 1987 crash. Some of the more serious weaknesses included the following:

- the Commodity Trading Commission, which was set up to oversee the derivatives industry, lacked direction and played a passive role;
- the Office of the Commissioner for Securities and Commodity Trading, which was established to service the Commissions, was under-resourced

---

[108] Id., para. 1.4.
[109] Id., Appendix 1, para. 7.
[110] See Harrison, above n. 49, para. 10.1: 'Thanks to booming stock turnover as the 1990s commenced, the levies were finally suspended in August 1993.'
[111] See Hay Davidson Report, above n. 106, Appendix 1, para. 15.
[112] Id., para. 21.

and placed too much emphasis on vetting papers instead of active market surveillance;

- the tripartite structure of exchange, clearing house and guarantee corporation confused lines of responsibility and obstructed development of an adequate risk management system.[113]

The Committee was most scathing in its attack on the lack of regulatory supervision over the market:

We found that, while the entire system had originally been based on self-regulation by the Exchanges with "the support of an authoritative and impartial body to assist them in taking action themselves to curb questionable practices", the concept of self-regulation and market discipline had failed to develop in Hong Kong. What is equally unfortunate is that, faced with this, the supervisory bodies charged with overseeing the markets had lost effective control.[114]

It has been suggested that the system of self-regulation had failed in Hong Kong largely because of the structure of the derivatives market.[115] The Hong Kong market had an active investor base with a high retail element and there was a large gap between the public interest and the self-interest of the controlling group in the exchange. Not surprisingly, one of the Hong Kong Government's main priorities after the publication of the Committee's findings was to change the regulatory approach. This was achieved through the establishment of a new statutory body to assume the roles of the Securities Commission, Commodity Trading Commission and the Office of the Commissioner for Securities and Commodity Trading. With the establishment of the Securities and Futures Commission (SFC) by the *Securities and Futures Commission Ordinance* on 1 May 1989, self-regulation of the derivatives industry effectively came to an end.

Currently, HKFE offers a number of products for trading which include the following:

- HKFE Gold futures contracts
- Hang Seng Index (HSI) futures contracts
- Hang Seng Index (HSI) options contracts
- Hong Kong Inter-bank Offer Rate (HIBOR) futures contracts
- Individual Stock futures contracts
- Rolling Forex futures contracts.

In 1999, HKFE recorded a turnover of 6.331 million contracts, which represented a 25.4 per cent decline in volume from the previous year.[116] The

---

[113] Id., para. 1.7.
[114] Id., para. 1.6.
[115] See N. Gunningham, 'Futures Market Regulation in Australia' in G. Walker and B. Fisse (eds), *Securities Regulation in Australia and New Zealand* (Oxford University Press, Auckland, 1994), pp. 827–831.
[116] See 'Total HKFE Futures & Options Volume (1986–1999)' <www.hkfe.com/datasta/sta/s6.htm>, 16 February 2000.

exchange's two most successful products are the HSI futures and HSI options contracts, with the former accounting for the bulk of its business. In 1999, both products accounted for 92.3 percent of the total turnover for the exchange.[117] The HSI futures contract is one of the most actively traded equity index futures contracts in Asia. Trading in other derivatives products has been relatively thin.

In the first quarter of 1999, the Hong Kong Government publicly announced its plans to restructure the financial market as it had become outdated. The restructuring exercise would, among other things, involve the demutualisation and unification of the stock and futures exchanges into a new holding company. The impetus for change came from both internal and external sources.[118] The external pressure was seen as coming from competition from other Asian markets, alternative and proprietary trading systems, disintermediation of brokers, and the deregulation of national markets. Internally, the pressure came from the need to improve performance and the conflict of interests faced by the exchanges while acting simultaneously as market operators and self-regulating organisations.

On 6 March 2000, HKFE, the Stock Exchange of Hong Kong and the Hong Kong Securities Clearing Company became subsidiaries of the Hong Kong Exchanges and Clearing Limited. As a result of the merger, HKFE shareholders have been granted trading rights on the exchange, subject to them meeting certain requirements. Access to trading facilities is no longer tied to ownership of shares, but to possession of trading rights. Members of the exchange are now called Exchange Participants. There are four categories of exchange participants: Traders, Brokers, Futures Commission Merchants and Merchant Traders.[119]

Traders are either individuals ordinarily resident in Hong Kong or companies incorporated in Hong Kong and can only trade on their own account. Brokers on the other hand, are those who trade on their own account as well as act as floor agents for transactions of other participants. Futures Commission Merchants, the third category of participants, trade on their own account as well as for clients. They also sometimes act as floor agents for transactions of other participants. The last category, Merchant Traders, trade on their own account and act as merchants in a deliverable commodity traded on the exchange. All Exchange Participants are subject to ongoing obligations such as compliance with the CTO, the rules of the exchange and the exchange's financial requirements. There are no changes to the trading and settlement arrangements. The HKFE Clearing Corporation Limited (HKCC), a wholly owned subsidiary of the HKFE, undertakes the clearing of futures contracts.

---

[117] Ibid.

[118] See Clifford Chance, 'Hong Kong's Proposed Financial Market Reforms', (1999) 5 *World Securities Law Report* 35.

[119] For details about conditions and privileges, see 'Exchange Participantship' <www.hkfe.com/exchange/hkfemember.htm>, 29 May 2000.

2.3   OVER-THE-COUNTER DERIVATIVES MARKETS

2.3.1   Market Size

The over-the-counter (OTC) derivatives markets are principal-to-principal dealer markets. Unlike, exchange-traded derivatives markets, OTC derivatives markets do not regularly publish statistical information. It is therefore difficult to obtain accurate or timely information about the size of these markets in Australia, New Zealand, Singapore, Malaysia and Hong Kong (markets under study). The two main sources of information are the Bank of International Settlement (BIS) and the International Swaps and Derivatives Association (ISDA). BIS data is more useful as it has a wider coverage of institutions. On the other hand, ISDA data is based on the information provided by its members only. Preliminary data from the Bank of International Settlement Triennial Central Bank Survey of Foreign Exchange and Derivatives Market Activity in April 1998,[120] provides some indication of the level of OTC activity in the markets under study:

Distribution of OTC Derivatives Market Activity (Average daily turnover in billions of USD)

	April 1995		April 1998	
	Amount	*% Share*	*Amount*	*% Share*
Australia	3.8	1.4	4.6	1.0
Hong Kong	4.3	1.6	3.8	0.8
Malaysia	–	–	–	–
New Zealand	0.2	0.1	0.5	0.1
Singapore	18.1	6.7	11.3	2.4
Global Turnover	269.5	100	474.0	100

Notes:
1. The data is adjusted for local double counting.
2. Estimated coverage range between 75–100 per cent for OTC derivatives activity.
3. Where no figure is stated, it means that either no data is available or the amount is insignificant.

From the above information, the three largest OTC derivatives markets are Singapore, Australia and Hong Kong. The OTC markets in New Zealand and Malaysia are very small, compared to the other markets. Based on the data released by the central banks of Singapore, Australia and Hong

---

[120] See Bank of International Settlement's 19 October 1998 Press Release <www.bis.org/press/index.htm>, 21 February 2000. The survey covers 43 countries and is limited to OTC currency and interest rate instruments. It excludes information on exchange-traded business as well as the smaller OTC market segments such as equity, commodity and credit-related products.

Kong,[121] it is possible to make a number of comments about these markets. First, a significant proportion of the transactions were carried out with overseas counterparties, reflecting the international nature of these markets.[122] Second, market activity is still concentrated among a small number of dealers. This mirrors the situation in the other developed markets. Third, the OTC markets have generally developed in tandem with the exchange-traded markets. Fourth, the Asian Crisis had an adverse effect on the Singapore and Hong Kong markets, but not the Australian market.

Trading in OTC derivatives is unregulated, except to the extent that the market participants trading in such transactions are regulated. It has been argued that regulating OTC derivatives as securities or futures contracts is inappropriate given that the securities and futures laws were devised to address policy concerns not present in OTC markets.[123] However, it is incorrect to say that OTC markets are not regulated at all. There are various forms of market-generated regulation, ranging from codes of practice to standardised market documentation.[124] Market-generated regulation while lacking the force of law, have contributed significantly to the success of OTC markets. Contrary to belief, OTC markets have functioned remarkably well considering the fact that they are not subject to external regulation. While it is true that some end-users have suffered sizeable losses trading in OTC instruments, some OTC derivatives pose no greater risk than the average financial transaction. No discussion of OTC derivatives markets will be complete without mentioning the various international risk management initiatives undertaken to instil greater market discipline and the role played by standard market documentation in allocating risks between derivatives counterparties.

2.3.2 International Risks Management Initiatives

Recent policy initiatives relating to OTC derivatives markets fall into two broad categories. Under the first category are those initiatives that improve the functioning of markets, and under the second category are those that support the prudential soundness of the financial institutions, which are

---

[121] See the 29 September 1999 media releases of the following central banks: Reserve Bank of Australia <www.rba.gov.au/media/mr_98_12.htm>; Hong Kong Monetary Authority <www.info.gov.hk/hkma/new/press/others/980929e.htm>; Monetary Authority of Singapore <www.mas.gov.sg/newspeeches/290998-c.htm>, 21 February 2000.

[122] For Hong Kong, 72 per cent of all transactions were with overseas counterparties. As for Singapore, 69.5 per cent of foreign exchange transactions involved overseas financial institutions and customers. The number of foreign exchange contracts with overseas banks was much smaller for Australia—24.7 per cent.

[123] See, for example, W. E. Gibson, 'Are Swap Agreements Securities or Futures? The Inadequacies of Applying the Traditional Regulatory Approach to OTC Derivatives Transactions' (1999) 24 *The Journal of Corporation Law* 379, 410.

[124] For a useful discussion of market-generated regulation see T. Little and S. J. Berwin & Co., 'Regulation by Non-Regulators' in E. J. Swan (ed.) *Issues in Derivative Instruments* (Kluwer Law International, The Hague, 1999), p. 27.

major players in the markets.[125] The focus of international policy co-ordination in the derivatives area has been the Bank for International Settlements in Basle, Switzerland. Two other international bodies have also played an important role in the development of supervisory policies for financial institutions and they are the Basle Committee and the Technical Committee of the International Organisation of Securities Commissions (IOSCO). Although neither of them can claim global membership, they nevertheless exercise considerable influence over non-members since their agreements are widely regarded as benchmarks, which supervisors worldwide seek to emulate. Not surprisingly, the standards and rules laid down by these three bodies have sometimes been described as 'international soft law' since they have significant legal and economic consequences for international banking.[126]

MACRO-PRUDENTIAL POLICY INITIATIVES

Macro-prudential policy initiatives refer to those initiatives which improve the functioning of financial markets. They include measures that enhance market transparency and facilitate the monitoring of the macro-economic aspects of these markets. The main contributor of such initiatives has been the Bank of International Settlement (BIS). BIS, which has its headquarters in Basle functions as a forum for international and monetary cooperation. It hosts the meetings of central bankers and provides the facilities for various committees. In addition, it acts as a centre for monetary and economic research. Despite its name, BIS does not accept deposits or provide finance to corporate entities or private individuals. A number of Working Groups set up under the auspices of BIS produced several reports during the 1980s and 1990s that covered the general development of international banking and interbank relations.[127]

One of the earliest BIS initiatives was the establishment of a Study Group in early 1985 to examine the recent innovations which affected the conduct of international banking. Following extensive discussions with international banks, the Study Group published its report, *Recent Innovations in International Banking* (also known as the 'Cross Report' after the Chairperson of the Working Group, Sam Cross of the Federal Reserve Bank of New York) in April 1986 to stimulate public debate on the issues raised. The Cross Report examined the causes of financial innovation and some of the principal issues connected with it, such as its impact on financial stability, financial reporting and monetary policy. Its major finding was that the process of rapid innovation and the development of new financial

---

[125] This section on international risks management initiatives draws heavily from M. Taylor, 'International Policy Initiatives in the OTC Derivatives Markets' in E. Bettelheim, H. Parry, and W. Rees (eds), *Swaps and Off-Exchange Derivatives Trading: Law and Regulation* (FT Law & Tax, London, 1996), p. 332.

[126] See J. J. Norton (ed.), *Devising International Bank Supervisory Standards* (Graham & Trotman/ Martinus Nijhoff Publishers, London, 1995), p. xix.

[127] For a short summary of some these initiatives, see for example, G. A. Walker, 'Financial Derivatives—Global Regulatory Developments' (January 1996) *Journal of Business Law* 66, 72–77.

instruments such as derivatives had the potential to destabilise the financial system.

As a follow up to the issues highlighted by the Cross Report, a separate Working Group was established in 1991 to examine international interbank relations, especially in non-traditional markets like those trading derivatives. The Working Group's report entitled *Recent Developments in International Interbank Relations* (also known as the 'Promisel Report' after the Chairperson of the Working Group, Larry Promisel of the Federal Reserve Board), which was published in October 1992, recommended a host of measures to strengthen the structure of wholesale markets including the increased use of netting schemes and the reduction of legal uncertainties. The Promisel Report pointed to the need for more reliable and timely statistics on OTC markets worldwide.

A subsequent Working Group, chaired by Jan Brockmeijer of the Netherlands Central Bank was established to develop appropriate measurement concepts and monitoring techniques in view of the lack of reliable data on derivatives activities. It published its report entitled *Issues of Measurement Related to Market Size and Macro-prudential Risks in Derivatives Markets* (also known as the 'Brockmeijer Report') in February 1995. The Brockmeijer Report proposed two important initiatives to address central banks' information needs. The first was a system of collecting statistics regularly from a small number of leading dealers and the second, was a comprehensive survey of derivatives markets conducted on a less regular basis. The proposal for a comprehensive survey culminated in the April 1995 Central Bank Survey of Derivatives Market Activity. The results of the survey, which involved 26 countries, are described in the 'Central Bank Survey of Foreign Exchange and Derivatives Market Activity' released by the BIS in May 1996. A second survey, this time involving 43 countries, was undertaken in April 1998.

Although numerous reports have been published about the rapid growth of derivatives activities and their implications in terms of risks to banks and the financial system as a whole, none has provided a comprehensive survey of the practices adopted by OTC participants to manage counterparty risks. A Study Group chaired by Patrick Parkinson was set up to undertake this task and in September 1998, it released a report of its findings.[128] What the Study discovered was that practices for managing counterparty risks and processing trades were broadly similar in the G-10 countries. There is widespread use of standardised market documentation. Netting and to an increasing extent collateral agreements are used to mitigate counterparty risks. The vast majority of OTC derivatives transactions are settled bilaterally between the counterparties. The report also drew attention to three sets of issues that required further analysis, namely, delays in completing master agreements and confirmations; the rapidly expanding use of collateral; and the potential expansion of clearing houses for OTC derivatives.

---

[128] See Bank of International Settlements, *OTC Derivatives: Settlement Procedures and Counterparty Risk Management* ('BIS OTC Report') (Basle, September 1998).

SUPERVISORY POLICY INITIATIVES

Supervisory policy initiatives refer to those initiatives that improve the way in which financial institutions manage and control their risks. The Basle Committee on Banking Supervision (Basle Committee) has been responsible for most of these initiatives. It is a committee of banking supervisory authorities established by the Group of Ten countries in 1975. It has no formal relationship with BIS, except that it uses the latter's offices in Basle for its headquarters. The Basle Committee's primary aim is to:

[E]ncourage a gradual convergence of bank supervisory practices of the member regulatory institutions by enhancing the scope and effectiveness of supervisory techniques for international banking activities, by studying and making recommendations on specific areas of prudential concern in international banking, and by facilitating the exchange of information among bank supervisors so as to upgrade the quality of international bank supervision.[129]

Although initially the Basle Committee focussed on the supervision of the activities of banks operating in more than one jurisdiction, it later turned its attention to the substance of prudential regulatory norms.[130] The Basle Committee's most notable achievement has been the development of common minimum standards of capital adequacy for international banks.[131]

In July 1988, the Basle Committee published its key document entitled *International Convergence of Capital Measurement and Capital Standards*, which recommended the introduction of a minimum standard for the capital adequacy of internationally active banks and the establishment of a common measurement system.[132] The widespread use of derivatives in the years prior to 1988 had increased the credit exposure of banks without adding to their balance sheets.[133] There existed a need to devise a scheme which would associate an equivalent asset amount to off-balance sheet exposures for the calculation of capital adequacy ratios.[134] The proposals published by the Basle Committee were ratified by the G-10 central banks. This agreement, later known as the 'Basle Accord', has since been adopted by a number of countries outside the G-10 region. The banks were given until the end of 1992 to comply with a minimum risk asset ratio requirement set at eight

---

[129] See Norton, above n. 126, p. 177.
[130] See C. D. Hadjiemmanuil, 'Central Bankers' Club Law' and Transitional Economies: Banking Reform and the Reception of the Basle Standards of Prudential Supervision in Eastern Europe and the Former Soviet Union' in J. J. Norton and M. Andenas (eds), *Emerging Financial Markets and the Role of International Financial Organisations* (Kluwer Law International, London, 1996), p. 186.
[131] Ibid.
[132] See M. Hall, 'The Revised Supervisory Treatment of Netting and Potential Exposure for Off-balance-sheet Items under the Basle Capital Accord' (1996) 11 JIBL 93. For details of the various proposals see, Basle Committee, *Proposals for International Convergence of Capital Measurement and Capital Standards* (December 1987).
[133] See J. Jarrat, 'Allocating Capital' in E. Sheedy and S. McCracken (eds), *Derivatives: The Risks That Remain* (Allen & Unwin, St Leonards, NSW, 1997), p. 199.
[134] Ibid.

per cent because it reflected levels of capital maintained by the better capitalised banks at that time.[135]

In January 1996, the Basle Committee published its *Amendment to The Capital Accord to Incorporate Market Risks*. The Basle Committee's proposal for market risk allows for two methods of calculating capital for market risk: the 'standardised approach' and the 'model user approach'.[136] The 'standardised approach' had attracted considerable comment from users who had for some time been using considerably more sophisticated methods of capital allocation for market risks.[137] Under the 'model user approach' firms may use their own systems subject to compliance with certain quantitative and qualitative guidelines laid down by the Basle Committee. This concession on the part of the Basle Committee represents a shift in supervisory policy from one of independent risks measurements to assessment of the reliability of internal risk measurement systems.

The Basle Accord also recognised bilateral netting by novation for the same currency and same value date for supervisory purposes. In July 1994, the Accord was amended to include other forms of bilateral netting of credit exposure besides netting by novation, provided they complied with the following requirements: (1) the bank's supervisor must be satisfied that the netting agreement creates a single legal obligation; (2) written legal opinion has been obtained that the agreement is legally enforceable under the laws of the relevant jurisdictions; and (3) procedures are in place to ensure that the legal characteristics of netting arrangements are kept under review in the light of possible changes in relevant law.[138] Despite the introduction of the July 1994 amendments, no recognition was given to multilateral netting.[139] In April 1996, the position under the Accord in respect of the multilateral netting of forward value foreign exchange transactions was clarified with the publication of the Committee's 'interpretation' of the subject.[140] Through this recent 'interpretation' of the Accord, the Committee will now recognise multilateral netting of forward value exchange transactions provided certain conditions are met, thereby allowing for a reduction in capital charges.

Apart from its work in the allocation of capital to credit and market related risks of derivatives, the Basle Committee also worked with the Technical Committee of International Organisation of Securities Commissions (IOSCO) to develop common standards on systems and controls. These standards are contained in the *Risk Management Guidelines for*

---

[135] Ibid.
[136] Id., p. 217.
[137] Ibid.
[138] See Hall, above n. 132, 98.
[139] Multilateral netting is normally achieved by netting through a central clearinghouse, so that for every eligible transaction agreed by a pair of participants, the clearinghouse becomes the counterparty to each participant.
[140] See M. Hall, 'The Treatment of Multilateral Netting of Forward Value Foreign Exchange Transactions Under the Basle Capital Accord' (1997) 12 JIBL 333. See also, Basle Committee, *Interpretation of the Capital Accord for the Multilateral Netting of Forward Value Foreign Exchange Transactions*, (April 1996).

Derivatives, issued jointly by the Basle Committee and the Technical
Committee of IOSCO in July 1994. The guidelines are intended to provide
an outline of best practice in risk management. For example, the guidelines
assign risk management responsibilities to the board of directors, stress the
importance of internal controls and audit, and emphasise the need for regular reviews of risk management practices.[141] The guidelines are consistent
with recommendations on 'best practices' made by private-sector bodies
such as the Group of Thirty.

In September 1999, the Basle Committee released three papers as part of
its efforts to develop a new framework for international bank supervision.
The first paper is on enhancing bank transparency, the second on internal
control systems, and the third on operational risk management.[142] At the
same time, the Basle Committee announced that it was reviewing the 1988
Accord with the view to replacing it with more flexible rules that could prevent regulatory capital arbitrage. It has been suggested that the proposed
changes is an acceptance by the bank supervisors that the structure put in
place by the 1988 Accord has become dangerously outdated.[143] The recent
financial turbulence in emerging markets has cast doubts on the universal
validity of the existing framework for prudential supervision. It has also
reinforced the importance of proper internal controls and the management
of operational risk. The Basle Committee's new initiatives, which domestic
regulators are expected to follow, emphasise more flexible application of
rules to account for differences in institutional size and activities.

2.3.3   Standard Market Documentation

When over-the-counter (OTC) derivatives like swaps were first introduced,
they were individually negotiated and subject to a detailed agreement. A
significant amount of legal resources were involved negotiating and drafting complex documents. As OTC derivatives gained widespread usage the
legal documentation became simpler and more standardised.[144] Few would
dispute that there are advantages to be derived from using standardised
documentation.[145] Firstly, the use of standardised documentation saves time
and costs. Secondly, standardised documentation is more likely to be legally
safe since the terms would have been considered in depth. Thirdly, the
recognition of netting for capital adequacy purposes depends on the existence of signed master agreements approved by national regulators.

---

[141]   See Taylor, above n. 125, pp. 340–341.
[142]   See generally, C. M. Friesen and Others, 'The 1998 Basle Committee Supervisory
Initiatives and their Potential Consequences on International Banking Activities' (1999) 14 JIBL
56 for a discussion of these new initiatives.
[143]   See S. Gleeson, 'A Journey From Basel to Brussels' (1999) 14 JIBL 275.
[144]   See J. R. Day, 'The Documentation Revolution: From a Necessary Evil to a Crucial Business
Enabler' (1996) 2 *Derivatives Use, Trading & Regulation* 323, 324: While very weighty amounts of
documentation were written for the first swap transaction in 1981, a similar deal today would
require little no more than a 25-page master agreement and a confirmation of a couple of pages.
[145]   See Wood, above n. 1, para. 15–22.

The initial response to the need for standardised documentation was the development of codes of standard terms and conditions by industry associations, which could be incorporated by reference into new transactions.[146] While these codes were being developed, various financial institutions were creating their own 'master agreements', which allowed them to document deals involving no more than the exchange of letters or telexes containing the financial details. Although the use of in-house master agreements was much better than documenting transactions on an individual basis, there was still the difficulty of reaching agreement when both parties had their own standardised documents.

Dealers quickly recognised the need for standardised documentation that would be accepted industry wide. In 1984, a group of New York dealers got together to form the International Swap Dealers Association (now the International Swaps and Derivatives Association) or 'ISDA' as it is popularly referred to. A year later, ISDA published the Code of Standard Wording, Assumptions and Provisions for Swaps. This Code is like a menu of relevant provisions that could be adopted either in its entirety or partially by contracting parties as a basis for their contracts. It was replaced in 1986 by a revised Code, which contained an expanded menu of provisions. In 1987, ISDA published two master agreements and a set of definitions.[147] As the range of derivatives expanded, ISDA introduced new definitions, addenda and master agreements to supersede the earlier ones.[148]

ISDA documentation, which is based on Anglo-American law, is suitable for most derivatives transactions. According to the Bank of International Settlement, the master agreement developed by ISDA is the most widely used master agreement in the G-10 countries.[149] The important role played by ISDA documentation has even been recognised by the English courts. In *Bankers Trust Co. v PT Jakarta International Hotels & Development*,[150] Cresswell J not only commented about the extensive use of ISDA documents in international finance and international trade, but also explained the importance of giving effect to its clauses. The following discussion of standard legal documents will focus on ISDA documentation in view of its widespread usage in common law jurisdictions.[151] It is not the intention of this chapter to provide a detailed discussion of ISDA documentation. There are a number of definitive works on the subject that readers could consult.[152] Instead this chapter will attempt to provide an overview of the general structure and key features of ISDA documentation.

---

[146] This account of the early development of standardised documentation is largely derived from S. Das, *Swaps and Financial Derivatives* (2nd ed., LBC, Sydney, 1994), pp. 133–134.
[147] The 1987 Interest Rate Swap Agreement; the 1987 Interest Rate and Currency Exchange Agreement; and the 1987 User's Guide to the Standard Forms Agreements.
[148] For example, the 1991 ISDA Definitions, the 1997 ISDA Bullion Definitions, 1999 ISDA Credit Derivatives Definitions.
[149] See BIS OTC Report, above n. 128, p. 1.
[150] [1999] 1 Lloyd's Rep. 910, 915–916.
[151] Various industry groups such as the British Bankers Association and the Foreign Exchange Committee of New York have developed their own standard market documents.
[152] See for example, A. Hudson, *The Law on Financial Derivatives* (2nd ed., Sweet & Maxwell, London, 1998).

ISDA DOCUMENTATION

The ISDA documentation comprises the following: confirmation, master agreement, schedule, and credit support annex. ISDA publishes different sets of definitions that can be incorporated into the master agreement by means of the schedule or confirmation. Through the use of definitions, ISDA has been able to adapt the standard documentation to new products. The ISDA master agreement operates on the principle that all transactions form a single legal obligation. It provides that in the event of any inconsistency between the provisions in the master agreement and the provisions in the schedule, the latter will prevail. Similarly if there is any inconsistency between the provisions of the master agreement and the confirmation, the latter will prevail. This is to facilitate netting and to eliminate the risk of 'cherry-picking' in the event that one of the parties becoming insolvent. Although the basic ISDA forms are standardised, it does not necessarily mean that the provisions in the forms cannot be changed.

(1) CONFIRMATION

Most OTC derivatives transactions are executed over the telephone. Although under English law and New York law, oral contracts are binding, yet most parties still prefer to execute a confirmation in case there is any doubt as to when the contract was formed or what its precise terms are. The confirmation evidences in writing the details of the transaction. It will include the economic terms of the transaction, specify the governing law and make reference to the relevant definitions. ISDA publishes different forms of confirmation. For example, there is the 'short-form' confirmation and the 'long-form' confirmation. The confirmation is expressed as forming one single agreement with the master agreement. It is usually put into place before the master agreement. If, for some reason, the master agreement is not entered into later, the terms of the confirmation will govern the transaction. For this reason, counterparties are tempted to include as many terms and conditions as possible in the confirmation. But this only causes delays to the signing of the confirmation and creates the possibility that a transaction may remain undocumented for a long period of time. It could take up to a few days to produce a confirmation and have it signed by both parties. A recent survey undertaken by the Bank of International Settlements revealed that dealers generally send out confirmations between one to five days after the trade, either by telex or fax.[153] What is a greater source of concern is not the delay in the despatch of confirmations, but the fact that a significant proportion of them were neither returned nor matched the terms agreed orally.[154] Delays in the signing of confirmations only tend to heighten the risks associated with OTC derivatives transactions.

(2) MASTER AGREEMENT

It is not unusual for dealers to enter into several derivatives transactions with the same counterparty. The master agreement sets out the basic terms

---

[153] See BIS OTC Report, above n. 128, p. 2.
[154] Ibid.

common to all the transactions entered into by the parties. Although a master agreement is usually executed before the first transaction is entered into, this is sometimes not the case. Most dealers have backlogs of uncompleted master agreements and these backlogs could vary between five to twenty per cent of their counterparties.[155] The failure to execute master agreements affects a dealer's ability to benefit from close-out netting provisions. To overcome this risk, most dealers include in confirmations, key provisions in master agreements, including close-out netting provisions.[156] This practice leads to delays in the signing of confirmations and creates the risk that the additional terms may render the confirmations legally unenforceable.

The 1992 ISDA master agreement (multicurrency-cross-border) appears to be the most used standard master agreement.[157] It contains two parts: the body or the pre-printed form and the schedule. The body contains several pages of standard terms and conditions that are applicable to all the transactions covered under the agreement. It also includes a number of options that the parties are free to select from. The schedule contains those options in the body that the parties have elected to adopt. Below is a summary of some of the key provisions found in the ISDA master agreement:

- **Single agreement**: The parties enter into all transactions on reliance of the fact that the master agreement and all confirmations form a single agreement. It provides the legal basis for close-out netting of all the transactions covered by the agreement in the event of counterparty default.
- **Obligations to pay or deliver**: The parties are required to make all payments and deliveries as specified in the confirmation on the due date and at the specified place or in the customary manner. Payments on the same date and in the same currency in respect of the same transaction are netted automatically. The parties may elect to net payments arising from two or more transactions.
- **Representations**: Each party is required to make various representations relating to legal validity; authority and capacity; legality of the contract; official consents; absence of certain events; accuracy of specified information; and tax representations.
- **Deduction or Withholding for Tax**: All payments must be made without any deductions or withholding for or on account of any tax. Each party is required to gross-up for any compulsory deductions of tax. But, if withholding tax is introduced at a later stage, the party resident in that jurisdiction must provide the necessary certificates to the other party as evidence of the regulation.
- **Events of Default**: The following are 'fault events', which lead to the termination of the contract: the failure to pay (with a grace period);

---

[155] Ibid.
[156] Ibid.
[157] For a useful summary of the structure and features of the ISDA master agreement, see BIS OTC Report, above n. 128, Annex 3.

breach of a material term; failure to provide credit support; misrepresentation; cross default; deterioration in credit worth; corporate restructuring; and bankruptcy. They are regarded as 'fault events' because they may be attributed to the fault of one party.

- **Termination Events**: The following are 'non-fault events', which lead to the termination of the contract: illegality under the applicable law; tax event (for example, a withholding tax is introduced after the agreement is signed); tax event upon merger; credit event upon merger and additional termination event. They are regarded as 'non-fault events' because they are triggered off by circumstances beyond the control of both parties.

- **Early Termination**: Upon the occurrence of an event of default, the non-defaulting party has the right to designate an early termination date. This has the effect of terminating all transactions and payments on that date. But where a termination occurs because of a termination event, the non-defaulting party will provide notice of termination, unless the parties have agreed to automatic termination. Both parties will calculate amounts and make payment according to the method agreed upon.

- **Close-out netting**: After an event of default has occurred and the relevant notices given, all the covered transactions are closed out. A termination amount is calculated for each transaction or group of transactions. The termination amount is arrived at either using the 'market quotation method' or the 'loss method'. Under the first method, the termination amount is the mark-to-market value of the transaction, whereas under the second method, it is the amount of loss incurred by the non-defaulting party. Finally, the termination amounts of all the covered transactions are netted into a single net amount which could either be owed to the non-defaulting party or owed by the non-defaulting party. If the parties elect for one-way payment the defaulting party need to pay the non-defaulting party for any losses suffered. But if they elect for two-way payments, the non-defaulting party would also be required to pay the defaulting party any gains that it has received.

- **Transfer**: Any party, without the consent of the other party, may not transfer the master agreement including any interest or obligation in it. However, a clause will usually be inserted in the schedule to allow the parties to transfer the obligations to another entity within the group.

- **Governing Law and Jurisdiction**: The agreement will be governed by and construed in accordance with the law specified in the schedule, which is usually English law or New York law. If the agreement is expressed to be governed by English law, the parties agree to submit to the jurisdiction of the English courts, and if governed by New York law, to the non-exclusive jurisdiction of the courts of New York.

(3) SCHEDULE

The schedule is that part of the ISDA documentation that is subject to negotiation. It is used to customise the printed form of master agreement. Customisation is achieved though changing, adding or deleting the standard provisions. For example, the counterparties may include an arbitration clause in the schedule. The English courts have upheld the validity of such additional clauses. For example, in *Bankers Trust Co. v PT Jakarta International Hotels & Development*,[158] the English Commercial Court upheld the validity of an arbitration clause in the ISDA master agreement. Some of the issues negotiated by the parties and included in the schedule include:

- the proper law of the contract
- additional events of default
- scope of payment netting
- automatic early termination
- scope of payment netting; and
- additional representations and warranties.[159]

Although any provision may be the subject of negotiation, some provisions are more frequently negotiated than others.[160] For example, structuring the cross-default provision involves reaching agreement on a number of issues such as (1) whether the provision should apply to one or both parties; (2) the companies affiliated to the counterparties that should be covered by the provision; (3) the range of transactions that should included; and (4) the threshold amount that would trigger default.

Difficulty in reaching agreement over the terms in the schedule could have disastrous effects if one party defaults or becomes insolvent pending execution of the master agreement. As one commentator observed:

Too often, ISDAs remain unsigned for long periods of time because of intransigence over a specific point. This pursuit of extra 5 per cent protection in the form of "nice to have" clauses leads to deadlock and an unsigned agreement. As a result the parties are deprived of the other 95 per cent of the agreement's value for the duration of the entrenchment.[161]

(4) CREDIT SUPPORT DOCUMENTATION

Increasingly collateralisation is being used to reduce credit risk in OTC derivatives transactions. An important difference between the collateralisation of derivatives transactions and other credit transactions is the possibility that either of the derivatives counterparties might be the credit support taker as the valuations of net exposure fluctuate.[162] ISDA has developed a number of forms of documentation that may be used for collateralisation. These forms are commonly referred to as a credit support annex (CSA). Currently there are four different versions of the CSA: 1995 Credit Support Annex

---

[158] [1999] 1 Lloyd's Rep. 910, 915–916.
[159] See BIS OTC Report, above n. 128, p. 55.
[160] For a more comprehensive discussion of frequently negotiated provisions and the issues involved see for example, M. R. Rodgon and H. Meyerson, 'ISDA Documentation to Suit the Needs of End Users' (1997) 3 *Derivatives Use, Trading & Regulation* 45, 48–52.
[161] See Day, above n. 144, 330.
[162] See K. Tyson-Quah, 'Collateralisation v Clearinghouse: Credit Risk Management for OTC Derivatives' in E. Bettelheim and Others (eds), *Swaps and Off-exchange Derivatives Trading: Law and Regulation* (FT Law & Tax, London, 1996), p. 125.

(Transfer—English Law); 1995 Credit Support Deed (Security Interest—English Law); 1994 Credit Support Annex (Subject to New York Law) and 1995 Credit Support Annex (Security Interest—Japanese Law). The Credit Support Deed is a standalone document, whereas the Credit Support Annex (English Law and New York Law versions) is an annex to the schedule of the ISDA master agreement. There are differences between the various forms and ISDA has produced a user's guide for each version of the CSA. It is possible to identify two broad approaches to the establishment of bilateral mark-to-market collateral arrangements. The first approach is based on the creation of a security interest, whereas the second approach is based on the transfer of title.

DOCUMENTATION ISSUES

Despite the popularity of the ISDA master agreement, the precise scope of many of its provisions is far from clear. Derivatives litigation in the English courts has revealed that 'there is a wealth of as yet unexplored legal issues to be resolved.'[163] Two recent English cases will help illustrate this point. The first case is *Australia and New Zealand Banking Group Ltd. v Société Générale*.[164] In that case, *Société Générale* (SG) entered into three non-deliverable forward foreign exchange contracts (Transactions) with *Australia and New Zealand Banking Group Ltd.* (ANZ) in April and May 1998. It was agreed that for each contract, SG would pay ANZ if the Russian rouble appreciated against the United States dollar between the traded date and the settlement date. However, if the rouble depreciated against the dollar, then ANZ would pay SG. The contracts, which were contained in amended confirmations, were subject to the terms of an ISDA master agreement dated 17 February 1995. The master agreement provided for early termination of the contracts upon the occurrence of a defined additional termination event, which included a 'Russian Market Event'.

The contracts were terminated early as a result of the Russian banking moratorium announced on 17 August 1998. In accordance with the terms of the master agreement, the parties were obliged to split the difference between their respective losses. Section 14 of the master agreement defined 'Loss' suffered by one party as including 'loss or cost incurred as a result of its terminating, liquidating, obtaining or re-establishing any hedge or related trading position'. A dispute arose when SG claimed to be entitled to take into account losses on three hedging contracts that it had entered into with Banque Société Générale Vostok (Vostok). These hedging contracts were concluded in November 1997 on similar terms with the Transactions, except for some minor differences. When the financial crisis in Russia occurred, SG terminated the hedging contracts because Vostok was unable to perform its financial obligation. The Russian Government had imposed a banking moratorium in Russian banks.

---

[163] See 'Comment', *Nuova Safim SPA v The Sakura Bank Limited* [1998] Lloyd's Rep. Bank 142, 162.
[164] [2000] Lloyd's Rep. Bank 153.

If SG could take into account the losses incurred on the hedging contracts, the sum it would have to pay ANZ would be USD 8.596 million instead of USD 16.719 million. SG paid that sum and ANZ contested SG's right to take into account the losses on its hedging contracts. Aikens J awarded summary judgement to ANZ for the remaining USD 8.122 million on 21 September 1999. SG appealed against the order of Aikens J on the grounds that the confirmations agreed between the parties contained a Russian Market event clause. In dismissing the appeal, the English Court of Appeal held that the ISDA Loss Clause only covers losses arising from the termination or liquidation of hedging transactions, not those arising from the hedging counterparty's inability to perform.[165] Since the losses arose from Vostok's inability to pay because of the banking moratorium, the hedging losses could not be taken into account when calculating the early termination payment. The Court of Appeal also held that the meaning of the ISDA Loss clause could not depend on terms agreed by the parties under a specific confirmation.[166]

The second case is *Nuova Safim SPA v The Sakura Bank Limited*.[167] In that case, Nuova Safim (NS) a wholly owned subsidiary of Ente Partecipazioni e Finanziamento Industria Manifatturiera (EFIM) entered into an interest and currency swap with Sakura Bank (SB) in May 1991. EFIM was an Italian statutory corporation established by Presidential decree in 1962 and wholly owned and controlled by the State of Italy. The swap agreement, which was to terminate on 30 May 1996, was on a standard ISDA form and provided for English law and jurisdiction. Under the terms of the agreement, Sakura agreed to pay a fixed rate of 7.5 per cent per annum on JPY 5,000 million, while NS agreed to pay a floating rate of USD LIBOR plus 0.3 per cent per annum on USD 36.3 million. Sakura as the fixed rate payer was obliged to pay on 30 May each year and NS as the floating rate payer had to pay twice a year, namely on 30 November and 30 May.

The agreement contained detailed provisions for early termination. These provisions were found in sections 5 and 6. Section 5 of the agreement provided for two different types of events that could bring about termination. The first type (events of default) included failure to pay, cross-default, and bankruptcy, while the second type (termination events) included illegality and tax events. Section 6 provided for the giving of proper notice for termination of the agreement. In July 1992, EFIM was dissolved by a Law Decree issued by the Italian President and other measures taken under Italian law to deal with the financial crisis faced by EFIM. The Law Decrees passed in October and December 1992 imposed a general suspension of payment of debts of EFIM and its subsidiaries. NS was therefore unable to make payment to Sakura on 30 November 1992. Under article 2362 of the Italian Civil Code, EFIM was legally liable for NS's debts. Both parties then proceeded to terminate the agreement.

---

[165] Id., at 157, per Mance LJ.
[166] Ibid.
[167] [1998] Lloyd's Rep. Bank 142.

What was at dispute was when the agreement was terminated and on what grounds. Sakura contended that it terminated the agreement in December 1992 consequent upon two events of default, namely failure to pay and cross-default. NS, on the other hand, contended that it terminated the agreement in April or May 1993 consequent upon a termination event, namely, illegality. If Sakura was correct it was not liable to make any further payments, but if NS was correct, it was entitled to claim about USD 8 million from Sakura. In October 1996, NS commenced proceedings by way of originating summons seeking the determination of various issues relating to the termination. The court held that the law decrees made the payment due on 30 November 1992 illegal by reason of an adoption or change in applicable law within the provisions of s. 5(b)(i) of the agreement. Although the failure to pay and the cross-default were events which would have given rise to an event of default under s. 5(a), they were not be treated as such because they resulted from illegality under foreign law. They could rightfully be treated under s. 5(c) as a termination event. However, because NS failed to give proper notice under section 6, it was not entitled to terminate the agreement on the ground of illegality.

2.4   CONCLUSION

The development of the derivatives exchanges of Australia, New Zealand, Singapore Malaysia and Hong Kong (jurisdictions under study) share one striking similarity. They all had their origins trading in futures contracts based on natural commodities. The Australasian exchanges were established to trade in wool futures contracts, but later diversified into the trading of financial futures contracts when world demand for wool declined. Similarly, the exchanges in Singapore, Malaysia and Hong Kong were originally commodity futures exchanges but later restructured to trade in financial derivatives. Despite their similar pattern of development, these exchanges have not developed at the same rate or in the same direction. The Australian and Singaporean exchanges are well developed and trade a diverse range of products, while the Malaysian exchanges are still relatively under-developed. Lying somewhere in between both extremes are the Hong Kong and New Zealand exchanges. Both are modest-sized exchanges, which are still heavily dependent on a few successful products. Like exchanges in other parts of the world, they have not escaped the twin forces of globalisation and advances in technology. Almost all the exchanges in the jurisdictions under study have adopted electronic trading. More and more of them are demutualising and contemplating either mergers or forming alliances with other exchanges.

In all the jurisdictions under study, the OTC derivatives markets have grown in tandem with the exchange-traded markets. Based on the 1998 Bank of International Settlements Survey, Singapore, Australia and Hong Kong have established OTC markets, while New Zealand and Malaysia have relatively small OTC derivatives markets. The OTC markets in all the jurisdictions under study are not regulated the way that exchange-traded markets are. However, it does not mean that OTC derivatives markets are not subject to any controls. They have to conform to various forms of market-generated 'regulation', ranging from industry codes and supervisory guidelines issued by international bodies such as the Bank of International Settlements, to standardised market documentation like those developed by the International Swaps and Derivatives Association. These various 'non-regulators'[168] exert an important influence on how OTC markets operate, but they are not without their own shortcomings. For example, there are still many unresolved issues arising from the use of standardised market documentation. OTC derivatives participants must recognise that in the final analysis, proper internal controls, prudent selection of counterparties, and the sensible use of derivatives, is the best form of regulation.

---

[168] See Little and Berwin & Co., above n. 124, p. 28.

3. Selected Legal Issues

3.1 INTRODUCTION

The widespread use, and occasional misuse, of derivatives has raised a number of complex legal issues, such as, the lack of legal capacity to enter into derivatives transactions, the nature of the duties owed derivatives dealers, and the validity of netting arrangements found in derivatives contracts. These legal issues, which have been the subject of considerable discussion in recent years, owe much of their existence to two factors. The first factor is the general lack of understanding of the legal nature of derivatives. This is not surprising considering that derivatives only gained prominence in the 1980s and the fact that derivatives come in very diverse forms. As at the time of writing, there is still no broad consensus on how to legally characterise derivatives. The second factor is the tendency for legal developments to lag behind market developments. Many of the existing legal rules were formulated well before the advent of derivatives, yet they are expected to be able to resolve issues arising from their use. The combination of both these factors has made derivatives, especially those transacted over-the-counter (OTC), particularly vulnerable to legal challenge.

Concern about the risks posed by derivatives prompted the Group of Thirty to sponsor a private study of the practices and performance of the derivatives industry. In July 1993, the study group published a report, widely referred to as the 'G-30 Report.' The report, among other things, recognised a need for clarification of the legal uncertainties arising from the use of derivatives and recommended that:

[D]ealers and end-users should work together on a continuing basis to identify and recommend solutions for issues of legal enforceability, both within and across jurisdictions, as activities evolve and new types of transactions are developed.[1]

This chapter will examine the main legal issues identified in the G-30 Report as well as a few other issues that have emerged since publication of the report.

---

[1] See Global Derivatives Study Group, *Derivatives: Practices and Principles* (Group of Thirty, Washington, DC, July 1993), p. 17.

It is necessary at the outset to mention that the ensuing discussion of the legal issues relating to derivatives is largely based on English law. Most of the leading cases on derivatives were decided in the English courts and therefore much of the discussion in this chapter will centre on them. Although these cases have little direct authority outside the United Kingdom (UK), they have persuasive authority in other common law jurisdictions. With the increasing use of standardised master agreements such as those developed by the International Swap and Derivatives Association, there is a tendency for more and more counterparties to choose English law as the proper law of their contracts. For comparison purposes, reference will also be made (wherever possible) to the existing legal rules in Australia, New Zealand, Singapore, Malaysia and Hong Kong. These jurisdictions share much in common because they were all at some time in the past either British colonies or protectorates. Their commercial laws are very similar to those in England and despite their independent status, they continue to 'receive' English law, albeit in modified form.

3.2   LACK OF LEGAL CAPACITY

According to Professor Gower, the expression 'ultra vires' is habitually used in three different senses.[2] When used in its strict sense, it is concerned with a corporation's legal capacity to act. In *Ashbury Railway Carriage & Iron Co Ltd v Riche*,[3] the House of Lords held that a corporation has no capacity to pursue any objects outside those stated in its memorandum of association.[4] The term 'ultra vires' is also used to refer to the lack of authority on the part of the persons who act on behalf of the corporation. For example, an agent of a company may enter into a derivatives contract when the agent is not authorised to do so. In its third sense, the term 'ultra vires' refers to any activity, which a corporation cannot lawfully undertake. An example of ultra vires in the sense of perverted power is when a corporation purchases its own shares in contravention of the capital maintenance rule, even though it may be expressly empowered to do so in its memorandum of association.[5]

We are concerned here with ultra vires in the sense of lack of legal capacity. The lack of capacity has proven to be an extremely contentious legal issue for derivatives participants. As a general rule, when one party lacks the legal capacity to enter into a derivatives transaction, the contract is void. If the contract is executory, both parties cannot enforce it and if money is paid or goods delivered, they cannot be recovered.[6] The ultra vires doctrine was originally

---

[2]   See L. C. B. Gower, *Gower's Principles of Modern Company Law* (Sweet & Maxwell, London, 1992), pp. 167–171.
[3]   [1874–80] All ER 2219.
[4]   A corporation's legitimate powers may also be defined by the statute under which it is formed, or the statutes that are applicable to it.
[5]   See for example, *Trevor v Whitworth* (1887) 12 App. Cas. 409, HL.
[6]   See N. Seddon, *Government Contracts* (2nd edn Federation Press, Leichhardt, N.S.W., 1995), para. 2.22.

intended to protect members and creditors of a company. Members and creditors were considered to have a right to ensure that the company used its funds to further its stated objects. However, the use of various drafting devices such as the 'independent objects clause' has effectively reduced its effectiveness.[7] The application of the doctrine is not confined to companies, but extends to other statutory corporations such as local authorities. In the case of local authorities, the doctrine exists for their better regulation.[8] The doctrine could cause problems for third parties, as in *Sinclair v Brougham*,[9] where a bank was unable to recover an ultra vires loan made to the company. A third party no matter how innocent cannot escape the consequences of lack of capacity.[10]

3.2.1 The *Hazell* Case

The level of awareness of the risk posed by a local authority's lack of capacity to enter into derivatives transactions was significantly raised by the *Hazell v Hammersmith and Fulham London Borough Council* case.[11] In that case the council was empowered by Parliament to borrow money to discharge its functions. As at 31 March 1989, it had borrowed approximately GBP 390 million from various financial institutions. The terms of the loan varied, but they were mostly at fixed interest rates. Between April 1987 and February 1989, the council entered into a number of swap transactions. It established a capital market fund for that purpose. For the majority of the swap transactions, the council would have stood to benefit had interest rates fallen, but would have incurred substantial losses had interest rates rose. By the end of March 1989 the council had entered into 592 swap transactions involving a notional sum of GBP 6,052 million, 297 of which were still outstanding.

The Audit Commission of Local Authorities in England and Wales issued a statement in July 1988 warning local councils that some swap transactions were ultra vires. The statutory basis of this was s. 111(1) of the UK *Local Government Act* 1972 which provided that:

Without prejudice to any powers exercisable apart from this section but subject to the provisions of this Act and any other enactment passed before or after this Act, a local authority shall have power to do anything (whether or not involving the expenditure, borrowing or lending of money or the acquisition or disposal of any property or rights) which is *calculated to facilitate, or is conducive or incidental to,* the discharge of any of their functions. [emphasis added]

Following the statement issued by the Audit Commission, the district auditor questioned the legality of the swap transactions. The council temporarily suspended all swap transactions on 25 July 1988 but continued to manage existing swap positions to minimise losses. The council decided to

---

7 The effectiveness of such a clause was upheld in *Cotman v Brougham* [1918] AC 514.
8 See *Westdeutsche Landesbank v Islington London BC* [1994] 4 All ER 890 at 915, per Hobhouse J: '[F]or the better regulation of local authorities in the public interest and, in relation to their revenue raising powers, for the protection of the rate-payers (or charge payers).'
9 [1914] AC 398.
10 See *Westdeutsche Landesbank v Islington London BC* [1994] 4 All ER 890 at 915, per Hobhouse J.
11 [1992] 2 AC 1.

desist from any further activity including making any payments on existing contracts in February 1989.

In May 1989, the auditor applied for relief under s. 19 of the UK *Local Government Finance Act* 1982. The auditor sought a declaration that the items of account appearing in the capital market fund for the 1988 and 1989 financial years were contrary to law, and for an order of rectification of the accounts. A number of banks involved in the local authority's derivatives activities were granted leave to be joined as respondents to the auditor's application in order to protect their commercial interest. The outcome of the proceedings was of great importance to the banks as there were another 77 local authorities that had entered into similar transactions. The Divisional Court held that the council acted ultra vires as it had no power to enter into the swap transactions. Accordingly, it granted the auditor the declaration that the items appearing in the capital fund were contrary to law. The banks appealed to the Court of Appeal who ordered that the declaration should stand, in so far as it related to transactions entered into before 25 July 1988, as some of the transactions carried out after July 1988 could have been incidental to the statutory functions of the council. The auditor then appealed to the House of Lords against the decision of the Court of Appeal.

The entire appeal rested on the issue of whether the council possessed the power to enter into any swap contract. Since the council had no express statutory power to enter into swap transactions, the House of Lords had to decide whether it had the implied powers to do so. Generally, a local authority can do anything which is 'calculated to facilitate, or is conducive or incidental' to its function of borrowing. The issue before the court was whether a swap transaction fulfilled any of these purposes. Lord Templeman who delivered the leading judgement, rejected the argument that swaps facilitated borrowing by reducing the interest burden, on the basis that:

A local authority when considering expenditure must carefully consider the amount required to be borrowed and the sums available for payment of interest and capital. A local authority which borrowed in reliance on future successful swap operations would be failing in its duty to act prudently in the interests of the [council's] ratepayers.[12]

His Lordship also rejected the argument that swaps were conducive to borrowing 'because local authorities should not be encouraged to borrow by the prospect of swap transactions.'[13]

On the issue of whether swaps were incidental to borrowing, Lord Templeman first pointed to the issue that 'a swap transaction is a separate collateral contract which may be undertaken long after a borrowing has been effected.'[14] His Lordship then went on to say that 'when a power is claimed to be incidental, the provisions of the statute which confers and limits functions must be considered and construed.'[15] Since Schedule 13 of

---

[12]   [1992] 2 AC 1 at 29.
[13]   Id. at 29–30.
[14]   Id. at 30.
[15]   Id. at 31.

the UK *Local Government Act* 1972 established a comprehensive code, which defines and limits the powers of a local authority with regard to borrowing and lending, there can be no incidental power to enter into swap transactions.[16] The House of Lords unanimously overturned the decision in the Court of Appeal and restored the judgement of the Divisional Court.

The *Hazell* case had far-reaching ramifications for counterparties entering into derivative transactions. Not only did it reach the conclusion that local authorities did not have the powers to enter into interest rate swaps, it also highlighted the risk of entering into such transactions with similar counterparties. The application of the ultra vires doctrine was extremely harsh to the banks and the other parties involved in swap transactions with local authorities. They were after all innocent parties, who believed all along that swap contracts were ancillary to the exercise of the borrowing powers of local authorities. Considerable pressure was applied by the banking industry to overrule the decision by statute, but this was resisted by the legislature.[17] Many of the banks were however able to recover the net amounts paid through the courts. These cases are discussed later in this chapter.

3.2.2 Companies

While the lack of legal capacity is still an issue, it is not a significant one for parties dealing with companies. The strict ultra vires doctrine has either been abolished or its effects have been watered down by statute in most common law jurisdictions. Generally, under English law, the validity of an act done by a company, regulated by the UK *Companies Act* 1985, may not be called into question on the ground of lack of capacity by reason of anything in the company's memorandum.[18] If a person deals with a company in good faith, the power of the board of directors to bind the company is deemed to be free of any limitation under the company's constitution.[19] The position with regards to the application of the ultra vires doctrine to companies in the other common law jurisdictions is broadly similar to that in the United Kingdom.

In Australia, the strict ultra vires doctrine has been abolished by statute. Section 124 of the *Corporations Law* gives a company all the powers of a natural person. In addition, a company's legal capacity to do something is not affected by the fact that the company's interests are not, or would not, be served by doing it. Prior to 1 July 1998, companies were required to have a constitution, which comprised the memorandum of association and articles of association. However, since the introduction of the *Company Law Review Act* 1998 on 1 July 1998, companies are no longer required to have a constitution or to lodge one when they register. Companies have a choice whether to adopt a specially drafted constitution, the 'replaceable rules' found in the *Corporations Law*, or a choice of both. If they do not have a constitution, the

---

[16] Id. at 33–34.
[17] See S. McCracken, 'Confronting the Legal Dimension' in E. Sheedy & S. McCracken (eds), *Derivatives: The Risks That Remain* (Allen & Unwin, St Leonards, NSW, 1997), p. 169.
[18] See the UK *Companies Act* 1985, s. 35(1).
[19] Id., s. 35A(1).

'replaceable rules' will automatically apply.[20] A company's constitution can displace or modify the 'replaceable rules'. Although a company may still include in its constitution an objects clause, an act of the company is not invalid merely because it is contrary or beyond any objects in the company's constitution.[21] Similarly, if the constitution contains an express restriction or prohibition on the company's exercise of power, the exercise of power is not invalid merely because it is contrary to the restriction or prohibition.[22]

The New Zealand approach to the ultra vires issue is similar to that adopted by Australia. As from 1 July 1997, all incorporated companies in New Zealand will be regulated by the New Zealand *Companies Act* 1993. Generally, a company has the 'full capacity to carry on or undertake any business or activity, to do any act, or enter into any transaction.'[23] But it may include in its constitution any restriction on its capacity, rights or powers.[24] No act or transfer of property by a company is invalid merely because the company did not have the capacity, right, or power to do so.[25] The fact that an act is not, or would not be, in the best interests of a company would not affect the company's capacity to perform it.[26] A company cannot assert, against a person dealing with the company that the constitution of the company has not been complied with.[27] It would therefore appear that the legislation confers upon a company the widest possible legal capacity. Nonetheless, if a company has entered into an ultra vires transaction that has not performed, it may be possible for a shareholder or director to obtain an order restraining any further performance.[28]

Singapore, on the other hand, has adopted a different approach from the Australasian jurisdictions. The ultra vires doctrine has not been abolished in relation to companies, but its effects have been diminished by legislation. A company incorporated under the Singapore *Companies Act*[29] is generally entitled to enter into derivatives transactions if authorised by its memorandum and articles of association. As derivatives are still relatively new as a financial management tool, it is highly unlikely that the constitutional documents would contain an express power to enter into derivatives transactions. However if the constitutional documents contain a general clause empowering the company to do the things, which are incidental or conducive to the attainment of the company's objects or the exercise of its powers, then it is possible that such a clause might be wide enough for the company to enter into hedge-related derivatives transactions.[30]

---

[20] See the Australian *Corporations Law*, ss. 134, 135.
[21] Id., s. 125.
[22] Ibid.
[23] New Zealand *Companies Act* 1993, s. 16(1).
[24] Id., s. 16(2).
[25] Id., s. 17(1).
[26] Id., s. 17(3).
[27] Id., s. 18(1).
[28] Id., s. 164.
[29] Cap. 50.
[30] See S. K. Tan and R. Liew, 'Behind the Barings Debacle' (May 1995) *Asia Law* 37, 39.

Even if the company lacks the capacity to enter into a derivatives transaction it is still possible for the aggrieved counterparty to enforce the contract under s. 25(1) of the Singapore *Companies Act*, which states that:

No act or purported act of a company (including the entering into of an agreement by the company and including any act done on behalf of a company by an officer or agent of the company under any purported authority, whether express or implied, of the company) and no conveyance or transfer of property, whether real or personal, to or by a company shall be invalid by reason only of the fact that the company was without capacity or power to do such act or to execute or take such conveyance or transfer.

The effect of this provision is that even if an act is ultra vires, it may still be valid and binding upon the company. Under s. 25(2)(a) of the *Companies Act*, an ultra vires act may, before it is fully performed by a company, be restrained by its members or (where the company has issued debentures secured by a floating charge over its property) debenture holders.[31] The court may, if it considers just and equitable, set aside the contract and grant compensation for any loss sustained.

Malaysia has adopted a similar approach to Singapore and this is not surprising given their close links. The effects of the ultra vires doctrine have also been diminished through legislation. Although a company is still constrained by its constitution, s. 20(1) of the Malaysian *Companies Act* 1965 provides that the validity of its acts can no longer be called into question on the ground of lack of capacity.[32] Section 20(2) recognises that the ultra vires doctrine may still be applicable, albeit, in limited circumstances.[33] Commenting on both provisions, V. C. George J said in *Bumiputra Merchant Bankers v Supreme-QBE Insurance Berhad*[34] that while s. 20(1) had abolished the absolute effect of the ultra vires doctrine, s. 20(2) had the effect of watering down the abolishment of the doctrine. There are no indications at this stage that this approach will be changed in the near future.

---

[31] Includes trustees for the debenture holders.
[32] According to s. 20(1) of the Malaysian *Companies Act* 1965:

No act or purported act of a company (including the entering into of an agreement by the company and including any act done on behalf of a company by an officer or agent of the company under any purported authority, whether express or implied, of the company) and no conveyance or transfer of property, whether real or personal, to or by a company shall be invalid by reason only of the fact that the company was without capacity or power to do such act or to execute or take such conveyance or transfer.

[33] According to s. 20(2) of the Malaysian *Companies Act* 1965, the ultra vires doctrine will still apply in the following situations:

- in proceedings against the company by a member or debenture holder to restrain it from acting ultra vires;
- in proceedings by the company or any of its members against the past and present directors of the company;
- in any petition by the Minister to wind up the company.

[34] [1988] 2 CLJ 445 at 449.

The ultra vires doctrine used to be very much alive in Hong Kong until the recent amendments to the Hong Kong *Companies Ordinance*.[35] A company now has the capacity and rights, powers and privileges of a natural person.[36] Although companies are no longer required to state their objects, those that were incorporated with objects clauses, will continue to be restricted by them. But any act carried out in contravention of the restrictions will not be invalid.[37] A member of a company may bring proceedings to restrain the doing of any restricted act. The doctrine of constructive notice has also been abolished in relation to both the memorandum and articles of association, and for any return or resolution lodged with the Registrar of Companies.[38]

3.2.3   Specially Constituted Corporations

It has been suggested that the increasing involvement of specially consti-tuted corporations and other government entities in derivatives contracts may be attributed to the rise of 'entrepreneurial government'.[39] Despite the increasing involvement of such entities in derivatives activities, doubts con-tinue to exist as to whether they have the capacity to enter into derivatives contracts. It is difficult to generalise about the legal capacity of such entities to enter into derivatives transactions. There is bound to be significant incon-sistency between different entities within the same jurisdiction, as well as between the same types of entities in different jurisdictions. For example, a survey carried out by a legal firm has shown that there are several govern-ment entities in Australia that have the express capacity to enter into deriv-atives transactions.[40] In contrast, a similar survey of government entities in Singapore revealed that only the Monetary Authority of Singapore appears to have the express power to enter into derivatives transactions.[41]

There is a strong likelihood that the *Hazell* decision will be followed in other common law jurisdictions. Two Malaysian decisions, dealing with the powers of statutory corporations, have arrived at findings which are similar to that handed down in the *Hazell* case. In the first case, *Public Prosecutor v Datuk Haji Harun and Ors*,[42] the Malaysian High Court held that:

A natural person has the capacity to do all things save such as forbidden or prohib-ited by law. But this rule is reversed in the case of a corporation ... and, in relation

---

[35]   Cap. 32.
[36]   Hong Kong *Companies Ordinance*, s. 5A.
[37]   Id., s. 5B.
[38]   Id., s. 5C.
[39]   See K. Bull, 'Does Government Have a Future in Derivatives?' (1997) 25 ABLR 246, 247.
[40]   See Mallesons Stephen Jaques, 'Enforceability Survey – Australia' in Global Derivatives Study Group, *Derivatives: Practices and Principles, Appendix II: Legal Enforceability: Survey of Nine Jurisdictions* (Group of Thirty, Washington DC, July 1993), pp. 12–14. See also Seddon, above n. 6, para. 2.20, for a survey of government owned corporations legislation in Australia.
[41]   See Allen & Gledhill, 'Enforceability Survey—Singapore' in Global Derivatives Study Group, *Derivatives: Practices and Principles, Appendix II: Legal Enforceability: Survey of Nine Jurisdictions* (Group of Thirty, Washington DC, July 1993), p. 275.
[42]   [1977] 1 MLJ 180.

thereto, what the governing statutory provisions do not expressly or impliedly authorise or permit is to be taken to be prohibited not by virtue of any express or implied statutory prohibition but by the doctrine of ultra vires.[43]

In the second case, *Aluminium Company of Malaysia Bhd v Ng Than Chai & Anor*,[44] the Malaysian High Court had to decide whether a guarantee given by Majlis Daerah Jasin, a corporate body established under s. 13 of the Malaysian *Local Government Act* 1976 was valid. The court held that although the Majlis (local council) was empowered to borrow under the *Local Government Act*, it did not have express or implied powers to give a guarantee. It went on to add that the intention of Parliament was to ensure that the Majlis was not unnecessarily saddled with debts that it could not pay and to safeguard its assets from improper disposal. Accordingly, the court held that the guarantee given by the Majlis was null and void.

Generally, the capacity of such bodies to enter into derivatives transactions has to be ascertained by reference to their enabling statutes or to those statutes which regulate their activities. While a corporation may be empowered by its constitution to enter into derivatives contracts, there may be other legislation, which restricts the exercise of its powers. An insurance company in the United Kingdom, for example, cannot carry on any activities, otherwise than in connection with or for the purposes of its insurance business.[45] It would appear that if an insurance company entered into a derivatives transaction other than for hedging, it might be acting for an improper purpose. Although it would seem unlikely that a breach of the above condition would render the relevant contract void, in the absence of authority on this point, uncertainty continues to exist.[46]

Financial institutions are another category of corporate entities that might be restricted in their dealings with derivatives. In Australia, building societies, friendly societies and credit unions have restricted powers to enter into derivatives transactions.[47] They may only enter into approved contracts and for specified purposes. In Singapore, finance companies cannot engage in currency swaps, forward foreign exchange contracts, commodity swaps or commodity futures involving gold or other precious materials.[48] This is because they are prohibited from entering into transactions dealing in foreign currency, gold or other precious materials.[49] In Malaysia, banking institutions are required to obtain central bank approval before they trade

---

[43] Id. at 205, per Abdoolcader J.
[44] [1994] 3 MLJ 544.
[45] See *Insurance Companies Act* 1982, s. 16(1).
[46] See Linklaters & Paines, 'Enforceability Survey—England' in Global Derivatives Study Group, *Derivatives: Practices and Principles, Appendix II: Legal Enforceability: Survey of Nine Jurisdictions* (Group of Thirty, Washington DC, July 1993), p. 160.
[47] See for example ss. 120–121 of the Australian *Financial Institutions Code*. Since July 1998, the responsibility for administering the Code has been transferred from the Australian Financial Institution Commission to the Australian Prudential Regulatory Authority. Some changes are expected to the provisions of the Code.
[48] See S. L. Tan, 'Swaps and Derivatives: Managing Legal Risks' (1996) 11 *Asia Business Law Review* 29, 30.
[49] Ibid.

or arbitrage in derivatives instruments for their own account.[50] Despite an easing of restrictions, only 'Tier-1 Banks' are permitted to trade in equity derivatives, while commodity derivatives continue to be disallowed.[51]

Counterparties dealing with trustees also encounter problems relating to capacity.[52] Since trusts have no separate legal personalities, trustees enter into contracts in their personal capacities. Trustees may be entitled to be indemnified for liabilities, which they have incurred in the proper course of carrying out their duties. It is therefore important that counterparties establish at the outset whether the trustees have the requisite authority to enter into derivatives transactions. Failure to do so could result in counterparties losing their rights to the assets of the trusts under the doctrine of subrogation. The trustee's authority to act in relation to the trust assets is derived from the trust deed. In the absence of express powers to invest in derivatives, the trustee's power to trade in derivatives will depend on whether derivatives would fall within the definition of 'investments'. This would in turn depend on the breadth of the definition. It has been pointed out that in Australia 'many trust deeds were not drafted with any thought in mind that funds may wish to trade in derivatives.'[53] This observation would probably be true of the great majority of trust deeds drafted in other jurisdictions.

The case *re Buckland; ANZ Executors & Trustee Co Ltd v Attorney General*[54] provides an insight into how an Australian court may construe the meaning of the term 'investments'. In that case, the trustee applied to the court to vary the trust deed to permit it, inter alia, to invest in futures contracts and options traded on the Australian Futures Exchange. Nathan J allowed the trustee to invest in options, subject to a ten per cent limit, but refused the application to invest in futures contracts on the grounds that it was highly speculative. In the course of his judgment his Honour made a number of interesting comments:

The categories of investments suitable for trustees will expand and contract as the shape of the market changes. All the Court can do is examine the facilities available at a given time, and assess them against the standard of a prudent investor committed to safeguarding the corpus, but obtaining an optimum return thereon, on a long-term basis. Futures remain too highly speculative, the perceived benefits, as a general rule do not outweigh the risks of loss.

While this decision demonstrates the willingness of the court to widen the range of financial products that may be regarded as 'investments', it also reflects the caution that a court will exercise in varying the terms of a trust

---

[50] See Bank Negara Malaysia Circular, 'Participation of Banking Institutions in KLOFFE and MME' (18 December 1995), p. 3.

[51] See Bank Negara Malaysia Circular, 'Minimum Standards on Risk Management Practices for Derivatives' (26 July 1996), p. 2. Tier-1 banks are the larger and better capitalised financial instututions.

[52] See McCracken, above n. 17, pp. 174–175.

[53] See M. Adams, 'Practical Issues for Trustees in the Application of Trust Fund Moneys in the Use of Derivatives' (1994) 5 JBFLP 20.

[54] Supreme Court of Victoria, 23 July 1993, No. 10536 of 1992, Nathan J, unreported.

instrument.[55] It would appear that according to Buckley J, options are more acceptable as investments because it is possible to limit the losses arising from their use.

3.2.4 Summary and Comments

Derivatives contracts involving companies are unlikely to be struck down on the grounds of lack of legal capacity. However, it is still possible for local councils, semi-government bodies and other specially constituted entities, to act beyond their powers. Prior to entering into derivatives transactions with such entities, it is important to establish whether they have the necessary powers to do so. The answer will normally be found in the enabling statutes or those statutes which regulate their activities. The *Hazell* decision has clearly demonstrated the risk of entering into derivatives transactions with specially constituted entities. It has also highlighted the antiquity of the laws governing the capacity of such entities to enter into modern financial transactions. Lack of capacity remains a vexatious issue because there is no immediate solution to the problem.

There are a number of adverse consequences that flow from the lack of capacity problem. Firstly, a large number of specially constituted and government entities are deprived of the use of a valuable risk management tool. There is no reason why such entities should not be allowed to use derivatives to hedge against adverse market movements. Debt management in the broad sense would cover activities designed to minimise interest costs. Secondly, those financial intermediaries willing to enter into transactions with such entities are likely to do so only if the profit margins reflect the higher risks. This may mean that these entities could end up paying a premium for the use of derivatives. Thirdly, the lack of capacity problem is undesirable for both end-users and dealers, and undermines the concept of contract autonomy.

However, there is no simple solution to the lack of capacity problem. Even if the ultra vires doctrine were to be completely abolished, it would still not resolve the problem for entities that are subject to detailed regulation, such as insurance companies and financial institutions. It has been suggested that certainty relating to the capacity of specially constituted entities may be achieved through clear enabling powers.[56] For example, legislation may be passed to extend the borrowing powers of local authorities to include the use of derivatives. Another approach that could be adopted is to introduce some measure of flexibility into the enabling legislation so that the enabling authority may increase the list of permitted transactions to keep up with market developments.[57] In New Zealand, local authorities have reduced the possibility of their transactions being struck down for lack of capacity by undertaking the transactions through a local authority

---

[55] See E. Lanyon, 'Derivatives and Modern Portfolio Theory: the Trustee's Duty of Investments' (1995) 6 JBFLP 58, 61.
[56] See Linklaters & Paine, above n. 46, pp. 165–166.
[57] Ibid.

trading enterprise.[58] While the lack of capacity issue requires some form of statutory intervention, it is clear that there is no universal solution, given the range of entities and the different regulatory frameworks.

3.3   RESTITUTIONARY ISSUES

It has been said that 'the main legacy of the [*Hazell*] decision, apart from incredulity on the part of many in the banking world, was the massive litigation' which it spawned.[59] In the wake of the *Hazell* decision, more than 200 suits were started with a view to establishing that sums previously paid to or by local authorities under void swap contracts could be recovered from the recipients.[60] Some of these actions, which later went on trial, raised several issues that have helped clarify some important principles in the law of restitution. As Lord Goff remarked in *Kleinwort Benson Ltd v Lincoln City Council*:

> The process of unravelling transactions of this kind has produced a host of problems, so much so that Professor Andrew Burrows stated in 1995 ... that "it is no exaggeration to say that one could write a book on the restitutionary consequences of the decision in *Hazell's* case."[61]

Before turning to some of these cases, it would be useful to make a number of preliminary remarks about the law of restitution. It is generally accepted that the underlying principle of the law of restitution is unjust enrichment.[62] Judicial recognition of this general principle of unjust enrichment may be traced to Lord Wright's often quoted statement in *Fibrosa Spolka Akcyjna v Fairbairn Lawson Combe Barbour Ltd*:

> It is clear that any civilised system of law is bound to provide remedies for cases of what has been called unjust enrichment or unjust benefit, that is to prevent a man from retaining the money of or some kind of benefit derived from, another which it is against conscience that he should keep.[63]

The emphasis of the law of restitution is on the provision of a remedy designed to prevent a defendant retaining a benefit derived from the plaintiff

---

[58]   See D. Wetherell and R. Smith, 'Local Authority Capacity and Related Matters' (1992) 3 JBFLP 228, 231: 'A LATE [local authority trading enterprise] can be one of several legal entities: a company in which a local authority (or any combination of local authorities) hold equity securities carrying 50 per cent or more of the voting rights at any general meeting, or any other organization (such as a partnership, trust or joint venture) through which a local authority (or local authorities) operates a trading undertaking with the intention or purpose of making a profit.'

[59]   See H. Picarda, 'Interest Rate Swap Agreements in the Courts' Part 1 (1996) 11 JIBFL 428, 430.

[60]   See *Westdeutsche Landesbank Girozentrale v Islington London Borough Council* [1994] 4 All ER 890 at 899, per Hobhouse J.

[61]   [1998] 4 All ER 513 at 523.

[62]   See A. Burrows, *Understanding the Law of Obligations: Essays on Contract, Tort and Restitution* (Hart Publishing, Oxford, 1998), p. 45.

[63]   [1943] AC 32 at 61.

with no intention to enrich the defendant.[64] According to Professor Burrows, it was not until Goff and Jones published their seminal text, *Law of Restitution* in 1996 that the law of restitution based on reversing unjust enrichment gained widespread acceptance.[65] The ensuing discussion on the leading local authority cases shows how the law of restitution was used in the English courts to minimise the harsh effects of the doctrine of ultra vires.

3.3.1 The *Islington* Case

The landmark English case on the recovery of money paid under a void contract is *Westdeutsche Landesbank Girozentrale v Islington London Borough Council*.[66] In that case, the defendant council had a revenue shortfall for the financial year 1987/88. It had limited means of raising revenue, as it was rate-capped. Yet, it was not, as a matter of policy, prepared to reduce its expenditure. So it arranged with a number of finance brokers to raise approximately GBP 19 million by way of up-front payments on interest rate swaps. The effect of these swaps was to increase revenue in the current year at the expense of the revenue for later years.[67]

One of the transactions involved an interest rate swap with the plaintiff bank. The swap, which was based on a nominal amount of GBP 25 million, was to run for 10 years commencing on 18 June 1987. As part of its hedging strategy, the bank entered into a matching swap with Morgan Grenfell & Company Limited. Under the terms of both swap contracts, the fixed-rate payer would pay to the floating-rate payer an up-front amount of GBP 2.5 million on the commencement date of the swap. Between June 1987 and June 1989, the council made four payments to the bank amounting to a total of GBP 1.35 million. Following the *Hazell* decision on 1 November 1989, the council did not make any further payments. The bank brought an action against the council claiming GBP 1.15 million, being the difference between the initial lump sum payment and the payments made by the council and interest from 18 June 1987.

On 12 February 1993, Hobhouse J gave judgment for the bank by ordering the council to pay to the bank the amount claimed plus compound interest from 1 April 1990 (the date the bank was out-of-pocket). The judge held that the bank was entitled to recover the sum either as money had and received or as money, which in equity belongs to the plaintiff and which it is entitled to trace in the hands of the defendant.[68] The basis of restitution was the absence of consideration as payment was made under a contract, which unknown to the parties was void and the plaintiff had not intended to make a voluntary payment.[69] As the council had been unjustly enriched

---

[64] See *Kleinwort Benson Ltd v Birmingham City Council* [1996] 4 All ER 733 at 745, per Morritt LJ.
[65] See Burrows, above n. 62, pp. 46–47.
[66] [1996] 2 All ER 961; [1994] 4 All ER 890.
[67] See H. Cohen, 'Swaps and Restitution' in E. Bettelheim, H. Parry and W. Rees (eds), *Swaps and Off-Exchange Derivatives Trading: Law and Regulation* (FT Law & Tax, London, 1996), p. 90.
[68] [1994] 4 All ER 890 at 955.
[69] Id. at 955–956.

at the expense of the bank, the council must therefore repay the bank the difference. The council appealed to the Court of Appeal against the order and the bank cross-appealed on the ground that compound interest should run from the date of receipt of the principal sum. The Court of Appeal dismissed the council's appeal and allowed the cross-appeal by the bank.

The council accepted its liability to repay the difference but appealed to the House of Lords against the award of compound interest. The House of Lords did not accept the argument that the council held the money on trust for the bank.[70] It held that in the absence of agreement or custom, the court had no jurisdiction to award compound interest at law or under the UK *Supreme Court Act* 1981.[71] Although courts of equity can award compound interest, in the absence of fraud they have never awarded compound interest except against a trustee or other person owing fiduciary duties who is accountable for profits made.[72] The bank was therefore only entitled to simple interest from the date that the council received the money.

Another important issue that was dealt with by the House of Lords was the juridical basis of recovery of the sum of money paid to the council. Lord Browne-Wilkinson, who delivered the leading speech for the majority said that:

The common law restitutionary claim is based not on implied contract but on unjust enrichment: in the circumstances the law imposes an obligation to repay rather than implying an entirely fictitious agreement to repay...In my judgment, your Lordships should now unequivocally and finally reject the concept that the claim for moneys had and received is based on implied contract. I would overrule *Sinclair v Brougham* on this point.[73]

His Lordship then went on to add that the swap moneys were paid on a consideration that wholly failed.[74] This decision was a significant victory for the banks involved in swaps with local authorities by paving the way for recovery of the sums paid under void contracts. In hindsight, had the banks adopted a more cautionary approach by checking whether the local authorities had the necessary powers to enter into swap contracts, they would not have found themselves in such a mess.[75]

3.3.2   The *Sandwell* Case

Another case that was heard at the same time as the *Islington* action was *Kleinwort Benson Ltd v Sandwell Borough Council*.[76] It raised additional issues that were not dealt with in the *Islington* action and is therefore worthy of

---

[70] Id. at 990–991.
[71] Id. at 984.
[72] Ibid.
[73] [1996] 2 All ER 961 at 993.
[74] Ibid.
[75] See R. Cranston, 'Banks , Liability and Risk' in R. Cranston (ed.), *Banks, Liability and Risk* (2nd edn, LLP, London, 1995), p. 3.
[76] [1994] 4 All ER 890.

mention here. In that case, the bank entered into four swap transactions with the council between 1983 and 1987. The first swap, which was entered into on 6 July 1983 was based on a notional sum of GBP 5 million and had a life of five years, with the last payment to be made on 15 July 1988. Under the terms of the swap, the bank was to pay the council a fixed rate of 11 and three-eights per cent half-yearly, while the council was to pay the bank a floating rate of LIBOR quarterly. The contract ran its full course and over the life of the swap, the bank made net payments to the council in excess of GBP 196,000.

On 10 September 1986, the bank and the council entered into a second swap. The swap was also based on a notional sum of GBP 5 million and had a life span of 10 years, with the last payment due on 11 September 1996. Under the terms of the swap, the bank was to pay to the council a fixed rate of 10.3125 per cent on half-yearly basis, while the council was to pay to the bank a floating rate of BBAIRS sterling settlement rate on a half-yearly basis. Payments were made on this contract until the autumn of 1989, by which time the council had made net payments of more than GBP 76,000.

The third swap was entered into on 11 November 1986 and was based on a notional sum of GBP 5 million. It was agreed that the bank would pay the council a fixed rate of 11.42 per cent half-yearly, and the council would pay the bank a floating rate of LIBOR half-yearly. The swap was to have a life of ten years with the first payment due on 11 May 1987 and the last payment due on 11 November 1996. Before the time arrived for making the first swap payment, the counterparties entered into a further agreement, which had the effect of reversing the third swap out. The 'reverse swap' was almost an exact reversal of the third swap, except that the bank was left with a net obligation to make semi-annual payments equivalent to interest at the rate of 1.04 per cent per annum on GBP 5 million.

The fourth swap, which was entered into on 10 November 1986 was in all respects the same as the third swap except that the fixed rate was 11.35 per cent instead of 11.42 per cent. The reverse swap was dated 19 February 1987 and was in all respects the same as that for the third swap with the exception of the fixed rate, which was 10.25 per cent. For both the third and fourth swaps the bank had made payments to the council, but the council had not made payments to the bank. In other words, payments were made 'one-way' for both the swaps. They were therefore different from the first two swaps, which involved 'two-way' payments.

Both parties sought recovery of the net amounts paid under the various swap contracts. Hobhouse J held that the bank was entitled to formulate a claim for money had and received on the basis of total failure of consideration, but was of the view that the correct basis was, as for the other swaps, the absence of consideration.[77] It was also held that it did not make any difference to recovery of the net amounts paid that the first swap contract had run its full course or the fact that payments were only made 'one-way'.[78] Another issue that was considered by the court was the meaning of the

---

[77] Id. at 930.
[78] Ibid.

words 'action founded on simple contract' found in s. 5 of the UK *Limitation Act*. Hobhouse J adopted a broad interpretation when he concluded that the words should be construed as including money had and received.[79]

3.3.3 The *South Tyneside* Case

It is not surprising that swap counterparties who received more than what they had paid under void contracts resisted any attempts to recover the net amounts. In *South Tyneside Metropolitan Borough Council v Svenska International plc*[80] the council tried to recover the excess payments that it made but the bank resisted by attempting to rely on the 'change of position' defence. The facts of that case were basically similar to all the other swap cases that came before the courts. The council entered into an interest rate swap agreement with the bank commencing on 2 June 1988 and terminating on 3 February 1995. Interest rate payments were payable on a half-yearly basis and were to be calculated with reference to the notional principal sum of GBP 15 million. The bank was aware of the risk that the local authority might not be empowered to enter into the transaction, but did not consider that there was any serious possibility that the contract would be invalid since it did not involve any up-front payments. When the House of Lords provisionally ruled on 31 October 1990 that interest rate swaps entered into by local authorities were void, the bank closed out its position.

As the net payer, the local council was owed more than GBP 236,000 by the bank. The council sought to recover the money it had paid as money had and received. However, the bank argued that it had changed its position because it had entered into the swap in good faith and relied on the validity of the original swap contract in committing itself to hedges and maintaining them. It should therefore be entitled to avail itself of the 'change of position' defence. However, the Commercial Court was not persuaded by the bank's argument and decided in favour of the local council. It held that the council was entitled to recover the net payments made as money had and received on the basis that it was the council's money in equity or on the basis that there is no consideration for the payment.

Clarke J explained in the following terms why the bank could not rely on the defence of 'change in position':

In my judgment in circumstances such as these the bank is not entitled to rely upon the underlying validity of the transaction either in support of a plea of estoppel or in support of a defence of change of position. This is because the transaction is ultra vires and void. It is for that reason that in cases of this kind, save perhaps exceptional circumstances, the defence of change of position is in principle confined to changes which take place after receipt of the money. Otherwise the bank would in effect be relying upon the supposed validity of a void transaction.[81]

---

[79] Id. at 942.
[80] [1995] 1 All ER 545.
[81] Id. at 565.

Had the bank entered into the hedging transactions after it received the payments, the outcome could have been different.

3.3.4   The *Birmingham* Case

The 'passing on' or 'windfall gain' argument was another defence that was used to resist repayment of the net amounts received under void swap contracts. In *Kleinwort Benson Ltd v Birmingham City Council*,[82] the council entered into an interest rate swap with the bank on 23 September 1982. The contract was subsequently ruled by the House of Lords to be void and the bank brought an action to recover GBP 353,000 in net payments on the basis of unjust enrichment. The council applied for leave to amend its points of defence so as to raise the defence of 'passing on' or 'windfall gain'. It argued that the bank had not suffered any substantial loss as a result of the swap transaction because the bank had entered into its own independent hedging arrangements with third parties to offset any risk arising from the contract with the council. To allow the bank to recover the net payments would result in the bank receiving a windfall gain. Gatehouse J refused the application and awarded final judgement for the bank and the council appealed to the Court of Appeal.

The council argued that to establish a claim in restitution the plaintiff had to show that the defendant had been unjustly enriched at the plaintiff's expense. The central issue was whether the phrase 'at the expense of' should be interpreted by reference to the payer/payee relationship alone or in relation to the overall transaction. The Court of Appeal adopted the former approach. Lord Evans explained why this interpretation was correct as follows:

This is because the payee's obligation, which is correlative to the payer's right to restitution, is to refund or repay the amount which he has received and which it is unjust that he should keep. "At his expense", in my judgement, serves to identify the person by or on whose behalf the payment was made and to whom repayment is due ... That person, having made the payment, is necessarily out of pocket to that extent, and the defendant's obligation is to replenish his pocket when the circumstances are such that the money should be returned.[83]

The Court of Appeal accordingly held that the defence of passing on or windfall gain was not available to the council and dismissed the appeal.

3.3.5   The *Kensington* Case

In the *Islington* action the swaps in question were 'open' swaps because they were not fully performed. In *Guinness Mahon & Co Ltd v Kensington and Chelsea Royal London Borough Council*[84] the court had to consider whether

---

[82]   [1996] 4 All ER 733.
[83]   Id. at 742.
[84]   [1998] 2 All ER 272.

restitution is available for 'closed' swaps. In that case, the council entered into an interest rate swap agreement with the bank on 23 September 1982. The council agreed to borrow GBP 5 million from a building society for a period of five years at an interest rate of 11.625 per cent. It was further agreed that the bank would pay the council, over the same period of five years, sums of money equal to the interest payments that the council made to the building society, while the council will pay the bank interest at a floating rate based on the notional amount of GBP 5 million. The five-year period ended on 22 September 1987 and by that date the council had received GBP 384,000 more than it had paid the bank. Following the declaration by the Queen's Bench Divisional Court in the *Hazell* case that such a swap was void, the bank commenced proceedings against the council to recover the net amount that the council had received under the swap. Judgment in the sum of GBP 102,000 and interest were awarded to the bank.

The council appealed to the Court of Appeal and the issue before the court was whether full performance of a void contract prevented a claim of recovery, which would have succeeded in the case of partial performance. The council argued that the *Islington* case involved an open swap, whereas the case before the court involved a closed swap.[85] As such, there was nothing unjust in refusing recovery because that was what the parties had exactly bargained for had the swap not been void. However, the court rejected this argument and dismissed the appeal. Morritt LJ saw no principle, which could justify drawing a distinction between a closed swap and an open swap.[86] According to his lordship, an ultra vires contract was devoid of any contractual effect. Payments made under it were for a consideration, which had totally failed. They were therefore recoverable as money had and received. The right to recovery of the net payment exists regardless of whether the apparent contract had been fully performed or not. Moreover, the fact that the contract has been fully performed is no defence or bar to the recovery of the net payment.

3.3.6   The *Lincoln* Case

The issue of whether payments made under void contracts could be recovered on the basis of mistake was raised in *Kleinwort Benson Ltd v Lincoln City Council and other appeals*.[87] In that case, the bank sought recovery of money paid to four different local authorities under void interest rate swap contracts. In each case, the transactions had been fully performed and the moneys in dispute paid more than six years previously. Section 5 of the UK *Limitation Act* 1980 provides that an action founded on a simple contract shall not be brought after the expiration of six years from the date on which the cause of action accrued. In the *Sandwell* action, the limitation defence

---

[85]   A closed swap is one where the prescribed period of the swap has expired. An open swap on the other hand is one, which is executory.
[86]   [1998] 2 All ER 272 at 284.
[87]   [1998] 4 All ER 513.

was raised and Hobhouse J held that s. 5 also applied to a cause of action for money had and received. Since the payments to the four authorities were made outside the limitation period, the bank had to rely on an alternative ground for recovery.

The bank argued that it was entitled to recovery of the net payments made to the four authorities on the ground of payment made under a mistake of law. Section 32(1)(c) of the UK *Limitation* Act 1980 provides that in the case of any action for relief from the consequences of a mistake, 'the period of limitation shall not begin to run until the plaintiff has discovered the...mistake...or could with reasonable diligence have discovered it.' By claiming that in each case the money was paid under a mistake, the bank could avoid the six-year time limit under s. 5. But since the mistake relied upon was a mistake of law, rather than a mistake of fact, the bank had to argue for the abrogation of the long standing rule that generally money is not recoverable in restitution if paid under a mistake of law. The bank's claim was struck out by the High Court on the basis of binding Court of Appeal authority that no action lay for recovery of money paid under a mistake of law.

The bank then appealed directly to the House of Lords. Lord Goff (with whom Lord Hoffman and Lord Hope agreed) held that 'the mistake of law rule should no longer be maintained as part of English law, and that English law should now recognise that there is a general right to recover money paid under a mistake, whether fact or law, subject to the defences available in the law of restitution.'[88] One of the sub-issues raised was whether money should be recovered as payment made under a mistake of law, if payment was made on the basis of a settled understanding of the law. Lord Browne-Wilkinson was of the view that if at the date of each payment, it was settled law that local councils had capacity to enter into swap contracts, Kleinwort was not labouring under any mistake of law at that date.[89] The subsequent *Hazell* decision could not create a mistake where no mistake existed at the time that each payment was made.

However, the majority of the House did not accept this argument. Lord Goff held that the *Hazell* decision had retrospective effect. Since the payer believed at the time the payer was making payment that it was the law, the money was paid under a mistake of law.[90] Therefore the payer is entitled to recover the money. His Lordship concluded that there is no principle of English law that payments made under a settled understanding of the law which is subsequently departed from by judicial decision should not be recoverable on the ground of mistake of law.[91] The decision of the House on this point has been criticised as having destroyed certainty and finality in commercial transactions.[92] Transactions may be re-opened long after the event and this could have undesirable consequences. It has also been

---

[88] Id. at 533.
[89] Id. at 517.
[90] Id. at 536.
[91] Id. at 544.
[92] See generally M. Bridge, 'Restitution and Retrospective Law: *Kleinwort Benson Ltd v Lincoln City Council*' (1999) 14 JIBFL 5.

suggested that the case leaves open the question of what kind of mistake of law will generate a claim in unjust enrichment.[93]

3.3.7 The *Glasgow* Case

Dealing with the treatment of restitutionary claims under English conflict of laws rules is difficult because there is little guidance on the subject. For example, it has been pointed out that the 1993 edition of *Dicey & Morris on the Conflict of Laws* devoted only 10 out of its more than 1,600 pages to restitution.[94] This is not surprising as the law of restitution, until recently, was barely recognised in England as an independent subject.[95] A case that highlights this difficulty is *Kleinwort Benson Ltd v Glasgow City Council*.[96] In that case, the council entered into seven swap agreements with the bank between 7 and 15 September 1982. Pursuant to these agreements, the bank made various payments totalling around GBP 0.807 million to the council between 9 March 1983 and 10 September 1987, and the council made payments to the bank totalling around GBP 79,000. Following the *Hazell* decision, the bank commenced proceedings on 6 September 1991 in the English High Court to claim restitution of the sums paid.

The council challenged the jurisdiction of the English court, claiming that it was entitled to be sued in Scotland, the place of its domicile under article 2 of the *Brussels Convention on Jurisdiction and the Enforcement of Judgments in Civil and Commercial Matters* 1968, which was incorporated into the UK *Civil Jurisdiction and Judgments Act* 1982.[97] The bank argued, inter alia, that the English court had jurisdiction by virtue of articles 5(1) and 5(3) of the Convention which provided that :

5. A person domiciled in a part of the United Kingdom may, in another part of the United Kingdom, be sued:

  (1) in matters relating to a contract, in the courts for the place of performance of the obligation in question ...
  (3) in matters relating to tort, delict or quasi-delict, in the courts for the place where the harmful event occurred or in the case of a threatened wrong is likely to occur ...

The council had a motive for putting forward this argument as the bank's claim was likely to be statute-barred in Scotland but not in England.

Hirst J granted the council's application and struck out the bank's claim holding that it did not fall within either article 5(1) or 5(3). The decision was

---

[93] See L. Smith, 'Restitution for Mistake of Law' (1999) 7 *Restitution Law* Review 148, 155.

[94] See P. Millett, 'Jurisidcition and the Choice of Law in the Law of Restitution' in K. S. Teo & Others (eds), *Current Legal Issues in International Commercial Litigation* (The Faculty of Law, NUS, Singapore 1997), p. 203.

[95] Ibid.

[96] [1997] 4 All ER 641.

[97] The first part of the Act incorporates the Convention into English law, while the second part of the Act has adopted the same criteria for allocating jurisdiction between courts of different parts of the United Kingdom as those applied by the European Court of Justice in allocating jurisdiction between the courts in different Contracting States.

based on the reasoning that since the contract was void, there was no contract. If there was no contract, the bank's claim could not be regarded as a matter relating to contract.[98] The bank then appealed to the Court of Appeal, which in turn referred the matter to the European Court of Justice for an interpretation of the provisions. However, the European Court of Justice held that it did not have the jurisdiction to make a preliminary ruling as to whether the claim fell within the provisions because England and Scotland were not two different Contracting States. The Court of Appeal reversed the decision of the judge, holding that the court had jurisdiction under article 5(1).[99] In a conference held in Singapore in late 1986, Lord Millett explained the reasoning of the Court of Appeal in the following terms:

> Applying what we hoped was the proper teleological approach which the European Court would adopt, we considered that the case did come within Article 5(1) because it related to a supposed contract with an intended place of performance. The parties purported to enter into a contract. They assumed obligations to each other and intended them to be legally enforceable. The payments were made and received on an agreed basis and were explicable only by reference to the supposed contract. If the contract had been valid as the parties plainly thought it was, the intended place of performance would have been a sufficient connecting factor. It did not become less strong a connecting factor because the contract was afterwards found to be void.[100]

The council then appealed to the House of Lords. However, the majority of the House of Lords did not agree with the Court of Appeal. They held that the claim could only fall within article 5(1):

> [I]f it can properly be said to be based upon a particular contractual obligation, the place of performance of which is within the jurisdiction of the court. Where however, as here, the claim is for the recovery of money paid under a supposed contract which in law never existed, it seems impossible to say that the claim for the recovery of the money is based upon a particular contractual obligation.
>
> ...
>
> In truth, the claim in the present case is simply a claim to restitution, which in English law is based upon the principle of unjust enrichment; and claims of this kind do not per se fall within art 5(1).[101]

The House of Lords also held that article 5(3) did not apply to a claim based on unjust enrichment. Such a claim did not, apart from exceptional circumstances, presuppose either a harmful event or a threatened wrong.[102] Based on these reasons, the House of Lords reversed the decision of the Court of Appeal. The significance of this decision is that it establishes that an action for restitution of money paid under a void contract does not fall within article 5(1).

---

[98]   See *Barclays Bank plc. v Glasgow City Council, Kleinwort Benson Ltd. v Glasgow City Council* [1993] QB 429 at 440–441.
[99]   For details of the decision, see *Kleinwort Benson Ltd. v Glasgow City Council* [1996] QB 678.
[100]   See Millett, above n. 94, p. 211.
[101]   [1997] 4 All ER 641 at 649.
[102]   Id. at 653.

3.3.8   Summary and Comments

From the above discussion, it is possible to formulate a number of broad propositions of law. It is now firmly established that the law of restitution based on reversing unjust enrichment allows recovery of net sums of money paid under void swap contracts. The net amounts may be recovered on the basis of failure of consideration or payment made under a mistake. It does not make any difference to recovery that the swap contract has been fully performed or is executory. Net payments may be recovered if the payments were made both ways or one-way. It is not just the banks that can recover net payments, but also the councils. The defence of change of position is not available to a counterparty that alters its position in reliance upon the supposed validity of a transaction. It is only available to party that alters its position after receipt of the money. Similarly, the defence of passing on or windfall gain cannot be used to resist a claim for recovery of money under a void swap contract on the basis that the plaintiff is not out-of-pocket. Finally, under conflicts of laws, the recovery of money paid under a void contract is treated as a matter relating to the law of restitution instead of the law of contract.

It is possible to conclude that the interest rate swap cases have made a significant contribution to the law of restitution. They have not only helped clarify some of the principles underlying the law of restitution, but they have also highlighted the need for more research on the subject. For example, it has been pointed out that an area where there is a real need for academic research is restitution in the conflict of laws.[103] While the above decisions may have little direct authority outside the UK, they are of persuasive authority in other common law jurisdictions. The commercial law of the jurisdictions under study in this book are based on English legal principles. Australia, for example, has recognised the law of restitution based on reversing unjust enrichment since 1986.[104] Recent English developments in the law of restitution have been accepted to a significant extent in Singapore.[105] It has been suggested that even the Malaysian *Contracts Act* has provisions that 'have at least limited restitutionary qualities as well as principles.'[106]

3.4   GAMING AND WAGERING CONTRACTS

The possibility that a derivatives contract may be regarded as illegal is another type of legal risk identified in the Group of Thirty Report. A contract may be illegal either because it is prohibited by statue or it contravenes public policy. However, the ensuing discussion will only focus on illegality

---

[103]   See Millett, above n. 94, p. 204.
[104]   See *Pavey & Matthews Pty. Ltd. v Paul* (1986) 162 CLR 221.
[105]   See A. Phang, *Cheshire, Fifoot and Furnstorm's Law of Contract* (Butterworths Asia, Singapore, 1998), p. 1138. For example, s. 57 of the Malaysian *Contracts Act* 1950 offers restitutionary remedies for non-performance of a contract and s. 66 for recovery of payments made under a void contract.
[106]   Ibid.

arising from contravention of the gaming and wagering laws. This is because there have been a number of reported cases where the losing counterparties have argued that their contracts are illegal because they are gaming and wagering contracts.[107] As a general rule, an illegal contract cannot be enforced and money or property transferred under it may not be recovered. Despite the introduction of legislation to protect derivatives transactions from the application of gaming and wagering laws, the scope of such legislation is limited. Statutory protection is normally extended only to regulated products such as exchange-traded derivatives. This would mean that over-the-counter (OTC) derivatives transactions, such as swaps and forward contracts, are still exposed to the possibility that they may be deemed to be wagering or gaming contracts.

3.4.1 Gaming and Wagering Defined

Many countries have laws which render gaming or wagering contracts void. It is important to point out at the outset that these laws do not render gambling illegal. All they do is prevent the enforcement of gaming or wagering contracts. In other words, the winning party cannot sue the losing party to recover the prize money. These laws were originally intended to protect individuals and to control speculation, but despite having outlived their original uses, they have not been repealed.[108] The great majority of common law jurisdictions have adopted gaming laws based on the UK *Gaming Act* 1845. Legislation in all Australian jurisdictions, for example, is based on s. 18 of the *Gaming Act*, which provides that contracts by way of wagering or gaming are null and void.[109] The gaming and wagering laws of Malaysia, Singapore, Hong Kong, and New Zealand are also modelled after the UK *Gaming Act*.[110]

The statutes provide little assistance with the meanings of 'gaming' or 'wagering', and often it is necessary to resort to decided cases for judicial guidance.[111] It is not uncommon for the terms 'gamble' and 'wager' to be defined as including payment by one party to the other of an amount based

---

[107] For example, see *Jackson Securities Ltd v Cheesman* (1986) 4 NSWLR 484; *Richardson Greenshields of Canada (Pacific) Ltd v Keung Chak-kiu and Hong Kong Futures Exchange Ltd* [1989] 1 HKLR 476; *City Index Ltd v Leslie* [1991] 3 WLR 207; *Morgan Grenfell v Welwyn Hatfield DC* [1995] 1 All ER 1.

[108] See P. R. Wood, *Title Finance, Derivatives, Securitisations, Set-off and Netting* (Sweet & Maxwell, London, 1995), para. 15-41.

[109] See P. Latimer, 'Futures Contracts and Gaming Laws' (1993) 14 *The Company Lawyer* 67.

[110] See the *Civil Law Act* 1988 Revised Edition (Singapore); the *Civil Law Act* 1956 (Malaysia); *Gaming Ordinance* (Hong Kong), Gaming Act 1710 (as amended in 1835) (UK); and *Gaming and Lotteries Act* 1977 (New Zealand).

[111] Although the terms 'gaming' and 'wagering' are used interchangeably, they have distinct meanings. *See Halsbury's Laws of England* 4th edn. (1992), vol. 4(1), para. 10: '...a wager is necessarily, but a gaming contract not necessarily, a bipartite agreement. If, therefore, there are more than two parties to an arrangement under which stakes contributed by the players are to change hands as a result of the game, this may be a gaming contract, but it is not a wagering contract.'

on the difference between the value of two items on a given date or on a contingent event.[112] For instance, in *Thacker v Hardy*, Cotton LJ said that:

The essence of gaming and wagering is that one party is to win and the other to lose on a future event, which at the time of the contract is of an uncertain nature—that is to say, if the events turn out one way, A. will lose, but if it turns out the other way he will win.[113]

The classic definition of a 'wagering contract' was formulated by Hawkins J in *Carlill v Carbolic Smoke Ball Co*:

...a wagering contract is one by which two persons, professing to hold opposite views touching the issue of a future uncertain event, mutually agree that, dependent upon the determination of that event, one shall win from the other and that other shall pay or hand over to him, a sum of money or other stake; neither of the contracting parties having any other interest in that than the sum at stake he will win or lose, there being no other real consideration for the making of such contract by either of the parties. It is essential to a wagering contract that each party may under it either win or lose, whether he will win or lose being dependant on the issue of the event, and, therefore, remaining uncertain until that issue is known. *If either of the parties may win but cannot lose, or may lose but cannot win, it is not a wagering contract.*[114] [emphasis added]

Two English decisions have caused concern among market participants that certain derivatives transactions may fall foul of the gaming and wagering laws. In *Universal Stock Exchange v Strachan*,[115] the court held that wagering contracts included contracts for differences. Halsbury's defines contracts for differences as:

Agreements between those who are only ostensible buyers and sellers of stocks and shares where the common intention of the parties is to pay or receive the differences between their prices on one day and their prices on another day.[116]

In the second decision, *City Index Ltd v Leslie*,[117] the court declared that contracts akin to cash-settled derivatives were 'contracts for differences.' In that case, the plaintiff company, a bookmaker and an authorised person under the UK *Financial Services Act* 1986, ran a business which included the acceptance of wagers on stock market movements. The defendant opened an account with the plaintiff and lost a large sum of money. When the plaintiff brought an action to recover the debt, the defendant claimed that the debt was irrecoverable by virtue of the *Gaming Act*. Although the transactions were 'contracts of differences' within the meaning of paragraph 9 of

---

[112] See S. Henderson and J. Price, *Currency and Interest Swaps* (2nd edn, Butterworths, London, 1988), p. 171.
[113] (1878) 4 QBD 685 at 695.
[114] [1892] 2 QB 484 at 490.
[115] [1896] AC 166.
[116] See *Halsbury's Laws of England*, above n. 111, para. 21.
[117] [1991] 3 WLR 207.

Schedule 1 of the *Financial Services Act*, the court held that they were exempted from the application of the gaming and wagering laws by virtue of s. 6 of the *Financial Services Act*. The combined effect of both decisions is that cash-settled derivatives are wagering contracts and therefore unenforceable, unless exempted by legislation.

3.4.2   The *Morgan Grenfell* Case

Both the above decisions left open the possibility that some derivatives contracts could still constitute gaming and wagering contracts, not only in the UK but also in other jurisdictions which have adopted similar legislation. It was not until *Morgan Grenfell & Co Ltd v Welwyn Hatfield DC (Islington London BC, third party)*[118] that there was greater certainty with regards to the legality of interest rate swaps. The facts in *Morgan* are similar to those in the other interest rate swap cases involving local authorities. On 22 June 1987 the plaintiff bank (Morgan), as the fixed interest ratepayer, entered into a ten-year swap with the defendant local authority (Welwyn), as the floating ratepayer. At the same time, Welwyn as the fixed ratepayer entered into a parallel contract with the third party (Islington) as the floating ratepayer. The notional principal in each contract was GBP 25 million, and both contracts commenced on 23 June 1987. Payments on each side were to be made on a semi-annual basis, and both contracts contained provisions for the netting of payments.

From Welwyn's point of view, it was not taking any risks, as the contracts were undertaken on a back-to-back basis. It received a cash sum of GBP 210,000, which represented the difference between the sums paid for both contracts, for acting as an intermediary. As for Islington, it's motive for participating in the transaction was to raise revenue because of a major shortfall in its 1987–88 budget. Despite being rate-capped, it was not willing as a matter of policy to reduce its expenditure. Islington entered into the contract as part of its overall strategy of obtaining more than GBP 19 million in up-front payments from swap contracts. Between 23 June 1987 and 23 June 1989, a number of payments were made under the two contracts. However, no payments were made after 23 June 1989 as a consequence of the legal ruling made in the *Hazell* case. At the time of default, Morgan had paid Welwyn a net sum of GBP 1.9 million, and Welwyn had paid Islington a net sum of GBP 1.7 million. Welwyn sought to recover the GBP 1.7 million from Islington in third party proceedings.

Islington pleaded that it had a defence as the swap contract was a wagering contract and therefore unenforceable under the *Gaming Act*. However, the court rejected Islington's defence, which cited the decision in *Hazell* as a basis for its argument. Hobhouse J held that the decision in *Hazell's* case did not support the argument that interest rate swaps were gaming or wagering contracts.[119] If it did, then there would not have been any need for the House of Lords or any of the lower courts to have considered the issue of

---

[118]   [1995] 1 All ER 1.
[119]   Id. at 9.

whether engaging in swaps was a legitimate activity of the authority. But Hobhouse J did leave open the possibility that interest rate swaps could be wagering contracts when he said that:

> Certain contracts are by their very character gaming or wagering contracts, such as a bet upon what horse will win a particular race. Entering into such a contract inevitably has the purpose of wagering. Other contracts may on their face appear to have nothing to do with any wager but it may be possible to prove that the purported contract was a sham and the true transaction was a wagering transaction. In between there are, as is visualised by the passages I have quoted, *contracts which may or may not be wagering contracts, depending on the interests of the parties and their purpose in entering into the particular contract.* Interest rate swaps are such contracts.[120] [emphasis added]

Based on the facts however, neither Welwyn nor Islington entered into the transaction for wagering. Therefore, Islington's argument that the transaction offended against the provisions of the *Gaming Act* failed. In the course of his judgement, the judge made the following comments:

> In the context of interest rate swap contracts entered into by parties or institutions involved in the capital market and the making and receiving of loans, the normal inference would be that the contracts are not gaming or wagering but are commercial or financial transactions to which the law will, in the absence of some other consideration, give full recognition and effect.[121]

The above comments did go some way to dispel the fear that ordinary capital market transactions would be treated as gaming and wagering contracts. Although the decision as a whole provided some relief to many market participants, it did not totally destroy the argument that swaps, and by implication, derivatives in general, are not gaming or wagering contracts. The decision raises a number of interesting issues such as whether there is any justification for using speculation as a basis for determining the legality of a transaction. Even if there was such a justification, how will the courts decide whether the parties' interests were speculative? The reality is that many counterparties daily enter into derivatives transactions on a purely speculative basis, even though this may not be apparent to many.[122]

3.4.3 Legal Survey

The legal position with regards to gaming and wagering in Australia is similar to that in the United Kingdom, but is subject to some minor variations. All States and territories in Australia have legislation, which invalidates

---

[120] Id., at 7.
[121] Id., at 10.
[122] See McCracken, above n. 17, p. 163.

gaming or wagering contracts.[123] For example, s. 16 of the *Gaming and Betting Act* 1912 (NSW) provides that:

All contracts or agreements, whether parole or in writing, by way of gaming or wagering, shall be null and void, and no suit shall be brought or maintained in any court of law or equity for recovering any sum of money or valuable thing alleged to be won upon any wager or which has been deposited in the hands of any person to abide the event on which any wager has been made.

The concern that a derivatives contract may be unenforceable stems from the fact that the State and Territory legislation does not define the terms 'gaming' or 'wagering'.[124]

Some of the earlier Australian authorities on the subject are not clear and appear to contradict each other. In *See v Cohen*,[125] the plaintiff entered into a written agreement to sell negotiable wheat certificates to the defendant at a certain price. It was agreed that delivery would take place on a specified date, but the seller would have the option of making or claiming a cash adjustment. The defendant refused to either accept delivery or make a cash adjustment, and asserted that the contracts were made by way of gaming or wagering. Reversing the decision of Starke J on this point, the Australian High Court held that since the intention of the parties was for the settlement of differences, the contracts were wagering contracts. In a later decision, *Morley v Richardson*,[126] the High Court treated contract for differences as legitimate commercial contracts. Although in that case the buyer of warrants for wheat never took delivery of either the wheat or the warrants, the High Court held that they were not wagering contracts because only one party had intention to wager.

The common law position in Australia has been modified by statute. Section 1141 of the Australian *Corporations Law* protects the following categories of derivatives contracts from the gaming and wagering laws:

- those made on the futures market of a futures exchange, or a recognised futures market,
- those made on an exempt futures market,
- those permitted by the business rules of a futures association, a futures exchange, or a recognised futures exchange,
- Chapter 8 agreements prescribed for the purposes of s. 72A(1)(b).

A similar statutory provision offers protection to option contracts traded on a stock market of a securities exchange, or an exempt market.[127] However,

---

[123] *Gaming and Betting Act* 1912 (New South Wales); *Gaming and Betting (Contract and Securities) Act* 1985 (Western Australia); *Gaming Act* 1972 (Queensland); *Lottery and Gaming Act* 1936 (South Australia); *Gaming Act* 1983 (Tasmania); *Lotteries, Gaming and Betting Act* 1966 (Victoria); *Games, Wagers and Betting-houses Ordinance and Gaming and Betting Ordinance* 1945 (Australian Capital Territory); *Lotteries and Gaming Act* 1982 (Northern Territory).

[124] See Mallesons Stephen Jaques, above n. 40, p. 7.

[125] (1923) 33 CLR 174.

[126] (1942) 65 CLR 512.

[127] *Corporations Law*, s. 778.

s. 1141 falls short of providing protection for all categories of derivatives contracts. Futures contracts made outside any of the above markets are not protected. This means that not all OTC derivatives contracts are excluded from the application of the gaming and wagering laws.

In Singapore, cash-settled contracts involving the future delivery of commodities used to be illegal. For instance, in *SE Mizrahe v Stanton Nelson & Co Ltd*,[128] the Singapore Court of Appeal held rubber contracts not involving immediate delivery were not real contracts for the sale of rubber. They were merely colourable transactions to enable the appellant to gamble in differences and were therefore void. This decision no longer represents the law, following the amendments introduced by the Singapore *Civil Law (Amendment) Ordinance* 1962. Although s. 6(1) of the Singapore *Civil Law Act*[129] provides that all contracts or agreements by way of gaming or wagering are null and void, it is qualified by s. 6(4), which states that:

[W]here any contract for the future delivery of any commodity is entered into in any exchange or market, the fact that the contract is entered into by one or both parties with no intention of actual delivery of the commodity but with the intention of realising a profit arising out of differences in the price of the commodity shall not affect the validity or enforceability of the contract.

It has been suggested that s. 6(4) only applies to derivatives contracts involving tangible commodities like gold.[130] But even if s. 6(4) is given a narrow interpretation, many categories of financial derivatives would still be protected by s. 58 of the Singapore *Futures Trading Act* 1986, which states that:

For the purpose of this Act and any other written law or rule of law a futures contract made at a futures market or leveraged foreign exchange trading shall not be regarded as a contract of gaming or wagering.

However, there is a degree of uncertainty whether swaps would enjoy similar protection under the law.[131] Swaps are essentially bilateral contracts for the exchange of future cash flows calculated by multiplying the notional principal sum against agreed reference rates. Swaps, apart from cross-currency swaps, are not contracts for the future delivery of commodities and might not fall within the ambit of s. 6(4) of the Singapore *Civil Law Act*. They are also unlikely to be 'futures contracts' within the meaning of s. 58 of the Singapore *Futures Trading Act* since they are not made pursuant to the rules or practices of a futures market.[132]

In Malaysia, s. 26 of the Malaysian *Civil Law Act* 1956 provides that:

(1) All contracts or agreements whether by parol or in writing by way of gaming or wagering shall be null and void.

---

[128]   [1958] MLJ 97.
[129]   Cap. 43.
[130]   See Allen & Gledhill, above n. 41, pp. 284–285.
[131]   Ibid.
[132]   Id., 286. See also, S. L. Tan, 'Swaps and Derivatives: Managing Legal Risks' (1996) 11 *Asia Business Law Review* 29, 31: 'It would appear the Futures Trading Act is not meant to cover over-the-counter swaps.'

However, there is no 'safe harbour' for derivatives contracts similar to that provided by s. 6(4) of the Singapore *Civil Law Act*. Apart from s. 26, s. 31(1) of the Malaysian *Contracts Act* 1950 also renders wagering contracts void. Section 31(1) is worded differently from s. 26(1) of the *Civil Law Act*:

Agreements by way of wager are void; and no suit shall be brought for recovering anything alleged to be won on any wager, or entrusted to any person to abide the result of any game or other uncertain event on which any wager is made.

Although both provisions achieve the same effect, it has been suggested that in the event of an inconsistency, s. 26(1) will prevail over s. 31(1).[133]

To remove the risk of derivatives contracts falling foul of the gaming and wagering laws, s. 100(2) of the Malaysian *Futures Industry Act* 1993 was introduced which provides that:

… a futures contract made or traded—

    (a)   on the futures market of an exchange company; or
    (b)   on an exempt futures market,

or anything done under such a futures contract, is not to be taken to be a gaming or wagering contract.

Since the Malaysian definition of 'futures contract' has been framed wide enough to cover most types of derivatives, regardless of where they are traded, there is less likelihood that a derivatives contract may be rendered void. However derivatives contracts, which are excluded from the definition of 'futures contract', are not protected by s. 100(2).

In Hong Kong, there are two relevant statutes that deal with gaming and wagering contracts. The first is the Hong Kong *Gambling Ordinance*,[134] which basically makes gambling unlawful in Hong Kong unless provided otherwise. As a result of a number of specific exemptions introduced as late as 1993, the *Gambling Ordinance* has ceased to be a major concern for derivatives participants in Hong Kong.[135] For example, contracts for differences listed on the Stock Exchange, Futures Exchange or other recognised stock or options market are exempted from the provisions of the Hong Kong *Gambling Ordinance*.[136] So are contracts for difference entered into by way of business by a registered or exempt dealer under the Hong Kong *Securities Ordinance or Commodity Trading Ordinance*.[137] The other relevant statute is the UK *Gaming Act* 1710 (as amended in 1835), which is deemed applicable in Hong Kong by s. 4 of the Hong Kong *Application of English Law Ordinance*.

---

[133] See Phang, above n. 105, p. 576.
[134] Cap. 148.
[135] See A. Wingfield and E. Cain, 'Hong Kong' in L. Burke and Others (eds), *International Derivatives Law* (Risks Publications, London, 1996), p. 109.
[136] *Gambling Ordinance*, s. 29.
[137] Ibid.

The illegality defence was raised in *Greenshields of Canada (Pacific) Ltd v Keung Chak-kiu and Hong Kong Futures Exchange*.[138] In that case the plaintiff sued the defendant for over HKD 500,000 in outstanding losses arising from the trading in Hang Seng index futures. The issue before the court was whether the transactions, which were transacted on the Hong Kong Futures Exchange, contravened s. 1 of the UK *Gaming Act* 1710. However, the defence failed because Sears J held that the fact that one party engaged in the transaction for a speculative purpose, does not convert it into a gaming contract if the other party entered into it as a genuine commercial transaction.[139] In any case, Sears J. declared that:

> What occurs either on the Exchange floor, or between broker and client, is not gaming.[140]

Although the decision involved exchange-traded derivatives, it would also be applicable to off-exchange derivatives.

In New Zealand, futures contracts are protected from the application of the gaming and wagering laws by statute. One of the principal purposes of the New Zealand *Securities Amendment Act* 1988 was to eliminate the risk that futures contracts would be unenforceable under s. 128 of the New Zealand *Gaming and Lotteries Act* 1977. Section 40 of the New Zealand Securities Amendment Act (as amended by the *Securities Amendment Act* (No. 2) 1997) provides that:

(1) Nothing in the Gaming and Lotteries Act 1977 applies to, or in respect of—
   (a) An authorised futures contract; or
   (b) An agreement or a contract of the kind described in section 37(2).
(2) Without limiting subsection (1), a contract referred to in that subsection is not a gaming or wagering contract for the purposes of any enactment or rule of law.
(3) A contravention of this Part of this Act does not affect the validity or enforceability of a contract referred to in subsection (1).

Following the recent amendments, s. 40 excludes from the application of s. 128 of the *Gaming and Lotteries Act* 1977 all authorised contracts and those contracts described in s. 37(2), such as interest and currency swaps and forward agreements to which a registered bank is a party. This would suggest that derivatives agreements, which are not subject to the *Securities Amendment Act*, could still face the risk of unenforceability as long as they are speculative in nature.

3.4.4   Summary and Comments

The risk that a contract may not be enforceable on the ground of illegality is one that needs to be addressed. Generally, there is little risk of exchange-traded derivatives falling foul of the gaming and wagering laws in either

---

[138]   [1989] 1 HKLR 476.
[139]   Ibid.
[140]   Id. at 485.

the UK or other common law jurisdictions. But, there are still varying degrees of uncertainty as to whether OTC derivatives contracts would constitute gaming and wagering contracts. The comments made by some English judges have been a source of concern for market participants. For instance, Lord Goff in *Westdeutsche Landesbank Girozentrale v Islington London Borough Council* said that swaps are in law wagers, but they have been saved by statute.[141] Regardless of the interests of counterparties, there is no justification for treating derivatives contracts as wagering or gaming contracts. They are no different from the other commercial contracts entered into by parties on a daily basis. It is true they are more risky than other commercial contracts and some parties are attracted to derivatives by the prospects of windfall gains. But these factors do not make them wagering or gaming contracts any more than contracts to undertake some highly speculative business. Apart from the need to remove the existing uncertainties, regulators should also address the broader question of whether it is appropriate for gaming and wagering legislation to be applicable in the realm of financial transactions.[142]

3.5 SUITABILITY

The scope of the legal duty owed by derivatives dealers to end-users is an issue that has attracted much attention in recent times. Since derivatives are usually marketed in the context of an established banker–customer relationship,[143] it would be convenient to begin by examining the nature of this relationship. According to Professor Weerasooria:

The general relationship that exists between the parties is a complex relationship consisting of reciprocal rights and duties founded on the practices and usages prevailing among bankers. The relationship consists of a general contract which is basic to all transactions, together with special contracts which arise only as they are brought into being in relation to specific transactions or banking services.[144]

The banker–customer contract is basically of an implied nature, but outside the ambit of the current account operation, the relationship may be subject to special arrangements, which are normally reduced to writing.[145]

The banker–customer relationship does not, in itself, create a duty to offer financial or investment advice.[146] But where a bank assumes responsibility

---

[141] [1996] 2 All ER 961 at 964:

[Interest rate swaps] are in law wagers but they are not void as such because they are excluded from the regime of the Gaming Act by s. 63 of the Financial Services Act 1986.

[142] See McCracken, above n. 17, p. 164.

[143] See for example, *Procter & Gamble v Bankers Trust Co* [1997] 6 Bank LR 330 at 343: Both parties had a long business relationship.

[144] See W. S. Weerasooria, *Banking Law and the Financial System in Australia* (5th edn, Butterworths, Chatswood, NSW, 2000), p. 270.

[145] Ibid.

[146] See J. O' Donovan, 'Lender Liability for Investment or Financial Advice' (1999) 11 CBLJ 1, 22.

for giving advice, the bank can incur liabilities not only under the general law, but also under any applicable consumer protection legislation. For example, if the bank provides wrong advice to customer, it may be liable in contract or tort. A bank could also be liable for breach of fiduciary duty. However, the courts are usually reluctant to find a fiduciary relationship in any 'arms-length' transaction.[147] It is therefore unlikely that the ordinary banker–customer relationship will give rise to any fiduciary duty. Generally, when a bank enters into a transaction with a customer, it is entitled to obtain the best terms for itself and it is under no obligation to ensure that the customer has made a correct decision.[148]

However, the nature of the banker–customer relationship when derivatives are involved is not so clear. This may have something to do with the nature of the products and the way that they are marketed. Banks are usually involved in the development and promotion of the products. Often the customer would first learn of the product from the bank. To further compound the problems, banks often act as counterparties to the transactions involving their customers. In view of the novelty and complexity of derivatives, customers tend to place significant reliance on the bank's opinion and expertise. Such a lop-sided relationship could work against the bank in a legal dispute. Where the customer has benefited from the transaction, no problem is likely to arise. Legal disputes only surface when customers suffer large losses and somehow feel that they have been misled by the bank.

In the early 1990s, some investors in the United States (US) engaged in a number of complex swap transactions which offered them the prospects of attractive returns if US interest rates remained constant, but open-ended losses if interest rates either rose or fell.[149] When the US Federal Reserve Board began a series of interest rate increases in February 1994, a number of derivatives counterparties found themselves with significantly higher losses than anticipated.[150] Several unsuccessful counterparties brought legal proceedings to invalidate their contracts.[151] These US cases may have encouraged other foreign counterparties to file similar lawsuits against their dealers.[152]

---

[147] See, for example, *Hospital Products International Pty. Ltd. v United States Surgical Corporation* (1984) 156 CLR 41 at 70, per Gibbs CJ.

[148] Id., 8.

[149] See S. K. Henderson, '*Bankers Trust v Dharmala*: The English Courts Inject Commercial Sense into the Debate over the Scope of a Derivatives Dealer's Duty to an End-User' (1996) 7 JBFLP 162.

[150] Ibid.

[151] See H. S. Scott, 'Liability of Derivatives Dealers' in F. Oditah (ed.), *The Future for the Global Securities Market* (Clarendon Press, Oxford, 1996), p. 271: More than 30 major lawsuits were brought by customers against US securities firms that advised them about derivatives or entered into derivatives transactions with them. Some of the cases included *Gibson Greeting v Bankers Trust*, which involved a claim for USD 32 million in compensatory damages; *Procter & Gamble v Bankers Trust Co.*, which involved a claim for USD 195 million; and *Orange County Investments Pool v Merril Lynch & Co.*, in which Orange County sued for USD 3 billion in damages.

[152] See *Bankers Trust International PLC v P.T. Dharmala Sakti Sejahtera* [1995] 4 Bank LR 381; *Bankers Trust Co. and Another v P.T. Jakarta International Hotel & Development* [1999] 1 Lloyd's Rep. 910.

Many of the lawsuits filed by unsuccessful counterparties involved Bankers Trust Company and its affiliate, Bankers Trust International.[153] Bankers Trust Company acted as the counterparty in most of its swap transactions with US counterparties, while Bankers Trust International acted as the counterparty in many swaps with foreign counterparties. An analysis of the claims made by unsuccessful counterparties reveals three broad arguments. First, the counterparties claimed that they lost money because the dealers had misrepresented or failed to disclose material facts to them. Second, they claimed that the dealers had failed to recommend suitable investments to them. Third, they claimed that the dealers owed them duties, which they had breached.[154] The various claims brought against dealers for selling malpractices are usually subsumed under the 'suitability' heading. [155]

Despite the broad meaning given to 'suitability' in financial markets, the term has a more restricted meaning under US securities law. It refers to a broker's duty to investors to make suitable recommendations regarding the purchase of investment instruments.[156] This duty has its origins in the US National Association of Securities Dealers' general suitability rule.[157] Under this rule, a registered representative or dealer may recommend a security transaction only if there is a reasonable belief that the transaction is suitable for the customer. Prior to the execution of the transaction, the registered representative or dealer must make a reasonable effort to obtain information on the customer's investment objective, financial and tax status.[158]

There are three cases that help shed some light on the duties owed by derivatives dealers to end-users. The first two cases involved the Bankers Trust Group, but one was heard in a UK court and the other in a US court. Despite some differences in the cases, both courts have taken a broadly similar stand with regards to the duties owed by a dealer to end-users.[159] The third and most recent case involved the Morgan Stanley Group and was

---

[153] See generally, S. K. Henderson, 'Derivatives Litigation in the United States' in E. Bettelheim, H. Parry and W. Rees (eds), *Swaps and Off-Exchange Derivatives Trading: Law and Regulation* (FT Law & Tax, London, 1996), p. 211.

[154] A similar observation was made in C. Style and S. Dutson, 'Financial Products, Foreign Counterparties and Disputes: Minimising Litigation Risk' (2000) 11 JBFLP 93, 93–94: There are three complaints which usually arise in financial products related litigation: misrepresentation, breach of duty of care, and lack of capacity.

[155] See A. Hudson, *The Law on Financial Derivatives* (2nd ed., Sweet & Maxwell, London, 1998), p. 168.

[156] See D. C. Sienko, 'The Aftermath of Derivative Losses: Can Sophisticated Investors Invoke the Suitability Doctrine' (1995) 8 *Depaul Business Law Journal* 107, 115.

[157] See J. A. Frederick, 'Not Just for Widows & Orphans Anymore: The Inadequacy of the Current Suitability Rules for the Derivatives Market', (1995) 64 *Fordham Law Review* 97, 109, footnote 73: 'In recommending to a customer the purchase, sale or exchange of any security, a member shall have reasonable grounds for believing that the recommendation is suitable for such customer upon the basis of the facts, if any, disclosed by such customer as to his other security holdings and as to his financial situation and needs.'

[158] Other major US exchanges such as the New York Stock Exchange have adopted similar suitability rules.

[159] See generally, W. Blair and C. D. Olive, 'Derivatives Sales Liability: Approach of the English and US Courts' (1996) 11 JIBL 283. One of the key differences between both cases was that the claims in the UK case were based exclusively on common law principles, whereas the US case attempted to invoke the liability provisions of State and Federal laws.

heard in a UK court. What is significant about this case was that the customer was able to avoid liability for losses suffered in derivatives trading. The English courts have generally been unsympathetic to customers who have tried to avoid liability for losses sustained as a result of trading commodities and derivatives.[160] It would be useful to examine each of these cases in greater detail as they provide some guidance on the approach that might be taken by Anglo-American courts when deciding on the scope of the dealer's legal duty to end-users.

3.5.1 The *Dharmala* Case

The decision of the English Commercial Court, sitting without a jury, in *Bankers Trust International v PT Dharmala Sakti Sejahtera*[161] provides a valuable insight into how the courts in England may approach the issues relating to derivatives sales liability. PT Dharmala Sakti Sejahtera (DSS), an Indonesian company, entered into a swap transaction with Bankers Trust International (BTI), through the Singapore branch of Bankers Trust Company (BC). The swap agreement was for two years and involved a nominal amount of USD 50 million. It was concluded following a meeting on 19 January 1994, and formalised by a signed confirmation dated 27 January 1994. Although the terms of the swap provided for the execution of an International Swaps and Derivatives Association (ISDA) Agreement, DSS did not countersign and return the agreement signed by BTI on 1 February 1994.

There were two parts to the swap transaction. Under the first part, DSS would pay BTI interest at the 6-month London Interbank Offer rate (LIBOR), while BTI was to pay DSS the same rate plus 1.25 per cent. This effectively gave DSS a 1.25 per cent margin per annum. Under the second part of the swap, DSS was to pay interest at 5 per cent per annum, while BTI was to pay interest at 5 per cent per annum multiplied by a factor. The factor was based on the number of days the LIBOR was determined to be less than 4.125 per cent. The net effect of the formula in the second part of the swap was that if interest stayed above 4.125 throughout the six-month reference period, DSS would not receive any interest from BTI, but it would still have to pay the 5 per cent. This would result in a maximum net loss of 3.75 per cent (5 per cent minus 1.25 per cent) from both parts of the swap.

On 4 February 1994, the Federal Reserve Board raised its rates leading to an increase in the six-month LIBOR. Following an agreement between both parties, the first swap was cancelled on 16 February 1994 and replaced by a second swap, which was aimed at limiting the losses in the first swap. The terms of the second swap were basically similar to the first swap, except that the interest payment formula was changed. DSS would receive interest at the 6-month US dollar rate plus 1.25 per cent per annum, but pay BTI interest at the six-month LIBOR less 2.25 per cent per annum plus 'spread'.

---

[160] See P. Hann, 'Morgan Stanley Group v Puglisi: The First Reported Case in which a Private Customer Has Avoided Liability for Losses Sustained in Derivatives Trading' (2000) 6 *Derivatives Use, Trading and Regulation* 467.
[161] [1995] 4 Bank LR 381.

There would be no spread if the 6-month LIBOR stayed below 5.25 per cent, but if the rate went above it, spread was to be established as follows: (the 6-month LIBOR divided by 4.5 per cent) minus 1. The formula for calculating spread did not lead to a percentage rate of interest (as DSS claimed it understood to be), but a decimal, which was applied to the swap amount.[162] To further complicate matters the swap was divided into two tranches with the barrier in one tranche at 5.25 per cent and the other at 5.135 per cent.

Unfortunately for DSS, US interest rates continued to rise. Each rise in rates led to a corresponding rise in 6-month LIBOR. BC wrote to DSS on 19 April 1994 quantifying the interest rate at around USD 19 million for each of the two years. DSS requested for another amendment to the barrier rates, which BTI agreed. On 10 May 1994 and at DSS's request, BC sent a fax quantifying the amended swap at just over USD 45 million. DSS replied on 13 May 1994 that it did not wish to proceed with the 'LIBOR barrier swap' alleging misrepresentation, wrong economic advice and disagreement with the calculation of the spread. In August 1994, DSS brought an action against BTI in Jakarta to set aside its liability under the swap and the Central Jakarta District Council found in favour of DSS. Meanwhile, BTI served notice of default on DSS under the ISDA agreement, which provided for English law as the governing law and the non-exclusive jurisdiction of the English courts. On 20 December 1994, BTI commenced action in England claiming the sum of USD 64.7 million from DSS. The Commercial Court found in favour of BTI and in doing so gave its opinion on a number of issues, which have considerable implications for market participants.

DSS claimed that BTI made various misrepresentations in relation to the two swaps, with regard to the following matters:

- profitability of Bankers Trust's products;
- suitability and reduction in exposure to interest rate movements;
- safety, 'limited risk and downside' and 'replacement at no cost'; and
- accuracy and reliability of the economic forecasts.[163]

These representations were allegedly made orally and in writing on various occasions. Before arriving at a decision, Mance J laid down the legal position with regards to the plea of misrepresentation. Generally, a person who is induced to enter into a contract by misrepresentation, whether innocently, negligently or fraudulently, may rescind the contract.[164] While traditionally distinctions were drawn between representations of fact and statements of opinion or statements as to the future, these distinctions were themselves dependant on the circumstances.[165] The central issue was not whether statements of opinion or statements as to the future were actionable as

---

[162] See J. Quitmeyer, 'Dealer Disclosure in Derivative Transactions' (1996) 2 *Derivatives Use, Trading & Regulation* 241, 244: 'The initial swap had not been leveraged. The replacement swap was premised on a not-readily-apparent leverage factor of more than 22 to 1.'
[163] [1995] 4 Bank LR 381 at 383–384.
[164] Id., at 391.
[165] Ibid.

misrepresentations, but whether it was reasonable for the representee to rely on the representor's statements.[166]

For the plea of misrepresentation to succeed, two conditions must be satisfied. First, the representation must be misleading and what is misleading requires the application of an objective test in the context of the particular relationship. A representation may be fair and adequate in one context, but not so in another context.[167] In considering the effect of a representation on the representee, it would be necessary to consider 'the recipient's characteristics and knowledge as they appeared, or ought to have appeared, to the maker of the proposal or presentation.'[168] Business is generally carried out on the assumption that both parties understand, or are able to avail themselves of advice, about the area in which they are operating.[169] Mance J said that while this was not an issue in normal commercial transactions, it was different in the case before him because of the novelty of the products in question.

The second condition that must be satisfied for a successful plea of misrepresentation is that not only must the representation be misleading; the recipient must also have relied upon it. Mance J provided an insight into how the court will go about determining whether the second condition was met:

[This] involves a subjective investigation of the actual impact of the representation on its actual recipient, having regard to his actual characteristics and knowledge, whether or not these were within the knowledge of the maker of the representation.[170]

Ascertaining whether the second condition has been met involves the application of a subjective test, unlike the first, which requires an objective test.

With regards to the claim that BTI had misrepresented the profitability of Bankers Trust's products, the court held that the comments made by BTI were commercial puffery and it was not conceivable that any reliance would be placed on it.[171] The court did not accept that DSS entered into the first swap on the basis that it was suitable or that it would reduce its interest rate costs.[172] As for the claim that BTI had made representations about the safety and replacement at no cost of the first swap, the court found that implausible, given the experience and intelligence of the recipients.[173] With regards to the allegations that the economic forecasts were not complete and inaccurate, the court found that they were reasonable and honestly held.[174]

---

[166]   Id. at 392.
[167]   Id. at 393.
[168]   Ibid.
[169]   Ibid.
[170]   Id. at 394.
[171]   Id. at 404
[172]   Ibid.
[173]   Ibid.
[174]   Id. at 405.

As for the second swap, the court held that what was crucial was not whether any misrepresentations were made, but whether DSS was actually misled by them. While Mance J found the representations made by BTI fell below the best standards, they were in his opinion the result of over-enthusiastic salesmanship and lack of sufficient thought rather than deliberate misrepresentation or misconduct.[175] What was important to note was that DSS was capable of looking after its own position and contrary to its own claims, did so. The court then went to find that DSS had failed to establish that the misrepresentations would have made any difference to its decision to enter into the contract.[176] It was for these reasons that the claims of misrepresentations failed in respect of the second swap.

Apart from allegations of misrepresentation, DSS also claimed that it was owed a duty of care by BC and BTI to explain fully and properly the workings of both swaps and the risks of using them.[177] This duty of care was breached by BC and BTI when they failed, among other things, to:

- establish the level of skill and knowledge possessed by DSS;
- give adequate warning of the risks inherent in the swaps;
- advise on the suitability of the swaps;
- consider the desirability of DSS achieving its objectives through different products;
- advise DSS about the need to seek independent advice;
- satisfy itself that DSS had understood the consequences of each swap.

Mance J rejected the argument that a bank negotiating and contracting with another party owed a duty to explain the nature or effect of the transaction to the other party.[178] But he added that if the bank does give an explanation or tender advice:

[T]hen it owes a duty to give that explanation or tender that advice fully, accurately and properly … How far that duty goes must once again depend on the precise nature of the circumstances and of the explanation or advice which is tendered.[179]

As long as BC and BTI had accurately presented the terms of the transactions, it was up to DSS to evaluate the risks. While conceding that BC and BTI had greater expertise and experience that DSS, Mance J said that the courts should not be 'too ready to read duties of an advisory nature into [a commercial] relationship.'[180] Since DSS showed itself capable of looking after its own interests and neither BC nor BTI had assumed an advisory role, the claim for breach of duty of care failed. The court also noted that BTI's letter of 1 February 1994 to DSS (which was written prior to the latter's entry into the second swap) was couched 'in terms, which militate

---

175 Id. at 417.
176 Id. at 419.
177 Id. at 391.
178 Id. at 394.
179 Ibid.
180 Id. at 419.

against the wide implied duties to investigate, inform, advise and warn suggested by DSS in this action.'[181]

3.5.2   The *Procter & Gamble* Case

Less than six months after the *Dharmala* judgement was handed down in England, the United States District Court of Ohio gave its opinion on *Procter & Gamble v Bankers Trust Co.*[182] Although the decision addressing the various issues was given before the case went on trial (and a settlement was reached shortly after that between the parties) it nevertheless warrants some attention. The significance of that decision was that it showed the similarity in approaches adopted by the English and US courts to some of the claims made by unsuccessful swap counterparties, especially in relation to the scope of a dealer's legal duty to end-users.

In January 1993, Procter & Gamble (P&G) entered into a master agreement on the International Swap Dealers Association standard form with Bankers Trust Co (BT). The master agreement stated that the contract would be governed by, and construed and enforced in accordance with, the laws of the State of New York. Following negotiations, the parties entered into a customised swap transaction on 2 November 1993. Under this transaction BT agreed to pay P&G a fixed rate of interest of 5.3 per cent for five years on a notional amount of USD 200 million. P&G in turn agreed to pay BT a floating rate interest according to a fixed formula. P&G agreed that for the first six months it would make floating rate payments equivalent to the prevailing US Commercial Paper (CP) interest rate minus 75 basis points. For the remaining life of the swap, it would make floating rate payments based on CP rate minus 75 basis points plus spread calculated according to an agreed formula at the end of the first six months.

P&G entered into a second swap with BT in February 1994 based on the value of the German Deutschmark. Under the terms of the four-year swap, BT was to pay P&G in the first year a floating interest rate plus 233 basis points and P&G was to pay the same floating rate plus 133 basis points. However, P&G was to add a spread to its payments if the four-year Deutschmark swap rate traded either below 4.05 per cent or above 6.01 per cent during the first year of the swap. In other words, the spread would be zero if the Deutschmark swap rate stayed within the band of interest rates.

When interest rates in the United States and Germany took a significant turn upward, P&G unwound both the swaps before their spread set dates. BT claimed that it was owed USD 200 million on both swaps, while P&G claimed that the swaps were fraudulently induced and executed. In October 1994, P&G filed its Complaint for Declaratory Relief and Damages, alleging fraud, misrepresentation, breach of fiduciary duty, negligent misrepresentation, and negligence in connection with the first swap. Later in February 1995, P&G filed its First Amended Complaint adding claims relating to its

---

[181]   Id. at 420.
[182]   [1997] 6 Bank LR 330.

second swap. The court allowed P&G to file a Second Amended Complaint in September 1995. Feikens J granted BT's motions to dismiss nine of the counts and awarded summary judgment on another three of them, which related to breach of fiduciary duty, negligent misrepresentation and negligence.

P&G contended that a fiduciary relationship of trust existed between the parties by virtue of their long relationship, the trust that it reposed in BT, and the assurances given by BT that it would look out for P&G's interests.[183] However, the court rejected P&G's argument that BT had breached its fiduciary duty on the grounds that under New York law, 'no fiduciary relationship can arise in a business relationship.'[184] The fact that BT had superior knowledge in the swap transactions, did not convert their relationship into one which fiduciary duties are imposed.[185] In other words, once it was established that the parties were in a commercial relationship, no fiduciary duty will arise.

On the issue of negligent misrepresentation, the court held that under New York law there is no cause of action in the absence of a special relationship of trust and confidence between the parties.[186] Since BT and P&G were 'sophisticated corporations whose dealings were on a business level', they did not have a special relationship that would support a claim of negligent misrepresentation.[187] With regards to P&G's claim that BT was negligent, the court held that 'where the parties' relationship is contractual, and the duty of good faith and fair dealing is implied in the contract, a negligent claim is redundant.'[188]

What is interesting to note is that Feikens J said that under New York statute law, every contract imposes an obligation of good faith in its performance and enforcement. In addition New York case law establishes an implied contractual duty to disclose in business transactions where:

- one party has superior knowledge of certain information;
- that information is not readily available to the other party;
- the first party knows that the second party is acting on the basis of mistaken knowledge.[189]

It has been suggested that this implied contractual duty to disclose may have been the reason which induced BT to settle its case with P&G.[190] However, because the case never went to trial, it is difficult to speculate whether the court would have found that the duty was breached. One commentator has suggested that had BT known that US interest rates were

---

[183] Id. at 342.
[184] Ibid.
[185] Ibid
[186] Id. at 344.
[187] Ibid.
[188] Ibid.
[189] Id. at 343.
[190] Id. at 254.

going to rise, they would have been deemed to be in possession of 'superior knowledge'.[191] The failure by BT to disclose this information to P&G would have resulted in the breach of BT's contractual duty.

3.5.3 The *Puglisi* Case

In *Morgan Stanley UK Group v Puglisi*,[192] the defendant investor, a wealthy Italian gentleman by the name of Puglisi, lost a considerable sum of money investing in Principal Exchange Rate Linked Securities (PERLS), which he claimed were recommended by the plaintiff bank. PERLS is a bond issued by a corporation or government agency, which is redeemable in US dollars. Its redemption value is calculated by reference to a formula based on a short position in one or more 'hard' currencies and a long position in one or more 'soft' currencies. PERLS represents a bet against the market because under normal market conditions, soft currencies get softer and hard currencies get harder. It is a highly leveraged investment for two main reasons. Firstly, the product had a built-in leverage. For example, the redemption value of the first investment was expressed as the original US dollar amount plus twice the spot exchange at maturity of the Italian lira against the US dollar less the spot exchange of the Swiss franc against the US dollar. Secondly, the transaction was leveraged because the bank provided 90 per cent of the financing, while the investor only provided the remaining 10 per cent of the funds.

In September 1991, the investor invested USD 10 million in a PERLS issued by the General Electric Corporation. The structure of the investment was that it was short in Swiss francs and long in Italian lira. The bank entered into a six-month repurchase contract with the defendant. Under the terms of the repurchase contract the investor would immediately sell the investment to the bank, but will buy it back in six months time for the same price plus interest calculated at six per cent per annum. In March 1992, the investor invested a further USD 10 million in a second PERLS issued by the Finnish Export Credit Limited. The second PERLS was similar to the first except that the redemption formula included an additional soft currency in the form of the Spanish peseta and an additional hard currency in the form of the Japanese yen. In April of the same year, the investor invested in a third PERLS issued by Svensk Export Kredit. It was again issued on similar terms, but this time it was short on Japanese yen, but long on Canadian, Australian and New Zealand dollars.

Shortly before 16 September 1992, the Italian lira and the Spanish peseta were devalued and on that day the pound sterling left the Exchange Rate Mechanism. Anyone who speculated on the basis that the weaker currencies would hold their value against the stronger currencies stood to lose substantially. Not surprisingly, the PERLS lost a considerable part of their

---

[191] See D. L. Horwitz, 'P&G v Bankers Trust: What's All the Fuss?' (1996) 3 *Derivatives Quarterly* 18, 22.
[192] Queen's Bench Division (Commercial Court), 29 January 1998, Longmore J, unreported.

values because they essentially went against the prevailing market wisdom. When the time for repurchase came, the bank informed the investor that it would not be willing to refinance the transaction. The investor refused to meet his repurchase obligations and the bank sold the PERLS at a considerable loss in the market. The bank sued the investor for USD 6.6 million (which represented the difference between the repurchase price and the sale price) plus interest.

Throughout his relationship with the bank, the investor who spoke no English conversed with the bank's trader in Italian. When sued by the bank, the investor argued that he was entitled to rescind the contracts for various misrepresentations made by the bank's trader The misrepresentations included that the transactions were consistent with his investment objectives of conserving capital growth and that the PERLS investment had no unusual or risky features. He also counterclaimed for damages for breach of statutory duty under s. 62(1) of the UK *Financial Services Act* 1986. The Commercial Court found that the bank had breached The Securities Association (TSA) Rule 730.[193] PERLS was not a suitable investment for the investor since it was relatively illiquid. Moreover, the bank's trader did not have reasonable grounds for believing that the investment was suitable for the investor, since he did not know how much the investor had or how much he was prepared to lose.

The court also held that since PERLS were contracts for differences, the bank had failed to send an appropriate risk warning to the investor. The Risk Disclosure Acknowledgement, which the bank asked the investor to sign, was insufficient as no product notes were sent. Even if the product notes were sent, the investor would not have understood them because of his poor command of English. Since PERLS were unsuitable for long term trading, the bank should have warned the investor that the bank might not refinance the investment on the repurchase date. The bank had therefore breached TSA Rule 960, which dealt with the giving of appropriate risk warnings for contracts of differences. The court was satisfied that the investor had relied on the advice given by the bank. If not for the recommendation of the bank's trader, it was unlikely that the investor would have entered into the transactions. The court also believed that had the investor been properly advised of the risks involved, he would not have invested in PERLS. However, the court found no evidence of undue pressure or influence on the investor. The court dismissed the plaintiff's claim as well as the defendant's counterclaim.

The decision is significant for a number of reasons. Firstly, it is the only reported case in which a court in England has allowed a private customer to avoid liability for losses sustained in derivatives trading.[194] Derivatives

---

[193] 'An employee of a firm shall not give investment advice to a private customer ... unless he has reasonable grounds for believing that the advice or transaction is suitable for the customer concerned.'

[194] See P. Hann, 'Morgan Stanley Group v Puglisi: The First Reported Case in which a Private Customer Has Avoided Liability for Losses Sustained in Derivatives Trading' (2000) 6 *Derivatives Use, Trading and Regulation* 467.

litigation in the English courts has generally produced unfavourable results for customers. Secondly, the decision has demonstrated that the court is likely to grant relief where the customer has little experience in the product, regardless of whether the customer is experienced in other business matters.[195] This would suggest that it is not just the inexperienced investor who may recover losses. Even experienced investors may recover their losses, provided they can establish that they had little knowledge of the product. Thirdly, the *Puglisi* case highlights the risk that a bank may face when introducing a new product to a customer, especially if the product is complex and not readily available in the market. It would be easier under these circumstances for the customer to later argue that the customer bought the product in reliance on the bank's recommendation. Lastly, it reinforces the importance of giving the right risks disclosure documents to customers. It is no longer sufficient for banks to merely provide generic risks disclosure statements. They must ensure that they give their customers disclosure statements that specifically address the risks inherent in the products marketed.

3.5.4   Legal Survey

The legal principles governing dealer liability in contract, tort and equity are broadly similar in all the jurisdictions under study. Despite recent political and legal developments, the commercial laws of the jurisdictions under study still rely on English legal principles. Some of these developments include Singapore's introduction of the *Application of English Law Act* 1993 to reduce reliance on English law. Although the legislation put an end to the automatic reception of English statutes, Singapore's commercial law still remains very much based on English commercial law.[196] Another significant legal development was the British handover of Hong Kong to the Chinese Government in July 1997. Despite Hong Kong's present status as a Special Administrative Region of the People's Republic of China, the 1984 Sino-British Joint Declaration guarantees the continuation of the institutions and values of a common law system for 50 years after 1997.

Although at common law, the scope of the dealer's duty is limited, end-users may still find relief under consumer protection legislation. For example, in Australia a bank may be liable for misleading and deceptive conduct under s. 12DA of the *Australian Securities and Commission Act* 1989 (Cth). According to Professor O'Donovan, a failure to warn or explain the risks inherent in a particular transaction may constitute misleading or deceptive conduct where there is a positive duty to offer this advice.[197] A bank may also be liable for misleading and deceptive conduct under s. 12BB if it makes a statement about a future event or expresses an opinion without reasonable grounds. (It should be mentioned here that since July 1998, the Trade Practices Act 1974 (Cth) provisions no longer apply to financial services.)

---

[195]   Id., 471.
[196]   See H. Chan, *The Legal System of Singapore* (Butterworths Asia, 1995), p. 17.
[197]   See O'Donovan, above. n. 146, 45.

It would therefore appear that in Australia, consumer protection legislation could also play an important role in protecting derivatives end-users.

3.5.5 Summary and Comments

Although the *Dharmala* and *Procter & Gamble* cases may have significantly limited the scope of a derivatives dealer's duty to end-users, dealers may still incur liabilities. For example, when a dealer volunteers advice or provides any explanation, the dealer is under a duty to ensure that the advice or explanation is accurate and complete. The recent *Puglisi* decision has demonstrated that the court is willing to enlarge the scope of the dealer's duty in certain circumstances. There the court held that the dealer has a duty not only to recommend suitable investments, but also to ensure that the investment is properly explained and the associated risks disclosed, where the investor is an individual who had no experience in the product in question. Apart from incurring liability under common law, a dealer may also incur liability under consumer protection legislation.

3.6 NETTING ARRANGEMENTS

Netting has gained widespread significance in recent years because of the need to reduce counterparty credit risk, and the desire by banks to comply with capital adequacy requirements without incurring additional capital charges.[198] It has been estimated that the reduction in credit risk as a result of netting can be more than 90 per cent.[199] Netting is most effective in reducing credit risk where a large number of transactions are involved, some of which have a positive value and others a negative value. Following the 1988 Basle Accord, a bank may calculate its notional exposure to a counterparty for capital adequacy purposes on a net basis, if it has entered has entered into a netting by novation agreement with the counterparty.[200] The Basle Accord was amended in June 1994 to include close-out netting agreements, provided certain conditions were fulfilled.[201] However, industry initiatives to extend the benefits of netting beyond bilateral netting arrangements to multilateral netting arrangements have not received any supervisory response.

---

[198] For a discussion of the benefits of netting see, for example, R. Cranston, 'Netting and Settlement' in G. Ferrarini (ed.), *Prudential Regulation of Banks and Securities Firms* (Kluwer Law International, London, 1995), pp. 197–198.

[199] See P. R. Wood, *Title Finance, Derivatives, Securitisations, Set-off and Netting* (Sweet & Maxwell, London, 1995), para. 10-2.

[200] For information on the Basle Accord, see M. Hall, 'The Revised Supervisory Treatment of Netting and Potential Exposure for Off-Balance Sheet Items under the Basle Capital Accord' (1996) 11 JIBL 93.

[201] See T. Shea 'The Basle Committee Consultative Papers on Netting' (1993) 8 JIBL 314.

3.6.1   Definition of Netting

Although the expression 'netting' is often used interchangeably with 'set-off', netting in many cases involves more than just set-off.[202] Set-off refers to the 'discharge of reciprocal obligations to the extent of the smaller obligation.'[203] For example, if A owes B $500 and B in turn owes A $200, A sets off the $200 against the $500 with the result that A pays B only $300. Set-off confers a number of advantages, which makes it particularly attractive. Assuming A is an unsecured creditor, set-off effectively allows A to stands ahead of B's other unsecured creditors. Set-off also eliminates the multiplicity of payments where two parties have entered into a number of transactions. If set-off was allowed, instead of A having to make several payments to B and vice-versa, only one payment representing the net balance would need to be made.

The Netting Sub-Committee established by the Australian Companies and Securities Advisory Committee to review the law relating to the netting of financial transactions defined 'netting' as follows:

The expression netting is a commercial expression which applies when parties owe quantified or quantifiable obligations to one another. The obligations are "netted-out" when those obligations are replaced by a single obligation calculated by deducting the value of the smaller obligations from the value of the larger obligations.[204]

There are several other definitions of 'netting', depending on the context in which it is used.[205] In financial markets, netting is used in a wide sense to denote the totality of contractual arrangements designed to produce or facilitate contractual set-off.'[206] Most derivatives agreements would therefore provide that, in the event of a counterparty default, the non-defaulting party would be able to accelerate and terminate all outstanding transactions and net the market values of the transactions so that only a single amount is owed to, or owed by, the non-defaulting party.

Netting arrangements may be classified according to whether they are bilateral or multilateral. Bilateral netting may be further sub-divided into payment or settlement netting; continuous account netting; netting by

---

[202]   See Wood, above n. 199, para. 10-2.
[203]   Id., para. 6-2.
[204]   See Netting Sub-Committee of the Companies and Securities Advisory Committee, *Netting in Financial Markets Transactions*, Background Paper ('Netting Background Paper') (December 1996), p. 5.
[205]   See, for example, Y. L. Chin, 'Set-off in Modern Banking' in G. Burton (ed.), *Directions in Finance Law* (Butterworths, Sydney, 1990), p. 82, note 22: ' "Netting-off" is financial jargon for setting one amount against another in foreign exchange and other similar contracts.'; S. J. Phillips & B. W. J. Rutherford, 'Netting—The Shape of Things to Come' (1994) 9 JIBFL 174: Netting means 'the reduction of credit risk between two parties by offsetting mutual obligations either as a result of a right under either common law or statutory rules or contractual rights.'; Wood, above n. 199, para. 10-1: ' ... netting is the ability to set off reciprocal claims on the insolvency of a counterparty'.
[206]   See R. M. Goode, *Principles of Corporate Insolvency Law* (Sweet & Maxwell, London, 1997), p . 173.

novation; and close-out or default netting.[207] The last two types of bilateral netting arrangements are most relevant for derivatives transactions. Under netting by novation, the parties agree that any new obligations between them in respect of a specified product are automatically amalgamated with all other obligations for the same. At any one time, there is only one amount owing, which represents the balance of the account between the parties. The main drawback of this arrangement is that it does not entitle a party to net its exposure across a range of derivatives. Under close-out netting, the parties agree that on the occurrence of a specified event of default, such as the commencement of winding up of one party, the unmatured obligations would be terminated, valued and netted. Close-out netting is the more favoured form of netting arrangement as it can cover a much wider range of transactions.

Unlike bilateral netting, multilateral netting, involves more than two parties. Multilateral netting has been defined as a system under which:

[M]arket participants agree that, not only will bilateral claims between mutual counterparties be netted out, but also that all claims owed between one party and all other counterparties are to be netted so that each party owes or is owed only a single balance to or by the rest of the market.[208]

Although multilateral netting exists in a number of contexts, its most common application is to payment systems.[209] Multilateral payment netting may be achieved through the use of either an agency clearing organisation or a counterparty clearing organisation.[210] Under the first kind of arrangement, the parties agree that the clearing organisation will settle their mutual payments obligations by acting as their agent. However, under the second arrangement, the clearing organisation acts as a principal. All payment obligations are owed by or to the clearing organisation. Most derivatives exchanges use the second type of arrangement to achieve multilateral netting.

3.6.2   Effectiveness of Netting

It is widely accepted that English law favours insolvency set-off.[211] Three broad principles govern the application of this rule and its bankruptcy

---

[207]   For a description of each type of netting arrangement, see Netting Background Paper, above n. 204, pp. 6–7.
[208]   See Wood, above n. 199, para. 12-12.
[209]   Ibid.
[210]   For a description of each type of clearing arrangement, see Netting Background Paper, above n. 204, pp. 8–9.
[211]   The right of set-off in company liquidations is found in rule 4.90 of the *Insolvency Rules* 1986 (UK), which provides as follows:

(1)   This Rule applies where, before the company goes into liquidation, there have been mutual credits, mutual debts or other mutual dealings between the company and any creditor of the company proving or claiming to prove for a debt in liquidation.
(2)   An account shall be taken of what is due from each party to the other in respect of the mutual dealings, and the sums due from one party shall be set off against the sums due from the other.

equivalent.[212] First, insolvency set-off is mandatory and cannot be excluded by agreement. Second, insolvency set-off is self-executing and operates automatically from the point of liquidation. Third, the courts look at post-liquidation events to determine that state of account as at the date of liquidation. Generally, insolvency set-off is unlikely to pose a problem in English law provided the claims on both sides are mutual but independent, and capable of quantification.[213]

Academics and lawyers have been debating the effectiveness of netting for some time. Despite widespread recognition of the benefits of netting, doubts continue to exist regarding its effectiveness in the event of insolvency. In common law jurisdictions, the crucial questions are whether netting arrangements are encompassed by the notion of 'set-off', and if so, what happens if they purport to extend the circumstances in which set-off is permitted to occur.[214] If the netting arrangements do not amount to 'set-offs', the courts might strike them down. This is a serious concern among dealers as it is only in the event of insolvency that it is crucial for netting arrangements to be valid. Not surprisingly, a number of countries including Australia, the US, Canada and Ireland have introduced legislation to clarify the netting laws. The fact that clarifying legislation has been thought appropriate suggests that there are legitimate concerns about adverse rulings by the courts, which may have disastrous consequences for high value derivatives transactions.

In the case of bilateral netting, there are a number of legal issues, which have caused concern.[215] One of them is that netting may be contrary to the public policy against divestment on insolvency. It is widely accepted that under common law, a contract may be struck down as contrary to public policy if it constitutes an attempt to evade the pari passu or creditor equality principle. This principle was upheld in an English case, *British Eagle International Air Lines Ltd v Compagnie Nationale Air France*.[216] In that case, a number of airlines, including the plaintiffs and defendants, were members of the International Air Transport Association (IATA). IATA had established

---

(3) Sums due from the company to another party shall not be included in the account taken under paragraph (2) if that other party had notice at the time they became due that a meeting of creditors had been summoned under section 98 or (as the case may be) a petition for the winding up of the company was pending.

(4) Only the balance (if any) of the account is provable in the liquidation. Alternatively (as the case may be) the amount shall be paid to the liquidator as part of the assets.

[212] See Goode, above n. 206, pp. 185–187, adopting the analysis of Lord Justice Hoffman in *MS Fashions Ltd v Bank of Credit and Commerce International S A* [1993] ch. 425 at 432–433.
[213] See *National Westminister Bank Ltd v Halesowen Presswork and Assemblies Ltd* [1972] AC 785.
[214] See McCracken, op. cit. n. 17, p. 166. See also Cranston, above n. 198, p. 202: 'A few jurisdictions look on it [close-out netting] with disfavour because it prevents the liquidator or trustee in bankruptcy from swelling the assets with profitable contracts, to be available for creditors generally. There is also a problem in jurisdictions with a "midnight hour rule", i.e. one which invalidates all transactions beginning from midnight of the day prior to the insolvency. Elsewhere it seems that it is only transactions after the commencement of the insolvency which are at risk.'
[215] For a detailed treatment of each of these issues, see Netting Background Paper, above n. 204, pp. 43–57.
[216] [1975] 1 WLR 758.

a clearinghouse for its members to facilitate monthly settlement of their mutual debts. When British Eagle went into liquidation it was a net debtor of the clearing organisation. However, had the positions of all the members been considered separately, some of the other member airlines would have been net debtors of British Eagle. The liquidator of British Eagle sued one of the member airlines for recovery of the net amount. The trial judge dismissed the action, which was affirmed by the Court of Appeal, but the plaintiffs appealed. Reversing the decisions of the trial judge and the Court of Appeal, the House of Lords held (by a majority of three to two) that the clearing house arrangement was contrary to public policy as it contravened s. 302 of the then *Companies Act* 1948 which provided for the pari passu treatment of unsecured creditors.[217]

Another source of concern is that the 'single contract' approach taken in some master agreements may not be able to prevent the liquidator of a failed counterparty from 'cherry picking'.[218] The rationale behind the 'single contract' approach is that all transactions entered into pursuant to the master agreement are treated as a single contract. However, it has been pointed out that the liquidator's power is to disclaim contractual rights rather than the contract itself, and it is arguable that each transaction constitutes contractual rights for the purposes of disclaimer.[219] A third source of concern is that if the rights and obligations were not mutual between the parties, the provisions of the netting agreement would not be effective. Any form of alienation of interests such as an assignment of contractual interests may have an adverse effect on netting arrangements.

Although broadly similar issues affect multilateral netting, there are a number of additional issues, which may not be relevant for bilateral netting.[220] It is common for the rules of a clearing organisation to provide for novation of the open contracts after they have been registered at the end of the day.[221] The object of novation is to create a bilateral relationship between the clearing organisation and each market participant. But if the participant becomes insolvent prior to the completion of the clearing process, the benefit of statutory set-off will not apply as there is no mutuality. Difficulties may also arise when payments are of a different character. For example, the rules of the clearing organisation may provide for the netting of margins, premiums, as well as settlement amounts. Some of these obligations or entitlements may be owed or held by the market participant as trustee. Once again the clearing organisation may be unable to take advantage of statutory set-off because of the absence of mutuality.

---

[217] Id. at 780, per Lord Cross.
[218] 'Cherry picking' refers to the ability of the liquidator to disclaim unprofitable contracts and to enforce only the profitable ones.
[219] See Netting Background Paper, above n. 204, p. 52.
[220] For an analysis of the legal issues involved in multi party agreements in the Australian context, see D. Everett, 'Multi Party Set-off Agreements' in J. P. G. Lessing and J. F. Corkery (eds), *Corporate Insolvency Law* (The Taxation & Corporate Research Centre 1995, Gold Coast, 1995), p. 156.
[221] See, for example, *Rules of the Singapore International Monetary Exchange* (March 1990), r. 803.

3.6.3   Legal Survey

The insolvency laws of Australia, Malaysia, Singapore and Hong Kong have a common heritage. They may be described as 'netting-friendly' jurisdictions since they are likely to adopt traditional English attitudes, which favour netting.[222] These jurisdictions regard it as inequitable that the insolvent should be able to insist on performance when the insolvent itself has refused to perform.[223] The weight of legal opinion in Singapore and Malaysia suggest that netting arrangements would not offend either the pari passu rule or be vulnerable to 'cherry-picking'.[224] Although New Zealand has broadly similar insolvency laws, its statutory management regimes[225] appear to undermine the efficacy of netting arrangements.[226] They impose a moratorium on the debtor's affairs when there is a substantial risk to the New Zealand financial system or where it is deemed in the public interest to do so.[227] One of the actions that the moratorium prevents is the exercise of a right of set-off, which may result in a successful challenge of any payment of a close-out amount under a netting agreement.[228] This prohibition on the exercise of the rights of set-off is therefore problematic for derivatives counterparties in New Zealand. The Reserve Bank of New Zealand issued a discussion paper on netting in August 1996 which among other things proposed the introduction of netting legislation that would amend New Zealand's insolvency set-off and statutory management laws to ensure the effectiveness of contractual netting arrangements.[229] However, none of the jurisdictions surveyed, with the exception of Australia, have enacted legislation which specifically deals with netting arrangements.

The Australian Parliament enacted the *Payments and Systems Netting Act* 1998 (Cth), and it came into effect on 2 July 1998. It not only validates bilateral close-out netting and market netting contracts, but also the existing

---

[222]   See, for example, Wood, above n. 199, para. 13-3; Allen & Gledhill, 'Enforceability Survey – Singapore' in Global Derivatives Study Group, *Derivatives: Practices and Principles, Appendix II: Legal Enforceability: Survey of Nine Jurisdictions* (Group of Thirty, Washington DC, July 1993), pp. 287–288.

[223]   See Wood, above n. 199, p. 165.

[224]   See, for example, Tan, above n. 48, p. 34: 'It is submitted that settlement netting is enforceable because it does not violate the fraudulent preference rule under s. 329 of the Companies Act because it does not improve the position of the creditor …. Although the legal position is not exactly clear, it is submitted that close-out netting under the ISDA does not violate the pari passu rule because it achieves the same result under the mandatory insolvency envisaged in the Companies Act. It is further submitted that close-out netting does not infringe the undue preference rule because the intention under the ISDA Master provisions is to reduce credit risk and not to give undue preference over other creditors.'

[225]   Statutory management may be invoked under Part III of the *Corporations (Investigation and Management) Act* 1989, which is of general application, or Part V of the *Reserve Bank of New Zealand Act* 1989, which applies only to registered banks. This chapter is primarily concerned with the former as the latter applies to a limited number of counterparties.

[226]   See J. Ross and Others, 'Overview of Netting in New Zealand' (1997) 8 JBFLP 149, 150.

[227]   See *Corporations (Investigation and Management) Act* 1989, s. 42(1).

[228]   Id., s. 42(1)(h).

[229]   See Ross and Others, above n. 226, 149.

multilateral netting arrangements used by Australian financial institutions.[230] The legislation is only applicable where Australian law governs the contract, or regulates the insolvency of one of the parties. In view of the significant interest in the validity of close-out netting agreements, it would be useful to make a number of comments about those aspects of the legislation that deal with these agreements. In essence, the legislation states that the termination provisions of a netting close-out contract are to apply according to their terms.[231] It does not list specific forms of financial contracts that fall within the definition of 'close-out netting contract'. Both monetary and non-monetary obligations are covered by the legislation. The provisions of the netting agreement can still operate, notwithstanding any breach of the agreement relating to the disposal of rights or the creation of any interests. It is useful to note that the legislation only applies to legally enforceable netting contracts. The legislation is a welcome relief to many market participants and may even encourage the greater use of derivatives.

3.6.4   Summary and Comments

Contractual netting arrangements offer substantial benefits to counterparties, yet there are doubts whether such arrangements would be effective if one or both counterparties are insolvent. There are fears that contractual netting arrangements may be wider than insolvency set-off and may be unenforceable on the grounds that they offend against public policy. Although the weight of legal opinion suggests that contractual netting arrangements may survive the insolvency of one or both counterparties, it is best that any remaining uncertainty be removed through legislation. Many countries including Australia, Canada, Ireland and the United States have introduced legislation to clarify the effectiveness of netting arrangements.[232] The introduction of similar legislation in New Zealand, Malaysia, Singapore and Hong Kong would provide greater certainty for market participants.[233] In view of the international nature of derivatives transactions, it is in the best interests of counterparties everywhere that there is greater uniformity in the national laws governing netting.

3.7   CONCLUSION

The widespread usage of derivatives has raised a number of legal issues. These issues have highlighted two important developments. The first

---

[230]   See *Payment Systems and Netting Act* 1998, s. 5 for definition of 'close-out netting contract' and 'market netting contract'.
[231]   See P. Willis, 'Set-off and Netting' in Mallesons Stephen and Jaques (eds) *Australian Finance Law* (4th edn, LBC, Sydney, 1999), p. 699.
[232]   For the current status of netting legislation in various countries, see International Swap and Derivatives Association Website <www.isda.org/c6.html>.
[233]   An alternative solution suggested by Professor McCracken involves structuring a netting arrangement as a combination instead of a set-off. See McCracken, above n. 17, pp. 167–168.

development is that financial innovation will continue to outstrip legal developments. This has been brought into sharp focus by the introduction of financial derivatives in the early 1970s. The second development is that there is an increasing tendency to rely on legislation instead of the courts to resolve these issues. Relying on the courts for guidance is not only slow but also expensive. Although there is now greater legal certainty, there are still a number of issues that require clarification. Pending clarification of the remaining areas of uncertainty, counterparties need to adopt various measures to minimise the risk of litigation. For example, dealers should carefully select their counterparties and ensure that they clearly define their roles. In view of the trans-border nature of derivatives transactions, greater harmonisation of legal rules will facilitate development of the global derivatives market. One area in particular which deserves greater attention is the enforceability of netting agreements. In view of the many benefits that may be derived from netting, regulators in different jurisdictions should work together to ensure the adoption of more standardised rules.

4. Regulation of Derivatives

4.1 INTRODUCTION

In recent years there has been considerable discussion about the regulation of derivatives. Yet a survey of some of the leading legal texts on derivatives law reveals that little has been written about the subject. This is in part due to the rapidly changing nature of derivatives regulation which makes it difficult for anyone to keep abreast of all the latest developments. However, as Dr Hudson has pointed out, it is not possible to study the legal problems arising from the use of derivatives without also considering the regulatory frameworks that surrounds these instruments.[1] There is no clear separation between the substantive law and the regulation of derivatives. Sometimes there is overlap between the two and one good example is in the area of dealers' duties to end-users. This chapter will attempt to fill this gap, despite the risk that this work may be out-of-date even before it is published. It will examine how derivatives are regulated in Australia, New Zealand, Singapore, Malaysia and Hong Kong (the jurisdictions under study). A study of how derivatives are regulated in these jurisdictions will provide a useful introduction to how derivatives are regulated in other common law jurisdictions. Before proceeding to examine how derivatives are regulated it would be appropriate to outline the scope of this chapter.

The expression 'derivatives' encompasses a wide range of financial instruments and includes options over securities and even some forms of collective investments.[2] As most jurisdictions have adopted product-based regulation, derivatives are often regulated under more than one regulatory scheme. For example, in the majority of common law jurisdictions, derivatives are regulated as 'securities' as well as 'futures contracts'.[3] Although the regulatory

---

[1] See A. Hudson, 'The Law on Financial Derivatives' (Sweet & Maxwell, London, 1998), p. 329.
[2] In *Carragreen Currency Corporations Pty Ltd v Corporate Affairs Commission* (*NSW*) 11 ACL 298, the court held that some derivatives could constitute prescribed interests.
[3] For instance, in Australia, derivatives such as warrants, stock options and collective investments are regulated as securities under Chapter 7 of the *Corporations Law*. Exchange-traded derivatives such as eligible commodity agreements, adjustment agreements, and futures options are regulated as futures contracts under Chapter 8 of the *Corporations Law*.

schemes for both products are broadly comparable, they are significant differences. Nevertheless, it would be impractical to examine how derivatives are
regulated under both the securities and futures laws. Since most of the regulatory debate has centred on the legal framework for futures contracts, this
chapter will focus on futures regulation. However, to illustrate the differences
in regulatory treatment, some discussion will be devoted at the end of this
chapter to how derivatives are regulated under existing securities laws.
Although strictly speaking the term 'derivatives regulation' is broader in
scope than the term 'futures regulation', both terms will be used interchangeably in this chapter. The existing laws of the jurisdictions under study make
no reference to 'derivatives, only to 'futures contracts'.

4.2   NATURE OF REGULATION

Prior to discussing the regulation of derivatives, it might be useful to provide an introduction to the nature of regulation. Defining 'regulation' is not
as simple as it might seem and it has been suggested that there are as many
as five different meanings.[4] Despite the different usage of the term 'regulation' it is possible to extract a core conception. According to Professor
Prosser, regulation consists of public interventions, which affect the operations of markets through command and control.[5] Understandably, regulation is often viewed as having interference as its central element.[6] It has
been suggested that the origins of financial regulation may be found in the
political mistrust of the financial community.[7] This was clearly the case in
the United States where mistrust of the activities of the East Coast financiers
spawned not only a great deal of rhetoric but legislation.[8] Generally, economic and political theory support regulation in terms of enhancing the
public interest.[9] The 'public interest' theory of regulation is based on the
belief that individuals acting on their own self-interest without regulation
would take actions that are more damaging than beneficial to society as a
whole.[10] However, not all subscribe to this 'public interest' theory and econ-
omists like Stigler, Posner and others belonging to the Chicago School generally believe that regulation is undesirable.[11]

---

[4]   See T. Prosser, *Law and the Regulators* (Clarendon Press, Oxford, 1997), p. 4. See also,
A. Ogus, *Regulation: Legal Form and Economic Theory* (Clarendon Press, Oxford, 1994), pp. 1–4.
[5]   Ibid.
[6]   See E. J. Swan, 'Competition for Futures and Derivatives Markets: The Role of Regulation' in
E. J. Swan (ed.), *Derivative Instruments* (Graham & Trotman/Martinus Nijhof, London, 1994),
p. 88.
[7]   See J. Kay, 'The Forms of Regulation' in A. Seldon (ed.), *Financial Regulation—or Over-
Regulation?* (Institute of Economics Affairs, 1988, London), p. 35.
[8]   Ibid.
[9]   See G. J. Benston, 'International Regulatory Coordination of Banking', in J. Fingleton and
D. Schoenmaker (eds), *The Internationalisation of Capital Markets and the Regulatory Response*
(Graham & Trotman, London, 1992), p. 199.
[10]   Ibid.
[11]   See D. Gowland, *The Regulation of Financial Markets in the 1990s* (Edward Elgar, Hants,
England, 1990), p. 2.

The main focus of financial regulation has always been the regulation of financial dealings and not the rights and obligation of the particular financial arrangement which continues to be determined by the general law.[12] There are some commentators who see financial regulation as having three main goals.[13] The first goal is the prevention of monopolistic exploitation. It is argued that monopolies are unhealthy because they hinder competition and encourage unhealthy pricing practices. The second main goal of regulation is the protection of retail clients as they are regarded as incapable of looking after their own affairs. Their lack of financial sophistication is exacerbated by the asymmetrical nature of market information. The third goal of financial regulation is the maintenance of systemic stability. It is widely believed that the failure of a single financial institution may have a systemic dimension.

Financial regulation is predominantly concerned with client protection and systemic stability and less with the prevention of monopolistic exploitation. Client protection is achieved through prudential regulation, conduct of business regulation and the application of different rules for wholesale and retail clients, while the maintenance of systemic stability is achieved though systemic regulation.[14] The regulation of derivatives exchanges raises additional issues such as market integrity. Market integrity is concerned with the maintenance of a fair, transparent and efficient market. Since regulation is mainly directed at exchange-traded derivatives, market integrity is an therefore an important objective of derivatives regulation.

There are two broad forms of financial regulation: statutory regulation and self-regulation. Statutory regulation refers to regulation that is externally imposed, as opposed to self-regulation, which is internally imposed. The structure of regulation may be organised along three main lines: institutional, functional and objective.[15] Under the institutional approach, regulation is directed at the type of financial institution, regardless of the mix of business undertaken by the institution. The functional approach focuses on the nature of business conducted, regardless of the type of institution involved. Under the objective approach, the regulatory structure is built around the objectives of regulation. For example, regulation and supervision may be structured on the basis of systemic stability and consumer protection, with separate agencies responsible for each broad objective. More than one approach may be adopted at any one time. For example, it is not

---

[12] See J. Fisher and J. Bewsey, *The Law of Investor Protection* (Sweet & Maxwell, London, 1997), p. 6.

[13] See C. Goodhart and Others, *Financial Regulation: Why, How and Where Now?* (Routledge, London, 1998), p. 5. For an alternative perspective of the role of financial regulation see, P. Fleuriot, 'Financial Regulation as the Safeguard of Balances in a Global Context' in A. Jeunemaître (ed.), *Financial Markets Regulation* (Macmillan Press, London, 1997), pp. 34–35: The role of financial regulation is to maintain four main balances: between economic interest and financial interest, between minority and majority shareholders, between international and national financial activity, and between rules and business freedom.

[14] See Goodhart and Others, id., pp. 4–9.

[15] For a detailed discussion of the three broad approaches see Goodhart and Others, above n. 13, p. 144 et seq.

unusual for banks to be regulated on an institutional basis for systemic and prudential reasons, and on a functional basis for conduct of business purposes. In some jurisdictions, one mega-agency is solely responsible for financial regulation, while in other jurisdictions more than one agency may be involved. Although statutory regulation is often seen as a counterbalance to agency capture in self-regulation, it is sometimes viewed as an impediment to market efficiency.[16]

Self-regulation[17] refers to either the delegation of rule making or the enforcement of rules to a private sector body, such as a derivatives exchange or stock exchange.[18] Under self-regulation the government usually provides support to the private sector body and only intervenes when the system fails. Self-regulation may be further categorised into 'voluntary self-regulation' and 'compulsory self-regulation' (sometimes also referred to as 'statutory self-regulation'). The Australian Code of Banking Practice is an example of voluntary self-regulation, while the regulation of exchange-traded derivatives in New Zealand is a case of compulsory self-regulation. One of the advantages of self-regulation is that it places greater focus on the needs of the industry and its customers. Another advantage of self-regulation is the flexibility it possesses over a detailed prescriptive regime. A common criticism of self-regulation is that it gives rise to 'regulatory capture', which may be explained in terms of effective control of the regulator by the regulated.[19] Regulatory capture is present at the outset for self-regulation as the regulators find it difficult to distinguish between the interests of the regulated and the interests of the public.[20]

While statutory or externally imposed regulation offers a number of benefits, it also raises a number of issues. One of the issues is that it increases the costs of doing business, which are passed on to the consumer. Much has been written, for example, about the outrageous costs of complying with the regulatory system established by the *Financial Services Act* 1986.[21] Since it is easier to calculate the costs than the benefits of regulation no account is taken of the savings achieved by regulation.[22] This leads to the perception that the costs of regulation far outweigh the benefits of regulation. The problem is accentuated by the absence of a reliable method of calculating the costs of compliance and the tendency to treat all firms alike. In 1995, a report funded by the UK IFA Promotions Limited on financial services regulation in the independent financial adviser sector estimated the annual

---

[16] See C. Wright, 'Financial Markets Regulation: The Role of a Separate Competition Authority' in A. Jeunemaître (ed.), *Financial Markets Regulation* (Macmillan Press, London, 1997), p. 46.
[17] Self-regulation is also sometimes referred to as 'practitioner regulation'.
[18] See Fisher and Bewsey, above n. 12, p. 53.
[19] See Kay, above n. 7, p. 35.
[20] Ibid.
[21] See R. Collins, 'Identifying the True Costs of Compliance: A Financial Institution's Perspective' (1997) 1 *Journal of Financial Regulation and Compliance* 11.
[22] See J. R. Franks & Others, 'The Direct and Compliance Costs of Financial Regulation' in E. J. Swan (ed.), *Issues in Derivative Instruments* (Kluwer Law international, The Hague, 1999), p. 161.

incremental compliance costs at an incredible GBP 330 million.[23] The estimated cost of compliance was calculated by multiplying the time spent on regulation by the opportunity hourly earning rate of an independent financial advisor. The use of such unrealistic approaches to the calculation of regulatory compliance costs is not only misleading but distorts the case for regulation.[24]

Apart from the costs of compliance, another issue is the impact of regulation on competition. The difficulty of complying with regulations and the high costs of compliance could drive business offshore. It is widely acknowledged that regulatory arbitrage was largely responsible for the creation of the Eurodollar market. Factors such as the introduction of Regulation Q, which placed a ceiling on interest paid by US banks caused US investors to seek higher returns in the Euromarkets where interest rates were not regulated.[25] There is also empirical evidence, which suggests that the costs of regulatory compliance are an important determinant of whether a firm does business in one particular market. In March 1993, the Corporation of London published a report prepared by the London Business School which concluded that the United Kingdom was a much more attractive location for securities and derivatives trading than the United States in view of its lower costs of regulation.[26] Conversely, investors may be attracted to a particular market because the laws are either lax or favour them. It is common knowledge that offshore tax-free havens have been successful in attracting investors because they offer better returns and less regulatory controls. Similarly, Swiss banks have in the past been successful in attracting depositors because of their strict secrecy rules.

The difficulty of securing compliance is another vexing issue related to regulation. It is widely acknowledged that while regulations deter certain types of behaviour or activities, they do not themselves secure compliance. Unless there are mechanisms in place to ensure compliance, regulations would serve no useful purpose. The collapse of the Singapore subsidiary of Barings substantiates this point. There were regulatory rules in place, which if complied with, would have led to the discovery of the fraud much earlier. However, there was no effective mechanism in place to ensure compliance with the rules. Related to the issue of non-compliance is the issue of 'creative compliance'. 'Creative compliance' has been defined as 'complying with rules without complying in substance, meeting the letter but not the spirit of the law.'[27] It refers to the use of innovative techniques, which on the face comply with the law but in reality, undermines the policy behind it. A good example of creative compliance is the practice in the past of companies

---

[23] Id., 12.
[24] Ibid.
[25] See G. R. Walker and M. A. Fox, 'The Securities Industry and International Financial Integration' (1997) 7 *Canterbury Law Review* 239, 242.
[26] See Swan, above n. 6, pp. 121–122: The findings revealed that the cost of regulation, borne by industry, was between USD 150–500 less per industry employee in the UK than in the US.
[27] See D. McBarnet and C. Whelan, 'International Corporate Finance and the Challenge' in J. Fingleton and D. Schoenmaker (eds), *The Internationalisation of Capital Markets and the Regulatory Response* (Graham & Trotman, London, 1992), p. 135.

using 'off-balance sheet' financing, to avoid reporting on the true extent of their borrowings.

Externally imposed regulation has the potential to create moral hazard because it gives the impression that less care is needed not only on the part of the investors but also on the part of the regulated institutions. It has been suggested that the regulator is perversely exposed to its own performance.[28] The more successful that the regulator is in preventing failure, the more likely that investors would regard the regulator as guaranteeing the safety and conduct of the regulated institutions. Many investors fail to realise that it is impossible for regulation to eliminate risk of loss entirely. Not surprisingly almost every market failure is accompanied by a call for more or better regulation. For the majority of investors regulation is a free good and there can never be too much of a free good.[29] Yet this is not entirely correct as the costs and burdens imposed by regulation could far outweigh the benefits.

4.3   DEVELOPMENT OF DERIVATIVES REGULATION

Prior to discussing the development of derivatives regulation in the jurisdictions under study, it would be useful to make a number of preliminary comments. Firstly, in most jurisdictions, self-regulation preceded statutory regulation, suggesting that self-regulation was not successful. Secondly, derivatives regulation in almost all jurisdictions is preoccupied with investor protection and market integrity. This emphasis on investor protection and market stability appeared to stem from a high level of mistrust of derivatives. Thirdly, derivatives regulation in most jurisdictions tended to mirror securities regulation in terms of structure and contents.

4.3.1   Australia

In its early years, the Australian futures industry operated on a self-regulatory basis. It was only in 1979 that the *Futures Markets Act* (NSW) was passed. The Act provided that the Minister might approve a body corporate as a futures exchange if its business rules satisfied specified criteria.[30] In addition, the Minister was empowered to disallow any business rules promulgated by the body corporate.[31] The Act gave the Corporate Affairs Commission (CAC) supervisory powers over the futures industry. For instance, CAC had the right of access to all records kept by the exchange and the clearinghouse.[32] The Act confirmed that futures contracts made at a

---

[28]   See Goodhart and Others, above n. 13, p. 15.
[29]   Id., p. 62.
[30]   *Futures Markets Act* (NSW), s. 3.
[31]   Id., s. 4.
[32]   Id., s. 5.

futures market maintained by a futures exchange were not gaming or wagering contracts.[33] In doing so it laid to rest concerns regarding the legality of futures contracts. It has been suggested by some commentators that this may have been the primary intention of the Act.[34] The Act had only nine sections and was very limited in scope when compared to the existing legislation. One of the Act's main drawbacks was that it did not give the exchange any control over non-members trading in futures contracts or members trading in futures contracts over-the-counter.[35]

By the early 1980s, a number of factors had emerged which created a favourable climate for the introduction of legislation on a national scale. These factors included the growing realisation that the futures industry was an integral part of the Australian financial industry, widespread concern about the lack of consumer protection, and the emergence of the Sydney Futures Exchange (SFE) as an international futures exchange.[36] The *Report of the Inquiry into the Australian Financial System* (Campbell Report) recommended the adoption of a national approach to the regulation of futures exchanges comparable to that applying to stock exchanges.[37] One of the principal concerns at that time was that state legislation would result in the futures market being relocated in another state. Another concern was that the exchange would be vulnerable to improper market practices such as market manipulation. Comprehensive regulation on a national level was therefore needed to maintain investor confidence and market integrity.

The exchange, surprisingly, appeared firmly in favour of the introduction of national legislation. In its submission on the second exposure draft of the Futures Industry Bill 1985, SFE expressed its support for the proposed legislation in the following terms:

The exchange strongly supports the implementation of the Bill at an early date and would not wish enactment of the Bill to be delayed. The Exchange believes that it is important that the industry is, and is seen to be, appropriately regulated and the Exchange is ready to perform its role in the co-regulatory process.[38]

In the middle of 1986, the Commonwealth Government of Australia enacted the *Futures Industry Act* and by June 1987, the Act and its supporting State and Territory Codes were operational throughout Australia. The *Futures Industry Code* (as the Act and its supporting Codes were collectively called) was the first comprehensive legislation to regulate the Australian futures industry. The *Futures Industry Code* remained in operation until Chapter 8 of the Corporations Law replaced it in June 1991. Chapter 8 substantially re-enacted the provisions of the *Futures Industry Code*.

---

[33] Id., s. 7.
[34] See J. O'Sullivan, 'Derivatives—A Survey of the Law and Practice' (1994) 5 JBFLP 89, 101.
[35] See J. S. Currie, *Australian Futures Regulation* (Longman, Melbourne, 1994), pp. 30–31.
[36] Ibid.
[37] See Treasury, *Australian Financial System: The Final Report of the Committee of Inquiry* (Campbell Report), (AGPS, Canberra, September 1981), pp. 367–368.
[38] See the Attorney General, *Explanatory Memorandum to the Futures Industry Bill 1986*, p. 16.

Australian futures legislation follows the general format of the *Securities Industry Act* (SIA) 1980[39] but with the necessary modifications to reflect the distinctness of the futures industry.[40] Some aspects of the legislation are modelled on the Ontario *Commodity Futures Act* 1978, while a number of provisions are based on those found in the US *Commodity Exchange Act*.[41] It was decided at the drafting stage that it would be impractical to incorporate the futures legislation into the SIA. To do so would make the SIA a complex and cumbersome piece of legislation and would fail to take into account the different roles of securities and futures markets. While securities markets are concerned with the transfer of title in property, futures markets facilitate the management of risk.[42] Although the *Corporations Law* is the main legislation, which regulates the futures industry, SFE members are also required to comply with the Business Rules of the exchange.

4.3.2   New Zealand

Prior to the stock market crash of October 1987, New Zealand was one of the best performing financial markets in the world.[43] The October 1987 crash had a disastrous effect on the New Zealand equity and derivatives markets. Trading volumes shrank and public confidence in the markets sank to its lowest.[44] It is widely accepted that the New Zealand stock market sustained a more severe erosion in market capitalisation, decline in company listings, and loss in confidence than other developed markets.[45] One of the main reasons why the October 1987 crash hit the New Zealand so badly was the overheating of the markets caused by excessive lending to the financial sector and market manipulation.[46] These causes were in turn brought about by a number of deficiencies in regulation at that time, and significant among them for the purpose of this chapter was the lack of effective regulation of the derivatives market.[47] While stock market participants

---

[39]   The SIA was the predecessor of Chapter 7 of the *Corporations Law*.

[40]   See the Attorney General, *Explanatory Paper on Exposure Draft of Futures Industry Bill 1985*, p. 10.

[41]   Ibid.

[42]   See the Attorney General, *Explanatory Memorandum to the Futures Industry Bill 1986*, p. 18.

[43]   See K. K. H. Park and S. A. Schoenfeld, *The Pacific Rim Futures and Options Markets* (Heinemann Asia, Singapore, 1994), p. 212.

[44]   See B. Gaynor, 'Securities Regulation in New Zealand: Crisis and Reform' in G. Walker and B. Fisse (eds), *Securities Regulations in Australia & New Zealand* (Auckland, Oxford University Press, 1994), pp. 10–12.

[45]   Id., p. 10; see also, W. Slatyer and E. Carew, *Trading Asia-Pacific Financial Markets* (Allen and Unwin, Sydney, 1993), p. 66.

[46]   See J. Lindroos and G. Walker, 'A Short History of Securities Regulation in New Zealand' in G. Walker and B. Fisse (eds), *Securities Regulation in Australia & New Zealand* (Auckland, Oxford University Press, 1994), p. 75.

[47]   Until the enactment of the *Securities Amendment Act* 1988, only the articles of association and by-laws of the NZFOE governed the derivatives market. See also P. McKenzie, 'Reforming Securities Regulation in New Zealand' in G. Walker and B. Fisse (eds), *Securities Regulation in Australia & New Zealand* (Oxford University Press, Auckland, 1994), p. 37: The self-regulated market attracted a number of fringe operators who came across the Tasman to escape from the provisions of the Australian *Futures Industry Code* 1986. Although the Futures Exchange

operated within a lax regulatory regime, the derivatives market and its participants were largely unregulated.

Since 1984, successive New Zealand governments have chosen light handed regulation of the economy in stark contrast to the previous governments that have adopted more interventionist policies.[48] The share market crash of 1987 provided the impetus for reform of New Zealand's financial markets. In an attempt to address the regulatory deficiencies, the government acting on the New Zealand Securities Commission's report on insider trading, enacted the *Securities Amendment Act* 1988. The Act comprised three parts: Part I introduced legislation requiring disclosure of nominee shareholdings and other interests; Part II provided for private civil remedies for shareholders and public issuers against insiders; and Part III laid the foundation for the regulation of the derivatives industry in New Zealand.

Unlike the Australian legislation, Part III is limited in scope and basically achieves three main objectives:

- it puts into place a self-regulatory structure for the derivatives industry;
- it eliminates the potential for derivatives contracts to be invalidated by the *Gaming and Lotteries Act* 1977, and unenforceable as contracts for gaming and wagering;
- it provides for the making of regulations for the receipt and handling of client money and property by derivatives dealers.[49]

The introduction of derivatives legislation in New Zealand was prompted by concerns about the activities of fringe operators who were reported to have caused the investing public to lose more than $20 million in futures contracts.[50] Since its introduction, Part III has been amended a number of times, but none of the amendments have brought about any substantial changes to the way that derivatives are regulated in New Zealand.

4.3.3 Singapore

Although the trading of financial derivatives in Singapore commenced in September 1984, it was not until the second half of 1986 that legislation was

---

maintained a healthy oversight over its members, these fringe operators (such as Carragreen Currency, Worldwide Futures, Morgan Roche, Togali International, and Global Currencies) who were not members of the Exchange were able to introduce by stealth a number of dubious products to the unsuspecting New Zealand investor. For a contrary opinion, see B. Wilkinson and A. Mandelbaum in G. Walker and B. Fisse (eds), *Securities Regulation in Australia & New Zealand* (Oxford University Press, Auckland, 1994), p. 792: '…corporate and financial collapses have occurred on a large scale in countries such as Australia, Britain, and the United States, which arguably had much more prescriptive regulatory regimes at that time.'

[48] See C. Mulholland and A. Lester, 'Regulation of Derivatives in Australia' in G. Walker and Others (eds), *Securities Regulation in Australia and New Zealand* (2nd edn, LBC, Sydney, 1998), p. 693.

[49] See T. Shreves, 'Secondary Market Regulation in New Zealand' in G. Walker and B. Fisse (eds), *Securities Regulation in Australia & New Zealand*, (Oxford University Press, Auckland, 1994), p. 522.

[50] Ibid.

introduced to regulate the industry. During this hiatus, the industry operated on a self-regulated basis. The Memorandum and Articles of Association of the exchange and the Rules prescribed by the board of directors bound members of the Singapore International Monetary Exchange (SIMEX), as the exchange was then called.[51] All transactions were governed by general law principles and in addition, those members that were companies, were regulated by the legislation governing companies. Exchange members were not subject to any licensing requirements, and breach of the exchange rules did not attract criminal liability.[52]

The Singapore Government's decision to introduce legislation was motivated by a number of factors. In his Second Reading Speech, the Minister of Finance, Dr Richard Hu, explained why it was necessary to introduce legislation:

[T]he Futures Trading Bill is proposed to ensure that our futures market is operated properly and that public interest is preserved. Furthermore, the Bill will provide investors, especially international investors with the confidence that our futures market is operated fairly. In this context, most members will be aware that to benefit from the US experience in futures markets, SIMEX has established a link with the Chicago Mercantile Exchange. As a result of this arrangement, participation from US investors in SIMEX has been relatively heavy. There was a general understanding between the Commodity Futures Trading Commission, the US regulatory authority for futures trading and MAS [Monetary Authority of Singapore] that we would introduce legislation in due course.[53]

The introduction of the *Futures Trading Act* (FTA) 1986[54] marked the end of self-regulation of the derivatives industry in Singapore. Coincidentally, the FTA came into force on 15 August 1986, at about the same time that Australia introduced legislation to govern derivatives trading on a national scale. It should be pointed out that the FTA, which is administered by MAS, only regulates the financial derivatives industry. The commodity derivatives industry is regulated by the *Commodities Futures Act* (CFA), which is administered by the Singapore Trade Development Board. The adoption of different regulatory regimes for derivatives is not as significant as it appears because they both have similar provisions. Arguably, it is only in the administration of the legislation that there may be differences because two different regulatory bodies are involved.

The FTA was modelled on the United States commodity trading legislation because Singapore had to assure American investors that the Singapore laws were similar to the United States laws.[55] Since its introduction, the FTA has undergone two major amendments. On 1 March 1995 the *Futures*

---

[51] See C. J. Chen and C. Ng, 'Financial Futures Markets: Singapore Regulatory Framework— Legal Issues and Problems' in K. L. Koh and Others (eds), *Current Developments in International Securities, Commodities and Financial Futures Markets* (Butterworths, Singapore, 1987), p. 356.
[52] Ibid.
[53] See *Singapore Parliamentary Debates Official Report*, Vol. 47, February–March 1986, p. 1434.
[54] Cap. 116.
[55] See Dr Richard Hu's Second Reading Speech on the Futures Trading Bill, *Singapore Parliamentary Debates Official Report*, Vol. 47, February–March 1986, p. 1440.

Trading (Amendment) Act 1995 was passed with the view to ensure the continued effectiveness of the FTA in the light of market developments. The amending legislation, among other things, extended the scope of the FTA by bringing leveraged foreign exchange trading and electronic trading systems within its regulatory purview. In March 2000, the FTA was further amended by the *Futures Trading (Amendment) Act* 2000. The amendments brought about a number of changes including the introduction of a new Part VIIA to enhance the level of cooperation between MAS and other futures regulators. Other changes included an increase in the fines for trading offences such as bucketing and extending the coverage of the fidelity fund.

4.3.4 Malaysia

Financial derivatives trading in Malaysia is governed by the *Futures Industry Act* (FIA) 1993. The FIA was enacted even before the trading of financial futures trading was introduced. It is structured along the lines of the Malaysian *Securities Industry Act* and has as its main objectives the maintenance of financial integrity, the promotion of market integrity and the ensuring of systemic stability.[56] Since its introduction the FIA has been thrice amended. It was first amended in 1995 by the *Futures Industry (Amendment) Act* to take into account overseas developments. The amendments substituted, amended or deleted 76 of the 109 sections of the Act, and introduced 31 new sections.[57] The Securities Commission explained that the purpose of the amendments was:

[T]o address conceptual issues, changes in both market and regulatory structures, and to reinforce the protection that [FIA] affords to the systemic integrity of the market and to investors.[58]

The FIA was amended a second time to harmonise the regulation of financial and commodity derivatives. Prior to the second amendment exercise, the commodity derivatives industry was governed by the *Commodities Trading Act* 1985 (CTA) and administered by the Commodities Trading Commission, reporting to the Ministry of Primary Commodities, whereas the financial derivatives industry was governed by the FIA and administered by the Securities Commission, reporting to the Minister of Finance. In early 1997, the government decided to rationalise the Malaysian regulatory framework by merging the Securities Commission and the Commodity Trading Commission. This exercise was effected through the *Futures Industry (Amendment and Consolidation) Act* 1997 which came into operation on 7 March 1997. As a consequence, the commodity derivatives industry is now regulated by the FIA, and the functions previously performed by the Commodity Trading Commission now undertaken by the Securities

---

[56] See C. K. Low, *Securities Regulation in Malaysia* (Malayan Law Journal Sdn Bhd, Kuala Lumpur, 1997), p. 176.
[57] See Malaysian Securities Commission, *Annual Report 1995*, p. 57.
[58] Ibid.

Commission. The third amendment exercise took place in November 1998, shortly after the introduction of capital controls in Malaysia. One of the main changes introduced was the prohibition on the setting up of a futures market for the trading of specified contracts within or outside the country.

4.3.5   Hong Kong

Between 1910 and 1977, the only commodities trading in Hong Kong took place on the Chinese Gold and Silver Exchange Society, which was completely self-regulated.[59] Up to 1973 there were no legal constraints on commodity or futures trading in Hong Kong. In June 1973, several parties expressed an interest in setting up commodity exchanges. The Government reacted by announcing a temporary ban on commodity exchanges. In August of the same year, the Government introduced the *Commodity Exchange (Prohibition) Ordinance* to restrict the establishment and operation of commodity exchanges until the enactment of further legislation to regulate the industry.

In 1976, the *Commodity Trading Ordinance* (CTO) was enacted to provide for the establishment of a commodity exchange and to control trading in commodity futures contracts.[60] The CTO, among other things, provided for the establishment of a Commodities Trading Commission (CTC) and vested in the Governor-in-Council powers to authorise a commodity exchange. In 1977, the Hong Kong Commodity Exchange was issued with a licence, which was renewable in five years. When the Government undertook a review of the exchange's licence in 1982, it found that the lacklustre performance of the exchange stemmed largely from severe management problems. It renewed the exchange's licence on condition that the exchange was reorganised and the CTO amended to improve prudential supervision. In 1984 the exchange was reconstituted as the Hong Kong Futures Exchange Limited with government-appointed membership of the board. The CTO was also amended to strengthen prudential regulation of the exchange.

The October 1987 stock market crash uncovered a number of inadequacies in the institutional structure of regulation. It revealed that the CTC, which was set up to oversee the commodity futures industry, had lost effective control. This led to further regulatory changes including the establishment of the Securities and Futures Commission in 1989. At present the laws regulating the trading of derivatives in Hong Kong are found in a number of ordinances and the main ones are:

- *Commodity Trading Ordinance,*[61]
- *The Protection of Investors Ordinance,*[62]
- *Securities and Futures Commission Ordinance,*[63] and

---

[59]   See the Securities Review Committee, *The Operation and Regulation of the Hong Kong Securities Industry* (The Hay-Davidson Report) (Hong Kong, May 1988), p. 399.
[60]   Id., p. 429.
[61]   Cap. 250.
[62]   Cap. 335.
[63]   Cap. 24.

- *Securities and Futures (Clearing Houses) Ordinance,*[64]
- *Leveraged Foreign Exchange Trading Ordinance.*[65]

Since 1989, there has been little change to the laws governing derivatives trading. But some significant changes can be expected in 2001. The existing regulatory arrangements are under review and a new composite securities and futures bill has been drawn up.

4.3.6 Summary and Comments

Except for Hong Kong and Malaysia, the history of derivatives market regulation in all the jurisdictions under study exhibits a remarkable degree of similarity. In the initial years of operation they operated largely on a self-regulatory basis. Statutory regulation followed a number of years later either because self-regulation was inadequate or had failed altogether. Hong Kong and Malaysia are an exception in that legislation preceded the establishment of the exchange. It appears that the main reasons for the introduction of statutory regulation were concern about the lack of investor protection and the prevention of market abuse. Other reasons included linkages with more developed markets and the fear of regulatory arbitrage. Although most of the regulatory schemes have undergone changes since they were first introduced, there have been no major changes to their regulatory approaches.

4.4   REGULATORY SCOPE

This section will examine the regulatory scope of each regulatory scheme. Under product-based legislation, the regulation of a particular agreement depends on whether it falls within the statutory definition of the regulated product. This is because answers to questions like whether a particular market should be authorised, or whether a particular intermediary should be licensed, depend on whether a regulated product is involved. Framing a suitable definition of the regulated product is often a difficult task. If the definition is too narrow it would exclude from regulation those agreements that should be regulated. But, if it is too wide, it may catch those agreements that the regulators had no intention of regulating in the first place. In all the jurisdictions under study, the futures contract definition plays an important role in delineating the regulatory ambit of the legislation.

4.4.1   Australia

Currently, only those financial instruments that fall within the legal definition of 'futures contracts' are regulated under Chapter 8 of the *Corporations*

---

[64]   Cap. 420.
[65]   Cap. 451.

Law. The statutory definition of 'futures contract' is found in s. 72(1), as expanded by s. 9, and includes:

- An 'eligible commodity agreement', which is a deliverable contract since the subject matter is capable of physical delivery;
- An 'adjustment agreement', which is a cash settled contract since physical delivery of the subject is neither permitted nor possible;
- A 'futures option', which is an option over an eligible commodity agreement or adjustment agreement; and
- An 'eligible exchange-traded option', which is an exchange-traded option over a specified commodity or index.

The futures contract definition covers not just futures contracts, but also options over futures contracts. Dr Hains has described the futures contract definition as the 'cornerstone' of the Australian derivatives legislation since it determines the scope of Chapter 8.[66] One of the major shortcomings of the definition is that it can only be properly understood by reference to other definitions. For example, establishing whether an agreement is a futures contract, involves determining whether it is an eligible commodity agreement, an adjustment agreement, a futures option or an eligible exchange-traded option. Not surprisingly, there has been some uncertainty about the width of the futures contract definition. A discussion of some of the Australian cases, which have examined the meaning of 'futures contract', provides an insight into the problem.

The scope of the definition of eligible commodity agreement has been the subject of dispute in a number of legal cases. Under the *Corporations Law*, for an agreement to be an 'eligible commodity agreement', it must be first be a 'commodity agreement.'[67] A 'commodity agreement' is a 'standardised agreement' and involves a 'commodity'. Section 9 defines 'standardised agreements' as agreements of 'the same kind'. No other assistance is provided by legislation. In *Shoreline Currencies (Aust) Pty Ltd v CAC (NSW) & Anor*,[68] Shoreline entered into a number of foreign currency agreements with its clients. Under the agreements Shoreline agreed to act as agent for its clients in the purchase and sale of foreign currency. Although the agreements provided for physical delivery of the foreign currency, the clients could close out the contracts before the agreed delivery date. The Corporate Affairs Commission (CAC), the predecessor of the Australian Securities and Investment Commission, wanted to hold a hearing under s. 82 of the *Futures Industry Code*. Section 82(2) of the Code empowered CAC to make certain orders in relation to the conduct of a person in relation to futures contracts. Shoreline commenced proceedings to restrain CAC conducting the hearing on the grounds that the agreements were not futures contracts

---

[66] See M. G. Hains, 'Futures Contracts: Do They Include Forwards and Swaps?' in G. Walker and B. Fisse (eds) *Securities Regulation in Australia and New Zealand* (Oxford University Press, Auckland, 1994), p. 847.
[67] See s. 9 of the *Corporations Law* for the various definitions.
[68] (1986) 4 ACLC 686.

as they were not standardised agreements. It was argued by Shoreline that the agreements were not standardised as they were not entered into with the same party. However, the court held that the agreements were standardised as long as they dealt with foreign currency purchases 'in the same way' and it did not matter that they were not with the same party.[69]

In *CAC (NSW) v Lombard Nash*,[70] the defendant placed advertisements offering investments that involved foreign currency and commodity trading. Upon payment of a sum in Australian dollars, the client received certain documentation including a 'Confirmation of Leveraged Position', which stated details such as the amount of Australian currency paid, the quantity of foreign currency or commodity involved, and the amount of US dollars required to purchase the foreign currency or commodity. The plaintiff sought interlocutory relief on a number of grounds and one of them was that the defendant was conducting a futures market in breach of s. 45 of the *Futures Industry Code*. The court held that no adjustment agreement was involved, as the clients did not have an obligation to pay further sums of money.[71] Neither was a commodity agreement involved because there was no obligation to make delivery of any commodity.[72] The court took the opportunity to comment on one of the arguments raised that the agreements were not standardised agreements because they were partly written and partly oral. In rejecting this argument, Young J said that:

It seems to me that the words "of the same kind" mean no more than the agreements are substantially the same and refer to the same type or nature of transaction and the words do not exclude cases where there are different terms in a series of agreements or some of the terms are oral ... [73]

Both the above decisions do not provide clear guidance on what would constitute a standardised agreement. They suggest the term 'standardised agreement' is capable of embracing a wide range of agreements. Not surprisingly, using standardisation as a device for differentiating futures contracts from other derivatives contracts has come under a great deal of criticism. Apart from its uncertain scope, the widespread use of standardised market documentation has increased the likelihood that over-the-counter (OTC) derivatives contracts may be construed as standardised agreements.[74] It has been suggested by some commentators that fungibility should replace standardisation as the main criterion for futures contracts. What facilitates trading is the fact that contracts are fungible, not that they are standardised. When contracts are fungible they are perfect substitutes for each other. Standardised contracts, on the other hand, are not necessarily substitutes for each other. Since the great majority of futures contracts

---

[69] Id., at 693.
[70] (1986) 11 ACLR 566.
[71] Id., at 569.
[72] Ibid.
[73] Ibid.
[74] See for example, M. G. Hains, 'FRAs, Swaps, Futures, Options and the Concept of Standardisation' (1990) 5 JIBFL 158.

are closed-out before settlement date, trading would not be possible if the contracts are not fungible.

Another part of the futures contract definition that has been the subject of litigation in Australia is the meaning of 'commodity'. An eligible commodity agreement as its name suggests must involve a commodity. 'Commodity' is defined in s. 9 as either 'anything that is capable of delivery pursuant to an agreement for its delivery' or 'an instrument creating or evidencing a thing in action.' In *Shoreline Currencies*, the issue before the court was whether contracts, in standard form, under which clients acquired an option to acquire foreign currencies on a fixed future date, were futures contracts. The plaintiff claimed that foreign currencies are not commodities as money is not capable of delivery. Since no commodities were involved, the agreements were not eligible commodity agreements and therefore not futures contracts. However, the court rejected this argument and held that foreign currencies were commodities provided their prices and delivery dates were specified in the underlying agreement.[75]

A more recent decision, which dealt with the meaning of commodity, was *Sydney Futures Exchange Ltd v Australian Stock Exchange Ltd*.[76] In that case the Australian Stock Exchange (ASX) announced its intention to list Low Exercise Price Options (LEPOs) for trading on the Australian Options Market. LEPOs are deliverable contracts usually covering 1000 shares of the underlying stock. They are call options typically having a strike price of between one and ten cents. The taker of a LEPO holds a position similar to the buying of the underlying shares without having to pay the total outlay upfront. The Sydney Futures Exchange (SFE) sought a declaration and injunctive relief to restrain ASX from listing or trading the LEPOs. SFE argued that LEPOs were futures contracts within the meaning of s. 72(1) and that ASX would be conducting an unauthorised futures market in breach of s. 1123. However, the court held that a share was not a 'commodity' as it was not a thing capable of delivery pursuant to an agreement for delivery since title was only acquired by registration.[77] Since shares do not fall within the definition of commodity, LEPOs were therefore not futures contracts. This decision appears to be inconsistent with the policy underlying the *Futures Industry Code*, which clearly contemplated regulating futures contracts based on securities.

Establishing the meaning of adjustment agreements has also not been an easy task for the courts. An adjustment agreement has been described as 'a cash form of futures contract' since it does not call for delivery of the underlying commodity or instrument.[78] For a contract to be an adjustment agreement, one of the criteria that must be satisfied is that a 'particular person will either be under a Chapter 8 obligation to pay, or will have a Chapter 8

---

[75]   (1986) 4 ACLC 686 at 694.
[76]   (1995) 16 ACSR 148.
[77]   Id. at 181, per Gummow J.
[78]   See J. S. Currie, *Australian Futures Regulation* (Longman, Melbourne, 1994), p. 39.

right to receive, an amount of money'. Hodgson J in *Carragreen Currency Corporation Pty Ltd v Corporate Affairs Commission (NSW)*[79] interpreted this provision to mean that the person must in one set of circumstances be under an obligation to pay money, and in another set of circumstances have a right to receive money.[80] Where the person only has the right to receive money without ever any obligation to pay any more money, then the contract is not an adjustment agreement. The reasoning of Hodgson J was adopted in *CAC (NSW) v Lombard Nash (No. 2)*.[81] In that case, the purchaser of the leveraged foreign exchange contracts was not bound to pay any sum of money beyond the initial investment. Cohen J accordingly held that the contracts were not adjustment agreements because the purchaser was not under any obligation to pay money on closing-out.[82]

Widespread industry concern over the width of the futures contract definition during the drafting of the Futures Industry Code led to the inclusion of the 'banking exclusion' provision. Under s. 72(1)(d), currency swaps, interest rate swaps, forward exchange rate contracts and forward interest rate contracts, to which an Australian bank or merchant bank is a party to, are not futures contracts. This provision was based on the submissions made by the Australian Banker's Association and the Australian Merchant Banker's Association to the Attorney General.[83] The underlying intention was to expressly exclude from regulation a number of transactions, which are typically transacted in the wholesale markets. Although four categories of contracts are expressly excluded from the futures contract definition, none of them are defined in the legislation. The Explanatory Memorandum is of little assistance. Instead of elaborating on the agreements excluded, it merely makes reference to the description of swaps and forward exchange contracts in a commercial text. The exclusionary limb of the definition has not been updated to accommodate market developments. It does not cover several categories of OTC derivatives such as equity swaps and credit derivatives. As such its value as a device for excluding wholesale transactions is somewhat limited.

4.4.2   New Zealand

Part III of the *Securities Amendment Act* 1988 regulates the activity of dealing in derivatives contracts in New Zealand. It ensures, through s. 38(1) that only properly authorised persons are allowed to deal in derivatives contracts. Authorisation is required when the contracts dealt with, fall within the definition of a 'futures contract'. It would therefore be necessary to examine the statutory definition of 'futures contract' in order to determine the scope of Part III.

---

[79]   (1986) 11 ACLR 298.
[80]   Id. at 311.
[81]   (1987) 11 ACLR 866.
[82]   Id. at 875.
[83]   See Currie, above n. 78, p. 43.

Section 37(1) includes the following categories of agreements under the definition of 'futures contract':

- An agreement under which one party agrees to deliver to another, at a specified time in the future, a specified commodity or a fixed quantity of a specified commodity, at an agreed price. However, it is contemplated or understood that the obligations of the parties may be satisfied by means other than actual delivery (in other words, by offset);
- An agreement under which each party has either an obligation to pay or receive a sum of money calculated by reference to the difference between the agreed price of a specified commodity and its market price on an agreed future date;
- An agreement under which each party has either an obligation to pay or receive a sum of money calculated by reference to the difference between the level of a specified index at the date the agreement is made and its level at an agreed future date;
- An option or right to assume rights and obligations under any of the above agreements.

The New Zealand Securities Commission (Commission) may declare that any agreement, option or right, or any class of agreements, options or rights, are futures contracts for the purpose of Part III. Section 37(2) excludes the following categories of agreements from the definition of 'futures contract':

(a) A currency swap agreement to which ... a registered bank is a party;
(b) An interest rate swap agreement to which ... a registered bank is a party;
(c) A forward exchange rate contract to which ... a registered bank is a party;
(d) A forward interest rate contract to which ... a registered bank is a party.

Although the term 'futures contract' is broadly defined, an agreement would only be caught by the definition if the 'underlying' is a commodity or index. The term 'commodity' has been defined as 'any type of goods; and includes foreign currency and financial instrument.'[84] It covers shares and would avoid the controversy surrounding the definition of 'commodity' in the Australian *Corporations Law*.[85] However, the term 'commodity' does not include utilities like water, gas, or electricity.[86] They are not goods, but more in the nature of services. Not surprisingly, when electricity futures contracts were first introduced in New Zealand, there were doubts whether they were futures contracts within the meaning of s. 37(1). The issue has been resolved with the Commission now treating wholesale electricity price

---

[84] *Securities Amendment Act*, s. 37(1).
[85] Australia has adopted a narrower definition because s. 9 of the *Corporations Law* defines 'commodity' as 'anything capable of delivery' or 'an instrument creating or evidencing a thing in action.' In *Sydney Futures Exchange Ltd v Australian Stock Exchange Ltd* (1995) 16 ACSR 148, the Full Federal Court held that a share was not a commodity.
[86] See C. Mulholland and A. Lester, 'Regulation of Derivatives in New Zealand' in G. Walker and Others (eds), *Securities Regulation in Australia and New Zealand* (2nd edn, LBC, Sydney, 1998), pp. 732–733, fn. 193.

hedges as futures contracts. Another definitional issue that has been raised is whether the term 'futures contract' covers derivatives such as 'collars', 'caps', 'floors', 'margin foreign exchange' and 'swaptions'.[87] Although the Commission has not provided any clarification, no major problems are anticipated as the Commission may declare any agreement or class of agreements to be subject to Part III.

4.4.3 Singapore

In Singapore, the *Futures Trading Act* (FTA) not only applies to the trading of futures contracts, but also to leveraged foreign exchange trading. Section 2 of the FTA provides that:

'futures contract' means a contract the effect of which is that—

(a) one party agrees to deliver a specified commodity, or a specified quantity of a specified commodity, to another party at a specified future time and at a specified price payable at that time pursuant to terms and conditions set forth in the business rules or practices of a Futures Exchange or futures markets; or

(b) the parties will discharge their obligations under the contract by settling the difference between the value of a specified quantity of a specified commodity at the time of the making of the contract and at a specified future time, such difference being determined in accordance with the business rules or practices of the Exchange or futures market at which the contract is made,

and includes a futures option transaction;

'futures option transaction' means a transaction which gives a person a right, acquired for a consideration, to buy or sell within a specified period of time a specified amount of commodity or a specified futures contract at a specified price in accordance with the business rules or practices of a Futures Exchange or a futures market at which the transaction is made;

'commodity' in relation to a futures contract, means—

(a) a financial instrument; and

(b) gold and such other items, goods, articles, services, rights and interests, which are the subject of futures contracts, as the Authority [MAS] may by order prescribe;

'financial instruments' includes currencies, interest rate instruments, share indices, a group or groups of share indices and such other financial instruments as the Authority may by order prescribe.

Thus defined, the term 'futures contract' covers a broad range of derivatives. Some of the main types of derivatives included under the definition are:

- Deliverable exchange-traded futures contracts, such as Brent Crude Oil and Gold futures contracts;
- Non-deliverable exchange-traded futures contracts, such as Nikkei 225 futures;

---

[87] See A. Abernethy, 'Regulation of the Futures and Options Market in New Zealand' (1996) 11 JIBFL 27, 28.

- Exchange-traded options over futures contracts, such as Options on Eurodollar futures contracts.

At first glance it would appear that over-the-counter (OTC) commodity options and forward agreements may also constitute 'futures contract' as the FTA does not require that derivatives contracts be traded on organised exchanges. All that is required for a derivatives contract to qualify as a 'futures contract' is that it is made according to the business rules of a futures market. However, despite the use of standardised International Swaps and Derivatives Association agreements, it may be difficult to hold that negotiated OTC products trade according to the business rules of a futures market. The likelihood of products like swaps, caps and floors qualifying as 'futures contracts' is even more remote because these products (possibly with the exception of currency swaps) do not involve the delivery of any commodity on a specified date. They are basically agreements to exchange cash flows at specified future intervals. The cash flows are calculated by multiplying the notional sums by agreed reference rates. It therefore appears that OTC derivatives are excluded from the scope of the FTA.

The definition of 'leveraged foreign exchange trading' is found in s. 2A of the FTA. A person engages in leveraged foreign exchange trading if that person enters into or offers to enter into, or induces or attempts to induce another person to enter into or offer to enter into, a contract or arrangement (other than a futures contract) on a margin basis whereby that person undertakes to:

- make an adjustment or payment to the other person according to whether a currency is worth more or less than another currency, or
- deliver to another person at an agreed price, a specified amount of currency, at an agreed future date.

The FTA only regulates the trading of foreign exchange on a margin basis, not other forms of foreign trading. Leveraged foreign exchange trading poses the same risks as futures trading since the initial outlay for investors may be as low as three per cent of the total value of the contracts. Since the definition of 'futures contract' is wide enough to catch activities like leveraged foreign exchange trading, it would seem that the amendments to the FTA relating to leveraged foreign exchange trading are unnecessary. It has been suggested that the amendments were introduced because MAS had previously taken the view that foreign exchange contracts were not futures contracts and that trading in them was outside the purview of the FTA.[88] The amendments would therefore remove any doubts as to whether the provisions of the FTA apply to leveraged foreign exchange trading. All foreign exchange houses are now required to obtain licences to engage in leveraged foreign exchange trading, unless they are banks or are exempted.

---

[88]   See S. K. Tan and R. Liew, 'Behind the Barings Debacle' (May 1995) Asia Law 37, 39.

4.4.4 Malaysia

The regulatory ambit of the *Futures Industry Act* (FIA) is determined by the definition of futures contract. An examination of the Malaysian definition would reveal that it closely resembles the definition found in the Australian *Corporations Law*.[89] This is in large part due to the fact that the Malaysian regulatory framework is modelled on the Australian legislation. However, unlike the Australian *Corporations Law*, the FIA uses 'eligible delivery agreement' instead of 'eligible commodity agreement' to refer to deliverable futures contracts.[90] It is possible that a different nomenclature may have been adopted to avoid any confusion as to whether the term 'futures contract' included commodity derivatives traded on KLCE, which until March 1977 was governed by a separate regulatory scheme.

The definition of 'futures contract' in s. 2 of the FIA comprises two parts. The first or inclusionary part of the definition states that a 'futures contract' is:

(a) an agreement that is, or has at any time been, an eligible delivery agreement or adjustment agreement;
(b) a futures option;
(c) an eligible exchange-traded option; or
(d) any other agreement, or any other agreements in a class of agreements, prescribed to be futures contracts under section 2B.

Each of the four species of futures contracts is further defined in s. 2 of the FIA. The Minister of Finance may prescribe any agreement or class of agreements to be a futures contract. 'Eligible delivery agreement' as defined in the FIA covers deliverable contracts, while the definition of 'adjustment agreement' covers non-deliverable contracts. Deliverable contracts are those that allow settlement by physical delivery. To date, there are no deliverable contracts listed on either of the two exchanges. Non-deliverable contracts may either be contracts based on an underlying instrument incapable of delivery or contracts whose terms preclude delivery. The KLSE CI Futures Contract would fall into the first category of non-deliverable futures contracts since the KLSE Composite Index is the underlying instrument. As for the KLIBOR futures contract, it would fall into the second category as it is designated as a cash-settled contract.

For an agreement to qualify as an eligible delivery agreement or an adjustment agreement, various statutory criteria have to be met. One of the criteria is that the agreement must be 'one of two or more standardised agreements.' The term 'standardised agreement' is not further defined in the FIA which will make interpretation difficult. For an agreement to be an eligible delivery agreement the underlying subject of the agreement must be an instrument within the meaning of s. 2 the FIA. 'Instrument' is defined as 'anything that is capable of delivery under an agreement for its delivery, including a commodity, or a document creating or evidencing a thing in

---

[89] See the Australian *Corporations Law*, s. 9.
[90] Id., s. 72(1).

action'. It also includes 'any other thing that is prescribed to be an instrument'. Since the Minister is empowered under the FIA to prescribe any other thing to be an instrument, any doubts regarding the status of shares is likely to be resolved easily.

A 'futures option' is defined as 'an option or right to assume, at a stated price or value and within a stated period, a long position or a short position, in relation to a futures contract.'[91] The term covers any options on futures contracts, although it is doubtful whether it would cover options on excluded futures contracts such as those involving commercial banks. Currently, there are no futures options listed on either of the two Malaysian exchanges. An eligible exchange-traded option (EETO) by definition covers options over a stated quantity of a named instrument such as a bond or share, as well as options over cash adjustments based on changes to the price or value of an instrument, index or reference rate. EETOs are no different from over-the-counter options except that they have to be 'entered into on a futures market of an exchange company.'[92] Unlike a futures option, an EETO is not an option over another futures contract.

It would appear that the existing definition of 'futures contract' is wide enough to cover over-the-counter derivatives transactions. This is in sharp contrast to the earlier definition of 'futures contract', which covered only exchange-traded transactions because it restricted the term to those agreements made in accordance with the business rules and practices of a futures exchange or market.[93] The Securities Commission made it clear that the underlying purpose of reformulating the previous definition of a 'futures contract' was to allow 'over-the-counter markets to come under the regulation of the [FIA].'[94] By including over-the-counter transactions under the definition of futures contract, the FIA would apply not only to the trading on-exchange products but also those traded in the wholesale markets, unless they are specifically excluded from regulation.

The second or exclusionary part of the futures contract definition excludes the following agreements from being categorised as futures contracts:

> (aa) [an agreement] which is
>> (i) a currency swap;
>> (ii) an interest rate swap;

---

[91] FIA, s. 2.
[92] Ibid.
[93] The old definition of futures contract is reproduced below:

[A] 'futures contract' means a contract the effect of which is that—

(a) one party agrees to deliver a specified instrument, or a specified quantity of a specified instrument, to another party at a specified future time and at a specified price payable at that time pursuant to terms and conditions set forth in the business rules or practices of the futures exchange or futures market; or

(b) the parties will discharge their obligations under the contract by settling the difference between the value of a specified quantity of a specified instrument at the time of making of the contract and at a specified future time, such difference being determined in accordance with the business rules or practices of the futures exchange or futures market at which the contract is made, and includes a futures option transaction ... '

[94] See Malaysian Securities Commission, *Annual Report 1995*, p. 57.

(iii)   a forward exchange rate contract; or
(iv)   a forward interest rate contract,
  authorised by Bank Negara and to which a licensed institution is a party;
(bb)   which when entered into, is in a class of agreements prescribed not to be futures contracts; or
(cc)   which is prescribed to be an agreement that is not to be traded in on a futures market.

'Licensed institution' is defined in s. 2 of the FIA as 'any institution licensed or deemed to be licensed under subsection 6(4) of the *Banking and Financial Institutions Act* 1989.' All commercial banks, merchant banks, finance companies, and discount houses are included in this category. None of the four types of excluded agreements are defined in the legislation. It appears that this shortcoming may have been imported from the Australian legislation, since FIA is based on Chapter 8 of the *Corporations Law*. An important legal consequence flowing from this banking exclusion is that any agreement, which is excluded from the definition of 'futures contracts', is not protected from the gaming or wagering laws by s. 100 of the FIA.

4.4.5   Hong Kong

The application of the *Commodity Trading Ordinance* (CTO) is dependant on the meaning of 'futures contract'. A 'futures contract' is defined as:

(a)   a contract executed on a commodity exchange the effect of which is—
  (i)   that one party agrees to deliver to the other party at an agreed future time an agreed commodity, at an agreed price; or
  (ii)   that the parties will make an adjustment between them at an agreed future time according to whether an agreed commodity is worth more or less or, as the case may be, stands higher or lower at that time than a level agreed at the time of making the contract, the difference being determined in accordance with the rules of the commodity market in which the contract is made; or
(b)   an option on a contract of the kind described in paragraph (a)(i) or (ii).[95]

The above futures contract definition covers deliverable and non-deliverable futures contracts, as well as options on them, so long as they are executed on a commodity exchange licensed under Part III of the CTO. There can be little doubt that the legislation is not intended to apply to off-exchange transactions. Over-the-counter (OTC) derivatives such as swaps, customised options, and forward agreements are excluded from regulation, unless they are caught within the definition of 'leveraged foreign exchange trading' as defined in s. 2 of the *Leveraged Foreign Exchange Trading Ordinance*. The definition of 'leveraged foreign exchange trading' currently covers most currency-based OTC derivatives.

A unique feature of the Hong Kong 'futures contract' definition is that it is framed as an inclusive definition. The current definition of 'futures contract' only includes contracts that relate to a commodity. 'Commodity' is

---

[95]   CTO, s. 2.

defined in s. 2 as any item, whether or not capable of being delivered, specified in Schedule 1 of the CTO.[96] It is unlikely that any unlisted item would
be regarded as a 'commodity' within the meaning of the CTO. The problem
with adopting this method of defining 'commodity' is its inflexibility. There
is a regular need to add new items to the list in the statutory schedule to
accommodate new products. Part 1 of Schedule 1, which originally listed
only cotton and sugar, has been amended several times because of the addition of items such as soybeans, stock indices, and interest rate futures.[97]

4.4.6 Summary and Comments

All the jurisdictions under study have adopted essentially product-based
legislation. Only derivatives that fall within the definition of the regulated
product are subject to regulation. The scope of futures regulation is generally
dependent on the definition of futures contract. In the case of Singapore, the
definition of leveraged foreign exchange trading is also important as the legislation governs both futures contracts and leveraged foreign exchange trading. A survey of the legal definitions of futures contract adopted by the
jurisdictions under study reveals some variations in their scope.

In Australia, the term 'futures contract' covers all exchange-traded futures
contracts and options, and possibly swaps and forward agreements.
Excluded from this broad definition are currency swaps, interest rate swaps,
forward exchange rate contracts, and forward interest rate contracts, to
which an Australian bank or merchant bank is party to. However, the
excluded contracts are not defined in the legislation. Whether a particular
contract is an excluded contract or not, depends very much on market usage.

New Zealand has adopted an even broader definition of 'futures contract'. The definition covers not only futures contracts, but also options and
swaps relating to commodities or indices. However, doubts continue to
exist as to whether the definition is broad enough to cover derivatives such
as collars, caps, and floors where no underlying financial instrument or
commodity is involved. The New Zealand definition of a futures contract,
like the Australian definition, is subject to a similar banking exclusion.

In Singapore only exchange-traded derivatives are included within the
definition of 'futures contract' As such, there does not appear to be any need
for a banking exclusion since derivatives such as swaps and forward agreements are almost always traded over-the-counter. The regulatory scheme
also applies to leveraged foreign exchange trading. However, leveraged

---

[96] The commodities are cotton, sugar, soybeans, gold, Hang Seng Index futures, three month
Hong Kong Interbank Offer Rate futures contracts, Hang Seng Finance Sub-Index futures contracts, Hang Seng Utilities Sub-Index futures contracts, Hang Seng Properties Sub-Index
futures contracts, Hang Seng Commerce and Industry Sub-Index futures contracts, stock
indices, and cash-settled stock futures contracts for differences.

[97] Soybeans (added L.N. 268 of 1979); Hang Seng Index futures contracts (added L.N. 111 of
1986); Three month Hong Kong Interbank Offered Rate futures contract (added L.N. 415 of
1989); and Stock Indices (added L.N. 399 of 1992).

foreign exchange trading involving banks is excluded from regulation under the *Futures Trading Act*.

The Malaysian definition of futures contract covers almost all derivatives and only excludes certain transactions entered into with banks and other licensed financial institutions. Malaysia like New Zealand and Australia, has not attempted to define the categories of excluded contracts in the legislation. It therefore appears that Malaysia has adopted wholesale, some of the weaknesses of the Australian definition.

In Hong Kong, a futures contract is one that is executed on a commodity exchange. Hong Kong, unlike the other four jurisdictions under study, has adopted an inclusive definition of futures contract. Only those contracts based on commodities included in the Schedule to the *Commodities Trading Ordinance* are regulated. The Hong Kong definition of 'futures contract', like the Singapore definition has no banking exclusion. Over-the-counter products such as swaps, forward agreements and options are excluded from regulation, unless they fall within the definition of 'leveraged foreign exchange trading'. Leveraged foreign exchange trading in Hong Kong, unlike in Singapore, is regulated under a separate legislation.

4.5   INSTITUTIONAL STRUCTURE OF REGULATION

In the past, research into financial regulation paid little attention to the institutional structure of regulation, but this has changed in recent years.[98] Now, it has become a major focus of public policy debate. There is renewed interest in issues such as, the role of regulatory agencies, the optimum number of agencies and the impact of institutional structure on costs. The trading of derivatives has traditionally been regulated on a co-regulatory basis. Regulation is normally shared between the exchanges and the regulatory agencies, but the balance of power varies with jurisdictions. In some jurisdictions, the self-regulatory ethos is deeply ingrained and exchanges play an important role. In other jurisdictions, the government regulator plays a more dominant role. There are also jurisdictions where the central banks exert considerable influence on the industry through the issue of policy guidelines.

4.5.1   Australia

The *Corporations Law* and the *Australian Securities and Investments Commission Act* 1989 provide the legislative framework for co-regulation by the Australian Securities and Investments Commission (ASIC) and the self-regulatory organisations. Currently, the regulation of the futures industry is shared between the Australian Securities and Investment Commission (ASIC) and the Sydney Futures Exchange (SFE). Their respective roles

---

[98]   See Goodhart and Others, above n. 13, p. 142.

within this co-regulatory structure has been described in the following terms:

[T]he day-to-day running of the futures market, and the detailed surveillance of market trends, is left to the futures exchanges, and essentially to the SFE itself, operating in conjunction with its clearing house, SFECH. The ASC [now ASIC] on the other hand, in addition to its information-gathering functions and powers, has what might best be termed reserve powers of examination, investigation and prosecution. Above all it is the central licensing authority for all institutions … as well as participants in the markets.[99]

Where the market participants are deposit-taking institutions, life and general insurance companies and superannuation funds, the Australian Prudential Regulation Authority (APRA) is also responsible for their regulation. It is important to note that that ASIC and APRA have related but distinct roles. ASIC is responsible for consumer protection and market integrity regulation, while APRA is responsible for prudential regulation.

In some respects the powers of the exchange with respect to market conduct are subject to the overriding powers vested in ASIC. For example, SFE must notify ASIC of any changes to its business rules and failure to give notice may cause the amendment to lapse.[100] If SFE breaches its obligation to ensure a fair and orderly market, ASIC is empowered to give a direction in writing to SFE to take a particular course of action.[101] This may include ordering SFE to close the futures market or to suspend dealing in a particular class of futures contracts. SFE is also required to provide such assistance to ASIC as is reasonably required for the performance of its functions. If SFE takes any disciplinary action against a member, of if SFE believes that a person has committed or is about to commit a serious contravention of its business rules or the *Corporations Law*, it must notify ASIC.[102]

4.5.2   New Zealand

Although, the New Zealand Securities Commission (Commission) is empowered to regulate all aspects of derivatives trading, the New Zealand and Futures Options Exchange (NZFOE) is largely responsible for the regulation of the derivatives industry. Under s. 41 of the *Securities Amendment Act* 1988, the exchange may make regulations for the following purposes:

- to regulate the business and operations of authorised futures exchanges;
- to regulate the business of dealing in futures contracts and to prescribe requirements to be met by dealers; and
- to regulate the segregation of clients' money and property;

---

[99]   See Currie, above n. 78, p. 63.
[100]   *Corporations Law*, s. 1136.
[101]   Id., ss. 1137–1138.
[102]   Id., s. 1139.

The Commission plays a mainly supervisory role and its regulatory philosophy is best summed up in the following statement found in its Annual Report:

We advocate self-regulation under competent, independent and preferably statutory oversight.[103]

The exchange is generally responsible for the conduct of its members and the monitoring of its own transactions, in accordance with its rules. It is required to submit its constitution and rules, including that of its clearinghouse, to the Commission for approval.[104] In the event the exchange exercises any of its disciplinary powers it must inform the Commission, and where the matter is serious enough, it must allow the Commission the opportunity to get involved.[105]

4.5.3 Singapore

The regulation of the financial derivatives industry in Singapore is divided between the Monetary Authority of Singapore (MAS) and Singapore Exchange Derivatives Trading Limited. MAS, which is Singapore's central bank, was established in September 1970 by the *Monetary Authority of Singapore Act* 1970.[106] It is has a much wider role than other central banks and acts as a kind of mega-regulator. Apart from the conduct of monetary policy and the management of the country's foreign reserves, it is responsible for supervising the banking, insurance, securities and futures industries. MAS supervises the derivatives industry largely through its powers to authorise futures exchanges, clearinghouses, and intermediaries. In addition, it has powers of investigation, examination and prosecution. Institutions regulated by MAS are required to comply with its various guidelines relating to the trading of derivatives. For example, on 6 September 2000 it issued Notice 627, which provides guidelines to banks on the capital treatment of credit derivatives.

The exchange, on the other hand, is responsible for the day-to-day supervision and surveillance of the market. It has its own set of rules which members are obliged to adhere to. Failure to do so may lead to suspension or expulsion from membership. For minor violations, fines may be imposed on the offending member instead. The provision relating to the licensing of brokers was recently amended to secure greater compliance. Now, in order to carry on business as a broker, a person must not only be licensed, but also trade in accordance with the business rules and practices of the exchange.[107] However, there is no requirement that a broker should be an exchange member to carry on broking business. This would mean that it is possible,

---

[103] See New Zealand Securities Commission, *Annual Report for the year ending 30 June 1996*, p. 21.
[104] See McKenzie, above n. 47, p. 39.
[105] Ibid.
[106] Cap. 186.
[107] FTA, s. 11(1)(b)(2).

although highly unlikely, that a broker who has been expelled from exchange membership for a rule violation may still remain in business.

MAS has considerable control over the exchange and clearing house. For example, it can revoke approval of the exchange if the exchange operates 'in a manner detrimental to the public interest'.[108] This is different from the position in Australia, where the Australian Securities Commission has no express power to revoke approval. The exchange and its clearinghouse must advise MAS of any amendments to their business rules within 10 days of making the amendments, or they will cease to have any effect.[109] MAS may within 28 days after receipt of notice disallow the amendment.[110] If it deems necessary, for the protection of traders or to ensure fair dealing in the market, MAS can alter or even supplement the business rules of the exchange and its clearing house.[111] MAS powers have been greatly strengthened by the 1995 amendments. For example, the exchange cannot acquire 20 per cent or more of the share capital of any corporation without the approval of MAS.[112] The exchange is required to obtain the approval of MAS before operating any electronic facility for trading.[113] In addition, the listing of futures contracts on an exchange, or the trading of futures contracts on an electronic facility operated by the exchange, must be approved by MAS.[114]

4.5.4 Malaysia

The regulation of the derivatives industry is shared between the exchanges and the Securities Commission (Commission). One of the principal objectives for setting up the Commission was the creation of a central authority for the regulation and development of the capital markets.[115] The Commission was established on 1 March 1993 by the *Securities Commission Act* 1993. It is modelled along the lines of the Australian Securities Commission and the Securities and Futures Commission of Hong Kong.[116] The Commission controls the authorisation of exchanges, clearinghouses, and market intermediaries. It has extensive powers of investigation, examination and prosecution. Where necessary, it may intervene in the market to preserve the integrity of the exchange and protect investors. The exchanges are responsible for the supervision of trading and the discipline of its members.

Banking institutions wishing to participate in the derivatives market are also required to adhere to the guidelines issued by Bank Negara Malaysia (BNM), the Malaysian central bank. BNM plays an important regulatory

---

[108] Id., s. 7(1)(c).
[109] Id., ss. 6(1)–6(2).
[110] Id., s. 6(3).
[111] Id., s. 6(4).
[112] Id., s. 39A.
[113] Id., s. 5(1).
[114] Id., s. 5(2).
[115] See K. Arjunan and C. K. Low, *Understanding Company Law in Malaysia* (LBC Information Services, Sydney, 1995), p. 390.
[116] Ibid.

role in view of the significant involvement of banking institutions in derivatives trading.[117] The important guidelines applicable to brokerage activities undertaken by banking institutions are:

- Approval from BNM is required before seeking exchange membership;
- Brokerage activities must be performed through a subsidiary of the banking institution;
- Foreign participation in the subsidiary should not exceed 30 per cent.[118]

There are separate guidelines covering proprietary activities undertaken by banking institutions. For example, Tier-1 commercial and merchant banks are permitted to engage in interest rate, foreign exchange and equity derivatives activities provided they comply with the minimum standards on risk management practices for derivatives issued by BNM. However, these banks are prohibited from engaging in commodity derivatives activities, presumably because they have no relevance to banking business.[119] The guidelines are aimed at ensuring that the solvency of banks remains intact and that derivatives activities are conducted in a knowledgeable and prudential manner.

4.5.5 Hong Kong

Hong Kong has also adopted a co-regulatory approach to the regulation of derivatives. Regulation of the derivatives market is shared between the Securities and Futures Commission (SFC) and the exchanges. The SFC is responsible for enforcing the provisions of the various ordinances governing the derivatives industry, while the exchanges are responsible for the supervision of the markets and their members. During its early days, the SFC met with resistance when it took steps to implement its role in the market.[120] Some of the factors that contributed to the initial criticisms of the SFC were the market's opposition to regulation, and the initial problems encountered implementing co-regulation.

In Hong Kong, institutions authorised under the *Banking Ordinance* are also required to comply with the guidelines issued by the Hong Kong

---

[117] See Bank Negara Malaysia, 'Minimum Standards on Risk Management Practices for Derivatives' (Guidelines dated 26 July 1996), p.i.: 'Derivative Instruments have become important both in managing risks and as a source of income for banks in Malaysia. ... In respect of interest rate and foreign exchange derivatives, banking institutions by virtue of their access to the money and foreign exchange markets will invariably be key players and providers of these instruments.'

[118] See Bank Negara Malaysia, 'Participation of Banking Institutions in KLOFFE and MME' (Circular dated 18 December 1995).

[119] See Bank Negara Malaysia, 'Participation of Banking Institutions in KLOFFE and MME' (Circular dated 26 July 1996).

[120] See J. O'Hare, 'Regulation of the Securities Industry in Hong Kong: The Securities and Futures Commission' (1996) 6 *Australian Journal of Corporations Law*, 178, 194–195.

Monetary Authority (HKMA). The HKMA issued its first set of guidelines for authorised institutions based on the Basle Committee on Banking Supervision's Risk Management Guidelines in December 1994.[121] In March 1996, the HKMA issued a further set of guidelines, which provided more detailed guidance on specific aspects of the process for managing the risks of authorised institutions' derivatives activities. Areas covered in the second set of guidelines include the following:

- risk management and corporate governance;
- board and senior management oversight;
- identification and measurement of risks;
- limitation of risks; and
- operational controls.[122]

All authorised institutions and the subsidiaries of all locally incorporated authorised institutions involved in the trading of financial instruments are expected to follow the risk management practices set out in the guidelines.

4.5.6 Summary and Comments

Australia, Singapore, Malaysia and Hong Kong have adopted similar statutory regulatory systems. In these four jurisdictions, there is comprehensive derivatives legislation in place, which is administered by a statutory body. Regulation is shared between a statutory body and the various self-regulating organisations such as the derivatives exchanges. Although all four jurisdictions have adopted a co-regulatory structure, the extent of co-regulation differs between jurisdictions. For example, in Hong Kong, the government has traditionally adopted a laissez-faire approach to financial regulation and therefore the exchange plays a more important role in regulation. By contrast, in jurisdictions like Singapore and Malaysia, the government regulator plays a more dominant role.

New Zealand, unlike the other four jurisdictions mentioned above, has adopted an essentially self-regulatory system. Although there is legislation in place, it is very much limited in scope. Apart from mandating self-regulation of the derivatives industry, the legislation exempts regulated derivatives transactions from the gaming and wagering laws. The New Zealand Securities Commission plays a supervisory role, with regulation almost entirely in the hands of the exchange. Although the New Zealand Securities Commission is empowered to regulate on all aspects of derivatives trading, it has to date adopted a 'light-handed' approach to supervision.

---

[121] See Hong Kong Monetary Authority, *Risk Management of Financial Derivatives: Guideline No. 12.1* <www.info.gov.hk/hkma/>, (15 June 2000).
[122] See Hong Kong Monetary Authority, *Guideline on Risk Management of Derivatives and Other Traded Instruments: Guideline No. 12.2* < www.info.gov.hk/hkma/>, (16 June 2000).

4.6 MARKET AUTHORISATION

Exchange-traded derivatives markets play an important economic role and therefore it is essential that they are transparent, liquid, orderly, secure and well supervised. Although they enjoy a significant degree of independence, there is still a need for some form of external control to ensure that the markets are properly regulated. Under existing arrangements markets in futures contracts have to be authorised, unless they are exempt markets. Markets in other types of derivatives, on the other hand, do not need to be authorised. Usually futures markets have to meet stringent criteria before they are authorised. The regulators may also impose conditions for the operation of futures markets. These conditions normally include the provision of adequate clearing facilities and the existence of rules to govern the behaviour of their members. In some jurisdictions, the government regulator or the responsible minister is empowered to revoke approval if the market is not conducted satisfactorily. However such a power is unlikely to be exercised lightly in view of its serious ramifications. As such significant importance is attached to the approval of markets.

4.6.1 Australia

In Australia, all futures markets have to be authorised, unless exempted. Any person who operates an unauthorised futures market would be committing an offence.[123] An unauthorised futures market is neither an approved futures exchange nor an exempt futures market.[124] There is provision for the Minister (now the Federal Treasurer) to declare a market an exempt futures market, subject to certain conditions.[125] Markets that do not trade in futures contracts do not require authorisation. As such, Chapter 8 does not regulate the over-the-counter (OTC) markets for derivatives since OTC derivatives do not fall with the statutory definition of futures contracts. The great majority of OTC derivatives markets are currently in currency options, forward rate agreements, interest rate swaps and interest rate options.[126]

A 'futures market' has been defined as a 'market, exchange, or other place at which, or a facility by which, futures contracts are regularly acquired or disposed of.'[127] In *Carragreen Currency*, the plaintiff provided the infrastructure in the form of personnel, means of communication and access to foreign currency information to its clients to enable them to trade in futures contracts. Hodgson J held that the provision of the infrastructure amounted to the provision of a facility.[128] This broad interpretation of

---

[123] *Corporations Law*, s. 1123.
[124] Id., s. 9.
[125] Id., s. 1127(1).
[126] Treasury, *Financial Markets and Investment Products* ('CLERP Paper No. 6') (AGPS, Canberra, December 1997), p. 16.
[127] *Corporations Law*, s. 9.
[128] (1986) 11 ACLR 298 at 312.

'futures market' coupled with the uncertainty surrounding the scope of the definition of 'futures contract' has caused a number of banks to apply for exempt market status despite the banking exclusion.

In an effort to allay the concerns of market participants, ASIC introduced a 'safe harbour' policy for professional OTC derivatives markets. The policy is meant to be an interim measure, pending a complete review of the law governing derivatives. ASIC Policy Statement 70 was issued in July 1993 and outlines the guidelines that the Minister would adopt when granting approvals for exempt futures market status. It provides for the approval of exempt market status applications without extended investigation if certain conditions are fulfilled. The test used for approving exempt futures market status is a predominantly participant-based test. It basically excludes from regulation transactions involving financially sophisticated wholesale participants.

There are specific criteria that must be satisfied before the Minister would approve a futures exchange. The criteria for approval includes the following:

- the exchange is a body corporate,
- it has satisfactory business rules and compensation arrangements,
- the Minister has approved its clearing arrangements, and
- the interests of the public will be served by granting the application.[129]

In addition, the futures exchange must establish a fidelity fund to provide compensation to persons who suffer loss because of defalcation or fraudulent misuse of funds.[130] 'Defalcation' includes the failure to account for funds entrusted to a firm as trustee, even if the failure was due to negligence rather than dishonesty.[131] The person responsible for the loss must be an exchange member or an employee, director or partner of the member.[132] Additionally, the loss must have been suffered in respect of funds placed at the hands of person in connection with dealings in futures contracts.[133] If a client suffers loss arising from the insolvency of the broker, the client cannot claim from the fidelity fund.

4.6.2 New Zealand

Part III of the *Securities Amendment Act* 1988 does not contain a definition of 'futures market'. The New Zealand Securities Commission (Commission) may declare a body corporate that conducts, or proposes to conduct, a futures market or exchange in New Zealand to be an authorised futures exchange.[134] To date, the Commission has authorised only two exchanges, the New Zealand Futures and Options Exchange (NZFOE) and its successor

---

[129] Id., s. 1126.
[130] Id., ss. 1228(1), 1239(1).
[131] See *Daly v Sydney Stock Exchange Ltd* (1986) 160 CLR 371, 381, per Gibbs J.
[132] *Corporations Law*, s. 1239(1).
[133] Ibid.
[134] Section 37(8).

company, which operates the exchange.[135] However, Part III is silent as to whether the Commission may make such a declaration, subject to such terms and conditions as it thinks fit. This has created doubts whether the Commission may require that the exchange regulate its members and the conduct of business in accordance with the standards and rules approved by the Commission. As a result Commission had to obtain undertakings from the exchanges instead and this has proven to be a cumbersome process.[136] This is an obvious weakness of the existing regulatory scheme. The Commission has recommended that the legislation be amended to deal with this issue but the recommendations have yet to be acted upon.[137]

4.6.3 Singapore

The Singapore legislation states that no person may operate a 'futures market' without authorisation. Section 2 of the *Futures Trading Act* (FTA) provides that a futures market is:

(a) a market, Futures Exchange or other place, whether in Singapore or elsewhere, at which trading in futures contracts regularly takes place;

(b) an electronic system, whether operating in Singapore or elsewhere, through which trading in futures contracts is carried out; but excludes an electronic facility which merely provides price or other information … and which does not permit users of the facility to channel orders for, execute transactions in, or make a market in, futures contracts.

The definition of 'futures market', prior to the 1995 amendments, did not include an electronic system. But, now it covers computerised trading facilities like the exchange's Automated Trading System and other alternative market arrangements. 'Futures market' as defined in the FTA refers not only to the exchange and other approved futures markets in Singapore, but also to overseas futures exchanges and markets. Section 3(1) of the FTA provides that, unless exempted, it is an offence to maintain or establish a futures market in Singapore that has not been approved by MAS.[138]

One issue, which arises with regard to providers of over-the counter (OTC) contracts, is whether they may be deemed to be operating unauthorised futures markets. In *Carragreen Currency Corporation Pty Ltd v CAC (NSW)*[139] the court gave a broad interpretation to the term 'futures market'. Hodgson J held that it extended to the infrastructure provided by a broker to facilitate trading in futures contracts.[140] If this reasoning is adopted in

---

[135] See Shreves, above n. 49, p. 522.
[136] See New Zealand Securities Commission, *Recommendations for Amendment of Part III Securities Amendment Act* 1988, Discussion Paper (Wellington, July 1994), para. 6.
[137] Ibid.
[138] Under s. 3(3) of the FTA, MAS may by a notification in the *Gazette* declare any futures market exempt, subject to such conditions or restrictions it may think fit to impose.
[139] (1986) 11 ACLR 298.
[140] Id. at 313: 'In my view, the infrastructure of the plaintiff does constitute a facility by means of which futures contracts are regularly made, and in my view the office of the plaintiff is a

Singapore, financial institutions and large corporations, with their own dealing rooms, may technically be operating unauthorised futures markets. However, it should be pointed out that there are differences between the Australian and Singapore definitions of 'futures market'. The Australian *Corporations Law* defines a 'futures market' as a 'market, exchange or other place at which, or a facility by means of which, futures contracts are regularly acquired or disposed of.'[141] On the other hand, the definition of 'futures market' in the FTA omits any reference to 'a facility'. It has been argued that because of this omission, it is unlikely that OTC providers in Singapore would be regarded as operating futures markets.[142] So far there has been no clarification from MAS on this issue.

Under s. 4(2) of the FTA, MAS may approve a body corporate to operate a futures exchange, provided certain criteria are met. Since the exchange will be responsible for the day-to-day supervision and regulation of the market and its participants, the FTA requires that the business rules of the exchange must provide for:

- qualifications for membership;
- grounds for expulsion, suspension and disciplining of members;
- fair trading practices and proper supervision;
- terms and conditions under which contracts may be made;
- clearing arrangements and financial safeguards; and
- establishment of a fund to compensate customers that have suffered losses through the defalcation of a member or employee.[143]

In addition, MAS must also be satisfied that 'the interests of the public will be served by approving the application.'[144] The FTA does not elaborate on what is meant by 'the interests of the public' and any determination by MAS is unlikely to be subject to review.

4.6.4 Malaysia

Under the *Futures Industry Act* (FIA) all trading in futures contracts must take place on the futures market of an exchange company approved by the Minister. Section 3(1) of the FIA provides that:

No person shall establish, operate or maintain or assist in establishing, operating or maintaining or hold himself out as providing, operating or maintaining a futures market that is neither a futures market of an exchange company nor an exempt futures market.

---

place at which futures contracts are regularly made, within the meaning of the definition of "futures market".'
[141] *Corporations Law*, s. 9.
[142] See Tan and Liew, above n. 88, 38.
[143] FTA, s. 4(2)(a).
[144] Id., 4(2)(b).

In addition, s. 3B prohibits the establishment or operation of a futures market either within or outside Malaysia for the trading of futures contracts based on instruments such as stocks traded on the Kuala Lumpur Stock Exchange, futures contracts traded on the Malaysian derivatives exchanges, and the Malaysian currency. It would appear that s. 3B, which was introduced in November 1998, is aimed at preventing other exchanges from trading in derivatives that would destabilise the Malaysian currency or stock prices. At around that time, the government had just imposed capital controls and s. 3B is seen as part of the package of measures to insulate the Malaysian economy from further financial turbulence.

A futures market is further defined in s. 2 as 'a market, exchange or other place at which, or facility by means of which, futures contracts are regularly traded.' The combined effect of a wide definition of a futures contract and the rule against off-exchange trading is that OTC market participants like financial institutions may run the risk of operating unauthorised futures markets if they trade in derivative contracts not covered by the banking exclusion. To avoid the risk of operating an unauthorised futures market, banks can seek exempt futures market status. When granting approval, s. 3A empowers the Minister to grant approval subject to such terms and conditions as the Minister thinks fit. The Minister may therefore impose rules on exempt markets, similar to those imposed by the FIA on regulate markets.

Approval for the operation of a futures exchange will only be given if the Minister is satisfied that the applicant meets the following criteria:

- include in its constitution an object to act in the public interest;
- provide in its constitution for the making of business rules;
- maintain adequate and properly equipped business premises and facilities;
- establish and operate futures markets at places approved by the Minister;
- arrange with a clearinghouse to provide clearing facilities for its markets;
- arrange for the establishment of a fidelity fund.[145]

The FIA is silent on the matters that the business rules should cover, although there is a disallowance procedure for amendments to the business rules.[146] The exchange company should as soon as practicable submit to the Commission any proposed amendments to its business rules with an explanation of the purpose of the change.[147] The Commission shall within six weeks or a mutually agreed longer period notify the exchange company of its decision. In addition, the Commission is empowered to amend or supplement the business rules. The Commission or any aggrieved person may apply to the court to order compliance or enforcement of any of the business rules.[148]

---

[145] FIA, s. 4(3).
[146] The same procedure also applies to changes to the exchange company's constitution.
[147] FIA, s. 6.
[148] Id., s. 11A.

In Malaysia, unlike in Australia, the Minister may revoke approval of an exchange company.[149] This power of revocation is necessary since the Malaysian exchanges are organised as 'for-profit' companies. The grounds for revocation range from company insolvency to non-compliance with the requirements and conditions of approval contained in s. 4 of the FIA. The Commission may also recommend to the Minister to revoke approval if it is of the opinion that the exchange company's failure to enforce any of its business rules, or to comply with any provisions of the FIA, are serious enough to warrant revocation.[150] Instead of revoking approval, the Minister may suspend trading until such time the requirement is complied with.[151]

The Minister is also empowered to temporarily close an exchange in an emergency. Under s. 9 the Minister may close an exchange for a period not exceeding five days if the Minister:

... is of the opinion that an orderly and fair market is being or is likely to be prevented because—

   (a)   an emergency or natural disaster has occurred in Malaysia; or
   (b)   there exists an economic or financial crisis or any other circumstances in Malaysia or elsewhere.

The exercise of a similar power to close Hong Kong's stock and derivatives exchanges during the October 1987 stock market crash drew international condemnation and adversely affected the reputation of Hong Kong's financial markets.[152]

A company that proposes to provide clearinghouse facilities must obtain the approval of the Minister. Approval will only be granted if the Minister is satisfied that the following clearinghouse criteria have been satisfied:

- the constitution of the clearinghouse includes an object to act in the public interest; and
- the applicant complies with the prescribed requirements.[153]

The prescribed requirements for clearinghouses are contained in the *Futures Industry Regulations* 1995. Some of these requirements are similar to those imposed on the futures exchange company. The clearinghouse must have 'adequate capital and suitable systems, procedures and arrangements in place to manage the risks, liabilities and obligations with respect to futures contracts cleared by it.'[154] There is also provision under the FIA for the Minister to revoke the approval granted to the clearinghouse.[155]

---

[149] Id., s. 7.
[150] Id., s. 11.
[151] Id., s. 8.
[152] See O'Hare, above n. 120, 178.
[153] FIA, s. 6B.
[154] Regulation 8.
[155] FIA, s. 7A.

4.6.5   Hong Kong

Under s. 2 of the CTO, a 'commodity market' is defined as:

a place provided and maintained by the Exchange Company for the trading in commodities generally or in particular commodities, whether under futures contracts or otherwise.[156]

Currently the Hong Kong Futures Exchange (HKFE) is the only exchange in Hong Kong where it is possible to trade in futures contracts. The CTO has adopted a narrow definition of 'commodity market' because it restricts the term to a physical market. As such, the existing definition does not cover exchanges with electronic screen-based trading systems. With the increasing popularity of screen-based trading systems, the definition would certainly have to be changed to keep pace with technological developments. A commodity market can trade in futures contracts that are based on specified commodities only, unless otherwise authorised in writing by the Securities and Futures Commission (SFC).[157]

The Chief Executive in Council may issue a licence to an exchange company to establish and operate the commodity exchange, if it satisfies the various requirements set out in s. 13(3) of the CTO. Generally, the exchange company must satisfy SFC that it will:

- maintain an adequate and properly equipped place of business,
- provide and maintain commodity markets at places approved by SFC,
- have satisfactory clearing and settlement arrangements in place,
- have an authorised share capital of not less than HKD 25 million and an issued capital of not less than HKD 3 million,
- provide in its constitution for the exclusion from membership of any person disqualified from becoming a shareholder,
- meet minimum financial requirements, and
- have rules to regulate its members and trading practices.

Any amendments to the constitution or rules of the exchange company or its clearinghouse will have no effect unless approved in writing by SFC.[158] No person may be appointed as chief executive of an exchange company unless approved by SFC.[159] This provision was introduced in 1989, and may have been prompted by the events following the October 1987 crash.[160]

---

[156] The terms 'commodity' and 'futures' are used inconsistently in the CTO, which could give rise to confusion and uncertainty. For example, while the legislation makes reference to 'futures contract', it does not make any reference to either 'futures exchange' or 'futures market'. Instead, it only makes reference to 'commodity exchange' and 'commodity market'.
[157] CTO, s. 16.
[158] Id., s. 14.
[159] Ibid.
[160] See Hay Davidson Report, above n. 59, Appendix 1, para. 23: 'On 2 January 1988, Mr. Ronald Li, who had then retired as Chairman of the SEHK ... was arrested ... and charged, on 15 January, under the Prevention of Bribery Ordinance with unlawfully accepting an advantage, namely a beneficial interest in an allotment of shares in a construction company.'

SFC may revoke the licence of the exchange company on a number of specified grounds, including the failure to comply with the requirements laid down by s. 13(3) of the CTO.[161] In addition, SFC may close the exchange for up to five days, if after consultation with the exchange company it is of the opinion, that orderly trading is likely to be affected by an emergency, natural disaster, economic or financial crisis in Hong Kong or elsewhere.[162]

It is interesting that the CTO does not specifically deal with the recognition of clearinghouses. Instead the legislation on clearinghouses is found in another legislation, the *Securities and Futures (Clearing Houses) Ordinance*. This anomaly has been highlighted and will be addressed by the new legal framework, currently under consideration. Under the existing arrangements, the SFC may with consent of the Financial Secretary, declare a clearinghouse to be a recognised clearinghouse if it is 'satisfied that it is appropriate to do so in the interest of the investing public or in the public interest, or for the proper regulation of services for the clearing and settlement of transactions in securities or futures contracts'.[163]

4.6.6 Summary and Comments

In Australia, Singapore, Malaysia and Hong Kong, trading in 'futures contracts' may take place only on an approved 'futures market' or an exempt 'futures market'. What this means is that all derivatives markets, which fall within the definition of a 'futures market' (or 'commodity market' in the case of Hong Kong) must be authorised. Authorised markets include specified exchanges, such as approved overseas derivatives exchanges. In addition, no person may operate a clearing facility without proper authorisation. However, the legal position is different in New Zealand. Under the present laws, there is no requirement for an exchange to be authorised to conduct a market for the trading of futures contracts. As such, the New Zealand legislation does not contain any legal definition of 'futures market'. There is also no requirement in New Zealand for a person to obtain approval to operate a clearing facility.

Generally, for any person to obtain approval to operate an authorised exchange or clearinghouse they must satisfy the approval criteria laid down in the legislation. Although the regulatory objectives of Australia, Singapore, Malaysia and Hong Kong appear similar, there are variations in the approval criteria. For example, the Malaysian legislation is silent on the matters that should be included in the business rules of an exchange. On the other hand, the Australian, Singapore, and Hong Kong legislation specifically mention what the business rules must provide for. What is clear is that the existing approval criteria for exchanges in all jurisdictions are unsuitable for alternative market arrangements such as non-intermediated exchanges. None of the approval criteria deals with issues like clearing arrangements and documentation where the customer deals direct with the exchange.

---

[161] CTO, s. 18(1).
[162] Id., s. 21(1).
[163] *Securities and Futures (Clearing Houses) Ordinance*, s. 3(1).

Currently, there is no requirement for over-the-counter derivatives markets to be authorised in Australia, Singapore, Malaysia or Hong Kong. This has been achieved by either the legislation specifying that certain derivatives may only be traded on an authorised exchange, or exempting certain categories of customised contracts from the definition of 'futures contract'. However, the existing legal definitions of 'futures market' are far from satisfactory. There are still some doubts whether certain activities would constitute the operation of a futures market. For example, the Australian definition of 'futures market' is broad enough to cover even the trading activities of frequent derivatives end-users and the treasury operations of large corporations.

4.7   LICENSING OF INTERMEDIARIES

As the licensing of derivatives intermediaries is an important aspect of the regulatory function, the lack of a proper licensing system could put investors at risks. Generally, licensing is aimed at ensuring intermediaries are not only competent and financially sound, but also fair and honest. These objectives are usually achieved through limiting the categories of persons who should be allowed to undertake derivatives activities and by requiring them to fulfil certain obligations as a condition for retention of their licences. There are two broad systems of licensing: positive licensing and negative licensing. Under a positive licensing system all intermediaries must be licensed unless they are exempted, whereas under a negative licensing system, any person may be permitted to act as an intermediary, unless prohibited. The licensing of derivatives intermediaries adopts the former approach. In most cases, the government regulator is responsible for the licensing of intermediaries. The two main categories of intermediaries who require to be licensed are futures brokers and futures advisers. But in some jurisdictions, futures funds mangers must also be licensed.

4.7.1   Australia

In Australia, all intermediaries who fall within the definitions of 'futures brokers' or 'futures advisers' must be licensed, unless exempted.[164] They must satisfy a specified number of criteria, ranging from solvency to educational qualifications and experience for the grant of a licence.[165] Additionally, they must be members of a futures organisation and currently this means the Sydney Futures Exchange (SFE), as there is no separate futures association in Australia.[166] Futures brokers who trade on their own account are exempt from the licensing requirement. Trading on a person's own account extends to trading on behalf of an associate of the person or a

---

[164] *Corporations Law*, ss. 9, 1142–1143.
[165] Id., ss. 1144A, 1145.
[166] Ibid.

body corporate in which the person has a controlling interest. The expression 'acting on another person's behalf' includes acting on implied instructions of another person. 'Dealing' is given a wide meaning and covers not only the acquisition and disposal of futures contract, but also offering and inducing to acquire and dispose futures contracts.[167] Since it is not unusual for futures transactions to involve several intermediaries, the concept of dealing would embrace the activities of these intermediaries.[168] An exempt futures broker is not required to comply with the statutory provisions relating to the segregation of accounts, or to those relating to a broker's accounting and auditing obligations.[169]

A person is prohibited from carrying on a futures advice business, or from holding out as a futures adviser, unless that person is licensed or is an exempt futures adviser.[170] Futures brokers who also involved in the giving of advice on futures contracts do not require a futures adviser's licence. The *Corporations Law* specifically exempts certain categories of persons from licensing and they include proprietors and publishers of newspapers or periodicals, which are 'generally available to the public, otherwise than only as subscription.'[171] In *Australian Securities Commission v Dempster*,[172] the respondent, who was neither a licensee nor an exempt futures adviser, provided information about commodity prices to about 200 farmers for an annual charge. Those who subscribed to his service received, among other things, copies of a newsletter produced by him. In the newsletter, Dempster monitored commodity prices, made predictions about their future movements, and gave opinions about the desirability of acquiring put options on futures contracts. Dempster was not licensed and the issue before the court was whether his activities fell within the exemption found in s. 71(5). The court held that the newsletter was disseminated as part of a business and involved the proffering of advice about futures contract.[173] Even though the newsletter was made available from time to time to a substantial number of farmers who were not subscribers of his service, yet the evidence did not suggest that it was so widely distributed as to be a publication 'generally available to the public.'[174]

Representatives of futures brokers and advisers need not be licensed but must hold proper authority.[175] Futures representatives are natural persons who are either employed by, or act for or by arrangement, with a broker or adviser. Not all employees are regarded as representatives, only those who assist in the execution of futures business or those who tender advice about futures trading. A body corporate cannot act as a futures representative.[176]

---

[167] Id., s. 25(1).
[168] Id., ss. 26–28.
[169] See Currie, above n. 78, pp. 187–188.
[170] Id., s. 1143.
[171] Id., s. 71.
[172] (1992) 10 ACLC 1,050.
[173] Id. at 1056.
[174] Ibid.
[175] *Corporations Law*, ss. 1172–1173.
[176] Id., s. 1175.

Representatives must be registered with SFE and satisfy certain skills requirements. They must hold proper authority from a licensed broker or adviser. A proper authority is a copy of the broker's or adviser's licence on which are endorsed statements by the licensee that the holder is the licensee's representative. Brokers and advisers are responsible for their representatives and cannot contract out their liability, even if the representatives act outside the scope of their authority.[177] They may be required, for example, to pay damages to clients who have suffered losses as a result of the actions of their representatives. Licensees are required to keep a register of holders of proper authorities and the register must contain information such as the holders' names and addresses.[178]

ASIC has powers to revoke or suspend a licence on a wide range of grounds. In some instances, ASIC may revoke a licence without a hearing, such as when the licensee is convicted of a serious fraud or is insolvent.[179] But in most cases, revocation can only take place after a hearing.[180] Currently, there is no provision preventing the licensee from acting for clients, pending the outcome of the hearing. A person who enters into an agreement with a non-licensee is entitled to rescind the agreement, subject to the fulfilment of certain criteria.[181] The non-licensee cannot recover any fees or brokerage from the client in respect of the agreement, nor enforce the agreement against the client.[182] When ASIC revokes or suspends the licence of a natural person, it can also make a banning order against him or her.[183] The banning order may be temporary or permanent. It is made under certain circumstances such as when the licensee has engaged in egregious conduct. The effect of a banning order is that person is ineligible for the grant of a broker's or adviser's licence.[184] Alternatively, ASIC may apply for a disqualification order after a licence has been revoked.[185] A disqualification order is applicable to both natural persons and corporations.

4.7.2 New Zealand

The key authorisation provision is s. 38(1) of the *Securities Amendment Act 1988* (as amended by the *Sharebrokers Amendment Act*) which provides that:

No person shall carry on the business of dealing in futures contracts unless that person is, or is a member of a class of persons that is, authorised by the Commission by notice in the *Gazette* to carry on the business of dealing in futures contracts.

In other words, dealers may be authorised individually or as a class of persons. A class of persons may be members of a particular futures exchange.

---

[177] Id., ss. 1183–1188.
[178] Id., ss. 1176(1)–1176(3).
[179] Id., s. 1190.
[180] Id., s. 1191.
[181] Id., s. 1164.
[182] Id., ss. 1167–1168.
[183] Id., s. 1192A.
[184] Id., s. 1194.
[185] Id., s. 1201.

Authorisation may be for futures contracts generally, or for specified futures contracts or a specified class of futures contracts.[186]

The Securities Commission (Commission) may also authorise a dealer on such terms and conditions as the Commission thinks fit.[187] Conditions that have been attached to authorisations have varied. Most authorisations may require a continuing association with NZFOE, while some authorisations may require that the dealers provide financial statements to the Commission.[188] By making membership of an authorised exchange a condition of authorisation, the effect of Part III is to confer upon an authorised exchange the power to regulate its own members. In the past, the Commission had no express power to revoke, vary or suspend any authorisation under s. 38. This meant that any non-compliance with the exchange's rules would not have resulted in the revocation of authorisation. Under s. 38(3), the Commission may, by notice in the *Gazette*, vary or revoke, in whole or in part, any authorisation given. Contravention of s. 38 is an offence and a person is liable on summary conviction to a fine or imprisonment.[189]

Any determination of who should be authorised to deal in futures contracts depends on the meaning of the term 'dealing'. Section 37(5) defines 'dealing' in the following terms:

For the purposes of this Part of this Act, a person deals in a futures contract if that person—

   (a)   Acquires or disposes of the futures contract on behalf of another person; or

   (b)   Offers to acquire or dispose of the futures contract on behalf of another person; or

   (c)   On behalf of another person induces, or attempts to induce, a person, to acquire or dispose of the futures contract; or

   (d)   Advises or assists a person in connection with the acquisition or disposition of the futures contract; or

   (e)   Does any other act or engages in conduct declared by the Commission by notice in the *Gazette* to constitute dealing in a futures contract for the purposes of this Part of this Act.

Based on the above definition, the term 'dealing' only extends to situations when a person is acting on behalf of another person. A person who deals in a futures contract on the person's own account would not be regarded as dealing in a futures contract. The definition of 'dealing' also covers the provision of advice and assistance in connection with the acquisition or disposition of futures contracts. As a consequence, futures advisers would also be required to be authorised under the Act. However, any person who provides advice or assistance in a professional capacity, such as a solicitor or chartered accountant, would not be regarded as giving advice or assistance within the meaning of s. 37(5)(d) of the Act.[190]

---

[186] *Securities Amendment Act*, s. 38(2).
[187] Ibid.
[188] See D. Parker, 'Regulatory Environment of Derivatives in New Zealand Continues to Evolve' (1996) 11 *Derivatives* 282, 283.
[189] *Securities Amendment Act*, s. 39.
[190] Id., s. 37(6).

The New Zealand Futures and Options Exchange (NZFOE) has expressed dissatisfaction with the wide scope of the term 'dealing' as it has the potential to catch many activities either unintended by the legislation, or which do not involve any dealings with the public. For example, any person who has access to NZFOE through the use of a computer terminal may be deemed to be dealing in futures contracts. This would mean that Australian brokers who have access to the New Zealand exchange would be required to seek authorisation and also comply with the futures regulations relating to the handling of clients' funds. NZFOE has therefore recommended that the operation of s. 37(5) be limited to dealing in futures contracts in New Zealand.[191] It has also expressed concern that the term 'dealing' may cover activities such as dealing on behalf of a related company, as well as activities undertaken by a dealer's employees, directors, or contractors that are associated with the dealing in futures contracts.[192]

Currently, NZFOE is responsible for reviewing each application for admission as a dealer to ensure that only suitable applicants are admitted. In other words, the exchange is principally responsible for determining which persons may deal in futures.. However, this approach is not entirely satisfactory given the width of the futures contract definition. In view of the complexity and range of products traded by exchange members, it is unlikely that the exchange is in a position to supervise and regulate all the trading activities of its members. As such, a dealer should not be allowed to trade in all futures products (some of which are not traded on the exchange) by virtue of membership of an authorised exchange alone.

When trading in electricity futures began, many of the electricity distributors and generators sought authorisation from the Commission. They were concerned that their activities would constitute 'dealing in futures contracts'.[193] In view of the large number of potential dealers the Commission decided to issue a class authorisation. Under *The Authorised Futures Dealers Notice 1997 (No. 2)*, the Commission has authorised a specific group of dealers to deal in electricity futures contracts provided that their clients belong to specific classes of persons. The classes of persons consist of habitual investors, which are viewed by the Commission as being of sufficient financial worth to understand the complexity of futures contracts.

4.7.3 Singapore

In Singapore, all brokers, trading advisers, pool operators, and their representatives must be licensed. Section 11(1) of the *Futures Trading Act* (FTA) states that:

Subject to any regulations made under this Act, no person, whether as principal or agent, shall—

---

[191] See New Zealand Futures and Options Exchange, 'Recommendations for Amendments of Part III Securities Amendment Act 1988' (Memorandum addressed to the Securities Commission, 9 September, 1994), para. 10.1.
[192] Id., para. 10.2.
[193] See Mulholland and Lester, above n. 48, p. 733.

(a) carry on business as a futures broker; or
(b) hold himself out as carrying on such a business, unless such person—
     (i)   is licensed as a futures broker under this Act; and
     (ii) in relation to the business of futures trading trades in accordance with the business rules and practices of an Exchange or futures market on which the trading takes place.

Contravention of s. 11(1) is an offence, which is punishable on conviction, by a fine not exceeding SGD 30,000, or by imprisonment for a term not exceeding three years, or both.[194] The requirement that a broker must trade in accordance with the rules and practices of the exchange was recently introduced. Since the rules of the exchange now have legal backing, it will be easier for the Monetary Authority of Singapore (MAS) to take action against brokers who breach the rules.

'Futures broker' is defined in s. 2(1) as:

[A]ny person, whether as principal or agent, who—

(a) carries on the business of soliciting or accepting orders, for the purchase or sale of any commodity under a futures contract on any Futures Exchange or futures market whether or not that person accepts any money, securities or property (or extends credit in lieu thereof) to margin, guarantee or secure any contract or transaction that may result therefrom; or
(b) carries on the business of leveraged foreign exchange trading,

whether the business is part of, or is carried on in conjunction with, any other business.'

By expanding the definition of 'futures broker' to include a person who carries on the business of leveraged foreign exchange trading, foreign exchange brokers are now required to obtain licences under the legislation.

Under s. 11(2), the following categories of persons are exempted from the licensing requirement, provided they comply with the regulations prescribed by MAS:

(a) a person who carries on the business of futures trading or leveraged foreign exchange trading only with accredited investors;[195]
(b) a person who carries on the business of futures trading or leveraged foreign exchange trading for his own account, or for the account of a related corporation or related person;[196]
(c) a person licensed under the *Securities Industry Act* or exempted under that Act or any of its regulations, and who carries on trading in futures or leveraged foreign exchange wholly in connection with or incidental to the trading or hedging of securities.

---

[194] FTA, s. 11(3).
[195] Accredited investors are either individuals with net personal assets in excess of SGD 5 million or companies with net assets in excess of SGD 10 million.
[196] The term 'related corporation' has the same meaning as in the Singapore *Companies Act* (Cap. 50). Section 11(4) of the FTA defines 'related person' in relation to an individual as a member of the individual's immediate family, and a firm or corporation in which the individual or a member of the individual's immediate family has control of not less than 50 per cent of voting power in the firm or corporation.

By exempting those who carry on the business of trading with accredited investors and confining the licensing requirement to those who deal on behalf of others, the FTA is giving recognition to the need for minimal regulation at the wholesale end of the market. To avoid the need for dual licensing for securities brokers who deal in futures contracts in connection or incidental to their business, the FTA exempts them from licensing. However, it is important to recognise that the MAS can impose conditions for exemption from licensing.

The following categories of persons are also required to be licensed: futures broker's representatives; futures trading advisers; futures trading adviser's representatives; futures pool operators; and futures pool operator's representatives.[197] In line with the changes to the coverage of the FTA, the definition of 'futures trading adviser' now includes any person:

- who carries on the business of advising other persons concerning futures contracts, foreign exchange trading or leveraged foreign exchange trading;
- as part of a regular business issues or publishes any report or analysis of futures and foreign exchange markets; or
- who under an arrangement or contract with a client, undertakes trading in futures contracts and foreign exchange for the purpose of managing the client's funds.[198]

The following categories of persons are excluded from the futures trading adviser definition: (a) licensed commercial and approved merchant banks; (b) accountants and solicitors who carry on the business incidental to the practice of their profession; (c) newspaper publishers, journalists, and writers; and (d) futures brokers and pool operators who carry on the business of advising on futures contracts incidental to their main business. The term 'futures pool operator' refers to any person who carries on the business in the nature of a unit trust or other interest to which Division 6 of Part IV of the *Companies Act* applies. (This Division regulates interests other than shares and debentures, such as collective investments.) Pool operators are basically persons who pool investors' moneys to trade in futures contracts, foreign exchange trading or leveraged foreign exchange trading.

Sections 12(2) and 12(3) have been amended so that only corporations may be granted licences to operate as futures brokers, futures trading advisers, or pool operators. As for their representatives, they may be licensed if they are individuals. It would appear from this that partnerships and sole proprietorships are ineligible for licences, since they are neither individuals nor corporations. As a result of expanding the definitions of 'futures broker's representative' and 'futures trading adviser's representative', directors, officers, and employees who act on behalf of brokers and advisers must now be licensed. The amendment was introduced to allow greater governmental control over the appointment of employees by broking firms.

---

[197] FTA, s. 12(1).
[198] Id., s. 2.

One of the requirements for the grant and retention of a futures broker's or futures trading adviser's licence is satisfaction of the minimum financial requirement test prescribed by MAS or provided under the business rules of the exchange.[199] If a futures broker becomes aware of any inability to meet the financial requirement, the broker must immediately notify MAS and cease carrying on its business, unless to give effect to any unfinished business.[200] The broker is deemed to be aware of an inability to comply with the requirement 'if any of its directors or officers is so aware or would, with the exercise of reasonable diligence, have been aware of such inability.'[201] The onus is therefore placed on the management of the broker to notify MAS. Section 21A was recently introduced to empower MAS to issue notices to licence holders to comply with the requirements of the notices. Failure to comply with such a notice is an offence and on conviction punishable by a fine of SGD 20,000. In the case of a continuing offence, a further fine of SGD 5,000 is imposed for every day the offence continues after conviction.

MAS may refuse to grant or renew a licence on a number of grounds and some of them may prove difficult to challenge. For instance, an application for a licence may be refused if MAS 'is not satisfied with the record of past performance or expertise of the applicant.'[202] MAS may refuse to renew a licence if the applicant fails the 'fit and proper' person test. Information that is relevant to fitness and propriety would normally include details of past and live convictions, awareness of any civil proceedings anywhere in the world, and previous failed applications to the regulator.[203] In addition, MAS is empowered to revoke a licence under a wide range of circumstances.[204] Before a licence is revoked, MAS is required to give the licensee an opportunity to be heard. A licence is revoked, in the case of an individual, if the individual dies, and in the case of a corporation, if the corporation is wound up.[205] Under s. 22 (2), the revocation or suspension of a licence shall not operate so as to avoid any agreement or transaction, or affect any right or obligation arising under such an agreement or transaction.

The meaning of s. 22(2) was considered in *Tokyo Investments Pte Ltd & Anor v Tan Chu Thing*.[206] In that case, the respondent applied for a declaration that he was entitled to possession of some shares that he had pledged to the second appellant (a dealer licensed in Hong Kong but not in Singapore) with whom he had maintained a trading account. The account was subsequently closed and all outstanding amounts were settled. However, the shares were not returned to the respondent on the ground that they were pledged as security for the trading account of the respondent's brother. The first appellant, who admitted to having acted as futures broker representative of the

---

[199] Id., s. 24.
[200] Id., s. 24A(1).
[201] Id., s. 24A(3).
[202] Id., s. 14(1)(ix).
[203] See J. Virgo and P. Ryley, 'Fitness and Propriety in Financial Services in the 21st Century' (2000) 8 *Journal of Financial Regulation and Compliance* 109, 116.
[204] FTA, s. 20.
[205] Id., s. 20(1).
[206] [1993] 3 SLR 170.

second appellant, later pleaded guilty to having carried on the business of trading in futures contracts in contravention of s. 11(1)(d) of the FTA. The registrar granted the respondent the declaration and the appellants appealed first to the High Court and then to the Court of Appeal. The Court of Appeal held that s. 22(2) was meant to save those transactions entered into by a futures broker after his or her licence has been revoked or suspended, and not those transactions entered into by a person who was never registered as a broker. Transactions entered into by a person who was never licensed are illegal and unenforceable.

4.7.4 Malaysia

The *Futures Industry Act* (FIA) broadly defines the activities of those who deal in futures, those who give advice on them, and those who manage futures funds for the purpose of requiring them to obtain authorisation from the Securities Commission (Commission). Excluded from these broad definitions are certain categories of persons such as court appointed receivers, liquidators, and trustees. The FIA also introduces a degree of flexibility by empowering the Commission to exempt certain categories of persons from licensing.[207] However, those persons exempted from licensing are still required to comply with the other provisions of the FIA, unless exempted by the Minister.[208]

Under the FIA, a person must hold a futures broker's licence to trade in a futures contract on another's behalf, or hold out as carrying on a futures broking business.[209] This means that a person who trades in futures contracts on the person's own account would not require to be licensed. In addition, no corporation may carry on a futures broking business unless its directors and accredited employees are licensed as broker's representatives. The requirement that accredited employees (that is, those authorised to trade in futures contracts on behalf of the broker) must be licensed gives the Commission the power to screen the appointment of directors and employees to prevent undesirable persons from engaging in futures trading activities. The holder of a futures find manager's licence is not required to be licensed as a broker, as long as the trading in futures contract is for the purpose of the holder's funds management business.[210]

Similarly, futures funds managers and futures trading advisers are required to be licensed if they carry out futures funds management business and futures advice business, respectively.[211] 'Futures funds management business' means the business of offering to any person for subscription; or inviting any person to subscribe for, interests to which Division 5 of Part IV of the *Companies Act* 1965 applies.[212] Division 5 regulates interests other than

---

[207] FIA, 20(1).
[208] Id., s. 20(2).
[209] Id., s. 16.
[210] Id., s. 16(2A).
[211] Id., ss. 16A, 17.
[212] Id., s. 2.

shares and debentures, such interests in managed investments schemes, time-sharing schemes and investment contracts. 'Futures advice business' means the business of advising other persons about trading in futures contracts; or a business in the course of which the person publishes futures reports. Certain categories of persons are excluded from the definition of 'futures adviser' and they include publishers and proprietors of newspapers.[213]

Initially, the responsibility of approving licences was entrusted to the licensing division of the Ministry of Finance and not the Commission. Such a division of responsibilities would have made supervision of market inter-mediaries difficult for the Commission. The FIA was later amended so that the Commission is now responsible for the approval of licences for all derivatives intermediaries.[214] Licences are granted for a period of one year and conditions may be imposed on them.[215] While licences for futures brokers and futures funds managers will only be issued to corporations,[216] a futures trading adviser's licence may be granted to either a corporation or an individual.[217] No detailed criteria have been laid down in the FIA for approval of licences. However, the *Guidelines for Application of Licence under the Futures Industry Act* 1993 developed by the Commission in consultation with the exchanges provide some guidance on the prerequisites for approval.[218]

Under the Commission's guidelines, if a corporation is a member of both KLOFFE and COMMEX, representatives of the futures brokers sponsored by that corporation may be licensed to trade in both the exchanges. This approval to trade in both exchanges will be indicated in the licence issued to them. Securities brokers licensed under the *Securities Industry Act* 1983 are permitted to participate in the futures industry. The previous restriction on securities dealers engaging in any business other than stock broking has been removed. Now, a securities dealer's representative may also be licensed as a futures broker's representative. However, the securities dealer's representative will only be considered for dual licences, if the sponsoring futures broking company is either a subsidiary of the holding company of member company of the Kuala Lumpur Stock Exchange (KLSE) or a subsidiary of a member company of KLSE.

It is interesting to note that the futures broker's licence may only be granted or renewed by the Commission with the approval of the Minister of Finance. This additional requirement suggests that the final decision rests with the Minister and not the Commission. No similar requirements are imposed on the approval of licences for other categories of intermediaries.

---

[213]   Ibid.
[214]   Id., s. 22(1).
[215]   Id., s. 22(2).
[216]   Id., s. 23(1).
[217]   Id., s. 23(2).
[218]   For example, an applicant for a futures broker's licence must comply with the following requirements: (a) maintain a 30 per cent 'Bumiputra' (the term for an indigenous person) equity in the company, (b) fulfil the minimum financial requirements prescribed by the Futures Industry Regulation and the relevant exchange, and (c) obtain approval in principle for admission to the relevant exchange.

The Commission may refuse to renew a licence, or it may revoke a licence on a number of grounds.[219] These grounds include financial insolvency, professional incompetence, or financial impropriety. A person whose licence has been revoked or refused renewal can appeal within 30 days to the Minister, whose decision will be final.[220]

The Commission is empowered under s. 28(1) to conduct an inquiry into any allegation that a licensed person is or has been guilty of any 'misconduct', or is no longer a 'fit and proper' person. There are two meanings ascribed to the definition of 'misconduct' in the legislation. It could either mean failure to comply with any provisions of the FIA, regulations, business rules or licensing conditions, or it could also mean any act or omission that is prejudicial to the interests of the person's clients or the public interest.[221] Whether the licensee is still a 'fit and proper' person depends on whether there are any circumstances, which have led or are likely to lead to an improper conduct of business. At an inquiry to hear any allegation the licensee will be given an opportunity to be heard.[222] If the allegation is founded, the licence can be suspended or revoked, or the Commission can fine the licensee in lieu of suspension or revocation.[223]

Part IIIA of the FIA deals with agreements with unlicensed persons. An 'unlicensed person' is defined as a person who does not hold a relevant licence.[224] This would suggest that the term covers both persons who were never licensed and those whose licences have been revoked. Part IIIA covers agreements with all categories of unlicensed intermediaries. Its underlying objective is to ensure that a client may give the unlicensed person written notice, within a reasonable period of becoming aware of his or her rights, to rescind the agreement.[225] The term 'client' has a restricted meaning and excludes futures intermediaries and their associates.[226] However, the client is not entitled to give notice if the client has affirmed the agreement, or if the unlicensed person advised the client before the agreement was concluded that he or she was not in possession of a relevant licence. The unlicensed person is not entitled to recover any outstanding commission or fee, and the client may recover any commission or fee paid to the unlicensed person.[227]

4.7.5   Hong Kong

The term 'registration', instead of 'licensing', is used in the *Commodity Trading Ordinance* (CTO) to refer to the process of authorising intermediaries. Any person who carries on, or holds out as carrying on, the business of trading in

---

[219]   FIA, ss. 25(3), 26(1)–26(2).
[220]   Id., s. 30.
[221]   Id., s. 28(7).
[222]   Id., s. 28(3).
[223]   Id., s. 28(1A).
[224]   Id., s. 35A.
[225]   Id., s. 35E.
[226]   Id., s. 35A.
[227]   Id., ss. 35J, 35L.

commodity futures contracts, whether on the person's own account or on behalf of another, must be registered as a dealer.[228] Currently the Securities and Futures Commission (SFC) is responsible for authorisation. No corporation or firm may be registered unless every director, partner or employee is registered as a dealer.[229] The criteria for registration of a dealer include possession of a trading right and payment of a cash deposit.[230]

Under the existing arrangements, SFC is also empowered to grant exemption from registration. It is possible to avoid registration if the person trades 'otherwise than as agent in commodity futures contracts only thorough a dealer registered under this Ordinance'.[231] It has been suggested that this is an exemption, which is open to exploitation under many types of customer documentation common in the market.[232] Any person who carries on, or holds out as carrying on, an advice business has to be registered as a commodity trading adviser.[233] It is an offence under the CTO to act as a dealer or adviser without first being registered.[234]

The phrase, 'trading in commodity futures contracts' is defined in s. 2 of the CTO as 'making or offering to make an agreement with any other person in Hong Kong, or inducing or attempting to induce any other person in Hong Kong to enter into or offer to enter into a futures contract.' It would appear that the focus is on where the counterparty is located, rather than where the trading business is carried out.[235] This means that a broker who enters into an agreement with a client in Hong Kong to trade in futures contracts overseas must be registered. However, if the same broker enters into an agreement with a client overseas to trade in futures contracts in Hong Kong, it would appear that the broker does not require to be registered.

'Commodity trading advice business' is defined as the performance of any of the following activities for remuneration:

- advising any other person concerning the purchase or sale of futures contracts,
- as part of a regular business, issues or circulates analyses or reports concerning the above, or
- pursuant to an arrangement, manages a client's portfolio of futures contracts, including arranging their purchase and sale.[236]

The existing distinction between a 'dealer' and 'adviser' for licensing purposes has been criticised. One of the criticisms is that advisers include those who manage clients' portfolios and since the management of a portfolio would necessarily include the buying and selling futures contracts, there is an

---

[228]   CTO, s. 26(1).
[229]   Id., ss. 26(2)–26(3).
[230]   Id., s. 31.
[231]   Id., s. 26(4)(a).
[232]   See A. Malcolm and J. Fidler, 'Legal and Regulatory Issues for Derivatives in Hong Kong' (January 1995) IFLR 38, 39.
[233]   CTO, s. 27(1).
[234]   Id., ss. 26(5), 27(4).
[235]   See Malcolm and Fidler, above n. 232, 39.
[236]   CTO, s. 27(1).

overlap in functions between both categories of intermediaries.[237] In addition, advisers may expose investors to more than the usual risks of taking advice because they also handle clients' funds.[238] As such any intermediary who holds clients' funds should be registered as a dealer and not as an adviser.

Every director and employee accredited to a corporation must be registered as a dealer before the corporation can carry on business as a dealer.[239] Similarly, every partner and employee of a firm should be registered as a dealer, before the firm can carry on business as a dealer.[240] A person is accredited to a firm or corporation, if the person is authorised to trade or advise on futures contracts on behalf of the firm or corporation.[241] In addition, it is an offence for a person to perform for a dealer or adviser any of the functions of a dealer or adviser for remuneration unless registered as a dealer's or adviser's representative.[242] In other words, all representatives of dealers and advisers must be registered. However, any work ordinarily performed by an accountant, clerk or cashier is exempted from registration. Presumably this exemption extends to other back-room staff such as secretaries, data entry operators, and computer staff.

SFC may revoke the registration of a registered person on a number of grounds contained in s. 35. These grounds include the death of the individual or dissolution of the firm; insolvency of the registered person; and any of the grounds on which SFC may refuse to register a person under s. 32. Before revoking the registration of a person, SFC must first give the person an opportunity to be heard.[243] If after making an inquiry SFC finds that a registered person has been guilty of misconduct, it may either revoke or suspend the registration of that person.[244] For the purposes of s. 36, 'misconduct' refers to a failure to comply with any applicable laws or conditions for registration; conduct of business as an intermediary which is prejudicial to the interests of the investing public; and a failure to comply with any rules made by SFC. The revocation or suspension of a person does not affect the validity of any agreement or arrangement relating to the trading of futures contracts, whether made before or after the revocation or suspension.[245]

Currently tribunals, appointed from the Securities and Futures Panel, are empowered to hear appeals against decisions of the SFC. Under s. 21 of the *Securities and Futures Commission Ordinance*:

s. 21(3)
(a) An appeal shall be made to the Panel within 30 days beginning on the day on which written notification of the decision to which the appeal relates is served on the appellant

---

[237]   See Securities and Futures Commission, *A Consultation Paper on a Draft for a Composite Securities and Futures Bill* (Hong Kong, April 1996), paras 58–59.
[238]   Ibid.
[239]   CTO, s. 26(2).
[240]   Id., s. 26(3).
[241]   Id., s. 2.
[242]   Id., ss. 28, 29.
[243]   Id., s. 35(4).
[244]   Id., s. 36.
[245]   Id., s. 37.

...

s. 21(4)

...a decision in respect of which an appeal may be made to this Panel...shall not come into operation until the time for making the appeal has expired or, where an appeal is made, the appeal is withdrawn or determined.

In other words, any decision to revoke or suspend the registration of a person cannot take effect until expiry of the period for lodging the appeal, or determination of the appeal. Since the minimum period before a decision made by SFC can come into effect is 30 days (and when an appeal has been lodged the period could be much longer) the public is put at risk for an unnecessarily long period.[246]

4.7.6 Summary and Comments

The method of licensing (or 'registration' as it is referred to in Hong Kong) is basically similar for Australia, Singapore, Malaysia and Hong Kong. The relevant legislation broadly defines the activities of those that deal in futures contracts, those who advise on futures contracts, and those who manage funds involving futures contracts for the purpose of licensing, but excludes from the broad definitions certain categories of persons, or permits the regulatory agency to exempt specific categories of persons. The regulatory agencies are responsible for the approval of licences except in the case of Malaysia, where the approval of futures broking licences requires the approval of the Minister. Generally, the approval of licences is subject to the intermediaries meeting specified criteria such as those relating to solvency; education and experience; and good fame and character. New Zealand has adopted a somewhat different approach to the authorisation of dealers. Dealers may either be authorised individually by the regulatory agency or through membership of an authorised futures exchange.

The licensing schemes although broadly similar in approach, differ in a number of aspects. Australia, New Zealand, Singapore and Malaysia require brokers to be licensed only if they deal on behalf of other persons, and not when they enter into transactions on their own account. Another variation relates to the authorisation of representatives of intermediaries. In Singapore, Malaysia, and Hong Kong, all representatives of brokers, advisers and funds managers are required to be licensed by their respective regulatory agencies. This allows the regulatory agencies greater control over who may be employed by broking firms. Certain categories of employees like cashiers, accountants and clerks are exempted from this licensing requirement. However in Australia, all representatives of intermediaries are only required to hold proper authority, provided they meet the skill criteria laid down by the Sydney Futures Exchange. With respect to the protection offered to investors dealing with non-licensees, there are variations too. Australia and Malaysia have specific statutory provisions to protect clients

---

[246] See Securities and Futures Commission, *A Consultation Paper on a Draft for a Composite Securities and Futures Bill* (Hong Kong, April 1996), para. 27.

dealing with unlicensed intermediaries, whereas there are none in the other three jurisdictions.

4.8   RISKS DISCLOSURE AND SUITABILITY

Licensed derivatives intermediaries are subject to various statutory obligations and one of the more important obligations is the duty to provide risk disclosure statements to their clients. The underlying purpose of risks disclosure is to make clients aware of the risks inherent in trading derivatives. Intermediaries are normally required to advise clients not only about the risks generally associated with derivatives trading, but also of the risks involved in the trading of particular types of derivatives. Generic risks disclosures are normally made at the commencement of the intermediary-client relationship and specific risks disclosures before transacting in a specific class of derivatives. Breach of the risks disclosure obligation is an offence under the existing laws. Despite the importance attached to risks disclosure, it is not without limitations. For example, there is no way of ensuring that the client has fully understood the risks or the potential financial exposure. The irony is that risks disclosure works best when the client is financially sophisticated and can appreciate the risks disclosed.

Derivatives intermediaries, unlike securities dealers, are rarely subject to a statutory 'know your client' obligation. This obligation, also known as the suitability obligation, was originally introduced for securities trading. The main thrust of the obligation is that before an intermediary makes a personal recommendation to his or her client, the intermediary must have a reasonable basis for doing so. An intermediary has a reasonable basis if he or she has met two main obligations. First, the intermediary has taken into account the client's investment objectives, financial situation and particular needs. Second, the intermediary has undertaken a reasonable investigation of the investment or product in question. The objective of this obligation is to ensure that intermediaries do not make unsuitable personal recommendations to their clients. There is however ongoing debate about benefits of imposing such a rule for derivatives intermediaries. One of the arguments against the introduction of this rule is that it could create moral hazard problems. Another argument is that it may discourage the provision of personal recommendations, which may disadvantage some investors.

4.8.1   Australia

Chapter 8 of the Australian *Corporations Law* specifically deals with risks disclosure. Section 1210 imposes the following risks disclosure obligations on brokers:

A futures broker shall, before accepting a person as client of the broker, give to that person:

   (a)   a document that:
        (i) explains the nature of futures contracts;

(ii) explains the nature of the obligations assumed by a person who instructs a futures broker to enter into a futures contract;

(iii) sets out a risk disclosure statement in the prescribed form; and

(iv) sets out the specifications, and details of the essential terms, of each kind of futures contract in which the broker deals on behalf of clients; and

(b) a copy of each agreement into which the broker proposes, if the broker agrees to accept instructions from the person in relation to dealings in futures contracts, to require the person to enter.

One of the main purposes of s. 1210 is to ensure that clients are aware that futures trading involve the risk of loss as well as the prospect of profit. The obligations imposed under s. 1210 are over and above the common law obligations relating to risks disclosure imposed on brokers. For example, under common law, a broker has a duty of care to explain the nature and effect of margin calls to a person unfamiliar with futures contracts.[247] The Sydney Futures Exchange has published a number of standard forms that may be used by brokers to satisfy the above requirements. Currently, no distinction is made between retail and wholesale clients and risks disclosures must be made even to financially sophisticated clients.

The *Corporations Law* does not impose any suitability requirement on futures brokers, only on securities brokers and advisers.[248] Although the First Exposure Draft of the Futures Industry Bill 1985 recommended the inclusion of a 'know your client' requirement, it was subsequently omitted from the Second Exposure Draft of the Bill on the grounds that it was too onerous and impractical.[249] It is interesting to note that one of the clauses in the Customer Agreement Form actually reverses the obligation by requiring the client to acknowledge that he or she has formed the opinion after taking into account his or her needs and situation that the trading of futures is suitable.[250]

4.8.2   New Zealand

In New Zealand, Part III of the Securities Amendment Act 1988 does not impose on intermediaries either risks disclosure or suitability obligations. The New Zealand Futures and Options Exchange's Rules require all dealers to obtain acknowledgments from clients (in a prescribed form) outlining the terms on which they may transact business for their clients and disclosing the risks involved in derivatives trading. The prescribed forms are different for public and introducing brokers.[251] Although the dealers prepare their own Client Acknowledgement Forms, the documents must contain as a minimum the provisions stipulated in the Rules of the Exchange.[252]

---

[247] See *Rest-Ezi Furniture Pty Ltd v Ace Shohin (Aust) Pty Ltd* (1987) 5 ACLC 10.

[248] *Corporations Law*, s. 851

[249] See P. Hanrahan, 'The Proposed Suitability Requirement for On-Exchange Derivatives Markets: A Critical Analysis' (1997) 8 JBFLP 5.

[250] See Companies and Securities Advisory Committee, *Law of Derivatives: An International Comparison* ('CASAC Research Paper') (Sydney, January 1995), p. 36.

[251] See Marketing Department of the New Zealand Futures & Options Exchange, *A Guide to Approved Dealer Status & Regulation of the NZFOE* (undated).

[252] Ibid.

4.8.3. Singapore

Under the *Futures Trading Act* (FTA), a futures broker is prohibited from opening futures trading or leveraged foreign exchange trading accounts for a customer unless the broker has:

- furnished the customer with a separate written risk disclosure statement in the prescribed format; and
- received a signed and dated acknowledgment from the customer stating that the risk disclosure document has been received and the nature and contents of it understood.[253]

Similar requirements also apply to futures pool operators and futures trading advisers.

No futures pool operator may accept or receive funds or other property from a prospective pool participant, until the customer has been furnished with the prescribed risk disclosure document and has returned the signed and dated acknowledgment.[254] In the case of futures trading advisers, this risk disclosure obligation only applies when the adviser solicits or enters into an agreement with a prospective client for the purpose of managing or guiding the client's futures trading or foreign exchange trading account, or where the adviser recommends specific transactions.[255] This means that where the adviser merely provides advice of a general nature, no such requirement applies. Since the term 'customer' has not been qualified, it would appear that the risk disclosure obligation would apply to all customers, including accredited investors, related corporations, and related persons. Currently, the FTA does not impose any suitability obligation on brokers, advisers or other intermediaries and there are no immediate plans to do so either.

4.8.4 Malaysia

Malaysia, like Australia and Singapore, have imposed on intermediaries a statutory duty to disclose to their clients the risks involved in futures trading. Section 53(1) of the *Futures Industry Act* (FIA) provides that:

A futures broker shall, before accepting a person as a client of the broker, give to that person—

   (a) a document that—
       (i) explains the nature of futures contracts;
      (ii) explains the nature of the obligations assumed by a person who instructs a futures broker to enter into a futures contract;
     (iii) sets out a risk disclosure statement in the prescribed form; and
     (iv) sets out the specifications and details of the essential terms of each kind of futures contract in which the broker trades on behalf of clients.

---

[253] FTA, s. 39(1).
[254] Id., s. 39(2).
[255] Id., s. 39(3).

A specimen of the prescribed risk disclosure statement is found in the Third Schedule of the *Futures Industry Regulations* 1995. The client is required to acknowledge that he or she has understood the risk disclosure statement by signing and returning it to the broker.

The FIA imposes a suitability obligation on all futures brokers, futures advisers, and futures funds managers. Under s. 52B(1), an intermediary who makes a recommendation in relation to trading in futures contracts to a person who may reasonably be expected to rely on it must have a reasonable basis for making it. An adviser has a reasonable basis for making a recommendation if the adviser has:

- taken into account the person's investment objectives, financial situation and particular needs; and
- conducted an investigation of the subject matter of the recommendation as may be reasonable in all the circumstances.[256]

Section 52B is similar in wording to s. 851 of the Australian *Corporations Law*, which requires Australian securities adviser to have a reasonable basis for making a securities recommendation.

Under the FIA, where a person suffers loss as a result of the adviser's recommendation, the adviser shall be liable to pay damages to the person in respect of that loss or damage.[257] No distinction is made between a retail client and a wholesale client. This makes it possible for large and financially sophisticated institutional investors to seek protection under s. 52B. The Securities Commission has not provided any guidelines on how to interpret the provision. Since s. 52B is similar in wording with s. 851 of the Australian *Corporations Law*, the guidelines issued by the Australian Securities and Investments Commission may prove useful for those interested in the application of s. 52B.[258]

4.8.5   Hong Kong

There are no provisions in the *Commodity Trading Ordinance* (CTO) which deal with mandatory risks disclosure statements. Neither are dealers required under the legislation to recommend suitable contracts to their clients. However, they are required under the rules of the exchange, to disclose to their clients the risks inherent in the derivatives contracts proposed to be traded. Registered intermediaries must also comply with the 'Management, Supervision and Internal Control Guidelines for Persons Registered with the Securities and Futures Commission', which were issued in May 1997. The Guidelines require registered dealers to provide their clients with adequate information about its services, charges as well as relevant documents like risks disclosure statements. It also requires a registered

---

[256] FIA, s. 52B(2).
[257] Id., s. 52B(3).
[258] See Australian Securities and Investments Commission's Policy Statement 122 issued on 3rd March 1997.

dealer who offers investment advice or makes any recommendations for remuneration to document (and provide a copy to the client) the rationale underlying the investment advice or recommendation. The advice or recommendation 'must be suitable taking account the client's particular investment experience and objectives and financial position'.[259] While the Guidelines do not have the force of law, failure to follow them 'may reflect adversely on the fitness and properness of the registered person' to continue to be registered.[260] It should also be mentioned that the Hong Kong Monetary Authority (HKMA) has issued guidelines on risk disclosure for authorised financial institutions such as banks.[261]

4.8.6 Summary and Comments

In Australia, Singapore and Malaysia, the law imposes on intermediaries an obligation to disclose to their clients the risks involved in trading in derivatives. This 'risks disclosure' requirement applies to all customers, with no distinction being made between wholesale and retail counterparties, or between different types of transactions. Malaysia and Singapore require that customers acknowledge that they have read and understood the disclosure statements by signing and returning them to the intermediaries. There is no similar requirement in the Australian legislation. In Hong Kong and New Zealand, the legislation does not impose any risks disclosure obligations on intermediaries. The exchanges impose their own risk disclosure obligations on their members. Additionally, in Hong Kong, registered persons are required to comply with the Securities and Futures Commission Guidelines on risks disclosure.

With the exception of Malaysia, none of the other jurisdictions have imposed any statutory suitability obligation on intermediaries dealing with regulated derivatives. In Malaysia, if a person makes a recommendation in relation to the trading of futures contracts to another person, who may reasonably be expected to rely on it, then that person must have a reasonable basis for making the recommendation. Any person who breaches this obligation is liable for damages. In Australia only securities advisers are subject to a similar suitability obligation. The imposition of a suitability obligation on derivatives intermediaries was considered in Australia, but subsequently rejected on the grounds that it was not suitable for derivatives trading.[262] Although Hong Kong has not seen it fit to introduce such an obligation, failure to comply with the Securities and Futures Commission's guidelines relating to the making of recommendations and giving advice are factors that are taken into account when determining whether a person is fit and proper to be registered.

---

[259] See Securities and Futures Commission, 'Management, Supervision and Internal Control Guidelines for Persons Registered with the Securities and Futures Commission' (May 1997), Appendix A(3)(c).
[260] Id., Introduction.
[261] See Hong Kong Monetary Authority, *Risk Management of Financial Derivatives: Guideline No. 12.1*.
[262] See generally, Hanrahan, above n. 249.

4.9   SEGREGATION OF CLIENTS' ASSETS

Brokers hold assets of their clients for various purposes. These assets are held for initial deposits, for variation margins, or for the operation of discretionary accounts. The assets may be in the form of cash or property. It is important that these assets are properly protected to ensure investor confidence in the derivatives markets. One of the biggest threats to clients' assets is the insolvency of the broker. As long as clients' assets are kept separately the broker's creditors cannot have access to them. Not all exchanges require the segregation of customers' assets and this could hamper the transfer of assets in the event that a broker becomes insolvent.[263] Brokers are obliged by law to hold clients' funds and property separately from their own. Related to the segregation of clients' assets is the need to maintain proper records. Failure to maintain proper records could result in the freezing of clients' assets in the event the broker goes into insolvency. Not surprisingly, brokers are also subject to statutory record-keeping procedures.

Clients' funds may be kept in either a segregated account or a trust account. There is an important distinction between a trust account and a segregated account. In a trust account, the funds of each client are separately identified and cannot be used to meet the margin or settlement requirements of another client. But in a segregated account, the funds of each client are commingled with the funds of other clients and may be used to meet the margin and settlement requirements of other clients. A trust account is more beneficial for clients as they are protected from the default of other clients. While a segregated account may disadvantage individual clients, it facilitates trading by giving the clearinghouse access to a larger pool of funds for meeting margin and settlement requirements. Currently, the legislation in most jurisdictions requires futures brokers to maintain only segregated accounts.

4.9.1   Australia

There are several provisions in the *Corporations Law* that deal with the segregation of clients' money and property. Section 1209(3) of the *Corporations Law* provides that where a client, in connection with dealings in futures, deposits money or property with the broker whether in Australia or overseas, then on or before the next day:

- the money must be deposited in a clients' segregated account of the broker maintained in Australia, or in the place where the money was deposited with or received by the broker; and
- the property must be deposited in safe custody, in Australia or in the place where the property was deposited with or received by the broker, in such a manner that the property is segregated from the property of the broker.

---

[263]   See S. C. Blair, 'Lessons from the Barings Collapse' (1995) 64 *Fordham Law Review* 1, 8: 'The process was complicated significantly by the fact that, while the Japanese regulatory structure

Although the term 'client' is defined as 'a person on behalf of whom the broker deals, or from whom the broker accepts instructions to deal, in futures contracts', there are some categories of persons who are excluded from the definition.[264] For example, employees, officers, partners, and directors of the broker are not clients for the purposes of the segregated account provisions. This is to ensure that anyone who is in some way related to the broker does not enjoy the benefit of this protection.

The clients' segregated account must be maintained with an Australian bank or an approved foreign bank, and must be designated as such unless required to be designated in some other way by the law in force.[265] There are several rules regulating withdrawals from the segregated account.[266] These rules ensure that the withdrawals made are in connection with client's dealings in futures contracts. The broker is required to keep proper records of the segregated account and the client's property.[267] Section 1209(14) of the *Corporations Law*, provides that neither the client's money nor property is available 'for the payment of a debt or liability of the broker or is liable to be attached, or taken in execution, under the order or process of a court at the instance of a person suing in respect of such a debt or liability.' A similar provision applies to client's money invested by a broker.[268]

4.9.2   New Zealand

Under s. 41 of the *Securities Amendment Act*, the New Zealand and Securities Commission (Commission) is empowered to regulate on a wide range of matters. To date the *Futures Industry (Client Funds) Regulations* 1990 (Regulations) is the only delegated legislation made pursuant to s. 41. These Regulations came into force on 1 October 1990.[269] Dealers are required to establish client bank accounts in New Zealand with one or more registered banks.[270] They may also establish client bank accounts outside New Zealand with one or more overseas banks.[271] These accounts must be maintained in the name of the dealer but should be designated as client bank accounts.[272] Apart from banks, dealers may maintain client funds accounts in New Zealand with a recognised clearinghouse or another dealer, and outside New Zealand, with a clearinghouse for a futures exchange or with a futures broker.[273] To ensure that client accounts are not used for illegitimate

---

in general requires separate accounting for customer and proprietary positions, it does not require actual segregation of customer funds at the exchange … On the Japanese exchanges, however, margin funds posted by Barings on its own positions were commingled with customer margin.'

[264]   *Corporations Law*, s. 1209(1).
[265]   For the definition of 'clients' segregated account', see id., s. 9.
[266]   Id., s. 1209(5).
[267]   Id., ss. 1209(11)–(12).
[268]   Id., s. 1209(17).
[269]   Reg. 1.
[270]   Reg. 3(1).
[271]   Reg. 3(2).
[272]   Reg. 3(3).
[273]   Reg. 9(1).

purposes, the term 'client' excludes the dealer or a related party of the dealer.[274] The term 'related party' in the case of an individual means his or her spouse and child, and in the case of a corporation, anyone who holds a majority of the voting rights or shares.

Prior to paying any client money into the client account, the dealer must obtain a written acknowledgment from the recipient that the account is being operated in accordance with the Regulations and that all money is held on behalf of clients of the dealer.[275] In addition the recipient has to acknowledge that it is not entitled to combine the client account with any other account, or exercise its rights of set-off.[276] It would appear that where the dealer is also a bank, the client account might be maintained with itself, on condition that it complies with all aspects of the Regulations.[277] There are various rules, which govern the operation of client bank accounts. For instance, dealers should ensure clients' accounts are not overdrawn, and that no money is paid out except as provided for in the Regulations.[278]

Client property must be deposited with a bank, clearing house or person designated by the Commission for that purpose.[279] The obligations imposed on the custodians of property are similar to those imposed on banks, which operate client accounts for dealers.[280] Client investments held in the name of a dealer remain the property of the client and must be designated as such by the issuer of the investment.[281] Dealers must maintain proper accounting and other records of client accounts, which must be made available on request for inspection by their auditors, or any person authorised by the futures exchange.[282] Client accounts records must be audited annually, and if the audit reveals any breach of the Act, the auditor is required to send a copy of the audit report to the Commission.[283]

Any person who without reasonable justification or excuse, contravenes or fails to comply with any of the provisions of the Regulations, commits an offence and is liable on summary conviction to a fine not exceeding NZD 5,000.[284] Where the offence is committed by any person acting as the agent or employee of another person, that other person will also be liable in the same manner and to the same extent.[285] Where any body corporate is convicted of an offence, the director and managers will also be guilty of a like offence, if it can be proved that they permitted or authorised the offence, knew of its commission, or failed to prevent its commission.[286]

---

[274] Reg. 2(1).
[275] Reg. 4.
[276] Ibid.
[277] Reg. 19.
[278] Reg. 5.
[279] Reg. 14.
[280] Regs 15, 16.
[281] Reg. 22.
[282] Reg. 23.
[283] Reg. 24.
[284] Reg. 25(1).
[285] Reg. 25(2).
[286] Reg. 25(4).

4.9.3 Singapore

The *Futures Trading Act* (FTA) provides that a futures broker must maintain all moneys, securities or properties received from, or belonging to customers in a designated trust account.[287] In addition, the broker must not commingle clients' moneys or properties with that of the broker's, or use them to margin, guarantee, or secure contracts belonging to another customer.[288] For the sake of convenience all moneys, securities, or properties received from customers may be commingled and deposited in the same account maintained with any of the following: a licensed commercial bank or approved merchant bank in Singapore; a clearinghouse (whether inside or outside Singapore); another futures broker; or any person approved by the Monetary Authority of Singapore (MAS).[289] However, it should be noted that the exchange and the clearinghouse, with the authority of MAS, may use the assets of customers placed in a trust account to meet the obligations of a defaulting broker where 'failure to use … might jeopardise the financial integrity of the Exchange or the clearing house.'[290]

It would appear that this segregation rule applies regardless of where the funds are received.[291] Doubts have been expressed as to whether a futures broker who is also a bank would be required to deposit customers' funds with another bank.[292] In Australia, the Sydney Futures Exchange Practice Note No. 12 has confirmed that where the broker is itself an Australian bank the account need not be maintained with another bank.[293] It would appear that this would also be the case in Singapore. This does not seem to be a sound practice as it could defeat the objective of putting the client's money out of reach of the broker's creditors in the event that the broker is insolvent, since the bank is not only the customer's broker but also the customer's debtor.

For the purpose of s. 39, the term 'customer' excludes: the broker itself; an employee, director or representative of the broker; and a related corporation.[294] This will ensure that the clients' account is not used for an improper purpose such as to defeat any creditors, or for money laundering. However, there is no requirement that the moneys, securities or properties, should be received in connection with trading in futures contracts or leveraged foreign exchange trading.[295] This would suggest that funds received for

---

[287] FTA, s. 37(1).
[288] Ibid.
[289] Id., s. 37(2).
[290] Id., s. 37(8)(b).
[291] This inference is supported by SIMEX Rule 917, which provides that a futures broker is required to segregate all customers' funds received, irrespective of whether the trades were effected on futures markets in or out of Singapore.
[292] See Chen and Ng, above n. 51, p. 360.
[293] See Currie, above n. 78, p. 151.
[294] FTA, s. 37(9).
[295] Compare s. 37(1) of the FTA with s. 1209(3) of the Australian *Corporations Law*. The latter imposes the segregation rule only for moneys and properties received in connection with 'dealings in futures contracts', whereas the former does not.

other purposes might also be kept in the account. Neither is there any mention in the FTA as to when the money or property should be deposited in the account, apart from Regulation 15, which states that clients' funds should be deposited without delay.

There are various restrictions imposed on the withdrawal or use of the assets received by the futures brokers.[296] For example, money may only be withdrawn in accordance with the customer's instructions, or for margining or settling any dealings in futures contracts. However the FTA recognises that sometimes a broker may advance the broker's own money to prevent a customer's account from being under-margined, in which case the broker can withdraw from the customer's account to the extent of the 'residual financial interest'.[297] Customers' moneys or properties are not available for payment of the broker's debts or to satisfy any execution order levied against the broker by another customer.[298]

4.9.4   Malaysia

Intermediaries in Malaysia are also required to segregate their clients' assets. Section 52A(1) of the *Futures Industry Act* (FIA) provides that a futures broker must maintain a segregated account for clients' money. Since the term 'client' only excludes the broker, it would appear that members of the broker's immediate family or related companies of the broker would also be treated as clients.[299] This requirement applies to money received in connection with the trading of futures contracts either in Malaysia or elsewhere. The clients' account must be maintained with a licensed or prescribed bank in Malaysia or elsewhere. Brokers are also required to deposit clients' property in safe custody in Malaysia or where the property was received in such a manner that it is segregated from the broker's own property.

The money or property must be deposited no later than the next day after the money or property is deposited or received.[300] There are strict rules governing the withdrawal of money or property by the broker. Basically the broker cannot use the money or property for purposes other than those relating to the trading of futures contracts. The broker can withdraw money for margining and settlement, payment of brokerage fees, any other payments authorised by law.[301] However, the broker cannot withdraw the funds to settle the broker's own debts. The broker may place clients' money on deposit with a licensed bank or with the clearinghouse, although the FIA is silent as to whether the interest earned on deposits should be given back to the clients. There are also rules regulating the keeping of proper records for segregated accounts.

---

[296]   FTA, s. 37(3).
[297]   Id., s. 37(3)(d).
[298]   Id., s. 37(6).
[299]   FIA, s. 52(1).
[300]   Id., s. 52A(1)(bb).
[301]   Id., s. 52A(3).

4.9.5 Hong Kong

Under the *Commodity Trading Ordinance* (CTO), dealers are required to maintain segregated accounts with either an organisation approved by the Securities and Futures Commission (SFC), a registered deposit-taking company, or a licensed bank into which clients' monies are to be paid.[302] The term 'client' refers to a person on whose account a dealer carries on any trading in commodity futures contracts as an agent. All amounts (less brokerage and other proper charges) received from clients are to be paid into a segregated account within four bank trading days after their receipt. The period should be reduced to one working day to be on par with other jurisdictions.

Unlike the Malaysian and Singaporean legislation, the CTO does not provide for the deposit of property (such as bank guarantees and letters of credit) received from clients into a segregated account. It provides that money held in a segregated account shall not be available for payment of the dealer's debts or taken in execution under the order or process of a court.[303] Any payment made in contravention of this ruling, shall be void ab initio and no person shall obtain any title to the money paid.[304] It is interesting to note that there are no provisions dealing with the withdrawal of funds from the segregated account, except that the dealer must keep records of all deposits to, and withdrawals from, the segregated accounts.[305] There are rules governing the maintenance of proper records for segregated accounts.[306]

4.9.6 Summary and Comments

In all the jurisdictions under study, customers' funds must be separated from the broker's funds. Except for Singapore the other jurisdictions only require that the funds be kept in a segregated clients' account. However, Singapore requires that the funds be kept in a clients' trust account. The principal purpose of keeping customers' funds separate from the broker's funds is to ensure that they are placed beyond the reach of the intermediaries' creditors. Generally, all funds received from customers must be deposited with an approved bank or institution. The time frame within which customers' funds should be deposited range from the next working day to four bank working days. A segregated account must be so designated, and the bank or depository institution with which the account is maintained must acknowledge that the funds to the credit of the account are held on trust. There are specific rules governing withdrawals from segregated accounts. A similar segregation requirement also applies to customers' property, except for the Hong Kong legislation which is silent on this issue. This would suggest that there is no requirement in Hong Kong

---

[302] CTO, s. 46.
[303] Id., s. 47(1).
[304] Id., s. 47(2).
[305] Id., s. 46(5).
[306] Id., s. 46(5).

that customers' property be kept in a segregated account. In all jurisdictions there are specific rules governing the keeping of proper records for segregated or trust accounts.

4.10   STATUTORY OFFENCES

Most regulatory schemes have rules to protect investors from dishonest intermediaries and to ensure that the markets operate in a fair, transparent and orderly manner. These rules are necessary to maintain public confidence and to promote the development of the markets. Since derivatives markets also act as a price discovery mechanism, it is all the more important that market prices are not distorted but reflect the true forces of demand and supply. Before examining the various statutory offences, it might be useful to provide an overview of the various forms of abusive market behaviour.

'Frontrunning', 'bucketing' and churning' are all different forms of improper market practice. 'Frontrunning' is the practice of brokers giving priority to their own orders over clients' orders. Since brokers are not prohibited from engaging in proprietary trading, the potential for 'frontrunning' to take place is great. Bucketing is the 'failure to execute an order on a recognised commodity exchange when required to do so.'[307] It can take a variety of forms, such as when the broker takes the other side of the client's transaction, with the consequence that the trade is made at a price other than the prevailing market price and the trade is not guaranteed by the clearinghouse.[308] 'Churning' is 'the excessive trading of an account for the purpose of generating commissions, without regard to the needs of and objectives of the client.'[309] To establish that a broker has engaged in 'churning' a number of conditions must be satisfied: (1) the broker had control of the account; (2) the account was traded excessively; and (3) there was intent to trade excessively on the part of the broker.[310] Generally, where the account is discretionary, 'control' is much easier to prove.

Another form of improper market behaviour is market manipulation. It is not a recent phenomenon and has been around for some time. One of the earliest reported cases was that of *R v De Berenger*.[311] In that case, De Berenger and seven others were convicted of a conspiracy to cause a public mischief by rumours and false reports. One of the false reports that they had spread was that Napoleon had been killed and that the allies had entered Paris. This had the effect of causing a major rise in the price of

---

[307] See D. A. Chakin, 'Futures Frauds in the Asia Pacific Region' in C. Lye and R. Lazar (eds), *The Regulation of Financial and Capital Markets* (SNP Corporation, Singapore, 1991), p. 252.

[308] See E. F. Frohlich, 'Some Features and Legal Aspects of the Futures Industry' (1986) 60 ALJ 224, 229.

[309] For a detailed discussion of churning, see Chakin, above n. 307, p. 260; M. G. Hains, 'Churning and Burning: A Futures Cause of Action?' (1989) 63 ALJ 608.

[310] See J. W. Markham, 'Commodity Market Malpractices', in P. Farmey and K. Walmsley (eds), *US Securities and Regulations Handbook* (Graham & Trotman, London, 1992), p. 359.

[311] (1814) 3 M&S 66; 105 ER 536.

government securities. Similar ruses have been reported in the derivatives markets. For example, on February 14, 1984, a rumour had spread that the then President of the United States, Ronald Regan, was dead.[312] It was alleged that the rumour was started by a number of derivatives traders who were 'long' (or over-bought) on silver when they saw the market price of silver falling. The rumour had an immediate effect on the market and sent the prices of gold, silver and copper soaring.

There are several ways of manipulating the market. A 'corner' is one method used to manipulate market prices. It occurs when a person controls the supply of the commodity on the physical market and holds 'long' futures contracts in excess of the available commodity.[313] The persons holding 'short' positions are then forced to buy at artificially higher prices. A 'squeeze' which is 'a less extreme form of corner' occurs when a person holding a 'long' position takes advantage of a scarcity of the commodity caused by factors such as drought and delivery problems.[314] 'False trading' is another form of market manipulation. It was reported to have taken place in the initial months following the launch of property futures on the London Commodity Exchange. A number of brokers were alleged to have traded significant volumes amongst themselves to create artificial liquidity in the market.[315]

Insider trading refers to the practice of trading on the basis of price sensitive information. It involves the exploitation by a person who has an informational advantage over others. This advantage may have been obtained by virtue of that person's position or association with a particular corporation. It has been argued that regulating insider trading offers a number of benefits including equality of access to information by investors and the maintenance of market integrity.[316]

In most jurisdictions, all the above forms of abusive market behaviour are illegal under the futures laws. It should be mentioned that those charged under the futures laws could also be prosecuted under the common law or other relevant legislation. However, the ensuing discussion will be confined to examination of those offences under the futures laws only.

4.10.1 Australia

In Australia, Part 8.7 of the *Corporations Law* contains the various statutory offences relating to derivatives trading. Front running is prohibited under s. 1266 of the *Corporations Law*. Section 1266 imposes a number of obligations on brokers. First, brokers are required to transmit their clients' instructions at or near the market price, and in the sequence they are received.[317]

---

[312] See Chakin, above n. 307, pp. 264–265.
[313] Id., p. 267.
[314] See *Cargill, Inc v Hardin*, 452 F. 2d 1154 at 1162.
[315] See J. Roche, *Property Futures and Securitisation—the Way Ahead* (Woodhead Publishing Limited, Cambridge, 1995), p. 108.
[316] See M. Ziegelaar, 'Insider Trading Law in Australia' in G. Walker and Others (eds), *Securities Regulation in Australia and New Zealand* (2nd edn, LBC, Sydney, 1998), pp. 556–557.
[317] Corporations Law, s. 1266(2).

Second, they are not allowed to compete with their clients where they have received instructions from their clients to trade in a particular class of futures contracts[318] Third, the exchange member responsible for executing the orders on the trading floor is required to execute the orders in the sequence they were received.[319] Section 1266 has been criticised for not covering the entire range of client instructions used in the markets. For example, since many brokers authorise their floor traders to operate discretionary accounts, the need to transmit house orders to the trading floor is eliminated.[320]

There is no offence in Part 8.7, which specifically deals with 'churning'. However, Currie has suggested that if the motive of the broker is to gain additional commission from excessive trading, it might be possible to make out a case of fraud under s 1264 of the *Corporations Law*.[321] Section 1264 deals with fraud committed by a broker, a broker's employee or agent, against a client in connection with dealings in futures contracts.

Bucketing is prohibited by s. 1258 of the *Corporations Law*. Under s. 1258, a futures broker shall not deal on behalf of another person unless the dealing is effected:

- on a futures market of a futures exchange;
- on an exempt futures market; or
- in accordance with the business rules of a futures organisation of which the broker is a member.

Section 1258 is reinforced by s. 1123, which prohibits the establishment or maintenance of an unauthorised futures market.

Section 1259 prohibits a person from being involved in any transaction which is intended or likely to have the effect of creating or maintaining an artificial price for contracts in a futures market. Generally, intent is not easy to prove in market manipulation offences. However, the term 'likely to have' suggests that it may not be necessary to prove intent. Establishing price artificiality is also difficult as it involves complex economic analysis.[322] Taking into account these various factors, it may be difficult to make out an offence under s. 1259.

Under s. 1260(1), it is an offence for a person to create, cause to be created, or do anything calculated to create a false or misleading appearance (1) of active trading in futures contracts, or (2) with respect to the market or price for dealings in futures contracts. In *Australian Securities Commission v Nomura International PLC*,[323] the Federal Court held that the respondent had contravened s. 1260(1) when it placed orders to sell a large parcel of securities in

---

[318] Id., s. 1266(3).
[319] Id., s. 1266(5).
[320] See S. Ansell, 'The Regulation of Insider Trading in Derivatives' (1995) 13 C&SLJ 476, 482.
[321] See Currie, above n. 78, p. 230.
[322] See *Great Western Food Distributors v Brannan* 201 F. 2d 476 (7th Cir. 1953); *Cargill, Inc v Hardin* 452 F. 2d 1154 (8th Cir. 1971).
[323] (1998) 29 ACSR 473.

the last-hour of trading in the Australian Stock Exchange. This was because the placing of the orders was intended to create a false and misleading appearance with respect to the market and price for Share Price Index futures contracts on the Sydney Futures Exchange. Sackville J provided some insight into what 'conduct calculated to create a false or misleading appearance' meant when he accepted counsel's argument that it should be construed as 'conduct intended or designed to create that appearance, rather than conduct adapted or suited to the creation of such appearance.'[324] Under s. 1260(2) it is also an offence to use any fictitious transaction or device to maintain, inflate, depress or cause fluctuations in the prices of futures contracts. In determining the fictitiousness or artificiality, it will not be conclusive that the parties to transactions intended it be genuine.[325]

Sections 1253 to 1257 deal with insider dealing involving futures contracts. The basic prohibition is that a person is precluded from dealing in a futures contract concerning a body corporate in which he or she possesses inside information. There is still a need to establish a connection between the insider and the corporation whose futures contracts are traded. Although the Chapter 7 insider provisions were substantially amended by the *Corporations Legislation Amendment Act* (Cth) 1991, the Chapter 8 provisions have not been amended accordingly.

Section 1251 states that a futures contract only concerns a body corporate if:

- the futures contract is a commodity agreement and the commodity that the contract relates to, is securities of the body; or
- the futures contract is an adjustment agreement and the state of affairs to which the contract relates to, is the price of the securities of the body or the prices of a class of securities that includes the securities of the body.

As a consequence, the insider provisions only apply to insider trading in equity futures. It has been suggested that there is justification for extending the insider provisions to futures contracts based on commodities.[326]

It is unlikely that any of the above offences have any extra-territorial reach because of the omission of Chapter 8 from s. 110D of the *Corporations Law*. Section 110D states that:

Chapters 1 to 6, inclusive, and 9, apply, according to their tenor, in relation to:

(a) natural persons, whether resident in this jurisdiction or in Australia or not and whether Australian citizens or not; and

(b) all bodies corporate and unincorporated bodies, whether formed or carrying on business in this jurisdiction or in Australia or not; and

(c) acts and omissions outside this jurisdiction, whether in Australia or not.

The wording of s. 110D suggests that the extra-territorial reach of the *Corporations Law* does not apply to Chapter 8.

---

[324] Id. at 573.

[325] See Currie, above n. 78, p. 229.

[326] See Ansell, above n. 320, 481: The example used to support his case was that if an executive of a mining company had inside information about a major gold discovery the executive would not be prohibited from purchasing gold futures contracts under Chapter 8.

4.10.2 New Zealand

Part III of the New Zealand *Securities Amendment Act* does not contain any statutory offences relating to the derivatives industry. The New Zealand Futures and Options Exchange (NZFOE) deal with improper market practices under its business rules.

4.10.3 Singapore

The rules relating to conflicts of interests are found in Part V of the *Futures Trading Act* (FTA). Part V prohibits activities like 'front running', 'trading against customers' and 'cross-trading', which prior to 1 April 1995 were only proscribed under the rules of the exchange. Part VIII of the FTA deals with fraudulent activities such as 'false trading' and 'cornering' that distort prices and the forces of supply and demand. The legislation does not have any provision to deal with insider trading.[327] The exchange has no futures contracts, which use shares as the underlying instrument, and this may be the reason why insider trading is not expressly prohibited. The gravity of the Part VIII offences is reflected in the higher penalties imposed on persons found guilty of them.[328]

It should be noted that the various statutory offences are not confined to acts carried out in Singapore only. This is because the definition of 'futures market' and 'foreign exchange market' include overseas markets. Section 66 provides that proceedings for any Part VIII offences may be taken only with the consent of the Attorney General. The Monetary Authority of Singapore (MAS) may, instead of instituting proceedings, impose a fine on any person who has admitted to an offence under the FTA. This is only applicable where the offence is punishable by a fine.

The prohibition against 'front running' is contained in s. 37A of the FTA. It provides that no futures broker should knowingly trade in futures contracts for its own account or for an account in which it has an interest, when the broker has received an order from a customer to trade in a similar contract at the same price or prevailing market price and has not executed that order, except in accordance with the rules of the exchange.[329] 'Front running' only applies to trading in futures contracts, but the term 'futures broker' extends to brokers who engage in leverage foreign exchange trading.

'Trading against the customer' is another market activity that is prohibited under the FTA. Under s. 37B it is an offence for a futures broker to knowingly enter into a transaction to buy or sell from a customer any

---

[327] Under Part 8.7 of the Australian *Corporations Law* there is a prohibition, albeit a limited one, on insider trading.

[328] For a comparison of the penalties imposed for Part V and Part VIII offences, see FTA, ss. 40 and 56.

[329] An account in which the broker has an interest includes an account belonging to a 'connected person'. The term 'connected person' is defined in s. 2 of the FTA and it includes the broker's immediate family and a firm or corporation in which the broker controls not less than 20 per cent of the voting power.

futures contract for its own account or one in which it has an interest, except with the customer's prior consent and in accordance with the rules and practices of the exchange. This prohibition is to avoid any possible conflict of interest on the part of the broker.

Apart from 'front running' and 'trading against the customer', the FTA also prohibits 'cross-trading'. Section 37C prohibits a futures broker from knowingly filling or executing a customer's order for the purchase or sale of futures contract on a futures market, by offsetting that order against another person's order, without effecting the customer's order on the trading floor or electronic futures trading system.

Section 50 creates the offence of 'false trading':

No person shall create or cause to be created or do anything that is calculated to create a false or misleading appearance of active trading in a futures contract on a futures market or leveraged foreign exchange trading or a false or misleading appearance with respect to the market for, or the price of trading in, futures contracts on a futures market or leveraged foreign exchange trading.

Activities prohibited under this provision would include 'wash sales'. 'Wash sales' are transactions undertaken merely for the sake of generating market activity, but where there is no beneficial change in ownership.

Related to the offence of 'false trading' is the offence of 'disseminating information about false trading'. Under s. 52 a person shall not circulate, disseminate, or authorise (or be concerned in the circulation or dissemination of) any statement or information, to the effect that the price of trading in a class of futures contracts or leveraged foreign exchange trading will rise or fall, because of activities conducted in contravention of s. 50 by one or more persons.[330] The person disseminating the information need not be the person involved in the illegal transaction.

The prohibition against 'bucketing' is found in s. 51(1):

No person shall knowingly execute, or hold himself out as having executed, an order for the purchase or sale of a futures contract on a futures market, without having effected a bona fide purchase or sale of the futures contract in accordance with the business rules and practices of the futures market.

The above provision covers only the 'bucketing' of futures contracts. There is a similar provision that applies to leveraged foreign exchange trading.[331]

Under s. 53 no person shall directly or indirectly manipulate, or attempt to manipulate the price of a futures contract, or the underlying commodity or instrument.[332] Price manipulation distorts the normal forces of supply and demand, and normally results in the creation of artificial prices. It is also an offence to corner, or attempt to corner, any commodity, which is the subject

---

[330] Compare s. 52 of the FTA with s. 1263 of the Australian *Corporations Law*. The offence in Australia is more widely framed and covers dissemination of information relating to activities undertaken in contravention of a number of other market manipulation offences.

[331] FTA, s. 51(b).

[332] Id., s. 53(a).

of a futures contract.[333] Since the term 'cornering' is not defined in the FTA, market practice would play an important role in its interpretation.[334]

Under s. 54, it is an offence to employ any device, engage in any act, or make (or omit to make) any statement of a material fact, which will defraud or is likely to defraud another person, in connection with any transaction involving futures trading or leveraged foreign exchange trading. An activity that may be covered under this provision is 'churning' as it may be regarded as a form of fraud.

Section 55 prohibits a person from inducing or attempting to induce another person to trade in futures contracts by making any false or misleading statement in relation to a material fact.[335] The offence can also be committed if the person induces or attempts to induce another to trade by making a statement, which by reason of the omission of a material fact, is rendered false or misleading.[336] Brokers as well as their employees could commit these offences.

4.10.4 Malaysia

The statutory provisions that deal with improper market behaviour are contained in Parts V and VII of the *Futures Industry Act* (FIA). Part V deals with conflict of interests, while Part VII deals with offences. It appears that in so far as the severity of the penalties is concerned, Malaysia makes no distinction between Parts V and VII contraventions. Both types of contraventions attract fines not exceeding one million ringgit or imprisonment for a term not exceeding ten years or both.[337]

The FIA imposes on brokers a number of obligations to ensure that they place the interests of their clients ahead of their own. First, a broker is not allowed to take the other side of a client's order without the client's consent.[338] Second, a broker is not allowed to use another broker to carry out his or her client's orders without the client's consent.[339] Third, a broker is required to send and carry out clients' instructions in the order they were received.[340] Fourth, a broker is required to allocate trading in the sequence they were effected and in the sequence the instructions were sent.[341] Fifth, the broker must give precedence to the client's orders over his or her own.[342]

There are also a number of provisions in the FIA that are aimed at preserving market integrity and preventing distortion of prices. For example, it

---

[333] Id., s. 53(b).
[334] In *Limako v H. Hentz & Co. Inc*, [1979] 2 Lloyd's Law Rep. 23, the English Court of Appeal affirmed the importance of mercantile usage and the understanding of mercantile men in the futures markets.
[335] FTA, s. 55(a).
[336] Id., s. 55(b).
[337] FIA, ss. 56, 88.
[338] Id., s. 50(1).
[339] Id., s. 54(2).
[340] Id., ss. 54(3), 54(6).
[341] Id., s. 54(7).
[342] Id., s. 54(4).

is an offence under s. 79 to do anything that is calculated to create a false or misleading appearance of active trading in futures contracts, or a false or misleading appearance with respect to the market for, or the price of, trading in futures contracts. Related to the offence of 'false trading' is the offence of 'dissemination of information about false trading', which is contained in s. 81. This offence is made out if a person is involved in the circulation or dissemination of any statement or information to the effect that, the price of a particular class of contracts will, or is likely to rise or fall, because of the market operations of one or more persons. The prosecution must establish that the person was aware that the market operations were in contravention of s. 79.

The two distinct offences of 'price manipulation' and 'cornering' are contained in s. 82:

No person shall, directly or indirectly—

   (a) manipulate or attempt to manipulate the price of futures contracts that may be dealt in on a futures market, or of any underlying instrument which is the subject of such futures contract; or

   (b) corner, or attempt to corner, any underlying instrument which is the subject of a futures contract.

According to s. 82(a) it is an offence not only to manipulate or attempt to manipulate the price of futures contracts but also that of the underlying instrument. As such it covers both price manipulation on the futures market and on the physical and cash market. How the offence of price manipulation is to be made out is not clear from the wording of the section. Section 82(b) prohibits 'cornering' but 'corner' is not defined in the FIA.

Section 80 prohibits a person from executing, or holding out as having executed an order for the purchase or sale of a futures contract on a futures market, without having effected a bona fide purchase or sale in accordance with the business rules and practices of that market. Since no legitimate transactions have taken place, the broker would normally inform the client that he or she has lost money. In many cases, the broker will explain to the victim that the losses were the result of adverse market movements, and in its most extreme form, the broker will abscond with the client's money.

Section 83 deals with fraud in connection with the trading of futures contracts. It contains three separate offences:

- to employ any device, scheme or artifice to defraud another;
- to engage in any act, practice or course of business to defraud or deceive another;
- to make any false statement, or omit any material fact.

It is also an offence under s. 84 to make any statement, which is false, misleading or deceptive with the intention of inducing the purchase or sale of a futures contract. This includes the omission of any material fact from a statement, which by reason of the omission is rendered false or misleading.

There is no specific insider trading offence in the FIA. However, the FIA has two provisions, which are aimed at preventing abuse of inside information. The first is the restriction on employees of the exchange or clearinghouse, from engaging in the trading in futures contracts.[343] An employee includes the Executive Chairman of the Board. Second, it is an offence for a person to use any information, obtained in an official capacity, to gain an advantage for himself or herself, or for any other person.[344] It is surprising that despite the introduction of trading of equity derivatives in Malaysia, the FIA has no insider trading offence.

4.10.5   Hong Kong

In comparison with other jurisdictions, Hong Kong has a limited number of statutory offences. This may partly reflect the policy of the Securities and Futures Commission (SFC) to allow the exchange to set and enforce its own rules for trading. The government of Hong Kong has in the past adopted a generally light-handed approach to the regulation of the financial sector.

The 'hawking' of futures contracts is an offence under s. 60A(1) of the *Commodity Trading Ordinance* (CTO). The offence is made out if a person calls from place to place, making or offering to make with any person, (1) an agreement to buy or sell futures contracts; or (2) an agreement with the purpose of securing a profit for that person from a futures contract. 'Call' has been defined to include a visit in person or a communication by telephone. It is also an offence to call from place to place to induce or attempt to induce a person to enter into a futures contract. However, if the person calls on a banker, solicitor, professional accountant, commodity trading adviser, or representative, s. 60A(1) will not apply. Once it is established that that a person did any of the prohibited acts on two or more occasions within any 14-day period, the person would be presumed to have been calling from place to place, until the contrary is proved.[345]

Under s. 62(1) of the CTO, it is an offence to do anything with intent to create a 'false or misleading appearance of active trading in any commodity on any commodity market.' It is also an offence under s. 62(2) to be involved in the circulation or dissemination of information that the price of any futures contract will, or is likely to, rise or fall because of the market operations of one or more persons. Before the offence can be made out, it must be proven that the person knew that the market operations were conducted in contravention of s. 62(1).

Section 63 of the CTO is a general fraud provision. It makes it an offence for a person to employ any device, scheme, or artifice to defraud another in connection with the purchase or sale of a futures contract. A person also contravenes s. 63 if that person engages in any act, practice or course of business, which defrauds or deceives another.

Under s. 64(a) it is an offence to make any statement, which is, at the time and in the light of the circumstances it is made, false or misleading with

---

[343]   FIA, s. 85.
[344]   Id., s. 86.
[345]   CTO, s. 60(5).

respect to any material fact, for the purpose of inducing the purchase or sale of a futures contract. However, it must be proven that the person knew or had reasonable grounds for believing the statement was false or misleading. Similarly it is also an offence under s. 64(b) to make a statement, which by reason of the omission of a material fact renders it false or misleading. The statement must be made for the purpose of inducing the purchase or sale of a futures contract, and the maker must know or have reasonable grounds for believing that the omission would render it false or misleading.

4.10.6   Summary and Comments

In all the jurisdictions under study there are rules in place to ensure that the interests of intermediaries do not conflict with that of their customers. While these rules have been placed on a statutory footing in Australia, Singapore and Malaysia, they only form part of the rules of the exchange in New Zealand and Hong Kong. In all the jurisdictions under study, there are also rules governing improper market practices that are aimed at preserving market integrity. These rules have also been placed on a statutory footing in all the jurisdictions, save for New Zealand.

The jurisdictions under study exhibit significant variations in their lists of offences. For example, 'bucketing' is currently is an offence in Australia and Singapore, but not in Hong Kong. Similarly, while insider trading is an offence in Australia, it is not in either Singapore or Malaysia. However, if a person in Malaysia obtains price-sensitive information in an official capacity, that person cannot use the information to benefit from derivatives trading.

One of the problems with this diversity exhibited by the jurisdictions under study is that it could facilitate cross-border fraud. For example, if market manipulation is an offence in one country but not another, it would be difficult to eliminate market manipulation carried off shore. The risk of cross-border fraud is not only real but also serious given the international nature of derivatives trading. It would therefore make sense for all jurisdictions, especially those with linkages, to have similar rules regarding improper market behaviour.

4.11   REGULATION OF DERIVATIVES UNDER SECURITIES LAWS

In all the jurisdictions under study, how a financial instrument is regulated depends on where it is traded. If it is traded on the futures exchange it is regulated as futures contract, but if it is traded on a stock exchange it is regulated as security. The problem with such an approach is that it could lead to different regulatory treatment of functionally similar products. Take for example, the regulation of derivatives in Australia under the existing legal framework. If derivatives constitute futures contracts, they are regulated under Chapter 8 of the *Corporations Law*. But if they constitute securities,[346] they are regulated under Chapter 7. The securities definition found in s. 92(1), as expanded by s. 9, covers Low Exercise Price Options, share ratios, equity options and warrants.[347] Although most options traded on the Australian Stock Exchange are arguably derivatives, yet they are regulated as securities.

Despite the broad similarities in the regulatory treatment of securities and futures contracts in Australia, there are some important differences. Firstly, the issue of securities must comply with the disclosure requirements laid down in Chapter 6D, unless exempted.[348] Futures contracts are only subject to risk disclosure requirements. Secondly, the short selling of securities are prohibited except in limited circumstances.[349] There is no similar prohibition on futures contracts. Thirdly, securities dealers are subject to a 'know your client' rule.[350] Again, futures contracts are not subject to this rule. Fourthly securities dealers are obliged to disclose to clients any pecuniary or other interests, which may affect their recommendations.[351] There is no obligation imposed on futures brokers. Fifthly, the insider trading provisions for securities are broader than those for futures contracts. The differences in regulatory treatment could create competitive inequality and encourage regulatory arbitrage. For example, if it is perceived that securities are more tightly regulated than futures contracts, there may be an incentive to structure a product as a futures contract instead of a security.

4.12   CONCLUSION

Based on the above review of how derivatives are regulated in Australia, New Zealand, Singapore, Malaysia, and Hong Kong (the jurisdictions under study), it is possible to make a number of observations. Firstly, the regulatory schemes of all the jurisdictions under study, save for New Zealand, have a number of common characteristics. They have all adopted fully

---

[346]   In Australia, securities is defined in s. 92(1) of the *Corporations Law* as:

   (a)   debentures, stocks or bonds issued or proposed to be issued by a government; or
   (b)   shares in, or debentures of, a body; or
   (c)   interests in a managed investment scheme; or
  (ca)   in Parts 7.3. to 7.6 (inclusive)—interests that would be interests in a managed investment scheme but for paragraph (h) of the definition of managed investment scheme in section 9; or
   (d)   units of such shares; or an option contract within the meaning of Chapter 7;
but does not include a futures contract or excluded security.

[347]   See M. Heffernan, 'The Economic Role of the Australian Stock Exchange' in G. Walker and Others (eds), *Securities Regulation in Australia and New Zealand* (2nd ed, LBC, Sydney, 1998), p. 135, for description of derivatives products traded on the ASX Derivatives Division (formerly known as the Australian Options Markets).

[348]   Under the new s. 92(3), the term 'securities' does not cover an option approved by a securities exchange as an exchange traded option.

[349]   *Corporations Law*, s. 846.

[350]   Id., s. 851.

[351]   Id., s. 849.

statutory regulation based on the United States model, while New Zealand has adopted self-regulation under statutory oversight based on the United Kingdom model. Secondly, there is a greater degree of regulatory standardisation among the three Southeast Asian jurisdictions than between the two Australasian jurisdictions. This is surprising considering the significant linkages between the Australian and New Zealand markets. Thirdly, all the jurisdictions under study including New Zealand have adopted product-based legal frameworks. Not surprisingly, their regulatory schemes suffer from the same weaknesses and limitations. Fourthly, in all the jurisdictions under study significant attention is given to the authorisation of markets and intermediaries. Fifthly, the over-the-counter derivatives markets in all the jurisdictions under study are not subject to the same degree of regulation as the exchange-traded markets. Finally, despite the fact that the various regulatory schemes studied are not perfect, they have worked well and have generally achieved the regulatory objectives set for them.

5. Future Developments and Challenges

5.1 INTRODUCTION

The financial markets have changed radically in the last thirty years. New financial instruments have proliferated. Markets have become increasingly global. Product and institutional boundaries have become less distinct. These changes have presented regulators with new and complex challenges. Even the lines between exchanges and intermediaries are blurring. As the interrelated forces of globalisation and technological advances continue to sweep relentlessly across the financial landscape, regulators must develop new ways of achieving the same goals. To stay relevant and effective, financial regulation must not only be flexible and innovative but also competitive. No longer are investors hampered by national boundaries and regulation will be an important consideration in the choice of markets. As one commentator has remarked:

We live in interesting times. This is the Chinese curse under which market regulation must operate.[1]

This chapter will examine the task of reforming derivatives laws in the light of these regulatory challenges. It will begin with a brief discussion of the major forces driving change in the financial markets. This will be followed by an analysis of some of the more significant developments that have taken place recently in global derivatives markets. Finally, this chapter will look at regulatory reform that is currently underway in Australia and Hong Kong.

5.2 FORCES DRIVING CHANGE

There are a number of forces driving change in global financial markets. But, it appears that there is no broad consensus on the main drivers of change. According to Professor Dale, globalisation, financial integration and financial innovation are the three key developments that have transformed

---

[1] See B. Steil, 'Introduction: Effective Public Policy in a World of Footloose Finance' in B. Steil (ed.), *International Financial Market Regulation* (John Wiley & Sons, Chichester, 1994), p. 14.

international financial markets in the past two decades.[2] Another commentator has attributed the changed global financial marketplace to a much wider range of factors, namely:

[T]he deregulation of many national economies in terms of abolition of exchange controls and liberalisation of capital flows; advances in information technology; the rise of institutional investors particularly pension funds; privatisation; the increasing internationalisation of investments; and the increasing competition for business and influence between different securities markets.[3]

The Australian *Wallis Inquiry Discussion Paper*, which canvassed options for regulating the Australian financial system, named four key forces driving change in the financial system:

- globalisation;
- technology;
- consumer needs and demands; and
- financial innovation.[4]

Despite the apparent diversity of views, it is possible to isolate three major forces driving change and they are: globalisation, technological advances and financial innovation. While this chapter will address these forces separately, it is important to recognise that they interact with, and affect one another.[5] For example, improvements in technology make it possible to trade stocks and derivatives 24-hours a day, tying together national and global markets more closely. Increasing global competition encourages product innovation and novel ways of delivering financial services. Similarly, cheap, fast and secure communications facilitates the growth of global commerce, which in turn, creates the competitive pressure for firms to invest in communications technologies to achieve a competitive edge.[6]

5.2.1 Globalisation

More than two decades ago, almost all activity on financial markets was domestic, and regulation was extremely restrictive and differed widely across national boundaries.[7] Today the picture is vastly different with a relatively high proportion of all financial transactions transcending national borders. This process of 'globalisation', as it is often referred to, presents

---

[2] See R. Dale, 'Regulating Global Markets' (1996) 11 JIBFL 407.
[3] See the Preface to F. Oditah (ed.) *The Futures for the Global Securities Market*, (Clarendon Press, Oxford, 1996), p. vii.
[4] See Treasury, *Financial System Inquiry Discussion Paper* (Wallis Inquiry Discussion Paper) (AGPS, Canberra, November 1996), p. 45.
[5] Ibid.
[6] See A. F. Simpson, ' "Bits" of Disclosure: Communications Technologies and Securities Regulation in Australia' (1997) 12 JIBL 371, 375.
[7] See the Foreword to J. Fingleton and D. Schoenmaker (eds), *The Internationalisation of Capital Markets* (Graham & Trotman, London, 1992), p. vii.

regulators with a unique set of problems and has prompted calls for greater international coordination of regulation. Before discussing some of the principal regulatory issues involved, it would be useful to explain what globalisation means. Although the term 'globalisation' has achieved great academic and popular currency, yet there is no universal acceptance of what it means.[8] The meaning of globalisation varies with those using the terms. In the broadest sense, globalisation refers to the process taking place 'when communications between peoples of different nations increase, when economic decision-makers develop a wider orientation taking into account a larger group of nations and the constraints of geography on economic, political, social, and cultural arrangements gradually become less important.'[9]

As an economic phenomenon, globalisation refers to the international integration of markets and the increasing interdependence of the economies of different nations.[10] It should be distinguished from 'internationalisation', even though both terms are often used interchangeably. Globalisation involves a process of denationalisation, whereas internationalisation refers to the cooperative activities of international actors.[11] The key feature distinguishing globalisation from internationalisation is the erosion and irrelevance of borders in international financial transactions.[12] Globalisation of financial markets has three broad facets and they are:

- cross-border delivery of financial services to foreign residents;
- penetration of foreign financial markets by branches and subsidiaries of multinational institutions; and
- transactions between banks and investment firms from different countries.[13]

In the process of transforming national markets into global markets, globalisation has created a whole host of regulatory problems. For example, it has increased the potential for systemic risk. The recent Asian financial crisis has shown how easy it is for a financial crisis in one market to spread to other neighbouring markets. The collapse of the Thai currency in July 1997 caused other regional currencies including the Filipino peso, the Malaysian ringgit and the Singapore dollar to fall. What began as an isolated currency crisis in Thailand soon developed into an economic crisis that enveloped the entire Asia-Pacific region. Globalisation has also brought into sharp focus problems such as the difficulty of regulating international banking and financial activities. The collapse of the Bank of Credit and Commerce

---

[8] See F. Carrigan, 'Globalisation and Legal Transnationalisation' (1999) 10 *Australian Journal of Corporate Law* 122.
[9] See F. L. Pryor, 'Internationalisation and Globalization of the American Economy' in T. L. Brewer and G. Boyd (eds), *Globalizing America* (Edward Elgar, Cheltenham, UK, 2000), p. 1.
[10] See Treasury, *Financial System Inquiry Final Report* (Wallis Inquiry Final Report) (AGPS, Canberra, March 1997), p. 122.
[11] See G. Walker and M. Fox, 'Globalisation: Meanings and Implications', in G. Walker and Others (eds), Securities Regulation in Australia and New Zealand (2nd ed., LBC, Sydney, 1998), p. 4.
[12] See Simpson, above n. 6, 375.
[13] See Dale, above n. 2.

International and Barings plc has revealed the inadequacy of existing regulatory arrangements to deal with financial conglomerates, which conduct the bulk of their business overseas.

5.2.2 Technological Change

Although technology has been credited with making globalisation a reality,[14] yet it is important to realise that globalisation and technology are interrelated trends. The relationship between globalisation and technology has been described as 'both chicken and egg'.[15] While globalisation drives technology, it is technology that facilitates globalisation. Technological advances in the last two decades have resulted in a dramatic reduction in the costs associated with the processing, storing and transmitting of data.[16] The reduction in costs of using technology has significant implications for the financial services industry. For a start it has encouraged more extensive use of technology in the financial markets. While the impact of technology is most visible in the delivery of financial services to the retail sector, technological advances have been responsible for much of the development in the backroom operations of financial markets. In relation to the derivatives markets, technology has radically transformed the nature of derivatives trading. It has led to the introduction of screen-based trading, permitted around the clock trading, and provided the impetus for the link-up of exchanges.

It would be useful to elaborate on electronic trading because of its powerful influence on the future direction of financial regulation. Few would dispute that electronic or screen-based trading of derivatives has gained significant momentum in the last decade. The number of exchanges worldwide using electronic systems in varying degrees has increased from eight in 1990 to about 40 in 1997.[17] From 1986 to 1996, the volume on electronic trading systems used by derivatives exchanges more than doubled, rising from seven percent of the world's trading volume to 14 per cent.[18] With more and more exchanges adopting electronic trading, it has been predicted that floor trading will completely disappear within a short space of time.[19] There are a number of reasons why exchanges have switched from the traditional floor or open outcry trading to electronic trading.[20] Firstly,

---

[14] See G. Walker and M. Fox, 'The Securities Industry and International Financial Integration' (1997) 7 *Canterbury Law Review* 239, 265.

[15] See Simpson, above n. 6, 375.

[16] See Wallis Inquiry Discussion Paper, above n. 4, pp. 54–55.

[17] See A. Sarkar and M. Tozzi, 'Electronic Trading on Futures Exchanges' (1998) 4 *Derivatives Quarterly* 7, 8: 'An automated trade execution system has three components: computer terminals, where customer orders are keyed in and trade confirmations are received, a host computer that processes trades, and a network that links the terminals to the host computer. Customers may enter orders directly into the terminal or phone in the order to a broker.'

[18] Ibid.

[19] See M. O'Hara, 'Electronic Trading Risk: What Can Go Wrong in Screen-Traded Derivatives Markets' (2000) 5 *Derivatives Use, Trading & Regulation* 316, 317.

[20] See P. M. Johnson and Others 'Adapting to Tomorrow's Markets' (1999) 5 *Derivatives Quarterly* 8, 9.

electronic trading does not require large investments in real estate. Secondly, it does not require the assembling of a well-organised group of talented and well-capitalised brokers. Thirdly, it offers greater product versatility because it is easier to provide variations of the same basic financial instrument at little additional costs. Finally, it is extremely convenient as traders can conduct business from anywhere at any time.

Probably, the greatest benefit conferred by electronic trading is its ability to promote cross-border trading.[21] It can provide for remote access for non-resident investors and form co-operative links with independent exchanges.[22] While electronic trading offers exchanges significant advantages and provides investors greater access to markets, it also poses problems for regulators. It makes regulation more difficult because regulators are constrained by laws, which often have no extra-territorial reach. Municipal laws, for instance, are powerless to prevent offshore manipulation of markets. Many of the regulatory issues thrown up by electronic trading reveal how legal developments have lagged behind technological developments. For instance, while derivatives end-users may soon have the means themselves to transact, satisfy clearinghouse margins and settle contracts electronically, without the need for brokers, yet the present approval criteria for derivatives exchanges in many jurisdictions are still designed for intermediated exchanges.

Not all electronic trading systems operate as an exchange. Over the last decade there has been a significant increase in alternative trading systems. These systems have developed in response to investor demand for different services and fee structures than are now provided by conventional exchanges.[23] Alternative trading systems are also sometimes referred to as electronic communication networks (ECNs). In simple terms, ECNs bring buyers and sellers together for electronic execution of trades.[24] Subscribers of ECNs range from retail investors and market-makers to other brokers-dealers. Regulators have found it difficult to deal with the regulation of ECNs within their existing legal frameworks. Some have chosen to regulate them as exchanges, while others have regulated them as broker-dealers.[25] Unless ECNs are regulated, there would be no assurance that investors, especially those at the retail end, would be adequately protected. The increase in number of ECNs has the potential to cause fragmentation of the market, thereby introducing inefficiencies in price discovery. Since ECNs

---

[21] See Sarkar and Tozzi, above n. 17, 11.
[22] Id., 13.
[23] See J. Kerbel and C. Wade, 'Canadian Securities Administrators Proposal on the Regulation of Alternative Trading Systems and Other Marketplaces' (1999) 5:9 *World Securities Law Report* 25.
[24] For a detailed discussion of ECNs and their regulatory implications see Division of Market Regulation of the US SEC, *Special Study: Electronic Communication Networks and After-Hours Trading* (7 June, 2000).
[25] See F. Champarnaud, 'Facing New Regulatory Challenges: The Case of Proprietary Trading Systems' in A. Jeunemaître (ed.), *Financial Markets Regulation: A Practitioner's Perspective* (Macmillan Press Ltd, London, 1997), p. 85.

can easily operate across national borders, they highlight the need for greater cooperation between regulators from different jurisdictions.

5.2.3   Financial Innovation

Financial innovation is to a large extent driven by competition and changing consumer needs. Competition heightens the need for costs reduction and improved product performance. This is turn places great pressure on financial service providers to innovate. Changing consumer needs have also played a major role in driving financial innovation. For example, the increase in interest and exchange rates volatility in the early 1970s created a need for financial derivatives. Before the introduction of interest and foreign currency futures contracts, derivatives were mainly based on natural commodities such as wool, gold and wheat. Similarly, the search by banks for a mechanism to hedge against customer insolvency led to the development of the bankruptcy futures contract.[26] This contract, which was launched by the Chicago Mercantile Exchange in November 1998, is a cash-settled contract to buy or sell an index tracking the current number of actual bankruptcies in the United States. It enables consumer lenders to hedge against unexpected default losses by freezing the default rates on their loan portfolios. Other new products that have developed in response to changing customer needs include derivatives to hedge against natural disasters. One such product is the weather derivatives contract, which enables corporations to hedge against a fall in demand for their products arising from adverse weather conditions.

Many of these new products are often difficult to understand, and sometimes exhibit hybrid characteristics. Characterisation of a product is crucial when determining the application of product-based rules. The blurring of traditional product lines places a great strain on many existing regulatory arrangements. In many jurisdictions, the regulation of financial services continues to be organised along product lines. Such an approach has a number of drawbacks. Products that do not fall easily into any particular legal category may either be excluded from regulation or subject to overlapping regulation. This in turn raises the costs of compliance and creates uncertainty among market participants. The problem is exacerbated when different regulatory agencies are involved in the regulation of financial products. For example in the United States the regulation of securities and the regulation of futures contracts are divided between the Securities Exchange Commission and the Commodity Futures Trading Commission. The uncertainty over the legal meaning of 'futures contract' has created considerable friction between both agencies.[27]

---

[26]   For an explanation of how a bankruptcy futures contract works, see R. Ray, 'Hedging Against Consumer Default: The New Bankruptcy Futures Contract' (1999) *Banking Law Journal* 382.

[27]   See, for example, J. T. Medero, 'Jurisdictional Issues in U.S. Regulation of Derivatives Products' (1994) 9 JIBFL 117 for a discussion of the various skirmishes between the two regulatory agencies.

5.3   MARKET DEVELOPMENTS

The interaction of the various drivers of change has radically altered the nature of the global financial landscape. They have given rise to a number of important market developments. The ensuing discussion will focus on three important market developments: the convergence of markets, de-mutualisation of exchanges, and merger of exchanges. While these developments offer considerable opportunities for market participants, they also pose difficult challenges for regulators. The existing regulatory arrangements were put in place to deal with a marketplace that was vastly different from the one we have now. In the past markets were physical places, exchanges were non-profit 'mutuals', and it was easy to differentiate one product from another. The financial marketplace today is a vastly different one, which is undergoing change, even as this chapter is being written. As such many of the existing regulatory schemes are unable to adequately deal with the problems and issues that have arisen. Before discussing some of the regulatory reform that is underway in two of the jurisdictions under study, it might be useful to briefly discuss each of these new market developments.

5.3.1   Convergence of Markets

One of the most widely discussed market developments is the convergence of markets. Not only is there a blurring of the traditional distinctions between over-the-counter (OTC) and exchange-traded markets, but also between securities and derivatives markets. More and more derivatives exchanges are now offering products such as options, which were previously only traded off-exchange. Conversely, OTC transactions are becoming more standardised and bearing greater resemblance to exchange-traded products. Technological developments are now making it possible for an individual market participant to offer centralised platforms competing directly with exchanges.[28] At the same time, OTC markets are increasingly looking at using clearing arrangements to reduce counterparty risks. Even the long-held view that securities and derivatives markets are different is increasingly coming under challenge.[29] Derivatives are now traded on both securities and derivatives exchanges. Some derivatives such as equity options give rise to the transfer of title if held to maturity. New products have also been introduced that exhibit characteristics found in both securities and derivatives, suggesting that maintaining the distinction may no longer be useful.

Currently, in many jurisdictions only exchange-traded markets are subject to detailed regulation. The reasoning behind such an approach is that these markets, which have a significant retail element, require a higher

---

[28]   See Wallis Inquiry Final Report, above n. 10, p. 281.
[29]   See Treasury, *Financial Markets and Investment Products* (CLERP Paper No. 6) (AGPS, Canberra, December 1997), p. 36.

degree of protection than markets catering for wholesale participants. But as products originally designed for wholesale end-users are adapted for retail end-users, there will be increased retail participation in OTC markets. When this happens, the justification for not regulating the OTC markets may no longer exist. The existing regulatory approach confers on OTC markets an advantage over exchange-traded markets. This creates the possibility that market participants may prefer to conduct an OTC market instead of seeking authorisation to operate an exchange. Not surprisingly, there are many who support a more level regulatory playing field for OTC and exchange-traded markets.[30] The United States Commodity and Futures Trading Commission is of the view that OTC markets may benefit from the risk management systems used by exchanges and that some convergence in regulatory methodologies may occur in the future.[31]

5.3.2   Demutualisation of Exchanges

Another important development that has gained momentum in the last few years is the demutualisation of exchanges. Traditionally, stock and derivatives exchanges operated as mutual or cooperative enterprises. They usually took the form of a company limited by guarantee and operated on a 'not-for-profit' basis. Profits made by the exchanges were returned to members in the form of lower fees and better services. These enterprises have no shareholders and they are owned and run by their members according to their constitution and operating rules. Demutualisation involves changing the corporate form of such enterprises from that of a company limited by guarantee to that of a public company limited by shares.[32] The reasons for demutualisation vary with exchanges. The following reasons cited by the Australian Stock Exchange is representative of some of the reasons behind demutualisation:

- A public company structure would enable the exchange to operate more efficiently in the face of intense competition;
- There are various stakeholders in the exchange and the mutual structure does not allow it to provide a proper standard of service to these stakeholders;
- The exchange's mutual structure inhibits a fair distribution of the benefits and risks of ownership among its members.[33]

Demutualisation has regulatory implications because exchanges play an important regulatory role. An issue that has frequently been raised in

---

[30] See A. M. Corcoran, 'Prudential Regulation of OTC Derivatives; Lessons from the Exchange-Traded Sector' in G. Ferrarini (ed.), *Prudential Regulation of Banks and Securities Firms* (Kluwer Law International, London, 1995), p. 161.
[31] Id., p. 179.
[32] See F. Donnan, 'Self-Regulation and the Demutualisation of the Australian Stock Exchange' (1999) 10 *Australian Journal of Corporate Law* 1.
[33] Id., at 8.

relation to the demutualisation of exchanges is whether a 'for-profit' public company will be able to adequately discharge its responsibilities as a front-line regulator. Exchanges run as 'for-profit' organisations have less motivation to spend resources on regulating those who use their services. This may call for a new approach to the sharing of the regulatory burden. One solution is to establish a private self-regulating organisation to regulate all exchanges. Another solution is for the government regulator to undertake the regulatory functions previously undertaken by the exchange. A third solution is to leave regulation entirely in the hands of the government regulator. This is an issue that needs to be addressed as more and more exchanges demutualise.

5.3.3   Merger of Exchanges

A development related to the demutualisation of exchanges is the merger of exchanges. Demutualisation is central to any merger and often any merger proposal would include a plan for demutualisation. The impetus for the merger of exchanges is often intense competition from other exchanges. There has been a wave of mergers in the Asia-Pacific region over the last couple of years. The Kuala Lumpur Commodity Exchange merged with the Malaysian Monetary Exchange in December 1998. In December 1999, the Singapore International Monetary Exchange merged with the Stock Exchange of Singapore. More recently, the Hong Kong Futures Exchange merged with the Stock Exchange of Hong Kong. Another reason that has contributed to the increasing numbers of mergers is the blurring of distinctions between securities and derivatives. This could give rise to turf wars similar to the one that took place when the Australian Stock Exchange decided to trade in Low Exercise Price Options and the Sydney Futures Exchange objected on the ground that the product is a futures contract. There is widespread belief that the merger of exchanges would improve efficiency and the competitive standing of a particular financial market. This may account for strong government support for the merger of exchanges.

When the stock and futures exchanges of a country merge, there are bound to be regulatory implications. In many jurisdictions, securities and futures contracts are regulated separately. Securities exchanges are not allowed to trade in futures contracts, while futures exchanges are not allowed to trade in securities. Any exchange that wishes to trade in both products would require separate authorisation. Similarly, their intermediaries would require dual licenses to deal in securities and futures contracts. Mergers would necessitate the introduction of new legislation. New criteria may have to be established for the establishment of such unified exchanges and for the licensing of intermediaries. While mergers result in bigger and better capitalised exchanges, they encourage the development of monopolistic practices. New legislation would have to be introduced to regulate improper practices such as unfair competition and excessive pricing. In the past, financial regulation paid little attention to anti-competitive behaviour, but with the growth in mergers, this may have to change.

5.4   REGULATORY REFORM

This chapter will discuss the regulatory reform that is currently being undertaken in Australia and Hong Kong. Although their regulatory schemes are not perfect, yet it appears that they have worked well. They have not only provided an adequate level of protection for investors, but have also succeeded in preventing market failure. Even the recent Asian financial crisis did not halt the trading of derivatives in either Australia or Hong Kong. In the past regulatory reform was often in response to market failure. But today, it is the changing marketplace that is driving the reform agenda. The Australian and Hong Kong regulatory authorities have recognised that regulation must not only be responsive to change, but it must also bring about change. Forces such as globalisation, liberalisation, and advances in technology have interacted to create a global financial market. Funds flow freely from one market to another and poorly regulated financial markets would find it difficult to survive, let alone succeed.

5.4.1   Australia

In March 1997, the Federal Treasurer launched the Corporate Law Economic Reform Program (CLERP). This program, which was developed with the assistance of a Business Regulation Advisory Group established by the Treasurer, saw as its main objective the introduction of business regulation that would promote economic efficiency and assist Australian businesses to adapt to change. The Treasury released a number of discussion papers that dealt with accounting standards, fundraising, directors' duties and corporate governance, takeovers, electronic commerce, financial markets and investment products, and simplified lodgements and compliance. CLERP Paper No. 6, which deals with financial markets and investment products, recommended very far-reaching changes to the regulation of financial services.[34] It builds on some earlier work undertaken by the Companies and Securities Advisory Committee, which between 1995 and 1997 produced several discussion papers and reports on the regulation of derivatives markets.[35]

The Federal Government released its draft Financial Services Reform Bill (Bill) to the public for comment in February 2000. The Bill is based on the broad policy direction set by CLERP Paper No. 6 and is generally consistent with the findings of the Inquiry into the Australian Financial System

---

[34]   See, generally, Treasury, *Financial Markets and Investment Products* (CLERP Paper No. 6) (AGPS, Canberra, December 1997).
[35]   See CASAC Research Paper *Law of Derivatives: An International Comparison* (January 1995), CASAC Discussion Paper *Regulation of the OTC Derivatives Market* (August 1995), CASAC Draft Report *Regulation of On-exchange Derivatives Markets* (June 1996), CASAC *Submission to the Financial System Inquiry* (January 1997), CASAC Final Report *Regulation of On-exchange and OTC Derivatives Markets* (June 1997).

chaired by Stan Wallis (Wallis Inquiry). In its final report, the Wallis Inquiry observed that :

The [Australian] financial system has entered an era of accelerated change that is likely to continue into the next century. Change in the financial system implies the need to adapt regulations imposed on financial institutions and markets. Regulation must adapt both to facilitate greater competition and efficiency in the financial sector and to secure the integrity and stability of its operations.[36]

The Government plans to introduce the Bill into parliament in the Winter Sittings of 2000 so that it could come into effect on 1 January 2001. However, there are widespread timing concerns and many would favour a later start date given the scope and significance of the proposed changes.

The central theme underlying the Bill is the uniform regulation of functionally similar markets and products. Harmonisation would be achieved through the adoption of a single licensing, conduct and disclosure regime for financial service providers offering products that fall within the statutory definition of financial product. The new framework would cover a wide range of financial products including securities, derivatives, general and life insurance, superannuation, deposit accounts and non-cash payments. Common obligations would be imposed on licensees dealing with retail clients. A new Chapter 7 will be introduced to replace the existing Chapters 7 and 8 of the *Corporations Law*. The new chapter 7 is expected to promote informed consumer decision-making, raise professionalism in the financial services industry and improve the functioning of financial markets, without hindering efficiency and innovation. The ensuing discussion will examine some of the main changes that directly affect the derivatives industry.

5.4.1.1   New Definitions

The Bill introduces a number of new definitions, which will replace some of the existing definitions in the Corporations Law. It will introduce a definition for 'financial product'. The financial product definition will delineate the scope of the new Chapter 7. A 'financial product' is defined as any facility through which (or through the acquisition of which), a person does one or more of the following:

   (a)   makes a financial investment;
   (b)   manages a financial risk,
   (c)   makes non-cash payments.[37]

A list of specific inclusions provides example of things that will fall within the general definition. The general definition is then narrowed by a list of specific exclusions. In addition there is a regulation-making power to add or remove any product from both lists.

---

[36]   See Treasury, *Financial System Inquiry Final Report* (AGPS, Canberra, March 1997), p. 1.
[37]   Financial Services Reform Bill, cl. 763A.

Derivatives are included under the list of specific classes of things that are financial products. A 'derivative' is defined as any arrangement, under which:

- a party to the arrangement must, or may be required to, provide at some future time consideration of a particular kind to someone; and
- the amount or value of that consideration is ultimately determined, derived or varies by reference to (wholly or in part) the value or amount of something else (of any nature whatsoever and whether or not deliverable).[38]

There are a number of classes of agreements, which are specifically excluded from the definition of derivative and they include arrangements such as those that relate to physical property (except Australian or foreign currency) that cannot be cash settled; regulated credit transactions; and contracts for the provision of future services.[39] There will no longer be a need for a definition of futures contract and it will be excluded from the new legislation.

The definition of 'security' has been redefined in the Bill to mean:

(a)   a share in a body;
(b)   a debenture of a body ;
(c)   a legal or equitable right or interest in a security covered by (a) or (b); or
(d)   an option to acquire by way of issue in a security covered by (a), (b) or (c).[40]

The definition of security excludes interests in managed investment schemes and options over securities, other than options over unissued securities. It is provided in the Bill that if something is a security then it is not a derivative.[41]

5.4.1.2   Uniform Licensing Scheme

Three new categories of licences will be introduced when the Bill becomes law. A person must not operate, or hold out that the person operates a financial product market,[42] unless that person has an Australian Market

---

[38]   Id., cl. 761D.
[39]   Ibid.
[40]   Id., cl. 761A.
[41]   Id., cl. 764A(1)(a).
[42]   A 'financial product market' is defined under cl. 767A of the Financial Services Reform Bill as:

[A] facility through which, or a place at which:
   (a)   offers to acquire or dispose of financial products are regularly made or accepted; or
   (b)   offers or invitations are regularly made to acquire or dispose of financial products that are intended to result or may reasonably be expected to result, directly or indirectly, in:
      (i)   the making of offers to acquire or dispose of financial products; or
      (ii)   the acceptance of such offers; or

Licence, or the particular market is exempted. There is also a prohibition on providing assistance to operate such a market, and holding out that the person is in possession of a licence or the market is exempted. While the proposed licensing regime for financial product markets will not apply to foreign markets, it will apply to a market that can be electronically accessed in Australia and the operator targets Australians as investors or participants.[43] Since payments made by the delivery of Australian or foreign currency do not fall within the definition of financial product,[44] transactional foreign exchange dealings will not constitute a financial product market and therefore will not require to be licensed. There will be no restrictions on the types of products that can be traded in a particular market.

Since it is possible that some markets may not operate their own clearing and settlement facilities, the Bill makes provision for the clearing and settlement function to be undertaken by an independent operator. A separate licence for the operation of a clearing and settlement facility[45] is therefore necessary to accommodate this new development. The Bill provides that a person must not operate or hold out that the person operates a clearing and settlement facility unless the person holds an Australian Clearing and Settlement Licence, or the particular facility is exempted.[46] There is also a prohibition on providing assistance to operate such a facility, and holding out that the person is in possession of a licence or the facility is exempted. The licensing regime will apply even to those clearing and settlement facilities which are incorporated in Australia but operate overseas.[47] However, it will not apply to clearing and settlement facilities with no physical presence in Australia.

A single licensing regime would also apply to all financial intermediaries. Any person (and this includes partnerships) who carries on a financial services business in Australia must have an Australian Financial Service

---

(c)   information is regularly provided that:
  (i)   identifies people who propose to acquire or dispose of financial products; and
  (ii) states the prices at which those people propose to acquire or dispose of those products.

In the case of (c) above, persons using the facility or place must have a reasonable expectation that they will regularly be able to effect transactions at the stated price. Excluded from the definition of financial product market are negotiated transactions between parties who accept counterparty risk, treasury operations between related bodies corporate and auctions of forfeited shares.

[43]   Financial Services Reform Bill, cl. 791C(2).
[44]   Id., cl. 763D(1).
[45]   A 'clearing and settlement facility' is defined under cl. 768A of the Financial Services Reform Bill as:

[A] facility that:
  (a)   is operated as a business; and
  (b)   provides a mechanism for all the parties to transactions relating to financial products to meet obligations to each other that:
    (i)   arise from entering into the transactions; and
    (ii) are of a kind prescribed by the regulations for the purposes of this section.[45]

[46]   Financial Services Reform Bill, cl. 820A(1).
[47]   Id., cl. 820A(4).

Licence.[48] Financial services is defined broadly and includes the provision of financial product advice, dealing in a financial product, making a market for a financial product, operating a registered scheme or providing a custodial or depository service.[49] However, a person who deals in a product on his or her own behalf is taken not to be dealing.[50] A licence is required regardless of whether the service is provided to a wholesale or retail client.[51] Licences may cover all financial services in relation to all products or a subset of products.[52] A licensee may authorise a person to provide financial service. Unlike the position now, corporations and partnerships and not just natural persons, may act as authorised representatives.[53] This licensing regime will apply even to persons who carry on business overseas, but intend to induce people in Australia to acquire financial services.[54]

5.4.1.3   *Compensation, Conduct and Disclosure Requirements*

The new regime provides that a licensed market through which participants provide services for retail clients must have in place approved compensation arrangements.[55] This requirement also applies to a licensed clearing and settlement facility. Part 7.4 of the Bill establishes the criteria that a compensation arrangement must meet in order to qualify for approval. The proposed compensation arrangements differ from those currently in place under Chapter 8 of the *Corporations Law* in several ways.[56] First, the proposed arrangements will cover only retail clients, while the existing arrangements make no distinction between wholesale and retail clients. Second, the proposed arrangements tie the loss to a transaction on the market or service provided by the facility, not whether the recipient is member of the exchange or an employee or director of one. Third, the proposed arrangements cover loss arising from a wider range of circumstances. The existing arrangements only cover loss arising from fraud or defalcation, but the proposed arrangements extend to insolvency.

---

[48] Id., cl. 881A.
[49] Id., cl. 766A(1).
[50] Id., cl. 766C.
[51] The Financial Services Reform Bill introduces for the first time a definition for 'retail client'. Under cl. 761G(1) a product or service is provided to a person as a retail person except in three instances:

- the price of the product or service equals or exceeds the prescribed amount;
- the product or service is provided for use in connection with a business employing at least 20 people (100 in the case of manufacturing business); or
- the person acquiring the product or service provides a certificate stating that the person has net assets of at least $2.5 million or a gross income of at least $250,000 a year in each of the preceding two years.

[52] Financial Services Reform Bill, cl. 796A(4).
[53] Id., cl. 887A.
[54] Id., cl. 881D.
[55] Id., cl. 851A.
[56] See Treasury, Financial Services Reform Bill: *Commentary on the Draft Provisions* (AGPS, Canberra, February 2000) (FSRB Commentary), p. 64.

All financial service providers must provide their retail clients with a Financial Service Guide. The purpose of this guide is to provide clients with the key information about the services provided. Before making a personal recommendation to a retail client, a provider must have a reasonable basis for doing so. The advice must take into account the client's objectives, financial situation and needs. In addition, the provider must give the retail client a Statement of Advice including the basis on which the advice was given, and information about any conflict interest that the provider may have. A provider must also comply with the disclosure requirements laid out in Part 7.8 of the Bill. This new disclosure regime will replace those obligations for futures contracts currently imposed by the existing Chapter 8 of the Corporations Law. Providers are required to establish and maintain a separate account in which to hold clients funds.[57] This requirement applies to providers of service dealing with both wholesale and retail clients. Where providers hold funds or assets on behalf of clients, they must provide their clients with periodic statements. In addition, providers must also give priority to clients' orders.[58] They must not, in or in relation to the provision of a financial service, engage in conduct that is, in all circumstances, unconscionable.[59]

5.4.1.4   Summary and Comments

Despite the possibility that the Bill may eventually take a slightly different form, it is possible to make a number of general comments at this stage. Derivatives will no longer be regulated depending on whether they are securities or futures contracts. Instead, one single regime will apply to all derivatives. Over-the-counter (OTC) activities, which are currently not governed by the *Corporations Law*, will be subject to some form of regulatory control. These broad changes would mean that the existing Chapters 7 and 8 of the *Corporations Law* would have to be replaced by a new Chapter 7. For the first time, the term 'derivatives' will be legally defined. It will replace the existing futures contract definition. The definition of security has been narrowed and options over securities will no longer constitute securities. The new regime also provides that if something is a security, then it is not a derivative. This will overcome problems that could arise when an instrument is both a derivative and a security. By removing the reference to 'commodity' in the definition of derivative and replacing it with 'of any nature whatsoever, whether deliverable or not', the new framework will be able to accommodate new products such as derivatives based on things such as electricity or weather. Under the new framework, a financial product market will be free to trade in wide range of products. By extending the provisions of the new Chapter 7 to OTC activities, the issue of competitive inequality between OTC and organised markets would to some extent be resolved.

---

[57]   Financial Services Reform Bill, Part 7.7 Div 2.
[58]   Id., cl. 951B.
[59]   Id., cl. 951A.

The new framework represents a significant departure from the existing approach to financial regulation. It is designed to introduce more flexibility into the regulation of financial products. Generally, the provisions are less prescriptive and allow greater discretion. It is also readily apparent that some of the regulatory changes introduced are aimed at facilitating competition, reducing compliance costs and accommodating transmission of electronic information. For example, market participants dealing with wholesale clients will be subject to lesser obligations than those dealing with retail clients. Employees of licensed financial service providers will no longer be required to be authorised representatives. It has been suggested that the regulatory proposals adopt the 'highest common denominator' approach by borrowing the best from the various regimes that it is intended to supplant.[60] The Government has shown its willingness to please various interest groups. For example, it decided to drop the earlier proposal to allow investors to opt out of the regime for retail investors. The Bill has already received widespread support from various interested groups. The Parliamentary Joint Statutory Committee on Corporations and Securities has endorsed the broad thrust of the Bill.[61] When the new framework is implemented, the Australian regulatory scheme for derivatives will more closely resemble the United Kingdom regulatory model than the United States model.

5.4.2   Hong Kong

Hong Kong is on the threshold of major changes to its outdated futures and securities laws. However, in view of the magnitude of the task, the proposed legislation is still at the public consultation stage. Currently, the statutory provisions governing the securities and futures industries are spread over ten different ordinances.[62] Many of the statutes are obsolete and this is not surprising as some of them are a quarter of a century old. The various statutes operate by reference to an increasing number of other statutes, making it very difficult to find the law. There is considerable duplication and inconsistencies of wording between the ordinances.[63] This creates uncertainty and could act as a trap for the unwary.[64] The original initiative for reform arose out of a recommendation made by the Securities Review Committee in 1988.[65] In 1990, the Securities and Futures Commission

---

[60]   See P. Hutley, 'The Financial Markets Reform Bill (CLERP 6): Will One Size Fit All?' (2000) *Butterworths Corporation Law Bulletin* No. 4, 25 February 2000, para. 69.

[61]   See 'Joint Statutory Committee Okays CLERP 6' in (2000) *Butterworths Corporation Law Bulletin* No. 17, 25 August 2000, para. 306.

[62]   Securities and Futures Commission Ordinance, Commodity Trading Ordinance, Securities Ordinance, Protection of Investors Ordinance, Stock Exchanges Unification Ordinance, Securities (Insider Dealing) Ordinance, Securities (Disclosure of Interests) Ordinance, Securities and Futures (Clearing Houses) Ordinance, Leveraged Foreign Exchange Trading Ordinance, and Exchanges and Clearing Houses (Merger) Ordinance.

[63]   See Securities and Futures Commission, *A Consultation Paper on a Draft for a Composite Securities and Futures Bill* (Hong Kong, April 1996), p. i.

[64]   Ibid.

[65]   See Securities Review Committee, *The Operation and Regulation of the Hong Kong Securities Industry* (Hong Kong, May 1988), para. 13.2.

(SFC) commenced a review of the relevant ordinances with a view to ratio-nalising and modernising the laws.[66] Following a period of public consul-tation, SFC prepared a draft of the composite *Securities and Futures Bill*. It was released for public comment in 1996 but laid dormant until it was reactivated in 1999.

The renewed push for regulatory reform was prompted by concerns that Hong Kong's status as a regional and international financial centre is under threat from other centres. A recent survey revealed that Hong Kong has slipped from being the eight ranking financial centre in the world to the thirteenth.[67] This was a serious blow to Hong Kong's reputation and sug-gested that the 1997 handover had in some way altered investor perception about its financial and capital markets. The Government recognised that retaining the status quo was no longer an option and urgent action was needed for Hong Kong to maintain its status as a leading financial centre.[68] In the March 1999 Budget Speech, the Financial Secretary of Hong Kong announced a number of major financial market reforms to enable Hong Kong to maintain its competitiveness in the face of global challenges. The Hong Kong Government proposed a three-pronged reform programme, which would involve the following: upgrading the existing market struc-ture through the creation of a single clearing arrangement, merging the stock and futures exchanges, and creating a modern regulatory framework. Following the Budget Speech, a new composite Bill was drawn up. It built on the first draft bill released in 1996, but included a number of new pro-posals to take into account recent market developments. The new compos-ite Bill was released to the public for comment in April 2000 and the public consultation period ended on 30 June 2000.

Unlike the proposed Australian framework, Hong Kong's new frame-work does not fundamentally alter the basic approach to financial regula-tion. The new legal framework consolidates the various ordinances governing the securities and futures industries. But in the process it updates the various laws and sets clearer regulatory objectives. Many of the new provisions are aimed at upgrading the standards of regulation to bring them on par with international standards. As the Chairman of the Hong Kong Securities and Futures Commission recently said: 'the whole purpose of the Bill is to ensure the regulatory framework delivers a level playing field in our market which is comparable to other major markets'.[69]

Some of the key changes introduced by the Bill include the following:

- The Bill sets out clear regulatory objectives, based on those estab-lished by the International Organisation of Securities Commissions,

---

[66] See Securities and Futures Commission, *A Consultation Paper on a Draft for a Composite Securities and Futures Bill* (Hong Kong, April 1996), p. i.
[67] See Clifford Chance 'Hong Kong's Plans for the New Hong Kong Exchanges and Clearing Ltd.' (1999) 5:9 *World Securities Law Report* 27.
[68] Ibid.
[69] See A. Sheng, 'The Securities and Futures Bill, 2000', speech presented at a seminar organ-ised by the Hong Kong Securities Institute, 5 September 2000 <www.hksfc.org.hk/eng/speeches/as000905.htm> (26/09/00).

for SFC. These objectives will act as benchmarks for evaluating the performance of SFC. SFC's powers will be enhanced to enable it to carry out its functions more effectively. But at the same time measures will be introduced to make it more accountable and transparent. For example, a full-time Securities and Futures Appeals Tribunal will be established to review important decisions made by SFC.

- Financial intermediaries will no longer be subject to a multiple-registration system. An intermediary will only require a single license to engage in activities regulated by SFC. The list of regulated activities includes dealing in securities and futures contracts, trading in leveraged foreign exchange trading, and advising on securities and futures contracts. Only corporations would be licensed to carry on business in regulated activities, while individuals who perform such an activities on behalf of a licensed corporation would require to be licensed as representatives.

- Currently, when an intermediary engages in improper conduct, SFC can either reprimand the intermediary, or suspend or revoke the intermediary's licence. The new Bill will provide SFC with two additional sanctions: civil fines, or suspension or revocation of the intermediary's license in respect of part of its business only. However, market misconduct will not be completely decriminalised. The Bill will preserve and expand on the list of activities that wil remain criminal offences.

- In view of the difficulty encountered proving market manipulation under the existing laws, the composite Bill will provide an alternative civil route to dealing with market manipulation. It will establish a Market Misconduct Tribunal (MMT) to deal with insider trading and other proscribed market behaviour. The Tribunal will apply the civil standard of proof and will have a range of sanctions at its disposal. For example, it will be able to order disgorgement of profits including interest.

- The Bill will provide a clear statutory private right of action against market misconduct. This will make it easier for a person who has suffered loss as a result of market misconduct to claim compensation and other remedies. It will assist investors in obtaining damages for loss as a result of market misconduct by clarifying the circumstances under which action may be brought and allowing a finding by MMT that a person has engaged in market misconduct to be admitted in evidence in a private civil action.

- In response to new market needs, the Bill will extend regulation to automated trading services (ATS). Even ATS based overseas who target Hong King investors would be brought within the regulatory net. Since ATS operate in very different forms, the Bill will adopt a pragmatic approach for authorisation and supervision. Rather than laying down rigid rules, it will leave it to SFC to decide how these services should be regulated. SFC will issue guidelines on how it will discharge its statutory functions at a later stage.

- Since the existing compensation funds for both the securities and futures exchanges provide an uncertain level of protection for clients, the new Bill will propose the introduction of a new scheme that will provide a 'per investor level' of compensation for retail investors. The new arrangements will be provided through a new and independent entity that would be subject to appropriate checks and balances.

The draft Bill is expected to undergo some further changes to take into account some of the feedback received from market participants and the Government. The Hong Kong Securities and Futures Commission is confident that the amended Bill will be presented to the Legislative Council in November 2000.

5.5   SUMMARY AND COMMENTS

Financial markets today are more integrated and complex than probably any other period of history. Forces such as globalisation, advances in technology and changing consumer needs have radically altered the financial landscape. New market developments such as the convergence of markets, the demutualisation and merger of exchanges, and the dominance of electronic trading have placed great strains on the existing regulatory arrangements. These developments have created the need for regulatory reform of financial markets. Australia and Hong Kong have unveiled their plans for reform and the new frameworks would be implemented sometime in 2001. Both reform programs are aimed at creating modern and flexible legal frameworks that would not only provide investor protection, but also promote growth and encourage innovation. However each jurisdiction has adopted its own approach to regulatory reform. Australia has opted for harmonised regulation of its financial services, while Hong Kong has stayed with the existing approach of adopting different regimes for securities and futures contracts. The other jurisdictions under study can be expected to reform their financial markets over the next few years. Like Australia and Hong Kong, the motivation for reform will be the need to stay on par with regulatory best practices rather the fear of market failure. Should New Zealand, Singapore and Malaysia decide to reform their laws there is a good likelihood that they may adopt the Australian regulatory model. There are a couple of factors that support this argument. Firstly, Australia and New Zealand have always enjoyed close political and business relations. There is now an even greater commitment among politicians on both sides of the Tasman to harmonise their business laws. Secondly, Singapore and Malaysia have in the past modelled their securities and futures laws after the Australian securities laws and there is no reason why they will not continue to do so in the future.

Conclusion

The last two decades have witnessed the remarkable growth and development of the global derivatives markets. But despite the enormous contributions made by derivatives, many still view derivatives with a great deal of suspicion. There are a number of reasons why derivatives have attracted significant negative publicity. The first is that many end-users of derivatives suffered crippling losses in the 1980s and 1990s and went to court to seek relief. In many cases the existing legal rules proved inadequate to deal with the legal issues thrown up by derivatives. The second reason is that there is a general lack of understanding about the nature of derivatives and how they operate. This has been made worse by the wide array of products that are included under the rubric of 'derivatives'. The third reason is that derivatives have grown at an almost exponential rate. This has alarmed regulators who fear that the massive volumes of derivatives traded daily would pose a major threat to systemic stability.

Concerns about the inadequacy of the existing legal and regulatory frameworks to deal with the risks posed by derivatives have generated significant debate about the proper regulatory response. Two main themes have dominated the global regulatory debate. The first is the regulation of over-the-counter (OTC) derivatives markets and the second is the reform of the on-exchange regulatory framework. Fears about the lack of enforceability of OTC derivatives agreements and increasing pressure from exchanges to level the playing field have largely contributed to calls for regulation of the OTC markets. Uncertainty about the ability of the existing regulatory frameworks to deal with the rapidly changing financial landscape has been mainly responsible for moves to change the way derivatives are regulated. This study examined both these themes in the context of the regulatory frameworks of Australia, New Zealand, Singapore, Malaysia and Hong Kong. In the course of this study a number of findings were reached from which the following conclusions are drawn.

There is no denying that derivatives, especially those which are highly leveraged, are more risky than other financial instruments. But if used wisely, derivatives are an invaluable tool for modern financial management and not likely to be harmful. The difficulty of characterising the legal nature of derivatives coupled with their novelty has given rise to a whole range of legal issues. This has in turn made derivatives transactions more vulnerable to legal challenges. Most of the legal issues have arisen because legal developments have generally lagged behind market developments. Many of the existing legal principles were developed well before the advent of derivatives and are often unsuited to deal with disputes involving derivatives. The last few years have witnessed a significant increase in legal cases involving derivatives. These cases have helped clarify some of the legal uncertainty surrounding derivatives, but there are still many areas of uncertainty remaining. However, relying on the courts for guidance is slow and expensive. Greater reliance is now being placed on legislation to promote greater legal predictability. This is most evident in areas such as lack of legal capacity, suitability and netting.

The analysis of the regulatory frameworks of the jurisdictions under study have revealed that with the exception of New Zealand, there is significant degree of regulatory harmony among the other four jurisdictions. This is surprising considering the differences in their markets. It is also interesting to note that the regulatory frameworks of the three Southeast Asian jurisdictions have more in common than the two Australasian jurisdictions have with each other. However, there is good likelihood that New Zealand will eventually adopt a similar legal framework as Australia. The Australian and New Zealand Governments recently signed a revised Memorandum of Understanding to reduce the costs associated with Trans-Tasman business operations.[1] This will pave the way for the removal of differences in business laws. The adoption of a common legal framework for derivatives is logical considering Australian ownership of the New Zealand exchange.

There is also now widespread acceptance that as markets become more global and the boundaries between exchanges and intermediaries become blurred, the existing regulatory approach may have to be replaced. While the objectives of financial regulation have not changed, the methods of achieving them would have to change. Since many of the regulatory challenges confronting regulators everywhere are similar, regulators would benefit if they cooperate more closely with each other. It makes more sense now than ever before for regulators to achieve regulatory harmony on an international basis. Regulatory harmony does not necessarily mean identical laws but the adoption of common minimum standards. National laws are no longer useful in regulating borderless transactions and will only lead to regulatory competition. There is already significant cooperation among international regulators in derivatives regulation. The next step is the adoption of a common legal framework that is universally acceptable. This is not too difficult considering that many jurisdictions have broadly similar laws. It appears that regulatory harmonisation in derivatives regulation is inevitable and the only question is 'When will it happen?'

---

[1] See ' "Common Sense Principles" Govern New Aust/NZ Business Law Accord' (2000) *Butterworths Corporation Law Bulletin* No. 18, 8 September 2000, para. 326.

Select Bibliography

1   Books and Legal Encyclopaedia

Australian Corporations Law: Principles and Practice, Vol. 3 (Butterworths Loose-leaf, Sydney).

Arjunan, K. and Low, C. K., *Understanding Company Law in Malaysia* (LBC, Sydney, 1995).

Banks, E., *The Emerging Fixed-Income Markets in Asia* (Probus Publishing, Chicago, 1994).

Banks, E., *Asia Pacific Derivative Markets* (Macmillan Press Ltd, United Kingdom, 1996).

Battley, N. (ed.), *The World's Futures and Options Markets* (Probus Publishing Co., Cambridge, 1993).

Bettelheim, E., Parry, H. and Rees, W. (eds), *Swaps and Off-Exchange Derivatives Trading: Law and Regulation* (FT Law & Tax, London, 1996).

Bhala, R. K., *Foreign Bank Regulation After BCCI* (Carolina Academic Press, Durham, 1994).

Black, J., *Rules and Regulators* (Clarendon Press, Oxford, 1997).

Brown, M. (ed.), *Managing and Disclosing Risks of Investing in Derivatives* (Kluwer Law International, London, 1996).

Burke, L., Glennie, D. and Melrose, J. (eds), *International Derivatives Law* (Risk Publications, London, 1996).

Burrows, A., *Understanding the Law of Obligations; Essays on Contract, Tort and Restitution* (Hart Publishing, Oxford, 1998).

Burton, G. (ed.), *Directions in Finance Law* (Butterworths, Sydney, 1990).

Burton, G., *Australian Financial Transactions Law* (Butterworths, Sydney, 1991).

Carew, E., *Derivatives Decoded* (Allen & Unwin, Sydney, 1995).

Carew, E., *Fast Money 4* (Allen & Unwin, St Leonards, NSW, 1998).

Cavalla, N., *OTC Markets in Derivative Instruments* (Macmillan Publishers Limited, Hants, England, 1993).

Cashmere, M., *Tax and Corporate Finance into the New Millennium* (CCH, Sydney, 1999).

Chan W. C. and Others (eds), *Current Legal Issues in International Commercial Litigation* (Faculty of Law, NUS, Singapore, 1997).

Chew, L., *Managing Derivative Risks* (John Wiley & Sons, Chichester, 1996).

Chicago Board of Trade, *Commodity Trading Manual* (1989).

Chorafas, D. N., *How to Understand and Use Mathematics for Derivatives, Volume 1: Understanding the Behaviour of Markets* (Euromoney Publications, London, 1995).

Corpus Juris Secundum, Vol. 79A (West Publishing Co., St. Paul, Minn., 1995).

Courtney, D. and Bettelheim, E. C., *An Investor's Guide to the Commodity Futures Markets* (Butterworths, London, 1986).

Courtney, D., *Derivatives Trading in Europe* (Butterworths, London, 1992).

Cranston, R. (ed.), *Banks, Liability and Risk* (2nd edn, LLP, London, 1995).

Crawford, G. and Sen, B., *Derivatives for Decision Makers* (John Wiley & Sons, New York, 1996).

Currie, J. S., *Australian Futures Regulation* (Longman, Melbourne, 1994).

Dale, R., *International Banking Deregulation* (Blackwell Finance, Oxford, 1992).

Dale, R., *Risk and Regulation in Global Securities Markets* (John Wiley & Sons, Chichester, 1996).

Das, S., *Swaps and Financial Derivatives* (2nd edn, Law Book Co., Sydney, 1994).

Das, S., *Exotic Options* (LBC Information Services, Sydney, 1996).

Das, S. (ed.), *Credit Derivatives* (John Wiley & Sons, Singapore, 1998).

Decovny, S., *Swaps* (Woodhead-Faulkner, London, 1992).

Dicey and Morris, *The Conflict of Laws* (13th edn, Sweet & Maxwell, London, 2000).

Dobbs-Higginson, M. S., *Asia Pacific: Its Role in the New World Disorder* (William Heinemann Australia, Port Melbourne, 1993).

Edwards, F. R., *The New Finance* (The AEI Press, Washington DC, 1996).

Farmey, P. and Walmsley, K. (eds), *US Securities and Regulations Handbook* (Graham & Trotman, London, 1992).

Ferrarini, G. (ed.), *Prudential Regulation of Banks and Securities Firms* (Kluwer Law International, London, 1995).

Fingleton, J. and Schoenmaker, D. (eds), *The Internationalisation of Capital Markets and The Regulatory Response* (Graham & Trotman, London, 1992).

Fisher, J. and Bewsey, J., *The Law of Investor Protection* (Sweet & Maxwell, London, 1997).

Fitzgerald, M. D., *Financial Options* (Euromoney Publications, London, 1987).

Ford, D., *The Investor's Guide to Traded Options* (Pitman Publishing, London, 1994).

Fox-Andrews, M. and Meaden, N., *Derivatives Markets and Investments Management* (Prentice Hall/Woodhead-Faulkner, London, 1995).

Galitz, L., *Financial Engineering* (Pitman Publishing, London, 1994).

Goodhart, C. and Others, *Financial Regulation: Why How and Where Now?* (Routledge, London, 1998).

Goode, R. M., *Principles of Corporate Insolvency Law* (2nd edn, Sweet & Maxwell, 1997, London).

Gower, L. C. B., *Gower's Principles of Modern Company Law* (5th edn, Sweet & Maxwell, London, 1992).

Gowland, D., *The Regulation of Financial Markets* (Edward Elgar Publishing Ltd, Hants, England, 1990).

Gringras, C., *The Laws of the Internet* (Butterworths, London, 1997).

Guest, A. G. (ed.), *Chitty on Contracts* (27th edn, Sweet & Maxwell, London, 1994).

Hadjiemmanuil, C., *Banking Regulation and the Bank of England* (LLP Ltd, London, 1996).

Halsbury's Laws of England, Vol 7(2) (4th edn, Butterworths, London, 1996).

Harrison, M., *Asia-Pacific Securities Market* (Longman, Hong Kong, 1994).

Henderson, S. and Price, J., *Currency and Interest Swaps* (2nd edn, Butterworths, London, 1988).

Hudson, A., *The Law on Financial Derivatives* (2nd edn, Sweet & Maxwell, London, 1998).

Jeunemaître, A. (ed.), *Financial Markets Regulation: A Practitioner's Perspective* (Macmillan Press Ltd, London, 1997).

Kaufman, P. J. (ed.), *Handbook of Futures Markets* (Wiley, New York, 1984).

Klein, R. A. and Lederman, J. (eds), *Derivatives Risk and Responsibility* (Irwin, Chicago, 1996).

Koh, K. L. and Others (eds), *Current Developments in International Securities, Commodities and Financial Futures Markets* (Butterworths, Singapore, 1987).

Langervoot, D. C. (ed.), *Securities Law Review—1996* (Clark Boardman Callaghan, New York, 1996).

Lastra, R. M., *Central Banking and Banking Regulation* (Financial Markets Group, London, 1996).

Leeson, N. W., *Rogue Trader* (Little, Brown and Co., Boston, 1996).

Lessing J. P. G. and Corkery, J. F. (eds), *Corporate Insolvency Law* (The Taxation & Corporate Research Centre, Gold Coast, 1995).

Low, C. K., *Securities Regulation in Malaysia* (Malaya Law Journal Sdn Bhd, Kuala Lumpur, 1997).

Lye, C. and Lazar, R. (eds), *The Regulation of Financial and Capital Markets* (SNP Printers, Singapore, 1991).

MacHarg, M. L. and Kameda, R. R. W. (eds), *International Survey of Investments Adviser Regulation* (Graham & Trotman/Martinus Nijhoff, London, 1994).

McCracken, S., *Banking and Finance in Singapore* (Longman, Singapore, 1993).

McCracken, S. and Everett, D., *Finance and Security Law: Cases and Materials* (Butterworths, Sydney, 1998).

Morison's Company and Securities Law (Butterworths Loose-leaf, Wellington).

Naisbitt, J., *Megatrends Asia* (Nicholas Brealey Publishing, London, 1996).

Norton, J. J. and Auerback, R. M. (eds), *International Finance in the 1990s* (Blackwell Finance, London, 1993).

Norton, J. J. and Others (eds), *International Banking Regulation and Supervision: Change and Transformation in the 1990s* (Graham & Trotman/Nijhoff Publishers, London, 1994).

Norton, J. J. (ed.), *Devising International Bank Supervisory Standards* (Graham & Trotman/Martinus Nijhoff Publishers, London, 1995).

Oditah, F. (ed.), *The Future for the Global Securities Market* (Clarendon Press, Oxford, 1996).

Ogus, A. I., Regulation: *Legal Form and Economic Theory* (Clarendon Press, Oxford, 1994).

Prosser, T., *Law and the Regulators* (Clarendon Press, Oxford, 1997).

Park, K. K. H. and Schoenfeld, S. A., *The Pacific Rim Futures and Options Markets* (Heinemann Asia, Singapore, 1994).

Phang, A., *Cheshire, Fifoot and Furmston's Law of Contract: Second Singapore and Malaysian Edition* (Butterworths Asia, Singapore, 1998).

Roche, J., *Property Futures and Securitisation* (Woodhead Publishing Ltd, Cambridge, 1995).

Schachter, B. (ed.), *Derivatives, Regulation and Banking* (Elsevier, Amsterdam, 1997).

Seddon, N., Government Contracts (2nd edn, Federation Press, Leichhardt, N.S.W., 1995).

Seidel, A. D. and Ginsberg, P. M., *Commodities Trading* (Prentice-Hall, New Jersey, 1983).

Seldon, A. (ed.), *Financial Regulation—or Over-Regulation* (Institute of Economic Affairs, London, 1988).

Sheedy, E. and McCracken, S. (eds), *Derivatives: The Risks that Remain* (Allen & Unwin, St. Leonards, N.S.W., 1997).

Slatyer, W. and Carew, E., *Trading Asia-Pacific Financial Futures Markets* (Allen & Unwin, Sydney, 1993).

Swan, E. J. (ed.), *Derivative Instruments* (Graham & Trotman/Martinus Nijhoff, London, 1994).

Swan, E. J. (ed.), *Derivative Instruments Law* (Cavendish Publishing Limited, London, 1995).

Swan, E. J. (ed.), *Issues in Derivatives Instruments* (Kluwer Law International, The Hague, 1999).

Steil, B., (ed.), *International Financial Market Regulation* (John Wiley & Sons, Chichester, 1994).

Teo, K. S. and Others (eds), *Current Legal Issues in Commercial Litigation* (Faculty of Law, NUS, Singapore, 1997).

Teweles, R. J. and Jones, F. J., *The Futures Game* (McGraw-Hill Book Co., New York, 1987).

Tomasic, R., Jackson, J. and Woellner, R., *Corporations Law: Principles, Policy and Process* (3rd edn, Butterworths, Sydney, 1996).

Tomasic, R. (ed.), *Company Law in East Asia* (Dartmouth Publishing, Aldershot, 1999).

Von der Heydt, K. and Kellar, S. (eds), *International Securities Law Handbook* (Graham & Trotman/Martinus Nijhoff, London, 1995).

Walker, G. and Fisse, B. (eds), *Securities Regulation in Australia and New Zealand* (Oxford University Press, Auckland, 1994).

Walker, G., Fisse, B. and Ramsay, I., (eds), *Securities Regulation in Australia and New Zealand* (2nd edn, LBC, Sydney, 1998).

Watters, R. F. and McGee, T. G. (eds), *Asia-Pacific: New Geographics of the Pacific Rim* (Hurst & Company, London, 1997).

Weerasooria, W. S., *Banking Law and the Financial System in Australia* (5th edn, Chatswood, N.S.W., 2000).

White, J., *Regulation of Securities and Futures Dealing* (Sweet & Maxwell, London, 1992).

Whittaker, A. and Morse, G., *The Financial Services Act 1986* (Butterworths, London, 1987).

Wood, P. R., *Title Finance, Derivatives, Securitisations, Set-off and Netting* (Sweet & Maxwell, London, 1995).

2   Journal Articles, Monographs and Book Chapters

Abernethy, A. A., 'Regulation of the Futures and Options Market in New Zealand' (1996) 11 JIBFL 27.

Adams, M., 'Practical Issues for Trustees in the Application of Trust Fund Moneys in the Use of Derivatives' (1994) 5 JBFLP 20.

Albrechtsen, J., 'Extraterritorial Implications of Australian Securities Laws' in Walker, G. and Fisse, B. (eds), *Securities Regulation in Australia and New Zealand* (Oxford University Press, Auckland, 1994), ch. 29, p. 730.

Alfon, I., 'Cost-Benefit Analysis and Compliance Culture' (1997) 5 *Journal of Financial Regulation and Compliance* 16.

Allan, R., 'Inside the Corporate Treasury' in Sheedy, E. and McCracken, S. (eds), *Derivatives: The Risks that Remain* (Allen & Unwin, St. Leonards, N.S.W., 1997), ch. 4, p. 77.

Ansell, S., 'The Regulation of Insider Trading in Derivatives' (1995) 13 C&SLJ 476.

Ansell, S., 'The Application of Equity Derivatives in Mergers and Acquisitions' (1997) 15 C&SLJ 218.

Ashall, P. and Brown, C., 'Regulatory and Legal Issues for Derivatives in the UK' (October 1994) IFLR 22.

Ayling, R. and Welch, J., 'Netting in Australia' (1992) 7 JIBFL 105.

Barcroft, P. A., 'Derivatives and Market Risk Disclosure—Leaving No Stone Unturned?' (1998) 3 JIBFL 131.

Barker, B., 'United Kingdom' in Burke, L., Glennie, D. and Melrose, J. (eds), *International Derivatives Law* (Risk Publications, London, 1996), p. 201.

Benston, G. J., 'International Regulatory Coordination of Banking' in Fingleton, J. and Schoenmaker, D. (eds), *The Internationalisation of Capital Markets and The Regulatory Response* (Graham & Trotman, London, 1992), ch. 10, p. 197.

Blair, S. C., 'United States Regulation of Derivative Instruments: Reflections from a Crucial Crossroads' in Swan, E. J. (ed.), *Derivative Instruments* (Graham & Trotman/Martinus Nijhoff, London, 1994), ch. 2, p. 13.

Blair, S. C., 'Lessons from the Barings Collapse' (1995) 64 *Fordham Law Review* 1.

Blair, S., 'Liability Risks in Derivatives Sales', (1996) 11 JIBL 18.

Blair, W. and Olive, C. D., 'Derivatives Sales Liability: Approach of the English and US Courts' (1996) 11 JIBL 283.

Blair, W., 'The Reform of Financial Regulation in the U.K.' (1998) 13 JIBL 43.

Blass, A., 'Lehman Discovers Derivatives Debt Has Chinese Characteristics' (February 1996) *China Law & Practice* 40.

Bradley, C., 'Competitive Deregulation of Financial Services Activity in Europe after 1992' (1991) 11(4) *Oxford Journal of Legal Studies* 545.

Breeden, R. C., 'Reconciling National and International Concerns in the Regulation of Global Capital Markets' in Fingleton, J. and Schoenmaker, D. (eds), *The Internationalisation of Capital Markets and The Regulatory Response* (Graham & Trotman, London, 1992), ch. 2, p. 27.

Bridge, M., 'Restitution and Retrospective Law: Kleinwort Benson Ltd. v Lincoln City Council' (1999) 14 JIBFL 5.

Brown, C., 'Report of the Board of Banking Supervision Inquiry into the Circumstances of the Collapse of Barings', (1995) 10 JIBL 446.

Brown, C., 'Legal, Documentation and Regulatory Issues of Credit Derivatives' (1997) 12 JIBFL 119.

Bull, K., 'Does Government Have a Future in Derivatives?' (1997) 25 *Australian Business Law Review* 246.

Carrigan, F., 'Globalisation and Legal Transnationalisation' (1999) 10 *Australian Journal of Corporate Law* 122.

Cecchetti, S. G., 'The Future of Financial Intermediation and Regulation: An Overview' (May 1999) 5 *Current Issues in Economics and Finance* 1.

Champarnaud, F., 'Facing New Regulatory Challenges: The Case of Proprietary Trading Systems' in Jeunemaître, A. (ed.), *Financial Markets Regulation: A Practitioner's Perspective* (Macmillan Press Ltd, London, 1997), p. 84.

Chakin, D. A., 'Futures Frauds in the Asia Pacific Region' in Lye, C. and Lazar, R. (eds), *The Regulation of Financial and Capital Markets* (SNP Printers, Singapore, 1991), p. 252.

Chen C. J. and Ng, C., 'Financial Futures Markets: Singapore Regulatory Framework—Legal Issues and Problems' in Koh, K. L. and Others (eds), *Current Developments in International Securities, Commodities and Financial Futures Markets* (Butterworths, Singapore, 1987), p. 356.

Chin, Y. L., 'Set-off in Modern Banking' in Burton, G. (ed.), *Directions in Finance Law* (Butterworths, Sydney, 1990), ch. 3, p. 76.

Chou, V. L., 'Derivatives and Dialectics: The Evolution of the Chinese Futures Market' (1997) 72 *New York University Law Review* 175.

Clifford, D., 'Proposed Close-Out and Market Netting Act' (1997) 8 JBFLP 75.

Clark, E., 'Comparative Research in Corporate Law' (1996) 3 *Canberra Law Review* 62.

Cohen, P. D., 'Securities Trading Via the Internet' (July 1999) Journal *of Business Law* 299.

Coffee, J. C., 'Competition versus Consolidation: The Significance of Organisational Structure in Financial and Securities Regulation' (1995) 50 *The Business Lawyer* 447.

Cohen, H., 'Swaps, Restitution and Compound Interest: Westdeutsche Landesbanke v Islington' (1995) 10 JIBL 106.

Coleman, E. A., 'Netting a Red Herring' (1994) 9 JIBFL 391.

Corcoran, A. M., 'Prudential Regulation of OTC Derivatives: Lessons from the Exchange-traded Sector' in G. Ferrarini (ed.), *Prudential Regulation of Banks and Securities Firms* (Kluwer Law International, London, 1995), ch. 11, p. 157.

Cullen, I., 'The Development of Regulation of OTC Derivative Business' in Swan, E. J. (ed.), *Derivative Instruments Law* (Cavendish Publishing Limited, London, 1995), ch. 1, p. 1.

Culp, C. L., 'Derivatives Regulation: Problems and Prospects' (1998) 4 *Derivatives Use, Trading & Regulation* 119.

Currie, J., 'Bank Use of Derivatives: More Ideas for Reform' (1994) 5 JBFLP 225.

Currie, J. and Lonie, J., 'LEPOs: Claytons Futures Contracts are Securities' (1995) 6 JBFLP 133.

D'Angelo, N. and Dow, S., 'Focusing on Regulation' in Sheedy, E. and McCracken, S. (eds), *Derivatives: The Risks That Remain* (Allen & Unwin, St. Leonards N.S.W., 1997), ch. 10, p. 259.

Dale, R., 'Regulatory Consequences of the BCCI Collapse: US, UK, EC, Basle Committee—Current Issues in International Supervision' in Norton, J. J. and Others (eds), *International Banking Regulation and Supervision: Change and Transformation in the 1990s* (Graham & Trotman/Nijhoff Publishers, London, 1994), ch. 10, p. 377.

Dale, R., 'Derivatives: The New Regulatory Challenge' (1995) 10 JIBFL 11.

Dale, R., 'Derivatives Clearing Houses: the Regulatory Challenge' (1997) 12 JIBL 46.

Dharmananda, K., 'Ultra Vires Goes Ultraviolet' (1997) 71 ALJ 622.

Donnan, F., 'Self-Regulation and the Demutualisation of the Australian Stock Exchange' (1999) 10 *Australian Journal of Corporate Law* 1.

Ebert, M, 'The Asian Financial Crisis and the Need for a New Global Financial Architecture' (1998) 13 JIBFL 454.

Edwards, F. R. and Canter, M. S., 'The Collapse of Metallgesellschaft: Unhedgeable Risks, Poor Hedging Strategy, or Just Bad Luck?' (1995) 87 *Journal of Applied Corporate Finance* 86.

Elderfield, M., 'Basle Publishes Final Market Risk Capital Standards' (1996) 11 JIBL 125.

Elliot, R. J. and Henshaw, A. R., 'Self-Regulation: Present and Future' in Swan, E. J. (ed.), *Derivative Instruments Law* (Cavendish Publishing Limited, London, 1995), ch. 2, p. 9.

Everett, D., 'Multi Party Set-Off Agreements' in Lessing J. P. G. and Corkery, J. F. (eds), *Corporate Insolvency Law* (The Taxation & Corporate Research Centre, Gold Coast, 1995), ch. 11, p. 156.

Forbes, D., 'Towards the "Pacific Century": Integration and Disintegration in the Pacific Basin' in *The Far East and Australasia 1996* (27th edn, Europa Publications Ltd, London, 1996).

Forster, D. M., 'The State of the Law after Procter & Gamble v Bankers Trust' (1996) 3 *Derivatives Quarterly* 8.

Franks, J. R. and Others, 'The Direct and Compliance Costs of Financial Regulation' in E. J. Swan (ed.), *Issues in Derivatives Instruments* (Kluwer Law International, The Hague, 1999), ch. 11, p. 159.

Frederick, J. A., 'Not Just for Widows & Orphans Anymore: The Inadequacy of the Current Suitability Rules for the Derivatives Market' (1995) 64 *Fordham Law Review* 97.

Gaynor, B., 'Securities Regulation in New Zealand: Crisis and Reform' in Walker, G. and Fisse, B. (eds), *Securities Regulation in Australia and New Zealand* (Oxford University Press, Auckland, 1994), ch. 2, p. 10.

Gengatharen, R., *Financial Futures Markets: Malaysian Regulatory Framework* (Occasional Paper No. 4/1996, Centre for South-East Asian Law, Darwin).

Gengatharen, R., 'Regulating Derivatives in a South-East Asian Market' (1998) 13 JIBL 93.

Gengatharen, R., 'Corporate Restructuring in the Malaysian Derivatives Market' (1998) 9 *Journal of Banking and Finance Law and Practice* 245.

Gengatharen, R., 'The Suitability Rule: How Suitable is it for Derivatives?' (1998) *LAWASIA Journal* 131.

Gengatharen, R., 'Regulatory Reform of the Australian OTC Derivatives Markets' (1998) 2 *Southern Cross University Law Review* 76.

Gengatharen, R., 'Bankers Trust Co. v P. T. Jakarta International Hotels & Development [1999] 1 Lloyd's Rep. 910' (2000) 28 *Australian Business Law Review* 62.

Golden, J. B. 'Regulating Derivatives: The Importance of Asking the Right Questions and Listening to the Answers' (1994) 9 JIBL 295.

Goldvasser, V. R., 'CLERP 6—Implications and Ramifications for the Regulation of Australian Financial Markets' (1999) 17 C&SLJ 206.

Gooch, A. C. and Klein, L. B., 'United States Case Law Involving Over-The-Counter Derivatives' 1992–1996: Part I' (1998) 4 *Derivatives Use, Regulation and Trading* 29.

Goodhart, C., 'The Costs of Regulation' in Seldon, A. (ed.), *Financial Regulation—or Over-Regulation* (Institute of Economic Affairs, London, 1988), p. 17.

Greenough, W., 'The Limits of the Suitability Doctrine in Commodity Futures Trading' (1992) 47 *The Business Lawyer* 991.

Gunningham, N., 'Futures Market Regulation In Australia' in Walker, G. and Fisse, B. (eds), *Securities Regulation in Australia and New Zealand* (Oxford University Press, Auckland, 1994), ch. 32, p. 819.

Hains, M. G., 'FRAs, Swaps, Futures, Options and the Concept of Standardisation' (1990) 5 JIBFL 158.

Hains, M. G., *Options: Should They be Treated as Futures Contracts*, Banking Law Association Special Report (1992).

Hains, M. G., 'Futures Contracts: Do They Include Forward and Swaps?' in Walker, G. and Fisse, B. (eds), *Securities Regulation in Australia and New Zealand* (Oxford University Press, Auckland, 1994), ch. 33, p. 846.

Hains, M. G., 'Reflections on the Sydney Futures Exchange Clearing House: The Rise of the Mirrored Contract Theory' (1994) 5 JBFLP 257.

Hains, M. G., 'The Two-Sided Nature of a Futures Contract: Its Meaning and Relevance to OTC Derivatives' (1997) 8 JBFLP 185.

Hains, M. G., 'Derivatives Regulation in Australia' in Walker, G., Fisse, B. and Ramsay, I., (eds), *Securities Regulation in Australia and New Zealand* (LBC, Sydney, 1998), ch. 18, p. 655.

Hall, M. J. B., 'The Revised Supervisory Treatment of Netting and Potential Exposure of Off-Balance Sheet Items under the Basle Capital Accord' (1996) 11 JIBL 93.

Hall, M. J. B., 'The Treatment of Multilateral Netting of Forward Value Foreign Exchange Transactions under the Basle Capital Accord' (1997) 12 JIBL 333.

Hammond, G. and Paterson, I., 'Additional Comments on Dharmala' (1996) 7 JBFLP 164.

Hammond, G. and Stumbles, J., 'Australia's Financial Regulation: A Blueprint for Change' (1997) 12 JIBL 311.

Hanrahan, P., 'The Proposed Suitability Requirement for On-Exchange Derivatives Markets: A Critical Analysis' (1997) 8 JBFLP 5.

Hay, Q., Taylor, M. and Webb, D., 'Trans-Tasman Mutual Recognition: A New Dimension in Australian-New Zealand Legal Relations' (1997) 1 INT.TLR 6.

Henderson, S. K., 'Swap Financing' in Norton, J. J. and Auerback, R. M. (eds), *International Finance in the 1990s* (Blackwell Finance, London, 1993), ch. 12, p. 344.

Henderson, S. K., 'Regulation of Swap and Derivatives: How and Why?' (1993) 8 JIBL 349.

Henderson, S. K., 'Bankers Trust v Dharmala: The English Courts Inject Commercial Sense into the Debate Over the Scope of a Derivatives Dealer's Duty to an End-User' (1996) 7 JBFLP 162.

Henderson, S. K., 'Procter & Gamble v Bankers Trust Company Resolved' (1996) 7 JBFLP 253.

Henderson, S. K., 'Derivatives as a Niche Area is Dead' (1997) 12 JIBL 351.

Henshaw, A. R., 'Derivatives Litigation Issues' in Swan, E. J. (ed.), *Derivative Instruments Law* (Cavendish Publishing Limited, London, 1995), ch. 8, p. 151.

Ho, C., 'The Capital City Vision: A Perspective from the Law on Financial Derivatives' (1997) 18 *Singapore Law Review* 98.

Horwitz, D. L., 'P&G v Bankers Trust: Whats All the Fuss?' (1996) 3 *Derivatives Quarterly* 18.

Hosking, L. V., 'Insight into the Global Futures Markets and Sydney Futures Exchange's Involvement' (December 1994) *Commercial Law Association* 23.

Hutley, P., 'The Financial Markets Reform Bill (CLERP 6) Will One Size Fit All?' (2000) *Butterworths Corporations Law Bulletin No. 4*, 25 February 2000, para. 69.

International Financial Law Review, *Special Supplement on Derivatives* (March 1994).

Jarrat, J., 'Allocating Capital' in Sheedy, E. and McCracken, S. (eds), *Derivatives: The Risks That Remain* (Allen & Unwin, St. Leonards N.S.W., 1997), ch. 8, p. 195.

Jacklin, N., 'Sales Practices in Over-The-Counter Derivatives Transactions' (1995) 10 JIBFL 181.

Jamison, N., 'Developments in Voluntary Self-Regulation' (1998) 6 *Journal of Financial Regulation and Compliance* 31.

Johnson, P. M. and Others, 'Adapting to Tomorrow's Markets' (1999) 5 *Derivatives Quarterly* 8.

Kay, R. S., 'Sovereignty in the New Hong Kong' (1998) 114 *The Law Quarterly Review* 189.

Knight-Ridder Financial, 'The Truth About Derivatives' (September 1995) *Asiamoney* 2.

Kojima, J. C., 'Product-based Solutions to Financial Innovation: The Promise and Danger of Applying the Federal Securities Laws to OTC Derivatives' (1995) 33 *American Business Law Journal* 259.

Lanyon, E., 'Derivatives and Modern Portfolio Theory; the Trustee's Duty of Investments.' (1995) 6 JBFLP 58.

LaPlante J. D., 'Growth and Organisation of Commodity Markets', in Kaufman, P. J. (ed.), *Handbook of Futures Markets* (Wiley, New York, 1984).

Latimer, P., 'Futures Contracts and Gaming Laws' (1993) 14(3) *The Company Lawyer* 67.

Lawrence, J., 'The Regulation of Derivatives and the LEPOs Litigation' (1996) 14 C&SLJ 90.

Levin, P., Luke, J. and Sundaravej, P., 'Recent Developments Affecting US Financial Derivatives', (November 1994) IFLR 10.

Lim, L., 'The Southeast Asian Currency Crisis and its Aftermath' (1997) 13 *Journal of Asian Business* 65.

Lindross, J. and Walker, G., 'A Short History of Securities Regulation in New Zealand' in Walker, G. and Fisse, B. (eds), *Securities Regulation in Australia and New Zealand* (Oxford University Press, Auckland, 1994), ch. 4, p. 59.

Linklaters & Paines Hong Kong, 'Legal Risk Management of Derivatives' (September 1995) *Asiamoney* 29.

Loh, H. S., 'SIMEX: Developing and Regulating a Futures Market' in Koh, K. L. and Others (eds), *Current Developments in International Securities, Commodities and Financial Futures Markets* (Butterworths, Singapore, 1987), p. 349.

Luke, R. D. and Burke, L. F., 'United States' in Burke, L., Glennie, D. and Melrose, J. (eds), *International Derivatives Law* (Risk Publications, London, 1996), p. 45.

Lynch, D. 'Growth in Asia-Pacific Markets' in Sheedy, E and McCracken, S. (eds), *Derivatives: The Risks That Remain* (Allen & Unwin, St. Leonards, N.S.W., 1997), ch. 1, p. 3.

Lynn, D. M., 'Enforceability of Over-the-Counter Financial Derivatives' (1994) 50 *The Business Lawyer* 291.

Malcolm, A. and Fidler, J., 'Legal and Regulatory Issues for Derivatives in Hong Kong' (January 1995) IFLR 38.

Markham, J. W., 'Commodity Market Malpractices' in Farmey, P. and Walmsley, K. (eds), *US Securities and Regulations Handbook* (Graham & Trotman, London, 1992), ch. 10, p. 351.

Markham, J. W., 'US Regulation of Futures and Options', in Farmey, P. and Walmsley, K. (eds), *US Securities and Regulations Handbook* (Graham & Trotman, London, 1992), ch. 8, p. 287.

Markham, J. W., 'Protecting the Institutional Investor—Jungle Predator or Shorn Lamb' in Langervoot, D.C. (ed.), *Securities Law Review—1996* (Clark Boardman Callaghan, New York, 1996), p. 633.

Markovic, M. 'The Legal Status of Futures Market Participants in Australia' (1989) 7 C&SLJ 82.

McBarnet, D. and Whelan, C., 'International Corporate Finance and the Challenge of Creative Compliance' in Fingleton, J. and Schoenmaker, D. (eds), *The Internationalisation of Capital Markets and The Regulatory Response* (Graham & Trotman, London, 1992), ch. 6, p. 129.

McCracken, S., 'Confronting the Legal Dimension' in Sheedy, E. and McCracken, S. (eds), *Derivatives: The Risks That Remain* (Allen & Unwin, St. Leonards, N.S.W., 1997), ch. 7, p. 155.

McKown, J. E. and Purcell, A. T., 'Enforcement Actions Involving Derivatives: BT Securities Corp. and Beyond' (1996) 65 *University of Cincinnati Law Review* 117.

McSherry, W. J. and Others, 'Litigation Involving Derivatives' in Klein, R. A. and Lederman, J. (eds), *Derivatives Risk and Responsibility* (Irwin, Chicago, 1996), ch. 22, p. 659.

Medero, J. T., 'Jurisdictional Issues in US Regulation of Derivative Products' (1994) 9 JIBFL 117.

Meer, C. J., 'Hybrid Instruments: Their Treatment Under Recent Commodity Futures Trading Commission Releases' (1991) 46 *The Business Lawyer* 405.

Moore, P. M., 'The Role of Regulation: A Case Study of the Emerging Regulation of Derivative Products' in *Securities Regulation: Issues and Perspectives; Papers Presented at the Queen's Annual Business Law Symposium 1994* (Carswell, Ontario, 1995), p. 427.

Mulholland, C. and Lester, A., 'Regulation of Derivatives in New Zealand' in Walker, G., Fisse, B. and Ramsay, I., (eds), *Securities Regulation in Australia and New Zealand* (2nd edn, LBC, Sydney, 1998), ch. 19, p. 686.

Mumford, V., 'Emerging Markets for Equity Derivatives in Asia' (1998) 3 *Derivatives Use, Trading & Regulation* 329.

Nankivell, P., 'The Liability of Australian Banks for Swiss Francs Loans' in Cranston, R., (ed.), *Banks Liability and Risks* (LLP, London, 1995), ch. 11, p. 297.

O'Donovan, J., 'Lender Liability for Investment or Financial Advice' (1999) 11 CBLJ 1.

O'Hara, M., 'Electronic Trading Risks: What Can Go Wrong in Screen-Traded Derivatives Markets' (2000) 5 *Derivatives Use, Trading & Regulation* 316.

O'Hare, J., 'Regulation of the Securities Industry in Hong Kong: The Securities and Futures Commission' (1996) 6 Aust Jnl of Corp Law 178.

O'Sullivan, J., 'Derivatives—A Survey of the Law and Practice' (1994) 5 JBFLP 89.

Ogus, A., 'Rethinking Self-Regulation' (1995) 15 *Oxford Journal of Legal Studies* 97.

Ottino, P., 'London Futures Markets: Self-Regulation, or Bureaucratic Centralism?' in Swan, E. J. (ed.), *Derivative Instruments Law* (Cavendish Publishing Limited, London, 1995), ch. 7, p. 138.

Parker, D., 'Regulatory Environment of Derivatives in New Zealand Continues to Evolve' (1996) 11 *Derivatives* 282.

Perry, M. J., 'Approaches to Market Regulation—The United Kingdom' in Oditah, F. (ed.), *The Future for the Global Securities Market* (Clarendon Press, Oxford, 1996), ch. 11, p. 179.

Philipp, M. and Nield, E., 'SwapClear: A New Mechanism for Enhancing Management of Counterparty Credit Risk from OTC Derivatives Transactions' (1999) 4 *Derivatives* 173.

Philips, S. J. and Rutherford, B. W. J., 'Netting—The Shape of Things to Come' (1994) 9 JIBFL 174.

Picarda, H., 'Interest Rate Swap Agreements in the Courts: Part 1' (1996) 11 JIBFL 428.

Picarda, H., 'Interest Rate Swap Agreements in the Courts: Part 2' (1997) 12 JIBFL 170.

Plews, T., 'Trading Places: The Inescapable Dilemmas Facing All Exchanges and Their Regulators' (2000) 15 JIBL 27.

Pryor, F. L., 'Internationalisation and Globalization of the American Economy' in Brewer, T. L. and Boyd, G. (eds), *Globalizing America* (Edward Elgar, Cheltenham, UK, 2000), ch. 1, p 1.

Ramsay, H. and Harwood, S., 'Analysis: Banking Supervision after Barings' (September 1995) *International Banking and Financial Law* 38.

Romano, R., 'A Thumbnail Sketch of Derivative Securities and Their Regulation', (1996) 55 *Maryland Law Review* 50.

Ross, J. and Craig, D., 'Overview of Netting in New Zealand' (1997) 8 JBFLP 149.

Ryland, M., 'Derivatives Regulation: The International Aspect' (1994) 5 JBFLP 173.

Samuelson, C. A., 'The Fall of Barings: Lessons for Legal Oversight of Derivatives Transactions in the United States' (1996) 29 *Cornell International Law Journal* 767.

Sarkar, R. and Tozzi, M., 'Electronic Trading on Futures Exchanges' (1998) 4 *Derivatives Quarterly* 7.

Sarker, R., 'Barings—The Singaporean View' (1996) 3 *Journal of Financial Crime* 366.

Schick, A., 'Financial Derivatives Instruments' (1989) 4 JIBFL 403.

Scott, H. S., 'Liability of Derivatives Dealers' in Oditah, F. (ed.), *The Future for the Global Securities Market* (Clarendon Press, Oxford, 1996), ch. 17, p. 271.

Shea, T., 'The Basle Committee Consultative Papers on Netting' (1993) 8 JIBL 314.

Shreves, T., 'Secondary Market Regulation in New Zealand' in Walker, G. and Fisse, B. (eds), *Securities Regulation in Australia and New Zealand* (Oxford University Press, Auckland, 1994), ch. 22, p. 504.

Sienko, D. C., 'The Aftermath of Derivative Losses: Can Sophisticated Investors Invoke the Suitability Doctrine' (1995) 8:105 *Depaul Business Law Journal* 107.

Simpson, A. F., ' "Bits" of Disclosure: Communications Technologies and Securities Regulation in Australia' (1997) 12 JIBL 371.

Smith, L., 'Restitution for Mistake of Law' (1999) 7 *Restitution Law* Review 148.

Sum, R., 'Exchange-traded Equity Options: Market Structure and Participation' (1996) 7 JBFLP 5.

Swan, E. J., 'Competition for Futures and Derivatives Markets: The Role of Regulation' in Swan, E. J. (ed.), *Derivative Instruments* (Graham & Trotman/Martinus Nijhoff, London, 1994), ch. 7, p. 85.

Swan, E. J. and McKenna, C., 'The Issue of Understanding Derivatives' in E. J. Swan (ed.), *Issues in Derivatives Instruments* (Kluwer Law International, The Hague, 1999), ch. 1, p. 1.

Starr, M., 'The CASAC Report on Derivatives—Implementation Prospects' (1997) 8 JBFLP 185.

Stickings, S., 'OTC Derivatives Regulation in Japan' in Bettelheim, E. C., Parry, H. and Rees, W. (eds), *Swaps and Off-exchange Derivatives Trading: Law and Regulation* (FT Law & Tax, London, 1996), ch. 13, p. 311.

Tan, S. L., 'Swaps and Derivatives: Managing Legal Risks' (1996) 11 *Asia Business Law Review* 29.

Tan, R., 'Trading Derivative Instruments—Malaysia' (1996) 7 JBFLP 180.

Tan, S. K. and Liew, R., 'Behind the Barings Debacle' (May 1995) *Asia Law* 37.

Taylor, M., 'The Financial Services Act after Ten Years: Have the 1986 Objectives Been Successfully Met?' (1996) 11 JIBFL 366.

Taylor, M., 'What Role Should Regulation Have in the Wholesale Markets?' (1996) 11 JIBFL 423.

Taylor, M., 'Redrawing the Regulatory Map: Why the Financial Services Act Must Not Be Reformed in Isolation' (1996) 11 JIBFL 463.

Taylor, M., 'International Policy Initiatives in the OTC Derivatives Markets' in Bettelheim, E., Parry, H. and Rees, W. (eds), *Swaps and Off-Exchange Derivatives Trading: Law and Regulation* (FT Law & Tax, London, 1996), ch. 14, p. 332.

Tunkel, D., 'Financial Services on the Internet: Can the Present Regulatory System Cope?' (1996) 11 JIBFL 193.

Tyson-Quah, K., 'Collateralisation v Clearing House: Credit Risk Management for OTC Derivatives' in Bettelheim, E., Parry, H. and Rees, W. (eds), *Swaps and Off-Exchange Derivatives Trading: Law and Regulation* (FT Law & Tax, London, 1996), ch. 6, p. 119.

Veljanovski, C., 'Introduction' in Seldon, A. (ed.), *Financial Regulation—or Over-Regulation* (Institute of Economic Affairs, London, 1988).

Virgo, J. and Ryley, P., 'Fitness and Propriety in Financial Services in the 21st Century' (2000) 8 *Journal of Financial Regulation and Compliance* 109.

Volkman, B. P., 'The Global Convergence of Bank Regulation and Standards for Compliance' (1998) 115 *The Banking Law Journal* 550.

Voorhees, P. and Henneman, A. L., 'CFTC Concept Release on Additional Regulation of OTC Derivatives' (1998) 13 JIBL 316.

Voorhees, P. and Henneman, A. L., 'SEC Release Proposing New Regulations for OTC Derivatives Dealers' (1998) 13 JIBL 312.

Vroegop, J., 'A Banker's Liability for Financial Advice' (1993) 8 JIBL 58.

Waldman, A. R., 'OTC Derivatives and Systemic Risk: Innovative Finance or the Dance into the Abyss', (1994) 43 *The American University Law Review* 1023.

Walker, D., 'Major Issues Relevant for Regulatory Response to the Internationalisation of Capital Markets' in Fingleton, J. and Schoenmaker, D. (eds), *The Internationalisation of Capital Markets and The Regulatory Response* (Graham & Trotman, London, 1992), ch. 1, p. 21.

Walker, G., 'The Policy Basis of Securities Regulation in New Zealand' in Walker, G. and Fisse, B. (eds), *Securities Regulation in Australia and New Zealand* (Oxford University Press, Auckland, 1994), ch. 9, p. 171.

Walker, G. and Fox, M., 'The Securities Industry and International Financial Integration' (1997) 7 *Canterbury Law Review* 239.

Walker, G., and Fox, M., 'Globalisation: Meanings and Implications' in Walker, G., Fisse, B. and Ramsay, I., (eds), *Securities Regulation in Australia and New Zealand* (2nd edn, LBC, Sydney, 1998), ch. 1, p. 4.

Walker, J. A., 'Financial Derivatives—Global Regulatory Developments' (January 1996) *Journal of Business Law* 66.

Walter, J., 'Close-Out Netting in English Law: Comfort at Last' (1995) 10 JIBFL 167.

Whetherell, D. and Smith, R., 'Local Authority Capacity and Related Matters' (1992) 3 JBFLP 228.

Whitby, D., 'Barings—A Culture of Greed?' (1996) 3 *Journal of Financial Crime* 377.

Whittaker, A. M., 'Tackling Systemic Risk on Markets: Barings and Beyond', in Oditah, F. (ed.), *The Future for the Global Securities Market* (Clarendon Press, Oxford, 1996), ch. 15, p. 257.

Willis, P., 'Set-off and Netting' in Mallesons Stephen and Jaques (eds) *Australian Finance Law* (4th edn, LBC, Sydney, 1999), ch. 28, p. 684.

Wingfield, A. and Cain, E., 'Hong Kong' in Burke, L., Glennie, D. and Melrose, J. (eds), *International Derivatives Law* (Risk Publications, London, 1996), p. 101.

Woon, W., 'Regulation of the Securities Industry in Singapore' (1995) 4 *Pacific Rim Law & Policy Journal* 731.

Wright, C. 'Financial Markets Regulation: The Role of a Separate Competition Authority' in A. Jeunemaître (ed.), *Financial Markets Regulation* (Macmillan Press, London, 1997), ch. 3, p. 46.

Yeo, H. Y., 'Kuala Lumpur Commodity Exchange (KLCE): Case Study of Crude Palm Oil Futures Market' in Koh, K. L. and Others (eds), *Current Developments in International Securities, Commodities and Financial Futures Markets* (Butterworths, Singapore, 1987), p. 291.

Zask, E., 'The Derivatives Risk Management Audit' in Klein, R. A. and Lederman, J. (eds), *Derivatives Risk and Responsibility* (Irwin, Chicago, 1996), ch. 2, p. 13.

'End-Users See Derivatives Dealers As Fiduciaries, Dealers See End-Users as Equals, Yet GAO Finds Few Problems Between Them' (1998) 3 *Derivatives* 158 (author unknown).

'IOSCO Analyses Regulation of Exchange-Traded Derivatives' (1998) 3 *Derivatives* 180 (author unknown).

'The Barings Debacle and SIMEX' (March 1995) *Asia Law* 9 (author unknown).

3   Reports, Official Documents and Unpublished Materials

Allen & Gledhill, 'Enforceability Survey—Singapore' in Global Derivatives Study Group, *Derivatives: Practices and Principles, Appendix II: Legal Enforceability: Survey of Nine Jurisdictions* (Group of Thirty, Washington D. C., July 1993), p. 273.

Attorney-General, *Explanatory Memorandum on the Futures Industry Bill* (1986).

Australian Securities Commission, *Report on Over-The-Counter Derivatives Markets* (Melbourne, May 1994).

Australian Treasury, *Financial System Inquiry Discussion Paper* (AGPS, Canberra, 1996).

Australian Treasury, *Corporate Law Economic Reform Program Proposals for Reform: Paper No. 6* (AGPS, Canberra, 1997).

Australian Treasury, *Financial System Inquiry Final Report* (AGPS, Canberra, 1997).

Bank for International Settlements, *Recent Developments in International Interbank Relations* (Basle, October 1992).

Bank for International Settlements, *Central Bank Survey of Derivatives of Market Activity*, Press Release (Basle, 18 December 1995).

Bank for International Settlements, *Central Bank Survey of Foreign Exchange Market Activity in April 1995: Preliminary Global Findings*, Press Release (Basle, 24 October 1995).

Bank for International Settlements, *Proposals for Improving Global Derivatives Markets Statistics* (Basle, July 1996).

Basle Committee on Banking Supervision, *Interpretation of the Capital Accord for the Multilateral Netting of Forward Value Foreign Exchange Transactions* (Basle, April 1996).

Bank Negara Malaysia Annual Report 1995 (Kuala Lumpur).

Bank of England, *Report of the Board of Banking Supervision Inquiry into the Circumstances of the Collapse of Barings* (July 1995).

Bank of England, 'Statistical Information about Derivatives Markets' (May 1995) *Bank of England Quarterly Bulletin* 185.

Companies and Securities Advisory Committee, *Law of Derivatives: An International Comparison* (Sydney, January 1995).

Companies and Securities Advisory Committee, *Regulation of the OTC Derivatives Market*, Discussion Paper (Sydney, August 1995).

Companies and Securities Advisory Committee, *Regulation of On-Exchange Derivatives Market*, Draft Report (Sydney, June 1996).

Companies and Securities Advisory Committee, *Regulation of On-Exchange and OTC Derivatives Markets*, Final Report (Sydney, June 1997).

Cravath, Swaine & Moore, 'Enforceability Survey—United States' in Global Derivatives Study Group, *Derivatives: Practices and Principles, Appendix II: Legal Enforceability: Survey of Nine Jurisdictions* (Group of Thirty, Washington D. C., July 1993), p. 291.

Global Derivatives Study Group, *Derivatives: Practices and Principles* (Group of Thirty, Washington D. C., July 1993).

Grenville, S. A., 'Exchange Rates and Causes' (February 1998) *Reserve Bank of Australia Bulletin* 29.

Gray, B., 'Supervision of Derivative Activities' (August 1993) *Reserve Bank of Australia Bulletin* 7.

Hong Kong Futures Exchange Annual Report 1995 (Hong Kong).

Linklaters and Paine, 'Enforceability Survey—England' in Global Derivatives Study Group, *Derivatives: Practices and Principles, Appendix II: Legal Enforceability: Survey of Nine Jurisdictions* (Group of Thirty, Washington D. C., July 1993), p. 173.

Mallesons Stephen Jaques, 'Enforceability Survey—Australia' in Global Derivatives Study Group, *Derivatives: Practices and Principles, Appendix II: Legal Enforceability: Survey of Nine Jurisdictions* (Group of Thirty, Washington D. C., July 1993), p. 1.

New Zealand Futures and Options Exchange, *Recommendations for Amendment of Part III Securities Amendment Act 1988* (Memorandum to the New Zealand Securities Commission, 9 September 1994).

New Zealand Securities Commission, *Recommendations for Amendment of Part III Securities Amendment Act 1988*, Discussion Paper (Wellington, July 1994).

Netting Sub-Committee of the Companies and Securities Advisory Committee, *Netting in Financial Transactions*, Draft Report (Sydney, November 1996).

Netting Sub-Committee of the Companies and Securities Advisory Committee, *Netting in Financial Markets Transactions*, Background Paper (Sydney, December 1996).

Phelps, L., 'Current Developments in Prudential Supervision' (Paper presented at the 1996 Banking Industry Congress, Sydney, February 1996).

Quinn, B., 'Derivatives—A Central Banker's View' (August 1994) *Bank of England Quarterly Bulletin* 277.

Reserve Bank of Australia, 'Australian Banks' Activities in Derivatives Markets: Products and Risk-Management Practices' (September 1994) *Reserve Bank of Australia Bulletin* 1.

Reserve Bank of Australia, 'Derivatives—Bank Activities and Supervisory Responses' (May 1995) *Reserve Bank of Australia Bulletin* 1.

Reserve Bank of Australia, 'Implications of the Barings Collapse for Bank Supervisors' (November 1995) *Reserve Bank of Australia Bulletin* 1.

New Zealand Securities Commission, *Annual Report for the year ending 30 June 1996* (Auckland).

Securities and Futures Commission of Hong Kong, *A Consultation Paper on a Draft for a Composite Securities and Futures Bill* (Hong Kong, April 1996).

Securities and Futures Commission of Hong Kong, *Main Proposed Revisions to a Draft for a Composite Securities and Futures Bill* (Hong Kong, December 1996).

Securities and Futures Commission of Hong Kong, *Consultation Paper on the Review of the Leveraged Foreign Exchange Trading Regulatory System* (Hong Kong, August 1996).

Securities Commission Annual Report 1995 (Kuala Lumpur).

Securities Review Committee (Mr Ian Hay Davidson, Chairman), *The Operation and Regulation of the Hong Kong Securities Industry* (Hong Kong, May 1988).

SIMEX Annual Report—Excellent 1994 & Beyond (Singapore).

Singapore International Monetary Exchange, *Rules of the Singapore International Monetary Exchange Limited* (Singapore, March 1990).

Sundram G. and Lee, F. M., 'Introduction to ISDA Documentation: Legal Issues Under Malaysian Law' (January 2000).

The Government of the Hong Kong Special Administrative Region, *Consultation Document on the Securities and Futures Bill* (April 2000).

The Report of the Inspectors Appointed by the Minister of Finance, Singapore (Ministry of Finance, Singapore, October 1995).

United States General Accounting Office, *Financial Derivatives: Actions Needed to Protect the Financial System* (Washington D.C., May 1994).

Index

INTERNATIONAL BANKING, FINANCE AND ECONOMIC LAW SERIES

1.   J. J. Norton, Chia-Jui Cheng and I. Fletcher (eds), *International Banking Regulation and Supervision: Change and Transformation in the 1990s.* 1994.
ISBN 1-85333-998-9

2.   J. J. Norton, Chia-Jui Cheng and I. Fletcher (eds), *International Banking Operations and Practices: Current Developments.* 1994.
ISBN 1-85333-997-0

3.   J. J. Norton, *Devising International Bank Supervisory Standards.* 1995.
ISBN 1-85966-1858

4.   Sir Joseph Gold, *Interpretation: The IMF and International Law.* 1996.
ISBN 90-411-0887-4

5.   R. Smits, *The European Central Bank: Institutional Aspects.* 1997.
ISBN 90-411-0686-3

6.   M. Andenas, L. Gormley, C. Hadjiemmanuil and I. Harden (eds), *European Economic and Monetary Union: The Institutional Framework.* 1997.
ISBN 90-411-0687-1

7.   T. Wan, *Development of Banking Law in the Greater China Area: PRC and Taiwan.* 1999.
ISBN 90-411-0948-X

8.   R. P. Buckley, *Emerging Markets Debt: An Analysis of the Secondary Market.* 1999.
ISBN 90-411-9716-8

9.   P. Cartwright (ed.), *Consumer Protection in Financial Services.* 1999.
ISBN 90-411-9717-6

10.   T. Traisorat, *Thailand: Financial Sector Reform and the East Asian Crises.* 1999.
ISBN 90-411-9734-6

11.   M. I. Steinberg, *International Securities Law: A Contemporary and Comparative Analysis.* 1999.
ISBN 90-411-9738-9

12.   M. Giovanoli and G. Heinrich (eds), *International Bank Insolvencies: A Central Bank Perspective.* 1999.
ISBN 90-411-9728-1

246

13.   K. N. Schefer, *International Trade in Financial Services: The NAFTA Provisions*. 1999.
ISBN 90-411-9754-0

14.   J. J. Norton, C. J. Li and Y. Huang (eds), *Financial Regulation in the Greater China Area: Mainland China, Taiwan and Hong Kong SAR*. 2000.
ISBN 90-411-9763-X

15.   Y. Shim, *Korean Bank Regulation and Supervision: Crisis and Reform*. 2000.
ISBN 90-411-9778-8

16.   A. Hudson (ed.), *Modern Financial Techniques, Derivatives and Law*. 2000.
ISBN 90-411-9781-8

17.   G. N. Olson, *Banks in Distress: Lessons from the American Experience of the 1980s*. 2000.
ISBN 90-411-9787-7

18.   R. M. Lastra (ed.), *The Reform of the International Financial Architecture*. 2000.
ISBN 90-411-9802-4

19.   G. A. Walker, *International Banking Regulation: Law, Policy and Practice*. 2000.
ISBN 90-411-9794-X

20.   R. Gengatharen, *Derivatives Law and Regulation*. 2001.
ISBN 90-411-9836-9

KLUWER LAW INTERNATIONAL – THE HAGUE, LONDON, BOSTON